TEACHING AND ASSESSING WRITING IN THE PRIMARY SCHOOL

The capacity to write well is fundamental to success in school and beyond. Yet many children struggle to become proficient writers. *Teaching and Assessing Writing in the Primary School* provides a comprehensive guide to the theory, practice and pedagogical research behind teaching children to write. Supported by case studies and real-world examples of teaching and learning writing in the classroom, this practical book proposes a whole-school, research-informed writing framework that engages children while building their writing skills. Readers will benefit from building their knowledge of the theory and research behind learning how to write successfully while discovering how they may apply this effectively to their classroom practice.

Firmly grounded in the theory of writing and with clear links to practical application, chapters explore:

- Effective pedagogies for teaching children aged 4–12 how to write
- The planned and received curriculum for writing, including a whole-school approach
- Formative and summative assessment of writing in the classroom
- Designing and organising a Writing Workshop for pupils
- Practical implementation of 'mini lessons' to support writing
- Supporting the needs of diverse writers within our schools

Filled with strategies for teaching, this practical and engaging book will be an essential resource for anyone working within primary schools, including classroom teachers (both new and more experienced), teaching assistants, subject leaders, literacy coordinators and senior leadership.

Eithne Kennedy is a teacher educator in the School of Language, Literacy and Early Childhood Education (LLECE), DCU Institute of Education and leads the DCU Centre for Literacy Research, Policy and Practice. She is a former primary classroom teacher with 14 years of classroom experience (K-12th Grade) in Ireland and the United States. As director of the *Write to Read* research initiative, she collaborates with schools designated as disadvantaged to create powerful literacy environments that motivate and engage children as readers, writers and thinkers.

Gerry Shiel, formerly a Research Fellow at Educational Research Centre, Dublin, has overseen several large-scale assessments at national level, including the OECD Programme for International Student Assessment and National Assessments of Reading Literacy and Mathematics. He has also been involved in the development of standardised tests in reading Literacy in English and Irish. He continues to collaborate with Eithne Kennedy on the *Write to Read* Project.

TEACHING AND ASSESSING WRITING IN THE PRIMARY SCHOOL

A Whole School Approach

Eithne Kennedy and Gerry Shiel

LONDON AND NEW YORK

Designed cover image: Getty Images

First published 2025
by Routledge
4 Park Square, Milton Park, Abingdon, Oxon OX14 4RN

and by Routledge
605 Third Avenue, New York, NY 10158

Routledge is an imprint of the Taylor & Francis Group, an informa business

© 2025 Eithne Kennedy and Gerry Shiel

The right of Eithne Kennedy and Gerry Shiel to be identified as authors of this work has been asserted in accordance with sections 77 and 78 of the Copyright, Designs and Patents Act 1988.

All rights reserved. No part of this book may be reprinted or reproduced or utilised in any form or by any electronic, mechanical, or other means, now known or hereafter invented, including photocopying and recording, or in any information storage or retrieval system, without permission in writing from the publishers.

Trademark notice: Product or corporate names may be trademarks or registered trademarks, and are used only for identification and explanation without intent to infringe.

British Library Cataloguing-in-Publication Data
A catalogue record for this book is available from the British Library

ISBN: 978-1-032-30119-8 (hbk)
ISBN: 978-1-032-30120-4 (pbk)
ISBN: 978-1-003-30351-0 (ebk)

DOI: 10.4324/9781003303510

Typeset in Interstate
by codeMantra

CONTENTS

	Preface	vii
1	**How Do Writers Write?**	1
2	**Effective Writing Pedagogy**	18
3	**Genre, Disciplinary Writing, Multimodal Texts and Writing Development**	40
4	**Curricula in Writing: The Intended, Implemented and Achieved**	56
5	**Assessment of Writing**	69
6	**Designing, Organising and Implementing a Writing Workshop**	90
7	**Process Mini Lessons: Generating, Planning and Drafting Writing Ideas across Genres**	106
8	**Craft Mini Lessons: Developing and Enhancing Writing Quality across Genres**	146
9	**Conventions Mini Lessons: Developing Accuracy in Writing across Genres**	178
10	**Process Mini Lessons: Evaluating, Revising and Publishing Writing across Genres**	208
11	**Addressing the Needs of Diverse Writers**	235
12	**Planning for Writing across a School**	258
	Appendix A: Partial W2R Writing Assessment Rubric – Word Choice	295
	Appendix B: Class-level Scoring Template for W2R Rubric (All Components)	301
	References	302
	Index	319

PREFACE

The capacity to write well is fundamental to success in school, which in turn supports individuals in discovering and reaching their potential in life. While few become literary giants, writing plays a fundamental role, be it major or minor, in whatever career path is chosen in life. Almost 20 years ago, the US National Commission on Writing referred to writing as the neglected R (2003, p. 11) and argued: 'disciplined writing is the most valuable job attribute of all: a mind equipped to think. Writing today is not a frill for the few but an essential skill for the many'. Today, writing remains the under-represented language form. There is a relative dearth of research on writing (compared with reading) and less time devoted to it in the classroom (Cutler & Graham, 2008; Kavanagh et al., 2015). More recently, in line with UNESCO (2021), Camacho et al. (2021, p. 214) consider writing to be 'a key skill in the twenty-first century and a gateway to lifelong learning, employment, and social inclusion', while Patino et al. (2020) posit that writing also provides the means for 'personal reflection, thought, creativity, creation of meaning and exchange of ideas, as well as a complement to other modes of communication in a world of multimodal texts' (p. 494).

Concerns about children's writing development are *'common across the globe…the typical teacher does not devote enough time to writing and writing instruction'* (Graham & Rijlaarsdam, 2019, pp. 278-281). Graham (2019) argues that children do not have access to the instruction they need and deserve. Teachers have reported finding it a challenge to meet the needs of all learners in today's diverse classroom and in particular, the needs of struggling writers (Troia et al., 2009). Additionally, though teachers report that they are aware of effective teaching practices and adaptations, they use them infrequently (about once a month), which research indicates is not often enough to truly impact on the quality of writing (Dockrell et al., 2016; Hertzberg & Roe, 2016). Thus, the depth and intensity of instruction required to master a complex skill such as writing are not accessible to all students. Furthermore, at the primary level, there is often an over-emphasis on grammar, handwriting and spelling and not enough emphasis on writing processes such as planning and revising (Cutler & Graham, 2008; Rietdijk et al., 2018). In addition, not enough attention is paid to persuasive and expository writing (Parr & Jesson, 2016) or to digital and multimodal composing (Dalton, 2012; Williams & Beam, 2019).

A number of paradigm shifts in the teaching of writing have occurred over time, with a shift from traditional approaches (pre-1980) to process-based approaches (e.g. Graves, 1983, 1994; Calkins, 1986, 1994) and genre-based writing instruction (Martin, 1985; Rothery, 1996,

Derewianka, 2015). Most recently, there has been a shift to more structured hybrid models that seek to achieve a balance between process and product, and between less-explicit and more-explicit teaching approaches. Recent developments relating to children's writing have also included an emphasis on digital and multimodal texts (Dalton et al., 2015; Mills & Exley, 2015; Williams & Beam, 2019), and a rebalancing between relative emphases on creative/imaginative and more functional writing, including writing in the disciplines and across the curriculum (e.g., Shanahan, 2019).

This book brings together theoretical perspectives, findings from meta-analyses, classroom research studies, assessment and policy, as well as discussion and application of models and pedagogical strategies in the realities and complexities of real classrooms. This book is directed at a teacher audience and dedicated to primary education (4-12 yrs.). In synthesising lessons from a broad range of perspectives and drawing on examples of practice from the Write to Read project (a longitudinal study conducted in high-poverty contexts with children aged 4-12 years) (see section on mission and scope of book below), it strengthens connections between theory and practice and seeks to support teachers in understanding how writing develops, in reflecting on their practice and in developing an evidence-based framework for their classroom context that can begin to meet the needs of the children they teach. It is concerned with developing writing in ways that honour the act of writing – not just as a task or skill to be mastered but as a creative and social process (regardless of genre) which enriches and nourishes. It adopts an integrated approach, capitalising on the interconnectedness of the forms of language (reading, writing, oral language) and the possibilities offered to connect writing across the curriculum in ways that honour both literary and disciplinary goals and the goals of the writer.

While individual teachers can and do make a difference to children's writing, the impact is magnified if a whole school vision for writing is developed and implemented (Graham, 2019). Our book considers how a school culture of writing, which balances the cognitive and affective dimensions and nurtures children as writers, can be created. It addresses whole school planning and the development of a coherent spiralling whole school framework that incorporates formative assessment so that the quality of children's writing can be monitored, improved and pushed to its potential, and ensuring teacher autonomy and creativity are not constrained or compromised.

Given that writing development is shaped by participation in various writing communities (Bazerman, 2016; Graham, 2018) and teachers' beliefs about writing and dispositions towards writing influence their practice (Brindle et al., 2016; Graham, 2019, this book also presents ways in which a school can evolve into a vibrant professional learning community. Our work with schools located in low-socio-economic communities over the last ten years highlights the importance of this and demonstrates that schools can make a difference to children's literacy development when a research-informed, responsive, cognitively challenging balanced literacy framework is designed and implemented. Particular attention is paid to supporting teachers to adopt an inquiry-as-stance approach (Cochran-Smith & Lytle, 2009) to planning, teaching and responding to children's assessed needs, and to engage in professional conversations with colleagues within and across grade levels in order to continually push the boundaries in the range and quality of children's writing from one grade level to the next.

Clearly, writing is a complex act and the teaching of writing is challenging. Our book can make a valuable contribution to the conversation on how to support teachers and schools in valuing writing, in understanding how it develops and contributes to overall literacy development, in enhancing teachers' expertise and in empowering them to develop a culturally responsive stimulating environment and whole school framework for writing.

This volume is divided into three sections. The first (Chapters 1-5) looks at models of the writing process, effective pedagogies for writing, curricula in writing and the assessment of writing. The second (Chapters 6-10) describes the implementation of writing instruction and assessment in classroom settings and includes exemplar mini lessons and anchor charts to support visibility and use of mentor texts. The final section (Chapters 11-12) addresses diverse communities of writers and whole-school planning for writing.

We are delighted that several of our literacy coaches have contributed vignettes and other materials to this book, including Stephen Brett, Rachel Hannify, Roisên O'Shea, Anne-Marie Roche, Caoimhe Shiel and Gillian Watson. We also wish to thank our families, especially Eddie and Mairéad, for their help as we worked on and completed the book.

Equivalency of Grade Levels

Throughout this book, reference is made to the class or grade levels in which children are enrolled or for which materials have been prepared, generally in the context of the Irish system. Readers are referred to the following for a list of equivalencies (e.g., the grade level in England or the United States corresponding to Third class in Ireland).

http://seandelaney.com/wp-content/uploads/2018/07/Comparing-Class-and-Grade-Levels-across-Countries.pdf

Further Reading

Dalton, B., Robinson, K., Lavvorn, J., Smith, B. E., Alvey, T., Mo, E., Uccelli, P.& Proctor, C. P. (2015). Fifth-grade students' digital retellings and the common core: modal use and design intentionality. *Elementary School Journal, 115*(4), 548-569. https://doi.org/10.1086/681969

Hertzberg, F., & Roe, A. (2016). Writing in the content areas: A Norwegian case study. *Reading and Writing: An Interdisciplinary Journal, 29*(3), 555-576. https://doi.org/10.1007/s11145-015-9607-7

Mills, K. A., & Exley, B. (2014). Time, space, and text in the elementary school digital writing classroom. *Written Communication, 31*(4), 434-469. https://doi.org/10.1177/0741088314542757

Parr, J. M., & Jesson, R. (2016). Mapping the landscape of writing instruction in New Zealand primary school classrooms. *Reading and Writing: An Interdisciplinary Journal, 29*(5), 981-1011. https://doi.org/10.1007/s11145-015-9589-5

Patiño, J. F., Calixto, A. L., Chiappe, A., & Almenarez, F. T. (2020). ICT-driven writing and motor Skills: A review. *International Electronic Journal of Elementary Education, 12*(5), 489-498. https://www.iejee.com/index.php/IEJEE/article/view/1074

United Nations Educational, Scientific and Cultural Organization. (UNESCO). (2021). *Reimagining our futures together: A new social contract for education*. Author. https://unesdoc.unesco.org/ark:/48223/pf0000379707.locale=en

US National Commission on Writing. (2003). *Writing and school reform, including the neglected R: The need for a writing revolution*. College Board. https://www.csun.edu/~rinstitute/Content/policy/national%20commission%20on%20writing%20report.pdf

1 How Do Writers Write?

Writing is a fundamental human activity. We write to fulfil many purposes in life: to create, amuse, inform, stay in touch, explain, understand, persuade, remember, learn, report, influence or discover new insights. Writing records our thinking, reaches through the mists of time and leaves our unique imprint (print or digital) on the world for generations to come.

Writing proficiency is a key aspect of student success during the school years, and can impact personal and work-related outcomes after school (Graham, 2006, 2019). In addition:

- Writing about what we learn helps with understanding and remembering, especially when writing leads readers to think deeply and make decisions about content, through such activities as summarising, describing, comparing/contrasting, connecting information within topics and/or texts, writing stories or poetry to extend ideas, making analogies, and developing graphic organisers or mind maps with text (McLean, 2022). These activities relate to writing to learn or disciplinary writing, which can be embedded in a discipline such as literature, mathematics or history.
- Writing about what we read enhances understanding. According to Graham and Herbert (2011), when students write about what they have read, comprehension of that material improves. Writing can be used to record, analyse, evaluate and modify the content or ideas in a text through such activities as summarising, note-taking, and generating or responding to questions.
- Writing improves reading and reading improves writing. Teaching writing and writing subskills improves reading comprehension, reading fluency and word-level reading. Reading instruction improves overall writing performance, writing quality, amount written and spelling (Graham & Herbert, 2011).

In this chapter, we consider writing from the perspective of young writers. We look at definitions of writing, models of the writing process, and motivation for writing. Associations between oral language, reading and writing are also considered.

After reading this chapter, you should be able to answer the key questions below.

> **Reflect and Connect**
>
> 1 What sources of knowledge do writers draw on when writing texts?
> 2 Which processes do writers engage in and how do these evolve as they develop as writers?
> 3 What motivates children to write well?
> 4 How can theories of learning inform children's writing development?
> 5 How do oral language and reading support children's writing (and vice versa?)

Broad Approaches to Teaching Writing

Think back to when you were in primary school. How were you taught to write? How was a typical writing class set up? Who decided what you would write about? What support did you receive as you wrote your text? With whom did you share your writing (who was the primary audience?)? What feedback was provided afterwards, and how did you use that feedback?

One approach to teaching children to write can be termed 'the traditional approach', also known as 'writing as a product', 'skills-based writing' or 'on-demand writing'. This typically involves the teacher setting a topic for writing, allocating a given amount of time to complete the text, and providing feedback afterwards, often focusing on such aspects as spelling, grammar and punctuation. Other aspects, such as purpose, structure and organisation, creativity/imagination and the writer's ability to engage the reader receive less attention. The primary audience is the teacher. On-demand writing is often associated with assessment contexts, where students are asked to write about a particular topic within a set time. A key element of this broad approach is to teach pupils to become proficient in discrete skills such as handwriting, spelling, punctuation and grammar, before moving on to writing whole texts (Daffern & Mackenzie, 2020).

A second approach to teaching writing is the 'process approach', popularised in the United States in the early 1980s by Donald Graves (1981, 1983, 1994), and by Lucy Calkins (1986, 1994). This approach can be summarised in five recursive cycles: previewing, composing/drafting, revising, editing, and publishing,[1] with pupils writing for real purposes and audiences, sometimes over an extended period (see Box 1.1). A related approach, the Writing Workshop (see Box 1.2), sets out an instructional framework for process writing that seeks to support students with different aspects of writing. This is achieved through direct instruction of key skills in a framework which typically includes a mini lesson (involving either a whole class or small groups), independent writing and conferencing, and a share session. The framework provides ample scope for attention to a range of skills, including topic choice, sentence construction, genres (see below), word choice, spelling and handwriting/ typing in real writing contexts. This is all underpinned by formative assessment, where the teacher assesses processes skills such as composing, revising and editing, as well as discrete skills such as spelling, grammar and punctuation, and provides relevant feedback to pupils. Research evidence (Graham & Sandmel, 2011; Chapter 2, this volume) supports the view that process approaches to teaching writing can improve the quality of pupils' writing.

BOX 1.1 ELEMENTS OF PROCESS WRITING

- Writing for real purposes and audiences, with some writing activities extending over several days
- Engaging in cycles of writing, including planning (setting goals, generating ideas, organising ideas), translating (putting a writing plan into action) and reviewing (evaluating, editing and revising)
- Emphasis on student ownership of writing, self-reflection and evaluation
- Collaboration among students
- Provision by teachers of a supportive and non-threatening writing environment
- Provision of personalised and individualised writing instruction, through mini-lessons, writing conferences and teachable moments

Source: Adapted from Graham and Sandmel (2011)

BOX 1.2 IMPLEMENTING THE WRITING WORKSHOP IN MY SCHOOL

By Caoimhe Shiel, Class Teacher, Support Teacher and Write to Read Coach

Having first experienced Writing Workshop on school placement as part of my initial teacher training, I was enthusiastic to implement this approach post-graduation. When I began teaching junior infants as part of a five-teacher stream in my current school, I was unsure of how to begin establishing the workshop with children at such an early stage of literacy development.

I researched effective conditions of Writing Workshop as part of my Masters of Literacy Professional Practice and felt confident enough to approach my principal about piloting this change. Initially, I implemented the Writing Workshop with my own class, which was useful for experimenting with which strategies worked, how lessons tied into reading genres across our school plans and resourcing lesson materials. Over time, I noticed a shift in the children's confidence and motivation when it came to writing. The desire to write spilled into other subject areas, and I set up a writing cart in the room for children to utilise whenever needed, e.g. during structured play time (called *Aistear*). The children made signs and props such as maps for the role play area, created cards and notes for family and friends and slowly became more independent at spelling and letter formation, no longer seeking adult reassurance as they wrote. Though children in the class were of mixed ability, I do think that the share session (where pupils share their writing with one another) helped the children recognise the value of their writing as a form of communication with others. The children's personal sense of pride in their work was very encouraging to see, and, combined with their overall writing development, justified the amount of time I devoted to writing workshop. My personal change in practice was cemented by the children's own enjoyment of writing lessons. I remember on the last day of school a child burst into tears because Writing Workshop was not on the daily timetable, and I had to explain how we didn't have time because it was a half day before the summer holidays.

Interest in the approach grew from colleagues, who asked me about the work on display and the anchor charts (describing different writing strategies) in my classroom, and from there I planned to implement the approach the following year with colleagues in my stream as part of a professional learning community. My principal facilitated this piloting through the PIEW (PILOT, IMPLEMENT, EMBED, WAITLIST) model recommended by the Irish Primary Principals Network, where she facilitated my modelling in other classes by providing cover to my class and supporting with resources. My colleagues on my stream were very accommodating and kept up the approach in their own classes after the initial period of support. It helped that we were able to plan together and collaboratively align lessons to learning outcomes in our literacy school plan.

In the years that followed, those four teachers continued to use this approach at other class levels. It was decided to implement and embed the workshop across the school, so as part of learning support, I was timetabled in every class across all three streams once a week to model and assist teacher planning using a writing workshop approach. This was beneficial as we often experience significant staff turnover and it helped ensure that our plans built on previous knowledge from year to year. The support of school leadership and colleagues was fundamental in ensuring lasting change to practice in our school setting.

A third broad approach to teaching writing is the 'genre' approach. This approach involves organising writing instruction around key social purposes of communication and their associated forms in particular social contexts (Rose & Martin, 2012). Thus, students might write (or indeed speak) to recount or recall, explain, entertain, inform, give instructions, narrate, persuade, and justify opinions. The broad formats associated with these purposes include narrative, explanatory, procedural and persuasive text subgenres. Writing instruction centred on the features of genres can be combined with process writing via a release of responsibility model, whereby teachers provide intensive support in the early stages of teaching a new genre, with the level of support reduced as students become more independent writers (see Chapter 3). Genre-based approaches are particularly relevant in the context of disciplinary or subject-based literacy, where children can acquire the language of specific subject areas through learning about the genre in which those subjects are written (or spoken) about (for example, recounting the procedures and outcomes of a science experiment).

An idea related to genre is that of text structure. This can be defined as the way information is organised within different genres or text types. It could include chapter headings, subheadings, table of contents, overviews, introductory and concluding paragraphs, sequencing, topic sentences and cause and effect. Hence, text structure refers to within-text language features designed to achieve coherence within a particular genre, such as how to sequence ideas within a historical recount.

In practice, writing instruction may draw on a number of different approaches, which may be combined in ways that are designed to achieve instructional goals. Chapter 2 looks at instructional practices in writing in more detail, while Chapter 3 examines genre in more depth, including approaches to teaching genre (sometimes called genre study).

Defining Writing

A good starting point for a book on teaching writing might be to define what writing is. According to Graham et al. (2013):

> Writing is a goal directed and self-sustained cognitive activity requiring the skilful management of (a) the writing environment; (b) the constraints imposed by the writing topic; (c) the intentions of the writer(s); and (d) the processes, knowledge, and skills involved in composing.
>
> (p. 4)

Hence, writing is a complex problem-solving process (McCutchen et al., 2008), depending, at least in part, on the writer's understanding of and experience with the writing process and the various skills involved in composing a text. The complexity of writing is also illustrated in a definition provided by Myhill et al. (2023a):

> Writing is a multidimensional construct, requiring mastery of multiple skills, ranging from transcription and orthography, the management of sentence and text structures; the generation of ideas; understanding the expectations of a genre; and navigating the relationship between reader and writer.
>
> (p. 1)

We can also cite definitions for specific types of writing. Barbot et al. (2012) define creative writing as involving students in drawing on their imagination and other creative processes to create fictional narratives or writing that is unusually original. Creative writing can also be viewed as an antidote to more structured forms of writing, which may lack a creative element because of the emphasis on getting the structure or form right. In a study by Myhill et al. (2023a), children valued opportunities to engage in creative writing, which was found to increase their agency and ownership of writing, and led to greater emotional engagement, compared with more structured forms of writing that sometimes involved preplanning.

Another way to think about writing, especially as it is practiced by children, is to reflect on what they can accomplish at different stages of development. For example, Clay (1993) has described children's early writing development with reference to the level of language (moving from the use of letters, words, phrases and sentences, to punctuated stories), message quality (from using signs, copying messages and using repetitive sentences to recording one's own ideas) and direction principles (from no understanding of direction through reversal of directional patterns, to correct directional patterns and spaces between words). A system such as this allows us to describe what is involved in writing at different points in early development.

Models of Writing

Based on what you have read so far, you will understand that, in order to be successful, young writers must develop knowledge about writing and hold positive dispositions about writing. In this section, we consider models of writing that highlight the key knowledge and dispositions that writers require and, in some cases, the contexts in which they operate as writers. Alamargot and Fayol (2009) note that writing (as composition) involves:

- Drawing on two main types of knowledge – the knowledge required by the topic of the text (topic knowledge); and linguistic knowledge (lexical, syntactical and rhetorical knowledge)[2]
- Short-term memory, to maintain and re-organise information
- A dynamic interaction, whereby the text being produced depends on the goals that have been set, the intended audience, the conditions of the writing task, and the text that has been produced so far
- Engagement in key processes of *planning*, *translating* ideas into mental linguistic representations, *transcribing* those representations into words, and *revising*
- The co-ordination and management of the writing task to ensure that processes are implemented appropriately, and writing is fluent (these are sometimes referred to as metacognitive or executive processes).

Three models of writing are described here: Berninger and Swanson's (1994) model of children's writing processes, Bereiter and Scardamalia's (1987) model of the transition from novice to skilled writer, and Graham's Graham's (2025) writers within community model. These models are not instructional or pedagogic models – rather, they focus on how writers write, and the knowledge, dispositions and processes they bring to the writing task. Chapter 2 (Key Messages on Writing Pedagogy) builds on the ideas about teaching writing discussed above and looks at how key knowledge, dispositions and processes can be developed during teaching and learning.

Berninger and Swanson's Cognitive Model of Writing

The earliest models of writing, dating back to the 1980s (e.g., Hayes & Flower, 1980), mainly described the writing processes of adults. Berninger and Swanson's (1994) model sought to extend this early work to younger writers (Figure 1.1). This model highlights the distinction between pre-planning (advance planning) and the planning that writers engage in as they write or review words and sentences (more localised planning). Pre-planning typically involves a consideration of the requirements of the writing task (topic, audience and plans for writing, such as specific genres or discourse types) and results in the generation of ideas, organisational schemas and goals (Berninger et al., 1996). Online (during writing) or offline (post-writing) planning can involve making decisions on word choice, sentence structure, and/or discourse or text structure.

In their model, Berninger and Swanson include translating or mapping ideas into grammatical strings of language, which are then transcribed into text by applying rules of spelling and good writing form (capitalisation, punctuation, well-formed letters, etc.). For adult

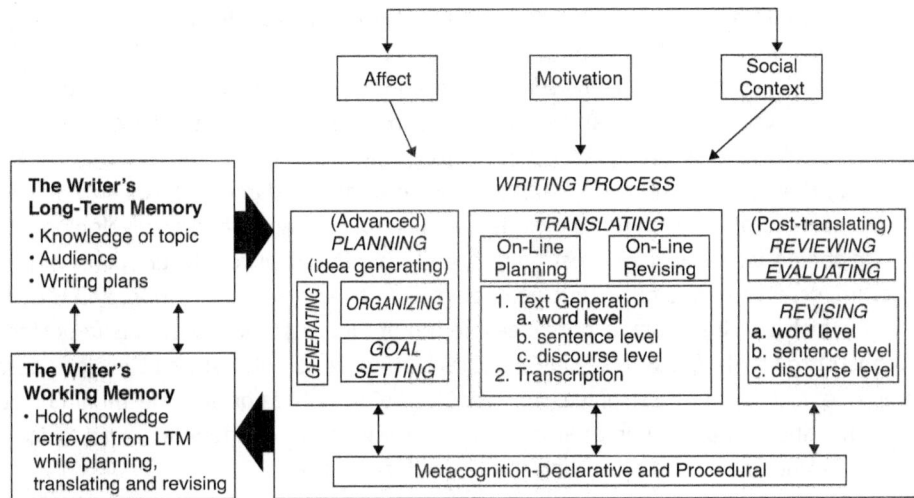

Figure 1.1 Berninger and Swanson's (1994) model of writing

writers, the translation process can be a bottleneck that slows down writing fluency as they struggle to come up with new ideas. For children, transcription can be a bottleneck (for example, if they are emergent writers or struggle with handwriting and/or spelling in senior primary classes) (Hayes & Olinghouse, 2015).

The reviewing stage of writing occurs post-translation (after a draft of the text has been written) and may involve revision of the text at the word, sentence and discourse levels. According to Graves (1983), young children are more likely to revise if teachers encourage multiple drafts, provide opportunities to revise, and do not expect a perfect draft at the first time of asking. The revision process includes problem detection and repair (Berninger et al., 1996), with beginning writers more likely to repair surface features of writing (spelling or grammar) rather than meaning-related features (sentence or discourse structures).

A useful distinction in thinking about writing processes is that between *long-term memory* and *working memory*. Long-term memory comprises knowledge of the (writing) topic, audience (who the piece of writing is for) and writing plans (often based on previous reading and writing experiences). Included are strategies for producing texts; knowledge about the properties of the text to be written (genre, length, format, tone); and knowledge of the properties of genres (arguments, narratives, expositions, etc.). Clearly, gaps in long-term memory (for example, lack of knowledge about the topic one is writing about) can have implications for other aspects of the writing process, such as the quality of ideas generated.

Working memory holds knowledge retrieved from long-term memory and is drawn on during planning, translating and revising (see left side of Figure 1.1). Young children with limited experience of writing may not have the short-term memory capacity to plan or revise their writing as they focus their efforts on transcription. Conversely, it has been argued that efficient management of the processes of writing within the limits of short-term memory is essential to producing good-quality texts (Breetvelt et al., 1994; Levy & Ransdell, 1995). According to Hayes (2006), working memory comprises a phonological loop for storing verbal information, a visuo-spatial sketchpad for storing visual information, and a central executive that controls the first two.

Goal setting is another important aspect of writing (see Figure 1.1, Planning). Goals guide all aspects of the writing process and strongly influence decision-making about what to write and how to write, while setting goals during writing may help children ensure that they produce writing that is consistent with the task, purpose and audience (Hayes & Olinghouse, 2015). Examples of goals for writing include planning for writing a report, developing a writing plan, planning for revising an existing text, and planning to write a future piece of text.

Other important aspects of writing include *affect* (attitude) and *motivation*, and the *social context* in which a writing task occurs (see the top of Figure 1.1). Motivation is important at each stage of the writing process (planning, translating, revising), but its key role is getting the writer to write in the first place. Activities to build motivation include pupil choice of topic, connecting to pupils' personal interests, cultures and communities; writing for real purposes and audiences; and observing the teacher as a writer.

Finally, Berninger and Swanson note the role of *metacognition* in managing the interaction or co-ordination between writing processes such as planning, translating and reviewing. Here, metacognition refers to the writer's awareness of writing processes. Declarative metacognitive knowledge refers to information about writing processes, while procedural knowledge refers to knowledge of procedures for planning, composing and evaluating/revising texts. The role of metacognition in writing is supported by research by Harris et al. (1996), who found that providing students with self-regulated strategy development (SRSD) instruction (see Chapter 2) significantly increased both students' effort and their intrinsic motivation. Children may become metacognitively aware as they discover that the benefits of planning a piece of writing in the pre-writing phase (by, for example, consulting a range of source texts) can lead to fewer interruptions (and hence to greater fluency) during transcription (Beauvais et al., 2014).

Bereiter and Scardamalia's Model of Writing Development

Several authors have described the development of children's writing through the primary and post-primary years or at different points in time. According to De Smedt and van Keer (2017), writers in Grades 5 and 6 (Years 6 and 7 in England) often struggle to engage in pre-writing planning, may have difficulties in generating sentences fluently and struggle to revise their texts as they focus for the most part on surface features such as spelling and handwriting. This represents a challenge to teachers in terms of ensuring that pupils develop proficiency in basic transcription processes, and also have an opportunity to engage in meaningful writing from an early stage. There is also a need to recognise that children will continue to develop as writers well beyond the end of primary schooling (Berninger et al., 1996).

In presenting their model of writing development for children, Berninger and Swanson (1994) describe how development progresses through three stages:

1 During the *lower primary grades* (1–3), low-level transcription processes such as handwriting, and high-level writing processes such as planning, translating, and reviewing

gradually emerge but operate on a very local level (i.e., there is limited interaction between them).
2   During *upper primary grades* (4-6), transcription gradually becomes automatic, reviewing (revision) starts to operate on higher-level aspects of the text and planning prior to writing begins to emerge, though it may not yet guide the generation of text;
3   During *lower secondary schooling*, all writing processes interact and become more complex, with metacognitive knowledge or executive functioning playing a more prominent role.

Berninger and Swanson (1994) note that, at first, planning for beginning writers tends to be local – sentence-by-sentence – before being more global and encompassing larger units of text. Similarly, for beginning writers, the reviewing process would first involve word-level activities, before moving on to larger units of discourse such as sentences, paragraphs and texts. By the senior primary classes, working memory is playing an increasing role, transcription has become more automatized, and text generation is now occurring at the discourse level, as well as at lower levels. Planning (and pre-planning in particular) is not yet fully integrated into the writing process, while revision is more often at the paragraph than at the whole text level.

Bereiter and Scardamalia (1987) compared less-skilled and more-skilled writers. They identified three broad strategies for writing that seem to emerge in sequence:

- Less-skilled writers engaged in a basic *knowledge-telling* strategy, where they generate content through association, with one idea prompting the next. At this stage, pupils' transcription skills may not yet be fluent: handwriting may be laborious, and spelling may require high levels of concentration. As pupils focus on these component skills, they may be unable to concentrate on the meaning of what they have written. They may be unable to focus on reader interpretation in the absence of a full understanding of what they have written. Because the relevant mental representations are not yet stable, they are less likely to use them when planning and reviewing, limiting their use of these processes.
- More skilled writers, on the other hand, engage in a strategy called *knowledge transforming*, where they develop elaborate writing goals, particularly goals related to content and form, which require complex processing strategies and ongoing adjustments until the text matches rhetorical and pragmatic goals. There is a constant interaction between the writer and the text as they write, with the writer changing what they wish to say, as a result of the process of writing. According to Needham (2021), as they read what they have written, writers at this stage strengthen representation of their writing, and activate additional planning and sentence generation. Writing is more about actively constructing knowledge.
- A third strategy identified by Bereiter and Scardamalia, *knowledge crafting*, represents a high level of proficiency and expertise. Writers think all the time about their readers, and how their written text will be interpreted. These writers may make extensive structural adjustments during writing and will attend to the form and shape of their arguments.

Needham (2021) characterises these strategies as mainly involving the writer (knowledge telling), the interaction between the writer and the text (knowledge transforming), and interaction between the writer, the text and the reader (audience) (knowledge crafting).

According to Alamargot and Chanquoy (2001), expertise in writing, such as that described in Bereiter and Scardamalia's knowledge-transforming and knowledge-crafting strategies, depends on making progress in the main writing processes (planning, translating and reviewing), and expanding knowledge about writing, including domain-specific information (content area knowledge) and linguistic and pragmatic knowledge (how language is used in different contexts for different purposes). They further note that, while the development of expertise in many domains not involving writing often means doing something more quickly or more efficiently, expert writers typically take longer to write than novice writers, as they deploy more complex processes. Alamargot and Chanquoy characterise the difficulties faced by young or novice writers as being related to a lack of awareness about writing problems (such as the consideration of a writing aim or audience), limited automatisation of appropriate procedures (including processes) and lack of experience in recognising errors. They further note that the development of expertise in writing can be related to an increase in working memory, arising from general cognitive development and a practice/training effect from implementing different writing processes more strategically.

While these models reflect children's general development as writers, they do not necessarily reflect the outcomes of a process approach to teaching writing, which may well expedite children's acquisition and development of key writing processes and strategies. Helping children move from a knowledge-telling to a knowledge-transforming approach and deepening the sophistication of their writing is discussed in subsequent chapters in this book.

Scoring rubrics, which are described in Chapter 5 in the context of assessing writing, also provide insights into children's writing development. For example, a rubric that includes organisation of writing at a key dimension will describe how children can be expected to improve the organisation of texts, including greater awareness of the characteristics of different genres, as they develop as writers, and move from one stage to the next. Similar insights can be generated for other dimensions of writing such as conventions (e.g., spelling, punctuation and grammar), ideas, word choice/use of language and voice.

Graham's Writer(s) within Community Model

Graham (2025) built on earlier and mainly cognitive models of the writing process (e.g., Flower & Hayes, 1981; Berninger & Swanson, 1994) by elaborating on his writer(s) within the community model (Figure 1.2). In addition to describing the cognitive architecture underpinning writing (e.g., attention, working memory, executive control, long-term memory and production processes), Graham describes how writing occurs within communities, adding a socio-cultural dimension to how writing is conceptualised. Graham argues that writing is shaped by the characteristics, capacity and differences in the writing community and is influenced by the cognitive characteristics (knowledge), capacity and individual differences among community members. These include those who compose a text (writers, collaborators), the readers who comprise the audience, and mentors and teachers who help writers

Figure 1.2 Basic components of a writing community (Graham, 2025)

acquire the knowledge, dispositions, strategies and modes of action needed to achieve the community's goals.

As outlined in Figure 1.2, the innermost circle includes the goals of the writer(s), their actions, their processes and the finished writing product. The second circle shows that the key actors involved in this are the writers, readers, mentors, teachers and, on occasion, their collaborators, if the composition is a shared activity. The third circle focuses on aspects of a writers' community that might impact how pupils perform on a writing task, including the purposes of the writing community, its collective history, its membership, and the physical/social environment in which writing takes place, whether the environment is a classroom or an online space. The outermost circle covers broad issues that can influence the activities of a writing community, such as social, historical, political and institutional influences. For example, in some countries, it may be illegal to write something that is critical of the ruling government (political, historical).

The Writers in Community model is especially relevant to classroom contexts in that a classroom of young writers comprises a writing community in development. Teachers need to be aware of the factors that can influence such a community, including the goals of the community (sometimes linked to broader curriculum goals – see Chapter 4, this volume), the tools that are available for writing, the skills or actions of members of the writing community, and the finished written product. An understanding of these, and related factors, such as how members of the community interact with and support one another, is important in devising activities that support pupils in their development as writers.

Self-Efficacy, Self-Regulation and Motivation to Write

According to Graham (2018), motivations for writing include beliefs about why one engages in writing, the importance of trying to outperform others, the value and utility of writing, attitudes and interest in writing, competence as a writer, determinants of writing success or challenges, writing identity or identities, and views about the communities where writing takes place.

Bruning and Kauffman (2016) note that self-efficacy for writing is important both because it can impact on whether a learner will undertake a specific writing task, and whether the learner will persist with the task if difficulties arise. Hence, the development of self-efficacy for writing should be a goal of writing instruction.

At a fundamental level, success in writing is the most basic way in which to develop writing self-efficacy (Pajares et al., 2007). Specific factors that have been associated with the development of self-efficacy that are relevant to writing, include:

- *Mastery experience* (the most important criterion for developing self-efficacy in a domain); the impact of mastery experience may be linked to the quality of the information or feedback that students receive when they perform successfully
- *Vicarious experience* (e.g., observing others' performances and assessing one's own capabilities in relation to what is observed); fellow pupils and teachers can serve as models of writing. Models who demonstrate the ability to cope in the face of difficulties are more effective than models who exhibit complete mastery (Zimmerman & Kitsantas, 2002).
- *Social persuasion* (e.g., others expressing beliefs that an individual can perform successfully). Teachers can offer suggestions for improvement and demonstrate their belief that the learner can improve; Bruning and Kauffman note that social persuasion should involve 'long term communication patterns in which teachers show their belief in learners' personal agency' (p. 160), rather than shorter pep talks.
- *Identifying and labelling physiological and emotional states linked to a domain* (e.g., identifying and addressing anxiety about writing in general, or about a particular writing task). Teachers can identify possible challenges to writing and seek to reassure students that they can overcome them.

Bruning and Kauffman (2016) identify a number of factors that need to be considered in understanding the development of writers' sense of self-efficacy, including writing goals and purposes related to a writing task; social, cognitive and linguistic contexts of a writing task; access to and use of resources for writing; form and frequency of feedback on writing; interaction of the writer's knowledge and interest with writing tasks and genres; and the teacher's own self-efficacy as a writer and teacher of writing.

Schunk and Zimmerman (2007) argue that self-efficacy in writing is not merely an outcome of writing successfully, but a consequence of how well students monitor how they are managing the writing process. They suggest that it is important to provide students with opportunities to observe a model writer (such as a teacher) because it helps with identifying the features of a writing task and its goals. In this regard, if particular writing strategies are taught, it would seem important to emphasise how to integrate and transfer them to independent writing. Modelling of strategies (by the teacher) is most effective if it is followed up by independent practice by students.

Self-efficacy for writing is often examined with reference to self-regulation for writing. Self-regulation (or self-regulated learning) refers to self-generated thoughts, feelings, and actions that are designed to affect one's learning of knowledge and skills (Zimmerman, 2000, 2001). Activities designed to enhance writers' self-regulation may also impact positively on their self-efficacy as writers. According to Santangelo et al. (2016), such activities include: goal setting, modelling and tutoring, cognitive strategies instruction, use of self-evaluative standards (such as scoring rubrics), prewriting, and use of mental imagery.

In sum, the research reviewed here suggests that building pupils' writing self-efficacy involves ensuring that they experience progress and success with their writing, that they are presented with successful models of writing, and that they receive and reflect on feedback provided by their teachers, their peers and their own self-evaluation.

As per Berninger and Swanson's (1994) model of writing (Figure 1.1), motivation is another key element of writing. It is associated with whether or not children will initiate and persist with a written text. Hayes (1996) notes that motivation can facilitate both short-term responses to immediate writing goals, and a long-term predisposition to engage in writing activities, even those that are quite challenging. Researchers (e.g., Wang & Troia, 2023) have established statistical links between measures of motivation and the quality of students' writing, with higher levels of motivation typically associated with stronger writing performance. However, neither self-efficacy nor motivation operate independently in terms of impacting the quality of a child's writing. They interact with one another, and with other factors such as working memory, long-term memory and writing-related strategies. Nevertheless, they can be viewed as important elements of writing that should be attended to during teaching, learning and assessment (see Chapter 2, this volume).

Activities to build motivation include pupil choice of topic, connecting to pupils' personal interests, cultures and communities, and writing for real purposes and audiences, including observing the teacher as a writer.

Not So Simple View of Writing

Some years ago, Gough and Tunmer (1986) proposed their simple view of reading, with the argument that performance in reading can be accounted for by two key factors: decoding (the ability to read words) and language comprehension. If children could decode the words in a text (D) and apply their language comprehension skills (LC) to understanding that text, they would be expected to comprehend the text. In other words, reading comprehension (RC) should occur. This relationship was expressed by the equation, $RC = D \times LC$. The model gained a new lease of life in England with the publication of the Rose Report (Rose, 2006), a government-commissioned independent review of the teaching of early reading. While acknowledging the complexity of reading, Rose noted that reading could be broken down into decoding and language comprehension. The model has some diagnostic value. For example, students with good decoding and poor language comprehension, or with poor decoding and good language comprehension can be expected to struggle with reading comprehension.

A model of writing produced by Berninger et al. (2002) has been viewed as embodying a simple view of writing. In that model, the authors described writing (W) as the product of lower-level transcription skills (spelling and handwriting/keyboarding) and text generation

> **BOX 1.3 THE SIMPLE AND NOT SO SIMPLE VIEWS OF WRITING**
>
> Simple view = Transcription Skills × Text Generation (Ideation)
>
> Not so simple view = Transcription Skills × Text Generation × Self-regulatory Processes × Working Memory
>
> Based on: Berninger et al. (2002); Berninger and Winn (2006)

(also called ideation). In this case, the relationship is described by the formula, Writing = Transcription Skills X Text Generation. In a subsequent article, Berninger and Winn (2006) portrayed writing as a more complex construct by adding such elements as executive functioning or self-regulatory processes (e.g., attention, goal setting, reviewing), working memory (required for planning) and revision. Hence, the formula might be adjusted to: Writing = Transcription Skills × Text Generation × Executive Functioning × Working Memory (Box 1.3). It is clear that it is difficult to capture the complexity of writing in one or two key processes or knowledge sources.

Scarborough (2001) published a graphic of a 'reading rope' depicting multiple components of language comprehension (background knowledge, vocabulary, language structure, verbal reasoning, literacy knowledge) and word recognition (phonological awareness, decoding, sight word recognition) as important components or interacting strands of reading. As children develop skills in these components, they become increasingly more strategic and automatic in their application, leading to strong reading comprehension. Sedita (2019) has extended the rope metaphor to writing, by including the elements below.

- Transcription (spelling, handwriting, keyboarding)
- Syntax (grammar, syntactical awareness, sentence elaboration and punctuation)
- Critical thinking (generating ideas, gathering information, organising, drafting, writing, revising)
- Text structure, including genre (narrative, informational and opinion structures, paragraph structure, patterns of organisation, linking and transition words and phrases)
- Writing craft (word choice, awareness of task, audience and purposes, and use of literary devices).

These are interwoven into the five strands of a rope. The elements of the rope and their interlinkages suggest that writing is indeed not so simple and takes time to develop, whether instruction is provided directly (through, for example, instruction in writing processes and strategies) or whether the writer acquires skills through observation and engagement with texts and ideas (for example, by learning about genres through reading, or by learning about the qualities of good writing by observing texts produced by the teacher and by other pupils).

Links among Oral Language, Reading and Writing

It is not surprising that synergies between oral language, reading and writing have been reported in the literature. After all, aspects of language such as vocabulary knowledge are important in expressive oral language (speaking), reading and writing. Similarly, knowledge about genres is implicated in all three processes – recounting a story orally, understanding a written text based on a particular genre, and writing a text around that genre. In some cases, oral language can act as a bond between reading and writing, as learners discuss texts they have read, or texts they have written or plan to write.

There has been an interest in capitalising on links between reading and writing for many years. According to Needham (2021), there are five aspects of knowledge in particular that are shared between reading and writing:

- *Domain or topic knowledge*, with learners who have high levels of domain (background) knowledge more likely to find both reading and writing easier, compared to those with low levels of such knowledge. For example, it is easier to understand a text about cricket, or to write one, if the rules of the sport are understood.
- *Meta knowledge*, or the functions and purposes of reading and writing, and how readers and writers interact; this implies that writers need to write with a reader in mind to ensure that their texts are coherent, while readers need to monitor their comprehension to ensure the ideas they generate cohere and make sense (as intended by the writer).
- *Knowledge about the functions and purposes of texts*, with readers drawing on such knowledge to help with the interpretation of texts, and writers using it to ensure that their writing fits the purpose on hand;
- *Knowledge of universal text attributes*, including, for example, the rules and grammar for composing sentences and using punctuation, which are drawn on by both readers and writers. Knowledge of text structures, formats and organisational elements is also shared by both processes.
- *Procedural knowledge*, which includes setting goals, retrieving relevant information from long-term memory and employing higher-level strategies such as questioning, drawing analogies, analysing and summarising. These can be deployed to support comprehension during reading and to support monitoring or executive functioning during writing.

Drawing on 89 experimental studies, Graham et al. (2018) investigated if literacy programmes balancing attention to reading and writing instruction improved students' reading and writing performance. They reported significant improvements in overall reading measures, and measures of decoding, reading vocabulary and reading comprehension following instruction in both reading and writing (compared with instruction in one or the other). Similarly, positive effects were found for overall writing performance, and for writing quality, writing mechanics and writing output as measured by the number of words written.

Oral language skills can be drawn on in various activities involving reading and writing (e.g., interactive book reading, literature discussion, writing processes and genres, inquiry-based learning, disciplinary literacy, critical literacy), with explicit intentional teaching linked to students' stages of development provided as required (Murphy et al., 2009; Wixson et al., 2020; Dobinson & Dockrell, 2021). Embedding oral language within such contexts enables children to develop a metalanguage to express their thoughts and responses while also supporting the development of key literacy skills (e.g. vocabulary, comprehension, composition) (Kennedy et al., 2022). For example, in discussing and justifying the linguistic choices made in their writing, children develop knowledge of language components and how their word choices shape and alter meaning (Myhill & Watson, 2014).

Jouhar and Rupley (2021) included 13 studies in their systematic review of the literature on reading-writing connections based on independent reading and independent writing (where students engage in these processes without help). According to the authors, the findings obtained from seven studies 'conclusively suggest that independent reading enhances overall narrative and descriptive writing quality, and increases output, mechanics, spelling accuracy, content, grammatical accuracy, and text organization' (p. 136). However, independent reading was not found to impact significantly on writing vocabulary, suggesting a need for more intensive instruction to enable this transfer. Independent writing was found to improve literal reading comprehension for beginning, low-performing and at-risk students and both literal and inferential reading for normally achieving students. The review strengthens the case to include independent reading and independent writing opportunities for students as part of a literacy framework that also includes systematic instruction in reading and writing.

Conclusion

The focus of this chapter has been on the sources of knowledge and the dispositions that contribute to writing development. Three main models of writing were presented: Berninger and Swanson's (1994) cognitive model, which outlined the different processes involved in writing, and the mental architecture (long-term memory, working memory) associated with implementing those processes; Bereiter and Scardamalia's (1987) model of writing development, encompassing knowledge telling, knowledge transforming and knowledge crafting strategies; and Graham's (2025) writer(s) within community model, which encompasses the broader social context in which writing occurs as well as the cognitive and motivational aspects. These models serve to underline the important role of knowledge in writing, as well as the complexity of the writing process, as also evidenced in the definition of writing proposed by Graham. However, descriptions of writing must also account for children's dispositions, and this chapter focused on three related aspects: self-efficacy (or confidence), self-regulation (ability to purposively control one's writing processes), and motivational beliefs. The notion that writing is a simple process was debunked, with, for example, Sedita (2019) arguing that it requires combining knowledge of transcription (spelling, handwriting, keyboarding), syntax, critical thinking, text structure and writing craft. Finally, links between oral language, reading and writing were highlighted, including research demonstrating that instruction in reading can improve writing and vice-versa. This information is useful in thinking about literacy programmes that integrate oral language, reading and writing, as opposed to teaching each element of language separately.

Chapter 2 builds on the theoretical perspectives presented in this chapter by focusing on how knowledge about the effective teaching of writing is generated, and on aspects of writing pedagogy that have been demonstrated to be effective.

Reflect, Connect, Act

Activity

Consider two writing samples on the same topic – one by a novice writer, and one by a more advanced writer (these can come from children in your class):

- Identify key differences between the two pieces, drawing on ideas in this chapter.
- What are some knowledge differences that can be inferred between the writers of the two pieces?

Suggestion for Further Reading

Barrs, M. (2019). Teaching writing badly. *English in Education, 53(1)*, 18–31. https://doi.org/10.1080/04250494.2018.1557858

Grahms (2025). https://www.guilford.com/books/Handbook-of-Writing-Research/MacArthur-Graham-Fitzgerald/9781462557271?srsltid=AfmBOoowvH3Lc-7EI9zC4QCWb-_A2rPb8CeA5g67O83r7xbat9bNh1DQ

Notes

1. These are sometimes summarised into three broad processes: planning, translating and reviewing, with composing/drafting and revising merged under 'translating', and publishing omitted.
2. Lexical knowledge refers to the meaning of words in a writer's lexicon. Syntactical knowledge is the knowledge of how words are combined in phrases and sentences (e.g., the order in which words are spoken or written); rhetorical knowledge refers to a writer's understanding of the audience, purpose or context of writing.

2 Effective Writing Pedagogy

This chapter examines how we learn about children's writing, and what we know about effective writing instruction. The chapter opens by looking at how children write, with reference to several approaches to research: case studies, which typically involve looking at individuals or small groups of students as they engage in writing and detailing their development; experimental research, which compares one or more methods of teaching writing and may include an experimental group, and a control group; meta-analyses of writing research, which combine the results of several experimental studies, and draw stronger conclusions about outcomes; process outcome studies, which link teacher and student activities designed to improve writing with changes in test scores; and policy-focused research reviews, which aim to inform policy on teaching writing (for example, curriculum development). The second section looks at the knowledge base needed by teachers for effective writing instruction, including knowledge about teaching grammar; how to support children's development as spellers; how to build students' self-efficacy as writers alongside their self-regulation, metacognition and motivation; how to build students' agency and identity as writers; and how to develop handwriting and typing/keyboarding. Overall, the research is viewed as providing insights into the types of classroom envionments that enable writing development. After reading this chapter, you should be able to answer the following key questions.

> **Reflect and Connect**
>
> 1 How has research on teaching writing to children been conducted?
> 2 What are some key messages that arise from recent research on teaching writing?
> 3 How can these key messages be translated into classroom practice?
> 4 What aspects of children's writing do we need to research in more detail to better inform teaching and learning?

Where Does Research on Children's Writing Come From?

Throughout this book, you will encounter studies on the effectiveness of various approaches to the teaching and assessment of writing. There are multiple ways in which we can learn about effective pedagogy and assessment in writing. In considering aspects of effective writing instruction, it is worthwhile to reflect on Hall and Harding's (2003) warning that there is no single critical variable that defines outstanding instruction, but that effective literacy instruction involves 'a complex interaction of many components, an intelligent weaving together of a lot of skills instruction with voluminous reading and writing' (p. 4). Gadd and Parr (2017) add that 'the apparent effectiveness of any particular dimension or move within the pedagogical context of the classroom may well be contingent on its inter-connectedness with other moves' (p. 1553). They also note that particular pedagogies (called instructional moves) may need to be modified to take into account the socio-cultural context in which they are implemented. This implies that there is no single roadmap for teaching writing that applies to all learning contexts.

Case Studies of Children Engaged in Writing

One of the most influential educators in writing pedagogy was Donald Graves, an American author and teacher, who popularised the process approach to writing. As noted in Chapter 1 (this volume), the key writing processes are previewing, composing/drafting, revising, editing, and publishing. These processes can be implemented through a Writing Workshop approach, where the teacher's role is to provide guidance to pupils on the quality of their work. Grave's (1983) book, *Writing: Teachers and Children at Work* did much to popularise process writing in Australia, New Zealand, the United Kingdom, and the United States. In that publication, he noted four components of a strong writing programme:

- Adequate provision of time, with writing instruction occurring at least 4-5 times per week, with frequent writing time allowing the teacher to maintain a connection between speaking (discussing writing) and writing.
- Learner choice of topic, with children generally knowing something about the topic they write about. Graves recommended that teachers write with children, to demonstrate where they get ideas from.
- Responsive teaching (to child meaning), where the teacher confirms what s/he understands in the text by asking key questions that can lead to the children valuing what they have written.
- Establishing a classroom community, where children assist and support one another. This recognises that writing is a social act.

Graves also articulated two basic principles for teaching writing:

- The teacher demonstrates how s/he learns, by gathering information from children - for example, in the course of a writing conference, a teacher might ask for clarification or additional information about what a child has written, as the teacher seeks to learn more.
- The teacher provides a highly structured classroom so that children who exercise choice have a predictable structure around them. The children know that the teacher will clarify their intentions and problems, rather than solve them. The teacher responds to children's writing in predictable ways and skills are taught with a view to enhancing meaning.

Graves had a particular interest in helping children with learning disabilities to improve their writing. Noting that such children often struggled with handwriting, spelling and language conventions, and a lack of ideas and information worth sharing, he observed that the instruction they received often focused on isolated skills, disconnected from meaningful writing. His research indicated that children with learning disabilities lacked confidence in themselves as writers, and benefitted from engagement with the writing process, with a focus on writing around a topic of interest (that is, a 'meaning-centred approach) rather than over-emphasizing handwriting or spelling, though difficulties in those areas also need to be addressed over time.

Prior to publishing *Writing: Teachers and Children at Work*, Graves observed writing instruction in an elementary school in New Hampshire (United States) as he tracked 16 children aged 6-8 years, over a two-year period. He conducted case studies of these children's progress as writers, describing their development in detail via narrative accounts. He also gathered video evidence. These approaches contrast with experimental research described below, which seeks to control the conditions under which writing is taught and tends to be mainly quantitative.

A critique of Graves' research by Smagorinsky (1987) claimed that the children Graves observed may not have been typical or representative of students in general and included some very talented children. He also criticised the model whereby beginning and emerging writers were expected to emulate the writing processes of professional authors. According to Smagorinsky, Graves and his colleagues also placed an overly strong emphasis on writing from personal experience, and an insufficient emphasis on planned writing or fiction.

Wyse (2019) revisited Graves' work and sought to address some of these criticisms. Drawing on interview data involving professional writers, he noted some parallels between the processes engaged in by professional writers, and those supported by Graves' work, including: a starting point that involves creating ideas for writing; the intense work that goes into translating those ideas into the text; the demanding skill of editing; and satisfactory publication. He contrasted these approaches with those sometimes prescribed for improving children's writing in classrooms that involve imitation, copying and reproduction. Wyse noted two other attributes of successful writing that seem to apply across all age ranges: the 'writer's ear', or the ability of the writer to learn by reading other writers' work, and the 'courage' to take risks, for example in the choice of words or sentence structures.

Experimental Studies of Writing Pedagogy

In recent years, some education systems and funders have questioned the value of qualitative research such as case studies, and favoured evidence arising from experimental research, where one group may be assigned to a new teaching approach, and another may be given a different one, or may function as a control or 'business as usual' group. Ideally, students (or teachers and their classes) would be assigned at random to one or another group.

An example of an experimental study designed to improve the quality of children's writing is one conducted by Madden et al. (2011). They looked at the implementation of Writing Wings with Multimedia (WWM), a programme that used a process approach, with a strong focus on multi-media segments (e.g., using puppets) to model the writing process, cooperative learning, writing genres and metacognitive strategies. Sixty-three teachers were randomly assigned to WWM or control conditions in 22 different schools, with 922 students in Third and

Fourth grades involved. The students worked in four-member heterogeneous writing groups to help one another plan, draft, revise, edit and publish compositions. The students completed writing assessments in October (the pretest) and May (the post-test). The researchers reported significant gains in total writing scores, writing styles and mechanics, but not in ideas and organisation, between pre-test and post-test. The findings were interpreted as providing some support for the use of cooperative learning and embedded multimedia to improve outcomes in writing process models.

In the WWM study, teachers received one day of professional development at the beginning of the school year, and four visits from coaches during implementation. The multimedia resources provided teachers (and students) with additional ideas for implementing different elements of the writing process in a cooperative setting and hence served as additional in-service support.

Meta-Analyses of Research on Teaching Writing

Meta-analysis is an important source of research evidence on the effectiveness of different approaches to teaching writing. It involves reviewing existing experimental studies such as the WWM study described above, and averaging the gains in writing quality (or other outcomes) across studies that have similar goals. In addition to allowing for the estimation of overall gains, a meta-analysis can examine the effects on subgroups such as students at primary and post-primary levels, or students with/without disabilities, if enough studies of sufficient quality are available. Graham and Sandmel (2011) reported on a meta-analysis involving 33 experimental studies across Grades 1-12 that compared a process writing approach to control or 'business as usual' conditions. They found a statistically significant effect for the process writing approach, with an overall effect size of 0.34 (indicating that process writing can be effective, but not powerfully so), with a stronger effect at the primary or elementary level (ES = 0.48), compared with secondary level (ES = 0.25). Process writing was not found to improve the writing quality of at-risk or struggling writers, nor was it associated with the reliability of the writing quality measure, the genre assessed or the quality of the studies.

Slavin et al. (2019) adopted a rigorous approach to selecting studies for inclusion in their meta-analysis on teaching writing in Grades 2-12. They found similar outcomes for writing programmes focused on the writing process (ES = 0.18), cooperative learning (ES = 0.16), and the integration of reading and writing (ES = 0.19). These authors noted the effectiveness of two approaches to process-based writing, Graham's Self-Regulated Strategy Development model, and Writing Wings with Multimedia (WWM). Key features of SRSD include teaching students both general and task-specific writing strategies, the necessary background knowledge to use those strategies, and procedures for regulating the strategies (e.g., goal setting, self-monitoring, self-instruction, and self-reinforcement), writing processes and writing behaviours. As noted above, WWM involves students working in writing teams to help each other through writing process activities in different genres, with teachers modelling key elements.

While the outcomes of meta-analyses are typically reported on in scholarly journals, they may also contribute to research summaries specifically targeted at schools and teachers. This is the case with the *What Works Clearing House Practice Guide* published by the

US Department of Education (see Graham et al., 2012/2018) and the guidance reports published by the Educational Endowment Foundation in England (Bilton & Tillotson, 2020; Bilton & Duff, 2021). The recommendations for writing instruction and related areas (e.g., assessment, inclusiveness) in these reports are summarised in Tables 2.1 and 2.2.

In addition to providing recommendations, the reports provide a research-based rationale for their recommendations, and, in the case of the Educational Endowment Foundation reports, support materials that teachers can use when working collaboratively at the school level to implement research-based instruction.

Process Outcomes Studies

An example of this approach, in which links are made between teaching and learning processes, and the learning outcomes achieved by the students, is a study by Gadd and Parr (2017). They examined the teaching practices of 9 upper-primary and middle-school teachers of writing in New Zealand, whose students had achieved greater than average gains ('accelerated progress') on the country's national assessment of writing. Data were based on observations of three lessons taught by each teacher, interviews with the teachers before and after observed lessons, and interviews with students after the observed lessons. The researchers found significant associations between two dimensions of writing instruction and student gains in writing:

- The nature of learning tasks (what teachers did and thought about as they devised learning tasks for and with learners),
- Direct instruction of writing (the approaches and strategies that teachers considered and used when providing instruction)

They also identified a third dimension that stood out as being among the practices of teachers whose students made the greatest gains in writing:

- Self-regulation (actions that teachers take to enhance learners' sense of ownership or responsibility and to support their development as independent learners)

Instructional actions and activities were found to be especially effective if regarded as purposeful by learners and if they incorporated meaningful opportunities for learner involvement. Gadd and Parr note that evidence for direct causality between strong application of these dimensions and learner gains is not claimed. Rather, they suggest that 'they are key levers within a learning context of all dimensions being applied in an integrated and flexible way' (p. 1563).

The other instructional dimensions identified in the literature by Gadd and Parr, and mentioned less frequently by interviewees, included:

- Expectations (the vision of achievement that teachers hold and communicate to learners, including achievement across the curriculum)
- Learning goals (what teachers do and think about as they formulate learning goals for and with learners)
- Responding to learners' work (how teachers give feedback and feed-forward information to learners, the nature of this information and how learners use it)

Table 2.2 Recommendations for teaching writing and supporting writing development in the key stage guidance reports

Key Stage 1 (Ages 5-7)	Key Stage 2 (Ages 7-11)
• Teach pupils to use strategies for planning and monitoring their writing. • Promote fluent written transcription skills by encouraging extensive and effective practice and explicitly teaching spelling. • Use high-quality information about pupils' current capabilities to select the best next steps for teaching. • Use high-quality structured interventions to help pupils who are struggling with their literacy.	• Teach writing composition strategies through modelling and supported practice. • Develop pupils' transcription and sentence construction skills through extensive practice. • Target teaching and support by accurately assessing pupil needs • Use high-quality structured interventions to help pupils who are struggling with their literacy.

Sources: Bilton and Tillotson (2020); Bilton and Duff (2021). Permission to reprint granted by the Educational Endowment Foundation.

Table 2.1 What Works Clearinghouse recommendations for teaching writing at primary level

Recommendations

1. **Provide daily time for students to write**
2a. **Teach students the writing process**
    - Teach students strategies for the various components of the writing process.
    - Gradually release writing responsibility from the teacher to the student.
    - Guide students to select and use appropriate writing strategies.
    - Encourage students to be flexible in their use of the components of the writing process.
2b. **Teach students to use the writing process for a variety of purposes**
    - Help students understand the different purposes of writing.
    - Expand students' concept of audience.
    - Teach students to emulate the features of good writing.
    - Teach students techniques for writing effectively for different purposes.
3. **Teach students to become fluent with handwriting, spelling, sentence construction, typing, and word processing.**
    - Teach very young writers how to hold a pencil correctly and form letters fluently and efficiently.
    - Teach students to spell words correctly.
    - Teach students to construct sentences for fluency, meaning, and style.
    - Teach students to type fluently and to use a word processor to compose.
4. **Create an engaged community of writers**
    - Teachers should participate as members of the community by writing and sharing their writing.
    - Give students writing choices.
    - Encourage students to collaborate as writers.
    - Provide students with opportunities to give and receive feedback throughout the writing process.
    - Publish students' writing, and extend the community beyond the classroom.

Source: Graham et al. (2012b, 2018). Reprint permitted by What Works Clearinghouse.

- Motivating and challenging learners (what teachers do to motivate learners in learning tasks and challenge them cognitively around tasks, at a level appropriate to their potential)
- Organisation, differentiation and management (what teachers do to organise, differentiate and manage instructional lessons effectively in the classroom).

The fact that these dimensions did not show significant associations with achievement gains does not mean that they are unimportant; rather, as Gadd and Parr note, they may work together with the statistically significant dimensions to support improvement in children's writing.

Policy-Focused Research Reviews

A final genre of studies that provide information on effective pedagogy and related issues (e.g., assessment of writing) are more traditional research reviews. While research reviews may include the outcomes of meta-analyses, they may also include outcomes from other studies such as experimental studies and case studies. One example of a research review is Kennedy et al.'s (2022) study on the teaching of literacy (oral language, reading and writing) in primary schools for a report designed to contribute to Ireland's next Literacy, Numeracy and Digital Literacy Strategy. Kennedy et al. conducted a systematic review of meta-analyses and related research to draw conclusions on effective instruction. Their recommendations on the effective teaching of writing are summarised in Table 2.3.

A second example of a policy-based review is a recent study of writing and writing instruction carried out by McLean (2022) on behalf of the Australian Education Research Organisation. This high-level or broad review focused on a number of key issues that, if addressed well, might be expected to contribute to effective writing via curriculum change. These included preservice preparation and professional development of teachers, the amount, frequency and quality of instruction, the development of writing curricula and programmes, use of 21st-century writing tools, and support for students with learning difficulties and disabilities. The author examined recently published studies dealing with these key issues, including some of the meta-analyses described above. As with most such reviews, McLean provided a set of key recommendations. Among these were:

- Improve access to high-quality and systematic professional learning options for school leaders and teachers in the writing domain.
- Align writing goals, curriculum, instructional methods and assessment practices.
- Provide additional scaffolding and instruction for students with learning difficulties and disabilities
- Create motivating and supporting writing environments where writing is valued, routine and collaborative.

Readers will notice some overlap between many of the studies reviewed in this section, whether based on observations, comparing instructional approaches in experimental contexts, meta-analyses or other approaches to gathering data. While several support process-based approaches to teaching writing, they also emphasise the importance of a balanced approach to writing instruction (with adequate attention to both composition

Table 2.3 Recommendations on teaching writing in primary schools – Kennedy et al. (2022)

Key Research-based Recommendations

- All children in primary school (ages 4–12) should have daily opportunities to engage in compositional writing for real purposes and audiences in authentic contexts.
- To enhance student agency, engagement and writer identity, students should have ownership over their writing through choice of topic and determination of time spent on a particular topic.
- Teachers should ensure conditions in classrooms (i.e., the learning environment) support students' motivation, engagement and self-efficacy, given how these are linked to writing quality.
- Teachers should adopt a process-based approach to writing and combine it with explicit teaching of strategies for planning, drafting, revising, editing and publishing writing on a regular basis. When teaching these strategies, teachers should combine self-regulated strategy development (SRSD) pedagogies and goal setting and also link strategies to the genre form.
- Students should be explicitly taught text structures for each genre of writing; Links should be made with reading text structures.
- Grammar should be taught in the context of authentic writing where it can be utilised as a 'design tool' for communicating.
- Instruction should be balanced between the higher-order dimensions of writing and the mechanics of writing (grammar, spelling and punctuation).
- Students should be explicitly taught how to assess their own and others' writing drafts, to give and receive feedback using insights gained from effective writing strategies taught. These need to be modelled by the teacher.
- Teachers should also give timely, focused and specific feedback to students on their writing quality.

Source: Kennedy et al. (2022).

and conventions), the value of teaching writing strategies, including self-regulated writing strategies, and the importance of providing feedback to pupils.

The Knowledge Base for the Effective Teaching of Writing

Myhill et al. (2023b) identified just seven studies that focused on content knowledge for teaching writing. Among the aspects identified in these studies were meaningful experiences as writers, with teachers learning how to be effective teachers of writing after engaging in writing themselves; explicit understanding of rhetorical structures for writing; and some understanding of revising and editing, the characteristics of texts and different written genres.

Based on the literature on writing development as well as some policy statements, it can be argued that teachers' content knowledge for writing should also comprise a number of areas discussed in Chapter 1, including:

- Stages or phases of writing development
- The roles of working memory and long-term memory in writing development
- Establishing links between reading and writing
- Understanding of writing as a craft.

In this section, a number of additional aspects of teachers' knowledge for writing are discussed, including: teaching grammar to improve writing; developing fluency in writing sentences;

supporting children's spelling development; supporting self-efficacy, self-regulation, metacognition and motivation to write; building writers' agency and identity; strategy instruction and writing development; and supporting the development of handwriting/keyboarding.

Teaching Grammar to Improve Writing

Historically, the teaching of grammar in many writing curricula has focused on the rules of grammatical usage. In contrast, modern linguistics takes a descriptive view of grammar, examining how language is used in different contexts, and how writers' choices around grammar can enhance writing quality (Myhill, 2021). In this view, grammar is not seen as a set of rules, but as a meaning-making system or a system of meaning potential (Halliday, 1978). Halliday's functional grammar looks at how grammatical forms such as verbs perform different meaning-making functions in different communicative contexts. This implies that the writer can exercise control over their syntactic and grammar choices, as well as choices related to vocabulary. Much has been made of the inclusion of the fronted adverbial in the National Curriculum in England. Fronted adverbials are words or phrases placed at the beginning of a sentence that describe the action that follows (e.g., Without warning, she jumped from the high wall; In the distance, they read a shrill cry). In Halliday's terms, the study of fronted adverbials involves assessing how a fronted adverbial alters the meaning of a phrase or sentence, and hence if it meets the writer's authorial intentions. This idea is encapsulated in a term coined by Myhill (2021, p. 269) – 'grammar as choice'.

Myhill and her colleagues (e.g., Myhill et al., 2020) have devised a pedagogical framework called the LEAD principles for heightening children's attention to the role of grammar in making writing meaningful:

- *Link* – Establish a link between the grammar being introduced, and how it works in the writing being taught – this represents Halliday's functionally-orientated meaning making
- *Example* – Explain the grammar through examples, rather than via explanations or rules
- *Authenticity* – Use examples of grammar in use from authentic texts to link young writers to the broader community of writers, thereby establishing reading-writing links
- *Discussion* – Build in high-quality discussion (dialogic talk or metatalk) about grammar and its rhetorical or communicative effects, to develop a sense of metalinguistic awareness.

Young and Ferguson (2022a) recommend that grammar be taught in the context of mini-lessons that occur during Writing Workshop, and argue that, where possible, grammar should be relevant to students' current writing or authorial intentions. Use of grammar is also linked to metalinguistic understanding, as it operates at a conscious level and involves the capacity both to engage in "reflection on language and its use" and to draw on that reflection "intentionally to monitor and plan their own methods of linguistic processing" (Gombert 1992, p.13). Discussion about language has been termed 'dialogic metatalk' by Myhill (2021). It is characterised by metalinguistic discussion which is not focused on "right" answers but involves open-ended thinking about language choices and possibilities. Generating dialogic metatalk appears to be a critical element of learning transfer, moving young writers from a dependence on what teachers suggest are effective choices in writing to a deeper understanding of children's own choices and greater authorial independence.

It might also be noted that spelling instruction, and the discussion of the structure of words in particular, offers additional opportunities to focus attention on grammar. For example, discussing inflectional endings in words (e.g., spying – spies- spied) provides an opportunity to consider the ways in which a word functions (as a noun, verb, adjective, adverb etc.), and, in the case of verbs, which tense is signalled.

Developing Fluency in Writing Sentences

Whereas the focus of much of Myhill's work has been on grammatical choices for writing, others (e.g., Graham et al., 2012; Bacon, 2019) have shown how children benefit from instruction in a related area, sentence structure. Indeed, there is substantial overlap between teaching grammar and teaching sentence structure, and both can be linked to the development of voice and style in children's writing (Young & Ferguson, 2023). Young and Ferguson also warn against approaches to sentence instruction that isolate it from other aspects of writing since only poor writers rely on sentence-by-sentence writing. More mature writers embed their sentences in a broader context that includes the purpose of writing, the audience, the genre, the text structure, and the writing style. Saddler (2018) notes a link between sentence structure and writer's style, or the writer's way with words. According to Saddler, 'the way in which writers convey what they consider the best syntactical arrangements in a given piece of writing relates directly to and reveals their particular style' (p. 23).

Young and Ferguson (2023) identify three main types of sentences:

- *Focused sentences* – these emphasise clarity in expression in terms of choosing suitable nouns and verbs to communicate knowledge or express their emotions.
- *Balanced sentences* – these deal with connections children want to make in their writing, helping 'children to share their reasoning, provide contrasts, establish conditions and discuss alternatives with their readers' (p. 12). This can be achieved through the use of co-ordinating conjunctions (*for, and, nor, but, yet, or, so*), subordinating conjunctions (*before, when, until, because, since*), complex sentences, and sentences involving semi-colons. Also included are comparisons and contrasts (*unlike, and yet, however, on the other hand, just as, in a similar way, in contrast, if we compare this to...*).
- *Developed sentences* – these more complex sentences are designed to 'push your reader's thinking, understanding and imaginings' and are 'about elaborating on or decorating meaning using artistic flair or poetic metaphor' (p. 12). According to Young and Ferguson, students can be supported to compose developed sentences by expanding noun phrases (e.g., *a long day* to *a long and worrisome day*), signalling the passing of time in a variety of ways (e.g., *finally, eventually, meanwhile, before long, without notice*), using fronted adverbials (*Back at the house*, Tom was sleeping peacefully), using prepositional phrases (She lost the book *with the red cover*), and using relative clauses (She's going to the museum, *which is full of interesting artefacts*).

Saddler (2018) identified two broad approaches to improving sentence writing: sentence construction (where the emphasis is on building simple sentences) and sentence combining (where the focus shifts to more complex sentences). Sentence construction can be linked to Young and Ferguson's 'focused sentences', while sentence combining can be linked to their 'balanced sentences', and, to a somewhat lesser extent, their 'developed sentences'.

According to Saddler, 'sentence construction activities help writers produce grammatically correct simple sentences through systematic, explicit instruction, active responding, immediate error correction, and praise during practice sessions' (p. 25). The premise is that, if struggling writers can learn to construct simple sentences with relative ease, this knowledge can support them in constructing more complex sentences. Among the instructional strategies identified by Saddler as being potentially useful, with a gradual shift from teacher-directed to pupil-directed construction, are: (a) identifying whether sentences are complete or incomplete; (b) fixing incomplete sentences by adding missing parts or correcting capitalization and punctuation errors; (c) constructing complete, simple sentences from picture-word prompts; (d) identifying the parts that are missing or present in incomplete sentences; and (e) creating complete sentences when given pictures and key words.

A second instructional approach involves combining sentences. According to Saddler (2018), sentence combining involves manipulating or rewriting short simple sentences into sentences that are more varied in terms of style, as revealed in the arrangement of words and word choice, and complexity, represented by sentence length and syntactic structure. Sadler recommends underlining words that must be retained in the new sentence as a guide to writers in the early stages of development. As students become more independent, it is no longer necessary to underline key words. As an example, consider the following sentences: Cheng was thirsty. He drank lemonade. Ways in which these sentences can be combined include:

- Chen was thirsty and he drank lemonade
- Chen drank lemonade because he was thirsty.
- Thirsty Chen drank lemonade.
- Chen drank lemonade to quell his thirst.

A discussion can follow to decide which is the best sentence, and why. Where appropriate, reference can be made to grammatical elements and how these may change (e.g., thirsty, thirst).

The Australian Education Research Organisation (2022) suggests the following steps (which closely align with Pearson and Gallagher's 1983 Gradual Release of Responsibility Model) to teach sentence combining:

1. Explain the purpose of sentence combining to students (e.g., to improve sentence quality, complexity and variety).
2. Explain that there is often more than one acceptable sentence combination.
3. Model how and why combinations are made using several worked examples. Start with simple sentences, narrate your thinking and justify your combination selections.
4. Explain that students can move words, add or delete words, or modify words to create optimal combinations.
5. Guide practice, supporting students to develop a range of solutions.
6. Students complete independent practice, followed by a supportive whole class discussion to evaluate different combinations.

Research on the impact of instruction on sentence combining (e.g., Graham et al., 2012) points to positive effects on sentence structure and on writing quality more generally. According to Saddler (2018), specific ways in which writing can improve when children learn about and manipulate syntactic options in their own writing, and engage in sentence combining include:

- A greater awareness of the reader
- Fewer sentence fragments, run-on sentences and choppy sentences
- Greater confidence about punctuation usage
- Stronger revision skills, as students also draw on sentence combining skills in revising their writing.

Supporting Children's Spelling Development

Spelling is an integral part of the orthographic knowledge that underlies efficient, automatic generation of words during writing, and efficient, automatic perception of words during reading (Kennedy et al., 2012). Difficulties with spelling can negatively influence writing quality as they may affect a student's motivation, sense of self-efficacy and confidence to write (Snowling, 2000) and may limit word choice as students are less likely to choose ambitious words they can't spell (Graham et al., 2012, 2012/2018).

Graham and Santangelo's (2014) meta-analysis of 53 studies investigated the extent to which spelling instruction made children in K-12th grade better spellers, readers and writers. Likewise, Kent and Wanzek (2016) examined the relationship between component skills (handwriting and spelling) and writing quality and production across Pre-K to 12th grade in the 38 studies they reviewed.

Graham and Santangelo (2014) consistently found that formal spelling instruction improved students' spelling performance, providing strong support for directly and systematically teaching students how to spell. They further recommended that teachers in the lower primary/elementary grades should continue to explicitly and systematically teach spelling, while teachers in the upper primary grades should place more emphasis on spelling instruction and schools should consider if spelling instruction should be extended into lower secondary schooling.

Kent and Wanzek's (2016) analysis confirmed moderate, significant correlations between handwriting, spelling and students' writing quality but generally weak relationships with the amount of writing produced. Student grade level and student ability level did not appear to moderate the relationship between spelling and writing quality.

There is debate in the literacy field as to whether spelling skills learned through formal instruction actually generalise to written composition. Graham and Santangelo (2014) found small non-significant effects of spelling instruction on writing quality, though they highlight that this result may be because writing and writing instruction in the six studies they reviewed occurred infrequently or not at all. According to Kent and Wanzek, the development of proficient transcription skills may free up cognitive resources for higher-level processes required for writing tasks. This correlates with research which highlights that young children's imagination, creativity and thinking capacities outstrip their transcription skills initially, and that providing invented spelling opportunities (defined below) within authentic writing contexts supports their agency as writers and assists them in capturing their thoughts in writing.

Providing opportunities for young children to compose using invented or approximate spelling has been found to benefit writing quality, and also contributes to later proficient reading development (Kennedy et al., 2012; Ouellette & Sénéchal, 2017) and supports children in acquiring the alphabetic principle (the understanding that there are consistent relationships between written letters and spoken sounds).

Box 2.1 describes the representations that children form in memory as they learn to spell, including phonological, orthographic and morphological representations.

BOX 2.1 TRIPLE WORD FORM THEORY

Triple words form theory (e.g., Daffern et al., 2015) posits that children formulate three types of representations as they learn to spell words, and that these develop together in a non-linear way, casting doubt on linear stage theories of spelling development such as those proposed by Gentry, 2000 and by Bear et al., 2012. Their theories base spelling instruction on the idea that phonological representations appear first, followed by orthographic representations (spelling patterns), and, finally, morphological representations):

Phonological representations – these are based on the letter-sound correspondences in a word and follow on from the alphabetic principle. Children require some level of phonemic awareness – the ability to segment words into their component sounds – in order to read and spell words phonologically.

Orthographic representations – these are based on patterns of letters in a word, which are often (but not always) rule-governed. This strategy requires sensitivity to letter clusters (patterns) and letter sequences in a word. Irregular words and silent letters in words may be represented in this way. Furthermore, as phonological representations become more embedded, they may be represented as orthographic patterns (e.g., *ought* in *thought*, and hence stored as orthographic representations).

Morphological representations – these are based on a learner's ability to analyse the morphemic elements in words (e.g., prefixes, inflectional endings, suffixes, base/root words). For example, a student might learn how words change when expressed in plural form (*cry, cries*), or changed to the past tense (*vet, vetted*). Sometimes these patterns may be governed by spelling rules. Learners may draw on etymology as part of this process, discovering, for example, that *visual, vision, revise* and *invisible* have a common origin.

A consistent recommendation across the Educational Endowment Foundation Guidance Reports for literacy at different key stages (Bilton & Tillotson, 2020; Bilton & Duff, 2021) is the need to provide systematic instruction in spelling, including teacher modelling, with a view to supporting the development of fluent transcription skills (Table 2.2).

In considering the spelling errors that students make in their writing, there is value in reflecting on the stages of spelling development presented by researchers such as Gentry (2000), who identified pre-communicative, semi-phonetic, phonetic, transitional and correct spelling stages, and Bear et al. (2012), who identified the emergent, letter-name alphabetic, within word pattern, syllables and affixes and derivational relations spelling stages (see Chapter 9). However, these models suggest a linear progression in spelling, moving from phonological to orthographic to morphological stages (see Box 2.1). Daffern et al. (2015) question whether spelling development is linear, and suggest that even the youngest writers can co-ordinate phonological, orthographic and morphological information, though this may relate to the opportunities that children have to engage in writing.

It is also useful to think about learning spelling as learning about patterns in written language, rather than memorizing words visually (Putman, 2017). While the most common irregularly spelled words should be memorised, much work on spelling will involve supporting pupils to discover the ways in which English spellings are regular and predictable. According to Putman, this involves studying the patterns of English word structure, word origins, and word meaning to discover predictable patterns of English spelling, word use and meaning. The Word Study Approach (Bear et al., 2012) is based on this, as it focuses on identifying predictable patterns of letters and sounds.

Chapter 9 (this volume) examines the teaching of spelling in the broader context of supporting children's efforts to write longer texts.

Supporting Self-Efficacy, Self-Regulation, Metacognition and Motivation to Write

Effective teachers of writing also need to understand the roles of self-efficacy, self-regulation, metacognition and motivation in children's writing, and how these elements are linked to writing quality.

As noted in Chapter 1, **self-efficacy** is important for writing development as it determines whether an individual will undertake to write in the first instance, the level of effort exerted and the degree to which they will persist in the face of difficulty (Bruning & Kauffman, 2016). Schunk and Zimmerman (2007) argue that self-efficacy in writing is not merely an outcome of writing successfully, but a consequence of how well writers self-regulate and monitor how they are managing the writing process. DeSmedt et VanKeer (2018) have shown how self-efficacy for ideation, regulation and conventions can impact cognitive aspects of writing (thinking, planning, revision and control strategies), and ultimately the quality of narrative writing.

Self-regulation concerns self-generated thoughts, feelings, and actions designed to affect one's learning of knowledge and skills (Zimmerman, 2000). Self-regulation supports writers in a multiplicity of ways, enabling them to 'attain greater awareness of their writing strengths and limitations and consequently be more strategic in their attempts to accomplish writing tasks' (Troia et al., 2009, p. 99).

BOX 2.2 THE CLASSROOM CONTEXT AND MOTIVATION AS A KEY TO WRITING ENGAGEMENT

by Rachel Hanniffy, Class Teacher and Write to Read Coach

As I look around the room, I see many enthusiastic, motivated writers diligently working on their stories. There's a subtle hum of chatter and a lovely sense of calm; writers exchanging ideas or getting feedback from peers, and others focused on getting ideas on the page. I glance at my handwritten notes on sticky labels, fresh from conferencing with the children and identify a mini-lesson for tomorrow. I encourage the children to read through their work before our share session, to which I am met with many eager responses from children volunteering themselves to share their writing. An important detail is that this is fifth class in an urban boys' school.

As I reflect on my teaching career to date, 15 years in, teaching writing wasn't always this enjoyable. Having taught in a variety of school settings and class levels, I observed many children experiencing frustration and resistance with writing as they were unmotivated and lacked confidence in themselves as writers.

Following a Masters of Education in Literacy, I adopted a Writing Workshop approach. If I could share some words of wisdom with my younger self all those years ago on how I could enhance motivation and create a classroom context that supports writing, here is what I would say:

- Motivation is everything. Creating a classroom culture where children want to write and are interested in writing, is critical. Find out their interests, hobbies, and what they like to read and write about. In recent years, I have started with non-fiction in September as I found boys in particular really enjoy this genre. They are motivated and engaged from the beginning.
- Implementing a Writing Workshop approach gives structure and allows children to grow as writers in a safe space. The routine is the same each day and children know what is expected.
- Create the time for children to write daily or four times a week. Opportunities for the children just to simply write. Writing that won't be covered in red pen, or circles around misspelled words.
- Allowing the children to write about what they know and are interested in will build up their confidence in themselves as writers. Increased exposure to high-quality mentor texts during mini-lessons and reading widely will support them to expand their writing topics.
- Encourage the children to read in the genre in which they are writing. The exposure to language and vocabulary within the genre will support the writer and generate ideas. Have a variety of high-quality texts available for the children to read and link in with the local library.
- Conferencing and talking to the children as they write is a lovely way to assess and support the writer. Praise their efforts and call the children writers. Celebrate their ideas and encourage and foster their creativity. These conversations build trust and take time to develop.
- Focusing on the children getting their ideas on the page is important. Children can lose motivation if there is an initial emphasis on the mechanics of writing. This will come during the revising, editing and publishing process.
- Explicitly teaching children what thoughtful writers do through mini-lessons and using high-quality mentor texts. The children know the mini-lesson is short and it is my time to teach one small element each day. Avoid the temptation to teach everything all at once.

- Assessing the children's writing becomes a daily habit and informs your practice. Anecdotal notes, reading the children's writing, conferencing and rubrics become part of your everyday practice across the curriculum. Using rubrics they have created themselves, the children are motivated to peer- and self-assess.
- Moving swiftly through the genres across the year ensures the children don't lose motivation and interest. I didn't realise how popular poetry would be!
- Creating a space where writers are comfortable and motivated to share their work with the class gives them a sense of achievement. This is invitation only! In time, the shy writer will share with the class or in a small group. Explicitly teaching children how to give focused feedback is essential.
- Publishing a favourite piece of writing within each genre gives the writer ownership and develops a sense of pride in their work. This can be done in a multitude of ways including using digital technologies.
- Creating a safe space where children are motivated to write and share their work leads to the creation of a community of writers. Time and consistency are needed in this enjoyable and worthwhile process.

Berninger and Swanson (1994) note the role of **metacognition** in managing the interaction or co-ordination between writing processes. They describe metacognition as referring to writers' understanding of the writing process (declarative information) and their knowledge of procedures for planning, composing and evaluating/revising texts (procedural knowledge). A notable omission from the model is a reference to the conditional level (knowing why a strategy is useful) which, arguably, is critical if writers are to value and internalise strategies and know when to use them (Paris, 2005). The development of metacognition can be emphasised in the course of self-regulated strategy development (SRSD, Graham & Perin, 2007; see below).

Wright et al. (2020, p. 153) define motivation to write as 'the variety of reasons a child may choose to engage in a writing task or decide to take steps to avoid the task'. Myhill et al. (2023b) describe motivation as involving beliefs, values, goals and dispositions that students bring to a writing task, and 'how these are dynamically shaped over time through student experiences in the classroom' (p. 2). According to Camacho et al.'s (2021) review of research conducted between 2000 and 2018 on writing motivation in schools, there is a moderate association between student motivation and measures of writing performance. They also found that students' writing motivation was associated with teaching practices such as SRSD instruction and the provision of opportunities for collaborative writing between peers and teachers.

The concepts considered here, self-efficacy, self-regulation, metacognition and motivation, are inter-related. For example, Bandura (1997, p. 122) noted that self-efficacy plays a central role in the cognitive regulation of motivation. Pajares and Valiante (2006) reported that meaningful writing activities, greater autonomy, choice in writing assignments, collaborative writing, self-regulation development, instruction well-matched to learning needs, less competitive writing environments and effective modelling practices all positively support the development of writing self-efficacy beliefs.

In an intriguingly titled article called 'The bright and dark side of writing motivation', De Smedt et al. (2019) reported that motivation to write is associated with the type of instruction provided to students. In their study, involving Grades 5 and 6, students, students in experimental conditions involving peer-assisted writing and extensive opportunities to write had stronger levels of autonomous (intrinsic) motivation (the bright side) than students provided with explicit instruction and opportunities to write individually, who were more externally-motivated ('the dark side'). This finding suggests that, while explicit instruction can play a role in writing development, other factors such as the social context and the frequency with which students write together may also be important.

Finally, at a practical level, it is worrying that the National Literacy Trust (Clark et al., 2023) reported that just 34.6% of children and young people in England aged between 8 and 18 enjoyed writing in their free time – down from 50.7% in 2016.

Building Writers' Agency and Identity

Two additional ideas are important for children's affective writing needs – agency (as a writer) and writing identity. Vaughn (2018) defines agency as 'a student's desire, ability, and power to determine their own course of action (whether that means choosing a learning goal, a topic to study, an activity to pursue, or a means of pursuing it)' (p. 63). Hence, agentic writers might be expected to develop an interest in and personal control over what they write about. Vaughan argues that agency can be developed by encouraging children to choose topics, texts, and activities that meet their linguistic, cultural, and instructional needs and interests. She suggests the following strategies for developing students' agency as writers:

- Teachers should be alert to students' readiness to assert themselves, guide their own learning, and make their own choices.
- Teachers should scrutinize their own classroom structures, materials, and assignments to make sure they allow students to assert agency.
- Teachers should err on the side of giving students too much choice and freedom. And if students aren't ready for it, then teachers should scale it back (rather than giving up on it entirely).

Young and Ferguson (2022b) define identity as a writer's belief in themselves as a writer and how they are perceived and valued as writers by their peers and teachers. According to Murphy (2016), a number of factors lead to the development of a writer's identity:

- Choice and agency as a writer
- Time to write every day
- A sense of enjoyment from having written
- A real audience
- Ownership over one's own writing process

Our goal as teachers of writing is to ensure that all of our students – not just the most enthusiastic ones – believe in themselves as writers. However, in addition to supporting children to develop their identity as writers, teachers can also build their own writing identities.

Cremin and Oliver's (2016) review of the literature from 1990 to 2015 on teachers as writers suggests that many writing teachers have negative writer identities, leading them to view writing instruction as 'problematic' (p. 2). Cremin and Oliver found some evidence of an impact of teachers' writing on student outcomes, with many teachers initially having a narrow concept of what counts as writing and being a writer. Among the tensions they documented were low self-confidence, negative writing histories, and the challenge of composing and enacting teacher and writer positions in a school. However, the authors were optimistic that initial teacher education and professional development could serve to reformulate teachers' attitudes and sense of self as writers. A subsequent project (Cremin et al., 2020) found that teachers' engagement with professional writers can enhance student achievement in writing. With strengthened writing identities, teachers made pedagogical changes that impacted students' motivation, confidence, sense of ownership and skills as writers (also see Cremin et al., 2024).

Strategy Instruction and Writing Development

A common theme in the recommendations arising from meta-analyses and research reviews covered in this chapter is the value of strategy instruction as an approach to teaching components of the writing process such as planning, revising and editing texts. According to Graham and Perin (2007), 'strategy instruction involves explicitly and systematically teaching students strategies for planning, revising and/or editing text, with instruction designed to teach students to use these strategies independently' (p. 449). They describe writing strategies as ranging from processes (such as brainstorming, which can be applied across all genres) to strategies devised for specific types of writing, such as stories or persuasive texts.

A variant of strategy instruction promoted by Graham and Perin is self-regulated strategy development (SRSD). The six stages are:

- Develop the background knowledge needed to use the strategy successfully.
- Describe the strategy, as well as its purpose and benefits.
- Model the strategy (the teacher models how to use the strategy).
- Memorise the strategy (the student memorises the steps in the strategy and accompanying mnemonic).
- Support acquisition of the strategy (the teacher may scaffold student acquisition of the strategy).
- Promote independent use of the strategy.

Graham and Perin also note that SRSD instruction is characterised by explicit teaching and individualised instruction, while students are treated as active collaborators in the learning process. Specific self-regulation skills that are taught as part of SRSD include:

- Goal setting.
- Self-monitoring.
- Self-instruction.
- Self-reinforcement.

These are intended to help students to manage writing strategies, the writing process and their writing behaviour.

According to Graham and Perin, examples of mnemonics taught in the context of SRSD include:

- POW – Pick an Idea; Organise my notes; Write and say more.
- PLAN – Pay attention to the prompt, List the main ideas, Add supporting details, Number your ideas.
- TREE – Persuasive writing strategy – Topic sentence; Reasons (3+); Explain reasons; Ending (wrap it up right).
- WRITE – Work from your plan to develop your thesis statement, Remember your goals, Include transition words for each paragraph, Try to use different kinds of sentences, and Exciting, interesting 10,000-dollar words.

McMaster et al. (2018) examined 15 studies of SRSD (K-3rd grade studies of children with learning difficulties) which they deemed to be high quality, and found that pairing POW – a general planning strategy – with TREE – a genre-specific strategy – is a useful approach to improve young children's fictional and persuasive writing. They suggest that SRSD in these studies was successful as it emphasised critical writing strategies that are of particular focus in the early grades (e.g., planning, organizing, adding details), and that the strategy structure supports students' independent use of these strategies, which can be applied across multiple genres.

While SRSD is an effective approach for teaching aspects of process writing, it might be noted that not all process approaches to teaching writing involve an explicit focus on SRSD or on the use of mnemonics to teach strategies.

The SRSD approach overlaps with the apprenticeship approach to teaching literacy, including writing. According to Shuell (2021), there are six steps in the latter:

- Students observe an expert (usually the teacher) model the desired performance in an environment similar to the ones in which the performance is to occur.
- Coaching (hints, feedback, modeling, reminders, etc.) is provided.
- Conceptual scaffolding is provided with the student performing as much of the task as possible, and external support gradually fades as the student gains proficiency.
- Students are asked to articulate their knowledge and understanding of the task.
- Students are asked to reflect on their understanding and reasoning.
- Students are encouraged to explore new ways in which knowledge or skill can be used.

A recent study involving the implementation of the cognitive learning apprentice approach (CLAA) in Grades K-8 in Canada provides evidence that instruction based on a lesson design that focuses on cognitive apprenticeship increases students' ability to write in the early grades (Akhavan & Walsh, 2020). The authors concluded that CALA training increased teachers' ability to teach writing and that their students' overall writing had improved.

Supporting the Development of Handwriting and Typing/Keyboarding

Handwriting is a 'complex neuromotor skill that encompasses numerous cognitive and motor processes operating in concert….handwriting relies on the close articulation between orthographic (spelling) and motor skills' (Limpo & Graham, 2020, p. 316). Thus, fluency and automaticity in handwriting are key to the integration and consolidation of alphabetic knowledge. Like spelling, explicit attention to handwriting has been shown to impact positively on writing development and quality (Fancher et al., 2018; McMaster et al., 2018). Children who experience handwriting difficulties can develop low self-efficacy and a mindset that they cannot write, which can lead to them avoiding or resisting writing (Santangelo & Graham, 2016; Feng et al., 2019). Limpo and Graham (2020) report that difficulties with handwriting interfere with writers' ideas and text generation, place burdens on working memory, affect the sense of self-efficacy and can create difficulties for the reader if the product is illegible or challenging to read, which in turn can affect assessment outcomes.

Fancher et al. (2018) investigated handwriting acquisition and interventions in Preschool to 2nd grade, drawing on 15 studies. They reported that time for handwriting had declined with the advent of technology in classrooms. This trend is a cause for concern given the theorised link between handwriting and outcomes such as reading and writing instead of literacy. Drawing on functional magnetic resonance imaging (fMRI) technologies, there is increasing evidence that, for pre-school children, 'writing letters mediates neural specialization' (James & Engelhardt, 2012). This body of work has identified patterns of neural activation associated with common forms of early writing instruction (tracing, typing, and forming letters), providing new insights into instructional and environmental conditions linking handwriting and letter recognition in pre-school children.

Critically, in the early years, handwriting instruction should target the name and form of each letter (Limpo & Graham, 2020). Effective teaching requires visuals of each letter (with cues as to the nature, order and direction of the letter strokes), teacher modelling of the letter formation, and opportunities for children to write the letter from memory. Fancher et al. (2018) found tasks that required 'self-generated letter writing or approximation of letters or symbols resulted in neural activation of networks associated with known reading and visual perception networks' (p. 458) and that writing letters is more effective than just seeing or saying letters.

In their review of research on handwriting, Santangelo and Graham (2016) found that students in grades 5 and up made better writing fluency gains than children in grades 4 and below. They note that a certain level of competence is required before fluency gains can be maximised. Additionally, compared to students who received little or no instruction in handwriting, handwriting instruction produced statistically significant gains in the quality, length, and fluency of students' writing. Similar findings were reported by Feng et al. (2019).

Schwellnus et al. (2012) highlight that up to a quarter of North American students (predominantly boys) have handwriting difficulties which impact negatively their confidence and self-esteem. They questioned the wisdom of the current practice of teaching both manuscript and cursive writing to students in primary schools. Their review (69 studies met their inclusion criteria) investigated the origins of dual instruction and the degree to which research supports teaching both forms. The high level of variation amongst countries, schools and teachers makes it difficult to compare outcomes across studies. Historically, manuscript writing was introduced first as it was thought to be easier to learn and closer to the kinds of letters encountered in reading. Research is not conclusive on which format to begin with as there appears to 'be similar but different challenges associated with both manuscript and cursive formats, and there does not appear to be strong evidence to support the choice of one over the other or which one is selected in the case where only one format is taught' (Schwellnus et al., 2012, p. 254).

Graham et al. (2012) argue that being able to type is a valuable life skill and is increasingly necessary for school, and recommend teaching all students to touch type fluently and to compose on a computer. Feng et al. (2019) explored the associations between handwriting or keyboarding on writing quality across 19 studies involving 3014 students from Kindergarten to adolescence. Accurate, fluent transcription of the writer's ideas to text was found to rely on fluency in either handwriting or keyboarding. Both processes relied on making visually accurate representations of letters. In keyboarding:

> Movement patterns and keystrokes must be memorized so that the keyboarder may begin to recognize accurate typing based on kinaesthetic cues, rather than looking at the keyboard to find each letter....while writers executing handwriting must accurately and efficiently form each letter.
>
> (Feng et al., p. 37)

Feng et al. also reported that handwriting contributed as much to writing quality as keyboarding and concluded that students should 'develop handwriting skills and receive explicit instruction about the technology' (p. 56).

Conclusion

In this chapter, we have clear evidence of the complexity of teaching writing and the broad range of factors that teachers must take into account in planning instruction at different grade levels. In this regard, it is worth thinking about the classroom environment in which writing instruction occurs, and how it can be set up to ensure that children enjoy writing and that they are effective writers.

An effective classroom environment is one in which there is adequate time to teach writing. It is important to provide time to teach the skills of writing such as spelling, grammar, sentence construction and handwriting. For maximum transfer, these skills should, where possible, be taught in the context of children's own written texts, with texts written by children's authors drawn on if strong examples are required. There is also a need to set aside time for students to engage in continuous writing, as they implement different aspects of the writing process (planning, drafting, revising, editing and publishing) for different purposes and audiences.

The development of self-efficacy, self-regulation, metacognition and motivation to write are all associated with improved writing quality. In some cases, these can be developed in the context of teaching writing (for example, SRSD focuses attention on self-regulation, during strategy instruction, while collaborative writing allows students to work together on framing a text); in other cases, factors such as a choice of writing topics, feedback and encouragement from the teacher to try out different strategies, and the opportunity to share writing with other students can provide motivation and help students to build positive identities as writers.

Reflect, Connect, Act

Observe a writing lesson, and, if possible, interview the teacher afterwards (if you are unable to observe a lesson in person, reflect on the last writing lesson you taught. Share your findings with your colleagues):

- What learning outcomes did the teacher intend to achieve?
- Which specific writing skills (if any) were taught and were these supported by the research described in this chapter?
- What processes were taught? How?
- What feedback did the students receive on their writing?
- Was an explicit instructional approach used to teach skills or processes?

Suggestions for Further Reading

Daffern, T. (2016). What happens when teachers use metalanguage to teach spelling? *Reading Teacher, 74(4)*, 423-434. https://doi.org/10.1002/trtr.1528

Friddle, K. A., & Ivey, G. (2023). Motivate and engage our youngest writers. *Reading Teacher, 77(3)*, 300-309. https://doi.org/10.1002/trtr.2251

Graham, S. (2019). Changing how writing is taught. *Review of Research in Education, 43*, 227-303. https://doi.org/10.3102/0091732X18821125

3 Genre, Disciplinary Writing, Multimodal Texts and Writing Development

This chapter addresses key issues in writing instruction that have emerged in recent years, including text genre as a knowledge source for writing, the emerging emphasis on teaching disciplinary writing, and the authoring of multimodal texts, strengthened by an emphasis on online writing. The concept of genre is explored further in Chapter 7, where more specific instructional strategies are suggested. After reading this chapter, you should be able to answer the following questions:

> **Reflect and Connect**
> - What is a text genre and why is it important?
> - What are the main genres, subgenres and text structures?
> - How can teachers support writing development across subject disciplines?
> - How can the shift towards technology enhance students' engagement with writing and the quality of their writing?

Origins of Genre-Based Approaches to Supporting Writing Development

In this section, origins of genre-based approaches are described with reference to Halliday's (1978, 1985) seminal work on systemic functional linguistics and subsequent developments in Australia (Martin, 1985; Rothery, 1996). The key concepts of field, tenor and mode are described.

A genre can be defined as a category of writing that includes common goals, structures, styles and content. Genres have particular features that differentiate them from other genres such as tone, language, format and organisation. Genre can be viewed as relating to the broad social purpose of composing a text, as well as its broad format.

Curriculum documents in many countries make specific reference to genre. In Ireland, for example, the Primary Language Curriculum (NCCA, 2019) describes genre as:

> A selection of oral and written forms in order to recount, explain, entertain, inform, give instructions, narrate, persuade and justify opinions… More specifically, genres are types

of multi-sentence oral or written texts that have become conventionalised for particular purposes. They have expected organisational patterns, as well as language features related to register – e.g., narrative, informational, persuasive and multi-genre.

(p. 20)

Lists of text genres can be short, encompassing broad sets of genres such as narrative, informational and argumentative/persuasive texts. Extended lists may also include poetry (though narrative poetry may be subsumed under narrative), drama, hybrid texts (where narrative and information texts are integrated, often for the purpose of providing information in subjects such as history and science) and multimodal texts (texts that can include written language, visual imagery, audio, spatial arrangements and gesture). According to Bintz and Ciecierski (2017), design features of hybrid texts include marginalia (margins containing informational text to compliment a narrative), symbolism, illustrative chronology, multiple data sources, and fun facts and intriguing questions. These features are intended to supplement a narrative text by providing additional information in formats that appeal to young learners.

Broad text genres such as those found in narrative, informational and argumentative or persuasive texts may be divided into subgenres (see Table 3.1).

Table 3.1 Key genres and subgenres

Main Genre	Purpose	Subgenres (Forms)
Narrative	To entertain, to amuse, to relay fictional events in an engaging way	Fairy tales, fables, fantasy, anecdotes, short stories, graphic novels, personal recounts, ballads, historical fiction, science fiction, adventure, flash-fiction (short stories that still offer well-developed characters and a complete plot), fan-fiction (stories involving popular fictional characters that are written by fans), self-created adventure stories, poems with a narrative focus, myths and legends
Informational	To inform and provide information, facts and explanations about a topic	Explanations, discussion, non-fictional recounts, historical accounts/recounts, people's history (an account of historical events from the point of view of ordinary people), biography and reports (e.g., science reports), memoirs, diaries, notes, and lists. Also includes procedural texts (recipes, science experiments, directions)
Argumentative/ Persuasive	To persuade and influence, to share opinions, to negotiate, to resolve difference of opinion	Letters for personal gain, advertisements, opinion pieces (for or against a proposition), speeches

Source: Authors.

Genres can be viewed as comprising structural and language features. Structural features of narrative texts can include an orientation and a complication or problem, which is then resolved (or not), and perhaps a theme or moral (whether directly stated or implied). Structural features of informational texts may include sequence/process, description, time order/chronology, proposition/support, compare/contrast, problem/solution and investigation. The structural features of genres may be identified (and indeed taught) using graphic organisers. The graphic organiser (frame) for a narrative text (Figure 3.1) can be used as a pre-writing (planning) activity for almost any narrative text, with pupils invited to pre-fil the frame as a pre-writing activity, by either drawing or writing text corresponding to each cell. Abbreviations (words and phrases) can be used rather than full sentences, leaving scope for children to compose full sentences (including dialogue, where relevant) during writing. Figure 3.2 shows a pre-filled graphic organiser for an informational text on the causes of climate change. Pupils can add additional causes that they come across in their research, before proceeding to write a full text. They can also add examples related to each cell.

Setting (where and when): In the countryside.
Main characters: The three little pigs. The wolf.
Problem (conflict): The pigs were sent off by their mother to make their way in the world. They needed to build sturdy homes to protect themselves from danger.
Steps to solve the problem: The first pig was lazy and built a house of straw. The second pig was also lazy and built a house of sticks. The third pig was more careful and built a house of bricks.
Resolution (how the problem was solved): The wolf easily blew away the house of straw. The wolf easily blew away the house of sticks. The three pigs hid in the house of bricks. The wolf was unable to blow it away. The three pigs were safe.
Theme (message): Taking the time to do something correctly pays off.

Figure 3.1 Graphic organiser for a narrative text

Source: Authors

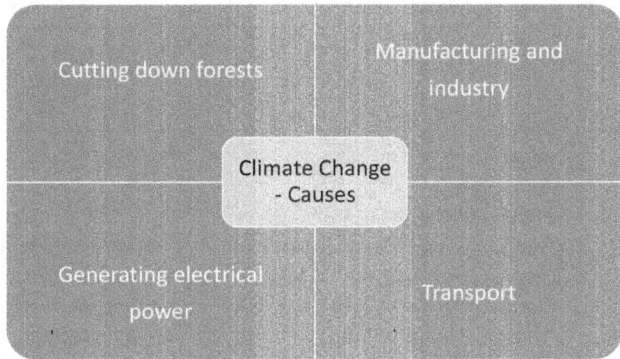

Figure 3.2 Graphic organiser for informational text on causes of climate change
Source: Authors

Language features are also important. Some authors refer to the language register associated with the social context in which a genre occurs. Halliday and Hasan (1989/1997) defined register as a system of meaning that relates linguistic choices to the context of the situation. Martin (2001) showed how language, register and genre are linked to one another, with language embedded in register and register embedded in genre. The genre approach (sometimes referred to as genre study) includes a focus on how the purpose and audience of a text influence the choices that are made regarding schematic structure and language features (Mackenzie & Scull, 2015).

Genre theory, the theoretical approach underpinning genre-based instructional approaches, has been a focus of international research since the early 1980s. It was originally inspired by Halliday's (1978, 1985) systemic functional linguistics, which posits that any text is contextualised within a particular environment, and the text's interaction with and influence on the environment leads to social action. Hence, purposes such as explaining, describing, arguing, reviewing, recounting and storytelling can be described as genres or social practices that writers adopt to achieve their goals. Halliday was especially concerned with what students read and write, and with 'providing access to powerful discourses for students from non-mainstream groups who might otherwise struggle with the demands of schooling' (Derewianka, 2015, p. 73). According to Halliday (1985), the register of a text is based on a combination of field, tenor and mode, which can be defined as they relate to functions of language. As the genre or purpose of the text changes, so too does the register, which, as noted above, includes the language of the text.

Field, tenor and mode are described in Table 3.2, with reference to a specific example (Writing a letter of complaint to the local council). For each function of language, the corresponding register is described. For example, the ideational function of language relates to the field (subject matter or topic) of the text, while the interpersonal function relates to the relationship between the writer and the reader or audience to whom the text is directed. The textual function is most closely related to the traditional concept of genre (or mode).

Young and Ferguson (2022) recommend that teachers use the register features of a genre as a basis for helping pupils to consider the purpose of their writing, and 'to generate rich conversation and discussion with their classes when reading mentor [exemplar] texts' (p. 26).

Table 3.2 Functions of language, corresponding features and examples of field, tenor and mode

Function of Language	Situational Context (Register)	Example (Letter of Complaint to Local Council re. Possible Loss of Playground Space)
Ideational	*Field*: the topic or subject matter of the text	Threat of loss of playground space
Interpersonal	*Tenor*: The relationship between the writer and the reader/audience	Formal style, reflecting the relationship between the writer (student) and the local council
Textual	*Mode*: The organisation and presentation of the text	A written text, organised as a letter (argumentative)

Source: Authors' table.

Perspectives on Teaching Genre

Understanding of genre, often combined with process writing, can be developed via a cycle based on a release of responsibility model (e.g., Pearson & Gallagher, 1983; Fielding & Pearson, 1994), whereby teachers provide intensive support in the early stages of teaching a new genre, and gradually reduce that support as students become more independent learners. This is reflected in Derewianka's (2015) key stages of teaching a genre (called the teaching/learning or curriculum cycle):

- *Deconstruction of the genre*: using a model (mentor) text, the teacher shows pupils how the text is structured to achieve the writer's purpose and how language features of the genre are applied.
- *Joint construction*: the teacher and pupils work collaboratively to write a text in the target genre, with pupils contributing their ideas while the teacher shows how they might be shaped to produce an effective, well-structured text, incorporating insights about language offered by the model text.
- *Independent construction*: when pupils understand what is required, they write independently of the teacher to produce a text similar to the model text using the same genre, though with a change in the field (for example, a description of a different animal than that provided in the model text).

These are summarised in Figure 3.3 where attention is given to the register variables of field, tenor and mode in each stage.

Research evidence suggests enhanced knowledge of genres can result in improved writing quality. Graham et al. (2015) reported that explicit instruction in the structures of different genres (narrative, informational and persuasive), and instruction on providing, discussing and emulating model texts for each genre, can significantly improve writing quality.

Overview of Main Text Genres

This section examines efforts to improve the quality of pupils' writing by improving their knowledge of different genres. It looks at narrative texts, recounts, informational texts, and

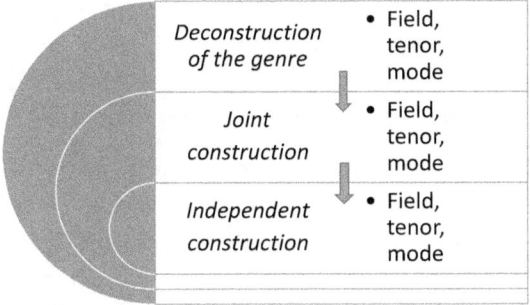

Figure 3.3 The teaching/learning cycle incorporating the register variables of field, tenor and mode

Source: Authors, based on Derewianka, 2015

argumentative/persuasive texts and poetry. It might be noted genre knowledge on its own may not be sufficient to improve children's writing. Another key factor is content knowledge or knowledge about the topic that children intend to write about. Hence, as Young and Ferguson (2022) note, knowledge transforming in writing requires the writer to combine content knowledge and genre knowledge.

Narrative Texts

Olson and Godfrey (2019) outline the many benefits of encouraging children to read and write narrative texts including:

- Imagining human possibilities that provide avenues for self-reflection and personal growth (In this context, Langer (2011, p. 5) refers to 'horizons of possibility thinking'; she contrasts this with 'points-of-reference thinking', which occurs when reading or composing an informational text, with the goal of acquiring specific knowledge about a topic).
- Promoting empathy and insight into the lives of others with differing backgrounds and experiences than our own, thereby developing compassion, social skills and perspective-taking.
- Fostering growth in vocabulary development, morphology, sentence structure, and use of cohesive devices such as complex noun phrases, descriptive clauses, phrases and words, and verb tenses.
- Developing voice, audience awareness, organisational skills and ability to select and use specific concrete details that are important for reading and writing other genres such as informative and argumentative texts.
- Motivating pupils and building their confidence, as they become interested in specific images, characters, conflicts, settings or themes.

A key challenge for writers of narrative texts is to familiarise themselves with narrative text structure. The term 'story grammar' is sometimes used to describe narrative text structure, and can include such elements as:

- Exposition, which introduces the setting, characters, and conflict in the story.
- Rising action, which introduces the challenges and obstacles that the characters face.

- Climax, or the turning point of the story, where the conflict is resolved.
- Falling action, which describes the aftermath of the climax, as the characters deal with the consequences of their actions.
- Resolution: ties up any loose ends and brings the story to a close.

Narrative texts can also include many of the common text structures found in other genres such as description, cause-effect, chronology/sequence, and problem-solution. Pupils' narrative writing may be enhanced by providing instruction on point of view, use of dialogue and showing (rather than telling).

Telling can be described as providing information directly (e.g., in the form of a summary), whereas showing involves providing clues that allow the reader to make inferences. For example, instead of stating that a character is tall, the writer might note that everyone looks up when speaking to them, or that they need to bend down to go through a doorway. The inference is that showing, rather than telling, can make writing more interesting for the reader. Techniques associated with showing include reference to body language, use of dialogue, unmasking of a character's thoughts, and use of sensory details.

There is evidence that explicit instruction in the elements of narrative text structure can improve the quality of pupils' writing. For example, a study by Fitzgerald and Teasley (1986) involving students in Grade 4 in the United States found positive effects of instruction in narrative text structure on organisation in story writing and on overall quality, but not on frequency of using temporal or causal links, or on creativity. A key reason why instruction in narrative text structure may be beneficial to students is that they acquire the meta-language of the narrative genre and can use this in their planning.

Informational Texts

Informational or explanatory texts are intended to convey information accurately (NGABP & CCSSO, 2010c). Specific purposes include:

- Increasing the reader's knowledge of a subject.
- Helping the reader better understand a procedure or process.
- Providing the reader with an enhanced understanding of a concept.

When writing informational texts, students typically draw from their background knowledge and experiences, and from primary and secondary source texts, including online texts.

A key element of informational writing is the selection of information that is important (that is, the reader must evaluate the importance of information in a text). This is especially evident when students write text summaries, requiring them to select the main ideas in one or more texts. Related skills include conveying relevant examples, facts and details in their writing, though these skills take time and practice to fully develop.

Among the techniques or structures that students use when writing informational texts are naming, defining, describing, differentiating different types, comparing/contrasting ideas or concepts, sequencing information, and presenting problems and solutions. Sub-genres of informational writing (as per Table 3.1) include literary analysis, scientific and historical reports, summaries, and functional writing (instructions, manuals, reports, applications and résumés). Biographies may also be categorised as informational texts. Students expand their range of genres as they progress over time, and they engage in writing tasks in different disciplines or subject areas.

According to Wyse et al. (2018), explanations are intended to support the reader's understanding of a topic (as opposed to persuading the reader in argumentative texts). Explanations provide information about causes, contexts, and consequences of processes or events.

We can specify the elements that are found in different informational subgenres. For example, an explanatory or expository text in history might be expected to include:

- Information about historic events.
- Information based on real people and events.
- Use of a compare-contrast structure to present factual information and ideas.
- Events organised and presented in chronological order.
- Use of headings and specialised vocabulary.
- Use of photos, captions, diagrams, illustrations, timelines and other graphs to convey information.

Similarly, we can specify the elements of procedural texts:

- A goal stating what the reader will make or do.
- Directions on how to make or do something.
- A series of steps, ordered by number.
- Text and graphic features that demonstrate and explain.

An important informational subgenre is the recount, which retells past events. Typical elements of informational recounts include:

- Information – the writer may outline the place, people and objects involved (who, what, when and where).
- Chronological narration – the recount may be narrated in the order in which events occurred.
- First- or third-person narration – the recount may be told by the writer as if they were present at the event, or the recount may be narrated by someone else.
- Descriptive language and imagery that bring events to life and create a vivid experience for readers.

The writer's purpose in authoring an informational recount is to support the reader in experiencing events as though they were present.

Informational recounts may be factual, where the writer informs readers about events through facts, or imaginative (fictionalised accounts with the purpose of helping readers to understand real-life events). Other subgenres include biographies, autobiographies, historical reports, newspaper reports and witness statements. Table 3.3 shows the main elements of an informational recount.

A consideration of the W2R rubric introduced in Chapter 5 for recount (under Organisation/Genre) will provide further insights into what to look for in children's recounts as they develop as writers.

Table 3.3 Key elements of an informational recount

Element	Focus
Orientation (opening paragraph)	The writer introduces the main elements of the account, including people, setting and other important information
Events/Experiences (main part of recount)	The writer retells events or experiences
Conclusion	The writer may communicate a message or moral, based on their experiences

Source: Authors' table.

Argumentative/Persuasive Texts

Arguments can be used for a range of purposes, such as changing a reader's point of view, motivating a reader to take action, or asking them to accept the writer's explanation or evaluation of a concept, issue or problem. According to the United States Common Core Standards (NGABP & CCSSO, 2010c, p. 23), 'an argument is a reasoned, logical way of demonstrating that the writer's position, belief or conclusion is valid'. In line with teaching genres that are relevant to the different disciplines, the Common Core makes a distinction between argumentation in English language arts (to make claims about the worth or meaning of a literary work or works), in history/social studies (to analyse evidence from multiple primary or secondary sources to advance a claim supported by the evidence), and in science (to draw on understanding of scientific concepts to argue in support of a claim). While recognising that young children up to Grade 5 are generally unable to offer fully developed logical arguments, the Common Core notes that they can 'develop a variety of methods to extend and elaborate their work by providing examples, offering reasons for their assertions, and explaining cause and effect' (p. 23). The Common Core also notes that the term 'opinion' is often used to refer to younger children's developing form of argument.

Although children begin to show some skill in argumentation at an early age (sometimes as young as two years of age!), they may ignore relevant information that is inconsistent with their perspective. According to Ferretti and Lewis (2019), they may:

- Be insensitive to potential criticisms of their opinions.
- Not consider alternative perspectives (my side bias).
- Lack standards for evaluating arguments.
- Fail to adapt their strategies to the communicative context.

Hence, the arguments of young writers (and indeed some adults) may be poorly developed and insensitive to alternative perspectives.

A dialogic approach has been identified as important in supporting argumentative writing (Ferretti & Lewis, 2019). Where pupils are preparing to defend their point of view in a written text, as part of an online discussion, or in an oral presentation, they can be challenged to:

- Work collaboratively with other students on the same side to identify reasons for their opinions on a topic.
- Identify alternative perspectives, and ways in which these might be challenged, if necessary.

- Reflect on the strengths (and weaknesses) of their arguments.
- Draw on what they have learned from the debate to inform their writing.

Wagner (1999) reported on a study in which students in Grades 4 and 8 engaged in writing persuasive texts. In preparation for writing, one condition involved dialogic interaction or role-playing, where pupils worked in pairs to roleplay a persuasive situation between a pupil and the school principal, with each pupil having an opportunity to play both the pupil's and principal's role, before writing to the principal about the topic. In another condition, pupils learned eight rules of effective persuasive writing, and analysed and discussed one exemplary and one poor model of persuasive writing, on a topic similar to the one they would write about. A third group (called the no-condition group) received the topic just before they wrote. Pupils in the role-play group outperformed their counterparts in the direct instruction group on argumentative letters, with students involved in role-play better adapting their letters to audience needs. Role play in this context can be interpreted as scaffolding the argumentative writing process.

When teaching argumentative writing to younger children, it is advisable to focus on topics with which they are already familiar. This allows them to focus their attention on the quality of their arguments and evidence. As they move through primary school, the focus will shift to argumentation in disciplinary subjects, where subject content knowledge will become an important prerequisite.

The following are typical components of a piece of persuasive writing in which an opinion is expressed:

- The writer presents facts about the topic in an organised way, and states an opinion.
- The writer supports the topic, and attempts to persuade the reader to accept or embrace his/her opinion.
- Reasons, evidence or personal experience support the opinion.
- The writer concludes by re-stating their opinion.
- The piece may include both sides of an opinion or argument.

Poetry

One genre that is often neglected in curricula is poetry. Indeed, it has been described by Hawkins and Certo (2014, p. 196) as the 'most feared and least understood literary genre'. This may arise because teachers are not very confident about teaching poetry, or because it tends not to be valued (it is rarely included in high-stakes assessments of literacy). Yet, poetry as a genre is usually part of a child's life since birth, and children build an early affinity with rhythm and rhyme as they memorise and sing simple verses again and again (Perfect, 1999). Concannon-Gibney (2019) notes that poetry can be more accessible to children with literacy difficulties than longer prose texts, which they may be less inclined to engage with. Perfect (1999) tells us that 'it is a genre especially suited to the unmotivated or struggling reader' (p. 728), while Duthie and Zimet (1992, p. 14) tell us that poetry 'can be the genre that excites children and motivates them to read and write'.

According to Concannon-Gibney, the writing workshop approach can be used to encourage children to write their own poems, by incorporating poetry into a broader genre study approach. Concannon-Gibney identifies the following steps in supporting children to write poems:

- Finding topics, with lists of possible topics being constantly updated. These often relate to children's everyday experiences.
- Understanding how poetry looks and sounds – for example, children need to understand that poets may not write complete sentences and may put line breaks in unexpected places.
- Selecting poetry forms – craft lessons/mini lessons can focus on various forms of poetry, with the teacher writing poetry, or the class working collaboratively to write a poem. Forms include simple rhyming texts, simile poems (where each line is structured around a simile), riddle poems, free verse and alliterative poems. They also include epitaphs, clerihews, haikus, limericks, shape poems, quatrains and palindromes.
- Celebrating – students share their poems and/or launch an anthology of their poems in a poetry café (Kovalcik & Certo, 2007).

An example of a poem written by one of the students in the Write to Read project – a project to support teachers to implement research-based reading and writing in disadvantaged schools in Ireland – is shown in Box 3.1. Sophia began by writing a historical report on the Belsen concentration camp in Germany during World War 2. Then she crafted the poem based on her report. This can be described as a found poem, since it is based on text composed in a nonpoetic context (https://poets.org/glossary/found-poem).

There are a number of features that combine to make the poem powerful, including the use of similes (*as yellow as the sun, dropping like flies*), strong imagery (**blanket of darkness, the silent sound of sadness**), powerful adverbs (**solemnly**) and adjectives (**faint** smile). The overall tone of the poem is also sombre, as Sophia projects herself as one of the victims. The poem does not follow any particular format (the words in each verse don't rhyme), but the tone – one of seriousness and fear – is just right.

BOX 3.1 BELSEN CAMP (BY SOPHIA KELLY, SIXTH CLASS, WRITE TO READ SCHOOL)

The camp was surrounded by sunflowers
As yellow as the sun
But the sun doesn't shine on this treacherous place
As it cannot break through this blanket of darkness.
I stared at them solemnly
As their limbs danced in the wind
To the silent sound of sadness
Hours I stood there standing
'They're just like the ones at home,' Father whispered
I stared at him with a faint smile

> The cabins were cramped
> And babies cried through the night
> The food was scarce
> All day and night I continuously pondered
> How long will we be here?
> Everywhere I looked Skeletons roamed around The look in their eyes would make you want to cry
> Everybody is dropping like flies
> The numbers of people were descending
> Every day I wondered
> Will we be next?
> Huddled together
> Like herds of sheep
> Rushing towards the giant room
> We clump together
> Not knowing what's next
> Screams of anxiety
> Soon turned to silence
> We stood in the darkness
> I held Father's hand
> We shut our eyes in unison
> Darkness

Challenges in Using Genre Study as a Basis for Writing Instruction

Some concerns have been raised about genre-based approaches to teaching writing. For example, it has been claimed that the stages in teaching a genre can be formulaic, leading children to implement them in a lock-step manner (e.g., an over-emphasis on analysing elements of a genre and extensive teacher modelling, with little time allocated to children writing in the genre). Derewianka (2015) points out that, while the main elements of a genre are relatively predictable (because of their function), there is ample room for creativity within their less-predictable sub-elements, allowing for flexibility and choice. It has also been argued that a narrow interpretation of the term 'genre' may lead to an instructional focus on a limited number of genres. Here, Derewianka argues that attention should be given to sub-genres such as historical recounts (under the broad umbrella of recounts), rather than focusing only on major genres. Finally, genres may be taught without attention to the register – to developing the language of the topic (field), the language for effective personal interaction (tenor) and the language and resources needed to compose coherent texts (the mode). The latter criticism can be addressed by attending to these important elements of language, in the context of listening to, reading and writing texts during genre study.

Disciplinary Literacy

In recent years, curricula have strongly embraced the concept of disciplinary literacy. This is defined as 'the specialised ways in which reading, writing and oral language are used in academic disciplines such as science, history or literature' (Shanahan & Shanahan, 2012). Each of these fields has its own ways of using text to create, communicate, and advance knowledge. In order to become proficient in the various disciplines, students must become acquainted with their unique or specialised ways of reading and writing (Shanahan, 2019). According to Shanahan, disciplinary literacy, which involves understanding how scientists, historians, mathematicians and other subject experts use literacy in reading and writing, takes years to develop. However, a number of authors have pointed out that children as young as five years of age can begin to learn aspects of disciplinary literacy such as the roots of scientific argument, in the context of developing oral language skills in science lessons (e.g., Wright & Gotwals, 2017). Shanahan also emphasises the social contexts of the disciplines in which disciplinary literacy occurs, noting that:

> Disciplinary literacy – including oral language – refers to literate practices that are specific to the particular social milieus of the various academic disciplines; milieus that are formed, at least in part, by the nature of what is studied, how it is studied, and what its rules of evidence may be
>
> (p. 3).

It is useful to make a distinction between content-area literacy and disciplinary literacy. While the former focuses on the transfer of literacy skills (such as generating questions or writing a summary) across a range of subject areas, the latter involves a focus on tools that discipline experts use as they engage in the work of that discipline – for example, thinking, reading and writing like a scientist or a historian. Such tools can include: de-constructing (and constructing) complex discipline-specific text structures; providing evidence to support and evaluate claims; writing journal entries to demonstrate understanding of another culture's way of live; writing newspaper articles to analyse a historical event; or writing a lab report (Chauvin & Theodore, 2015). Engaging children in such activities can be viewed as integrating literacy instruction and subject content knowledge (Dwyer et al., 2022).

Students in primary schools can be introduced to disciplinary writing, through engaging in writing activities in the different disciplines. For example, Colonnese et al. (2018) describe how students can be supported in writing four types of texts in mathematics:

- Exploratory, where they write to make sense of a problem or situation (e.g., what is a fraction?).
- Informative/explanatory, where they write to describe or explain their mathematical thinking.
- Argumentative, where they construct or critique an argument.
- Mathematically creative, where they document original ideas, problems or solutions, convey fluency and flexibility in thinking, and elaborate on ideas.

Also in mathematics, Welsh Kruger and Enriquez (2023) recommend the use of picture books to stimulate mathematical thinking. They note, for example, that a picture book on charts can stimulate children to develop (and write) a research question, create a survey, collect data, create charts and graphs, and analyse and present information orally or in writing.

Approaches such as these can lead to stronger mathematical reasoning and use of mathematical vocabulary, and greater conceptual and procedural knowledge (Cohen et al., 2015).

Another key approach to disciplinary learning, including disciplinary literacy, is inquiry learning. According to Clark and Lott (2017), this can be applied to science by supporting young students to:

- Ask and analyse (two to three days), where students' background knowledge is activated and questions are developed and recorded.
- Explore and collect (three days), where students gather information using print or online resources and write their findings in their journals.
- Experiment and record (two to three days), where students write their hypotheses and observe a phenomenon of interest or complete an experiment.
- Interpret and produce (two to three days), where students record findings using a graphic organiser[1] and write an informational text, perhaps guided by a model text provided by the teacher.

The use of inquiry-based methods is consistent with approaches to disciplinary literacy that use project-based methods. The latter have been associated with greater gains in content knowledge, higher levels of student engagement, and more positive perceptions of subject content when compared with traditional approaches (Dwyer et al., 2022).

More generally, researchers (e.g., Graham et al., 2020) have shown that there are strong benefits to be gained from integrating writing with learning in different subjects. Such writing should be supported by opportunities to read relevant disciplinary texts in a critical way. It should include the teaching of strategies to support planning, drafting and revision of texts. According to Dwyer et al., disciplinary writing can provide opportunities for students to 'engage critically with sources and to craft and hone their own thinking' (p. 2).

Multiliteracies and Multimodal Texts

From a young age, children encounter and engage with multimodal texts, or texts that include multiple modes of communication. These include storybooks with words and pictures, videos with animated characters and music, or online apps with interactive interfaces and a variety of sounds.

Multiliteracy theory was first put forward by the New London Group (1996) in response to rapid technological developments providing new modes for communication and the increasing cultural and linguistic diversity in society. Multiliteracies go beyond traditional understandings of literacy which emphasised reading and writing in standard English, and allow for a reconceptualisation of literacy as including several different modes, including visual, audio and text modes.

There are five semiotic systems that support understanding meaning from multimodal texts and the composition of such texts: Linguistic, Gestural, Audio, Visual and Spatial (New London Group, 1996; Kress, 2003). Linguistic refers to all aspects of written and oral language including features such as tone and stress, coherence and cohesion. The Gestural system includes such elements as body positioning, facial expressions and space between people. Audio refers to sound effects, music and even silence. Visual refers to symbols, images, colour and perspective. Spatial elements convey directional meaning.

Alberti et al. (2021) provide interesting examples of the types of multimodal texts that young children can construct, including:

- A multimodal story that provided an alternative ending to a well-known picture book. The lessons surrounding this activity show the teacher following the child's lead as the story develops, with the child selecting digital images, text, and background music for each scene.
- An investigation of how humans can care for the water system and work towards a sustainable future. The teacher followed a multisensory approach that enabled the learner to produce several artefacts, including a Powerpoint presentation that combined illustrations and reporting, with audio narrating.
- A multimodal presentation on a day at the beach that included storyboarding (constructing a set of graphic illustrations), listening to audio mentor texts, and audio recording, as a child created a text around the storyboard.

We can support children as they learn the semiotic systems to understand the meaning of multimodal texts and to compose their own. One approach to this is digital writers' multimedia design workshop (Dalton, 2012). This is a modification of the Writers' Workshop described in Chapter 2 and includes a strong element of design. The components are:

- Develop students' design identities – this recognises that students have modal preferences and talents, which they can pursue in-depth as they develop composing and technical skills.
- Build a designer's workshop community – the focus of the workshop shifts to design and media. The workshop involves a recursive movement across modes as children work to create a complete piece where the modes work together in creative and powerful ways. The focus of mini lessons shifts to the craft of multimodal composing. Multimodal work can be posted in a safe online location as work-in-progress, inviting feedback. Multimodal work may involve partners or groups of students working together in creative ways.
- Scaffold the composing process – Dalton suggests scaffolding students' composing by providing them with partially completed products, allowing them to focus on the newly taught skill, rather than completing the entire composition. She also emphasises the importance of collaboration among peers as a scaffolding tool and warns that too much scaffolding can be limiting.
- Teach metalanguage or technical vocabulary – for example, in preparing a soundscape, students can learn such terms as sound effects, audio narration, and, in the context of music, tempo, style and beat. Images (photographs) may lead to the use of terms like focus, intensity and contrast.
- Publish beyond the classroom walls – Dalton suggests publishing students' multimodal compositions on a restricted blog or website to which only students and their families have access.

Dalton (2014/2015) warns that digital multimodal teaching processes are complex, in large part because the final product is likely to be a combination of available modes, authoring and media tools, and devices.

Conclusion

The focus of this chapter was on genre as a basis for supporting students' development as writers, the emerging importance of disciplinary literacy, and the development of multimodal texts.

Historically, much of the early writing completed by children involved personal recounts or narratives. Now the emphasis has shifted towards ensuring that children are familiar with a broad range of genres as early as possible during their schooling. Curriculum frameworks, such as the Common Core Standards, emphasise a range of genres from kindergarten onwards. Similarly, there is now a clear understanding that children will read and write texts in the different disciplines from an early age. The same can be said of multimodal texts, with children as young as three years old able to construct such texts, if appropriate scaffolding is provided. It is noteworthy that genre-based writing instruction, disciplinary writing and the construction of multimodal texts can all be conducted using a broad set of principles associated with process approaches to writing, such as the writers' workshop. These include the use of mentor texts (often linking reading, writing and oral language during the planning stage), scaffolding of students' writing using a release of responsibility model, and reflection on and sharing of the finished product.

Reflect, Connect, Act

1. Plan an activity in a specific discipline (e.g., science) at a grade level of your choice that requires students to interact with a named mentor text (for example, an informational or non-fiction text).
2. Refer to specific literacy (reading and writing) and disciplinary (subject) outcomes for the activity.

Further Reading

Dahlström, H. (2021). Students as digital multimodal text designers: A study of resources, affordances, and experiences. *British Journal of Educational Technology, 53(2)*, 391–407. https://doi.org/10.1111/bjet.13171

Note

1. Graphic organisers can help with structuring written texts. They can include main idea webs, venn diagrams, sequence charts and problem-solving charts.

4 Curricula in Writing
The Intended, Implemented and Achieved

This chapter addresses curriculum development, implementation and evidence of achievement in writing. It describes national curriculum documents as the intended curriculum. Research on curriculum implementation in classrooms is cited as evidence of the implemented curriculum. Evidence from large-scale assessments of writing is drawn on in describing the achieved curriculum, though readers are advised on the limitations of such assessments for describing the full range of writing abilities. After reading this chapter, you should be able to answer the following questions:

> **Reflect and Connect**
>
> 1. What role does curriculum play in supporting teachers in planning and implementing writing instruction?
> 2. Why are there sometimes gaps between the content of writing instruction as presented in curriculum documents and instructional practices in classrooms?
> 3. What do national assessments tell us about how well writing curricula are implemented and how motivated children are as writers?

The writing curriculum is a key element of writing instruction in schools. Depending on the context, teachers may use the curriculum to identify which aspects of writing to teach, the sequence in which those aspects are presented, and how they are assessed. Curriculum documents may provide a basis for adopting particular instructional strategies and routines, and for curriculum planning in writing at school or classroom levels (see Chapter 12). Furthermore, school and teacher evaluation may look at the extent to which teachers are implementing curricula. Assessment of writing in classrooms may focus on those aspects of writing highlighted in curriculum documents. Hence, curriculum can have a key influence on the teaching and assessment of writing in schools.

In the first section in this chapter, components of national writing curricula are presented for selected lower- and upper-primary classes, with reference to relevant theoretical underpinnings outlined in Chapters 1–3. Examples of learning outcomes/statutory requirements/standards and key approaches to instruction and assessment highlighted in curriculum documents are given. In the second section, the concept of implemented curriculum is examined, drawing on descriptions of teachers' instructional practices from surveys as well as descriptions of writing pedagogy in classrooms based on observation by experts. Findings related to children's views about writing and their engagement in writing activities are also described. The final section of the chapter focuses on the achieved curriculum – what students have achieved in writing, based on national assessments (e.g., Key Stage 1 (teacher-marked) and 2 in England, the National Assessment of Educational Progress (NAEP) at Grade 4 in the US, and Years 3 and 5 in Australia's National Assessment Programme – Literacy and Numeracy (NAPLAN). A need to avoid 'formulaic writing' is highlighted, as is the importance of fostering creativity.

The Intended Writing Curriculum

The intended curriculum typically comprises curriculum plans developed at the national, state or regional level. It sets out what should be achieved as children learn to write.

America's Common Core Standards

Perhaps one of the most influential curriculum-related documents in recent years is the United States Common Core Standards (NGABP & CCSSO, 2010a). The Common Core Standards (CCSs) are descriptions of the skills students should have at each grade level in English/language arts and math in the US by the time they finish high school. They provide a broad outline of learning expectations from which state and district leaders and classroom teachers can formulate a curriculum. While the CCSs were initially well-received, they ran into difficulties over time, mainly because of political opposition. Aspects of the CCSs specifically related to writing state that:

- Students should demonstrate increasing sophistication in all aspects of language use, from vocabulary and syntax to the development and organization of ideas, and they should address increasingly demanding content and sources.
- Students advancing through the grades are expected to meet each year's grade-specific standards and retain or further develop skills and understandings mastered in preceding grades.

Growth or progression in writing from year to year is reflected in the Standards, and in annotated examples of student writing (NGABP & CCSSO, 2010b).

Table 4.1 shows the progression evident in the standards in opinion writing expected by the CCS over several grade levels and should be read in conjunction with the exemplar texts referred to above.

The CCSs for writing are significant for a number of reasons, including:

- Explicit links with corresponding anchor standards, related to college-level requirements (in the case of argumentative writing, the anchor standard is: Write arguments to support claims in an analysis of substantive topics or texts using valid reasoning and relevant and sufficient evidence.).

Table 4.1 Common Core Standards for argumentative writing (Kindergarten to Grade 4)

Grade	Common Core Standard for Argumentative Writing
Kindergarten:	Use a combination of drawing, dictating, and writing to compose opinion pieces in which they tell a reader the topic or the name of the book they are writing about and state an opinion or preference about the topic or book (e.g., My favorite book is...).
Grade 1	Write opinion pieces in which they introduce the topic or name the book they are writing about, state an opinion, supply a reason for the opinion, and provide some sense of closure.
Grade 2	Write opinion pieces in which they introduce the topic or book they are writing about, state an opinion, supply reasons that support the opinion, use linking words (e.g., because, and, also) to connect opinion and reasons, and provide a concluding statement or section.
Grade 3	Write opinion pieces on topics or texts, supporting a point of view with reasons. - Introduce the topic or text they are writing about, state an opinion, and create an organizational structure that lists reasons. - Provide reasons that support the opinion - Use linking words and phrases (e.g., because, therefore, since, for example) to connect opinion and reasons. - Provide a concluding statement or section.
Grade 4	Write opinion pieces on topics or texts, supporting a point of view with reasons and information. - Introduce a topic or text clearly, state an opinion, and create an organizational structure in which related ideas are grouped to support the writer's purpose. - Provide reasons that are supported by facts and details. - Link opinion and reasons using words and phrases (e.g., for instance, in order to, in addition). - Provide a concluding statement or section related to the opinion presented.

- A requirement that students write in a range of genres from the beginning of formal schooling. This contrasts with curricula that first emphasise foundational skills (transcription, in the case of writing) or narrative recounts in preparation for composition across multiple genres at higher grade levels.
- A recognition of the importance of increasingly complex subject matter content as students mature as writers (and readers). This includes the availability of standards for writing (as well as reading) in disciplines such as history, social studies and science from Grade 6 onwards. (Standards for disciplinary writing are built into the general standards for writing for lower grade levels). It also includes standards for research (for example, internet searches) to be used by children in their writing.
- Knowledge of conventions (English grammar and usage) and vocabulary acquisition are subsumed in a separate set of standards – those relating to Language. This sends the clear message that compositional writing is important in its own right from the beginning of schooling.

The CCSs can be criticised because they focus almost exclusively on cognitive aspects of writing and language more broadly, with almost no attention to attitudinal or motivational aspects. It has also been claimed that, because they focus on literacy and mathematics, they have negative effects on other subjects, which may receive less attention (Arold & Shakeel, 2021).

Unlike the United States, where individual states publish curricula, many countries, including England, Scotland, Northern Ireland, Ireland, Australia and New Zealand publish national curricula that all public schools are expected to follow. Here two curricula are described as they relate to writing: those of England and Ireland.

England's National Curriculum

The framework for the National Curriculum in England (Department of Education, 2013), covering Key Stages 1 (5-7 years) and 2 (7-11 years), outlines statutory requirements that must be met across various subjects by publicly-funded schools. Schools are required to incorporate the National Curriculum into their school curricula. The curriculum document sets out the content (knowledge) of literacy instruction. For the lower grade levels (Years 1 and 2), the knowledge is laid out for each Grade level, while for higher grade levels (Years 2-6 and beyond), it is set out for each pair of grade levels. Schools have some flexibility in the order in which they introduce content within and across grade levels, but they are responsible for teaching the relevant programme by the end of the Key Stage.

The curriculum document opens with a description of the aims of teaching English. The aims are student-centred. Those that relate most closely to writing include:

- Acquire a wide vocabulary, an understanding of grammar and knowledge of linguistic conventions for reading, writing and spoken language.
- Write clearly, accurately and coherently, adapting language and style in and for a range of contexts, purposes and audiences.

In the overview of the writing component of English, the curriculum document specifies that the programme of study for writing involves:

- Transcription (spelling and handwriting).
- Composition (articulating ideas and structuring them in speech and writing).

This represents the simple view of writing articulated in Chapter 1 of this book, which may under-represent the complexity of writing. However, the curriculum also states that pupils should be taught how to plan, revise and evaluate their writing. The introductory material also emphasises the teaching of writing in different subject areas (referred to in Chapter 3 as disciplinary writing). There are some important references to audience and purpose in the statement that 'Effective composition involves forming, articulating and communicating ideas, and then organising them coherently for a reader. This requires clarity, awareness of the audience, purpose and context, and an increasingly wide knowledge of vocabulary and grammar' (p. 15). It is further noted that 'writing also depends on fluent, legible and, eventually, speedy handwriting' (p. 15).

Table 4.2 shows the statutory requirements for Writing – Composition in Years 5-6. There are corresponding statutory requirements for Writing – Vocabulary, Grammar and Punctuation. A number of observations about the content of writing instruction can be drawn from Table 4.2.

Table 4.2 National Curriculum English – Statutory requirements for writing – composition – Years 5 and 6 Source: DE (2013, p. 47)

Pupils should be taught to:

- Plan their writing by:
  - Identifying the audience for and purpose of the writing, selecting the appropriate form and using other similar writing as models for their own
  - Noting and developing initial ideas, drawing on reading and research where necessary
  - In writing narratives, considering how authors have developed characters and settings in what pupils have read, listened to or seen performed
- Draft and write by:
  - Selecting appropriate grammar and vocabulary, understanding how such choices can change and enhance meaning
  - In narratives, describing settings, characters and atmosphere and integrating dialogue to convey character and advance the action
  - Précising [summarising] longer passages
  - Using a wide range of devices to build cohesion within and across paragraphs
  - Using further organisational and presentational devices to structure text and to guide the reader [for example, headings, bullet points, underlining]
- Evaluate and edit by:
  - Assessing the effectiveness of their own and others' writing
  - Proposing changes to vocabulary, grammar and punctuation to enhance effects and clarify meaning
  - Ensuring the consistent and correct use of tense throughout a piece of writing
  - Ensuring correct subject and verb agreement when using singular and plural
  - Distinguishing between the language of speech and writing and choosing the appropriate register
- Proofread for spelling and punctuation errors
- Perform their own compositions, using appropriate intonation, volume, and movement so that meaning is clear

---

Source: Department for Education (2013, p. 47)

First, key elements of the writing process – planning, drafting and writing, evaluating and editing, proofreading and performance/sharing – are included, though revision tends to focus on vocabulary and conventions (grammar, spelling and punctuation) rather than text structure.

Second, while some reference is made to narrative writing, other genres are not emphasised to any great degree, though the corresponding statutory requirements for reading make reference to poetry and informational texts, as well as a range of narrative text types.

Third, the requirement that pupils be taught to propose changes to vocabulary, grammar and punctuation to enhance meaning is consistent with the view that grammar is a design tool, with instruction in grammar centred on its use in written texts (e.g., Myhill, 2021). However, this seems to be contradicted by the strong emphasis on formal grammar in the statutory requirements for transcription in Years 5-6, where such elements as use of modal verbs and adverbs to indicate degrees of possibility, and use of the perfect form of verbs to mark relationships of time and cause are included and are also assessed in National Tests.

Fourth, some aspects of writing are absent from the statutory requirements, including writing poetry, and argumentative writing. As noted earlier, there is minimal or no reference in the requirements to enjoyment of writing, to motivation to write, or to self-regulation or metacognition. This contrasts with Scotland's Curriculum for Excellence, which includes a strand called 'Enjoyment and Choice'. Within this strand, the requirements for children at the primary level include 'I enjoy creating texts of my choice and I regularly select subject, purpose, format and resources to suit the needs of my audience' (Scottish Government, 2011).

In addition to learning programmes, the curriculum in England includes two statutory appendices – one on spelling and the other on vocabulary, punctuation and grammar – that provide an overview of the specific features of these elements that should be incorporated into teaching activities.

Ireland's Primary Language Curriculum

In Ireland, the curriculum for writing is embedded in the Primary Language Curriculum (NCCA, 2019), which includes English and Irish. Aims of the curriculum that relate to writing are formulated in terms of what is expected of teachers, and these are general rather than specific to writing. They include:

- Enable children to use language imaginatively and creatively and to appreciate its aesthetic aspects.
- Promote a positive disposition towards communication and language by fostering within children a lifelong interest in and a love of language learning for personal enjoyment and enrichment.

The curriculum framework identifies three strands of English (and Irish): oral language, reading and writing. Underpinning each of these are three elements:

- Understanding the content and structure of language (including conventions of print and sentence structure, vocabulary and spelling).
- Developing communicative relationships through language (including engagement, motivation and choice; purpose, genre and voice; writing process and creating text; and response and author's intent).
- Exploring and using language (including creative use of language, handwriting and presentation).

Figure 4.1 shows how the different elements interact – an approach that is consistent with an emphasis on relationships among oral language, reading and writing (see Chapter 1).

Under each of these elements are learning outcomes – what pupils what should be able to do, through appropriate learning experiences. The learning outcomes for writing are described for nine subareas, for each of four grade bands (Junior-Senior Infants, First-Second classes, Third-Fourth classes, and Fifth-Sixth classes) (Table 4.3).

Table 4.4 shows the learning outcomes for selected aspects of writing for Grades 3-6 for four subareas: motivation and choice; purpose, genre and voice; writing process and creating text; and handwriting and presentation. It might be noted that most of the outcomes, with the exception of handwriting and presentation among these examples, are spread

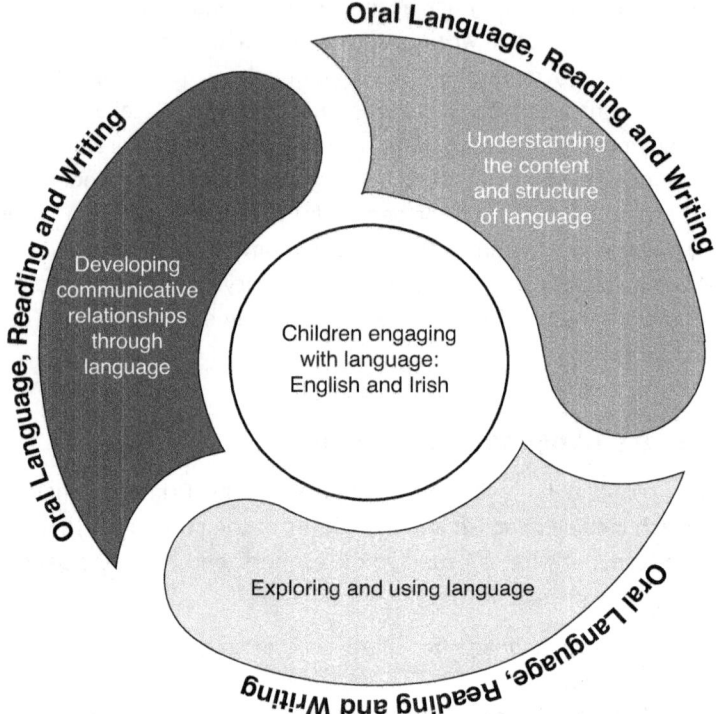

Figure 4.1 Elements of language in the Primary School Curriculum (Ireland)
Source: NCCA (2019)

Table 4.3 Structure of the curriculum for writing (Ireland)

Element	Subareas	Learning Outcomes
Understanding the content and structure of language	Conventions of print and sentence structure Spelling and word study Vocabulary	Separately for: Junior and Senior Infants First and Second Classes Third and Fourth Classes Fifth and Sixth Classes
Developing communicative relationships through language	Engagement Motivation and Choice	Separately for: Junior and Senior Infants First and Second Classes Third and Fourth Classes Fifth and Sixth Classes
Exploring and using language	Purpose, genre and voice Writing process and creating text Response and author's intent Handwriting and presentation	Separately for: Junior and Senior Infants First and Second Classes Third and Fourth Classes Fifth and Sixth Classes

Source: Authors' Schematic, based on NCCA (2019)

Table 4.4 Learning outcomes for selected elements of writing (Ireland)

Element and Subarea	Grades 3-4	Grades 5-6
	Through appropriately engaging learning experiences, children should be able to...	
Communicating/motivation and choice	• Evaluate and critically choose appropriate tools, strategies, content and topics to create text in a range of genres across the curriculum for a variety of purposes and audiences	
Exploring and using/ purpose, genre and voice	• Create text for a wide variety of authentic purposes, demonstrating an increasing understanding of the influence of the audience on their work. • Use, analyse and evaluate the typical text structure and language features associated with a wide variety of genres across the curriculum • Use a variety of writing techniques to further develop and demonstrate an individual voice in their writing, including awareness of dialect	
Exploring and using/ writing process and creating text	• Identify and evaluate skills and strategies associated with writing as a process and use them to create texts independently and/or collaboratively across a range of genres, in other languages where appropriate and across the curriculum for a variety of purposes and audiences • Use appropriate language to evaluate and discuss revisions and edits to texts created in a range of genres for a variety of purposes and audiences	
Exploring and Using/ Handwriting and presentation	• Write legibly and fluently in a chosen script using a personal style and present texts in a range of formats	• Select, justify, and recommend appropriate writing and presentation styles to create and present texts in a range of formats

Source: NCCA (2019) [Authors' table]

across all four grade levels (Grades 3-6). The outcomes for motivation and choice relate to the selection of tools, content and topics for writing across a range of genres. This implies a choice of topic on the part of students, with some teacher guidance on genres, purposes and audiences. The learning outcome for purpose, genre and voice link text genre to the purpose of writing, with particular reference to the audience, and also references text structure, with different text structures used in different genres. Reference is also made to voice, or the extent to which the writer's unique identity, including their dialect, comes through in a piece of writing.

The third example, the writing process and creating text, is of interest in terms of how it compares with the composition strand in England's national curriculum for the same age range. Table 4.4 refers to the implementation of the writing process across a range of genres, not only in English, but across subjects as well, with provision for both independent writing and collaborative writing. It might be noted that specific writing processes are not referenced. This is intended to provide some leeway to teachers (and their pupils) in terms of deciding which processes to draw on for a particular writing task. The fourth example in the table refers to handwriting and presentation. Unlike the previous subareas, slightly different outcomes are specified for Grades 3-4 (writing legibly and fluently) and Grades 5-6 (justifying and recommending appropriate writing and presentation styles).

The curriculum is not the only source of influence on how teachers in classrooms teach writing. Many countries provide a range of support to teachers to help them to interpret the curriculum and implement it effectively. In Ireland, these include an online primary language toolkit[1] that contains the following:

- Videos of children engaging in the writing process and authoring procedural texts and book reviews.
- Support materials (documents) on such topics as early handwriting patterns, cursive writing, the writing workshop and the development of functional literacy skills for children learning English as an additional language.
- Assessment continua, which describe children's expected progress in writing across grade levels (see Chapter 5).

In addition to these resources, teachers have access to school-based professional development provided by Oide, the national service charged with supporting teacher professional development. They also receive advice from members of the inspectorate.

The Implemented Writing Curriculum

A key question concerns how teachers implement writing curricula in their classrooms. Information about this comes from surveys that have asked teachers about their instructional practices, observational studies designed to describe how writing is taught in schools, and mixed methods studies designed to provide a detailed account of writing instruction in classrooms. Drawing on data from 28 studies involving 7,000 teachers across a range countries, Graham (2019) reached two broad conclusions that applied across countries and grade levels: Some teachers provide students with a solid writing programme, and in some classrooms, writing instruction is exemplary; however, writing and writing instruction in most classrooms can be described as inadequate. Examples of exemplary writing instruction include:

- Allocating adequate time to writing instruction.
- Use of a variety of instructional approaches, including evidence-based ones.
    - Writing for different purposes.
    - Teaching strategies for carrying out writing processes.
    - Conducting formative assessment to guide writing instruction.
    - Teaching foundational skills (spelling, handwriting, sentence construction).
- Making a variety of adaptations for struggling writers.
- Teaching writing to support learning across the disciplines.

Examples of inadequate writing instruction included:

- Allocating insufficient time to writing instruction.
- Minimal emphasis on some writing genres (persuasive, expository).

- Overemphasis on foundational writing skills such as spelling, grammar and handwriting.
- Little emphasis on teaching students how to carry out critical writing processes such as planning and revising.
- Notable absence of digital writing tools.
- Writing without composing in both English and subject classes (e.g., sentence length answers, worksheets).

A key question is the extent to which national or local curricula and related assessments emphasise features of exemplary writing, and, if emphasised, why these are not being implemented in practice.

In England, Dockrell et al. (2016) investigated the teaching of writing in a sample of ten primary schools. Drawing on data provided by 88 class teachers, they found that respondents enjoyed teaching writing and felt prepared to teach it. However, nearly half reported that supporting struggling writers was problematic for them, with teachers who had attended specialist training significantly less likely to report this as an area of concern.

Teachers reported more work at the word level, occurring several times a week than with transcription at sentence or text levels, which typically happened on a weekly basis. For the latter, no differences were found between teachers of younger students (4-7 years of age or Key Stage 1) and older students (8-11 years, or Key Stage 2). On the other hand, teachers of younger students focused more on phonic activities related to spelling, while teachers of older children focused more on root words, punctuation, word classes and the grammatical function of words, sentence-level work and paragraph construction. The data showed a lack of attention to teaching students how to plan and revise. Classroom resources for teaching writing were found to be inadequate, and the writing needs of students with a disability or who were learning a second language were not sufficiently addressed. Dockrell et al. noted a number of factors that might help explain these outcomes, including an emphasis in England on teaching phonics at Key Stage 1 and the requirements of a statutory assessment of writing at the end of Key Stage 2. Dockrell et al. predicted an increased emphasis on teaching grammar, as grammar, spelling and punctuation are now assessed separately from writing composition on national tests at the end of Key Stage 2.

Other studies also uncover some of the challenges associated with teaching writing in England. Barrs (2019) argues that the English curriculum focuses too strongly on content, and not enough on process. This, she argues, leads to teaching that does not improve the quality of children's writing, and results in writing that is 'inflated and unconvincing' (p. 18). She also notes that the writing curriculum and associated national assessments, especially at Key Stage 2, prioritise form over content, making 'grammatical complexity and ostentatious vocabulary the success criteria for assessment' (p. 18), weakening children's writing and learning, and teachers' instructional practices.

In a similar vein, in Australia, a survey of 301 primary-level teachers by de Abreu Malpique et al. (2023) found that, on average, most teachers spent less than 3 hours per week on writing practice in their classrooms, with large variability between estimates (ranging from 15 minutes to 7.5 hours). Teachers also reported placing more emphasis on teaching foundational skills such as spelling, over process skills such as planning and revising. A majority of teachers reported implementing only 6 of 20 different instructional practices included in the survey on a weekly basis (i.e., students engage in planning, students revise their writing products, teaching spelling, teaching grammar, teaching punctuation, and teaching capitalisation). Teachers reported that school-home strategies were used infrequently to foster students' writing development. Most teachers expressed positive beliefs about their preparation and self-efficacy for teaching writing though only self-efficacy made a statically significant contribution to predicting implementation of strategies to extend writing to the home environment.

Focusing on the attitudes of children towards writing, which might in part reflect the impact of school curricula on writing, Clark et al. (2023) reported that just one in three (34.6%) children and young people aged 8-18 in the UK said that they enjoyed writing in their free time. More children and young people in Wales said that they enjoyed writing in their free time (41.6%) compared with children and young people in England (34.3%), Scotland (32.4%) and Northern Ireland (23.2%), though the authors warn that the sample for Northern Ireland was small. More girls than boys (39.5% vs. 28.9%), more children aged 5-8 (72.0%) and 8-11 (51.6%) than those aged 11-14 (32.6%), and more children and young people who received free school meals (FSMs) than those who did not (38.6% vs. 32.9%), said that they enjoyed writing in their free time. The headline figure for England, 34.3%, is lower than in earlier surveys by the same team, suggesting a decline in enjoyment of writing over time. Clark et al. also reported that more children and young people aged 8-18 said that they enjoyed writing more at school than in their free time (43.9% vs. 34.6%). Clark et al. also noted that almost one-half of children and young people (48.2%) struggled with deciding what to write, and 2 in 5 (42.4%) admitted that they only wrote when they had to. Over 2 in 5 (42.7%) said that they continued writing even when they found it difficult.

Taking these studies together, it is clear that all is not well with the teaching of writing, with concerns about the allocation of time to teaching writing and the balance between transcription/foundation skills on the one hand and compositional or craft skills on the other. Yet, it seems that, in many cases, teachers feel well-prepared to teach writing and are confident about their ability to do so. This is problematic to the extent that change may be difficult to implement if teachers in general view themselves as being effective teachers of writing.

The Achieved Curriculum

An important test of curriculum implementation is the extent to which pupils can demonstrate what they have learned. In the case of writing, this typically involves an assessment based on a writing prompt (instructions to write a story on a particular topic). Conventions (spelling, grammar, punctuation, capital letters etc.) may be assessed in the context of the writing sample, or a separate test of these elements may be administered.

In England, pupils at the end of Key Stage 1 (age seven) may be administered a non-statutory assessment of writing and/or a non-statutory test of aural spelling, and written grammar, punctuation and vocabulary by their teachers (Key Stage 1 assessment is no longer mandatory since 2023-2024). At the end of Key Stage 2 (age 11), pupils sit a statutory test of English grammar, punctuation and spelling (EGPAS), which is externally scored. Pupils' compositional writing is scored by their teachers to determine if national curriculum standards have been met and outcomes may be moderated by the Local Education Authority, to ensure consistent application of standards.

Performance on Key Stage 1 tests is no longer reported at national level. However, in an analysis of data based on voluntary submission of outcomes, Thompson (2023) reported that 61% of pupils achieved 'the expected standard' in writing in 2023, up from 58% in 2022, but well below the pre-Covid level of 69% in 2019.

In 2023, 71% of pupils at KS2 reached the expected standard in writing (see Table 5.2, Chapter 5 for descriptions of standards), up from 69% in 2022 (GOV.UK, 2023). Before Covid-19, in both 2018 and 2019, this figure was 78%. In grammar, spelling and punctuation, 72% met the expected standard in 2023, the same proportion as in 2022, and the lowest since this assessment was introduced in 2016.

These data suggest that there is still a Covid-related lag in writing performance, and that, depending on grade level, between 30% and 40% do not reach the expected performance in writing for their age level. This is a matter of concern, though it should be acknowledged that factors other than the writing curriculum, such as socioeconomic disadvantage, gender, absence from school and disability status may impact on performance. For example, in 2023, 13% more girls than boys achieved the expected standard nationally at the end of KS2.

Another country that assesses writing at the national level on an annual basis in Australia as part of the NAPLAN assessment programme. Students in Years 3, 5, 7 and 9 in that country are provided with a writing stimulus or prompt – an idea or topic (see Chapter 5) – and are asked to write a response in a particular text genre (either narrative or persuasive). Separately, students are assessed on spelling and on grammar and punctuation. In 2023, a new reporting scheme was introduced, with students at each year level marked as exceeding expectations, strong (meeting challenging but reasonable expectations), developing (working towards expectations) and needs additional support (likely to need additional supports to progress satisfactorily) (ACARA, n.d.). In 2023, across Australia, 9.1% of Year 3 pupils were judged to be exceeding expectations in writing, 66.9% to be strong, 16.0% to be developing, and 6.1% to be in need of additional support. Just 1.8% were exempted because of special education needs. On the face of it, these results would seem satisfactory, with 75% either strong or exceeding expectations. However, McGaw et al. (2020) have pointed out that national NAPLAN scores in Writing in Years 3 and 5 did not change in the previous ten years, while scores in Years 7 and 9 declined, raising questions about how the results of the assessment are used to improve teaching and learning in schools.

In Scotland, pupils in Primary 1, 4 and 7, and Secondary 3 take the Scottish National Standardised Assessments or their equivalent in Scots Gaelic at any time during the school year. These assessments are taken on a computer, and are adaptive, meaning that items are selected to correspond to students' ability levels. The assessment of writing encompasses grammar, spelling and punctuation. There is no national assessment of compositional writing. In Ireland, there is no national assessment of writing either, though this does not preclude teachers from conducting their own assessments, using an appropriate scoring rubric (see Chapter 5).

Conclusion

In this chapter, we considered three dimensions of curricula for writing – the intended curriculum, the implemented curriculum, and the achieved curriculum. The intended curriculum can be examined by reviewing published curriculum documents issued by national or regional education departments or curriculum bodies. Such documents often make a distinction between transcription (variously defined as spelling, grammar, punctuation and sentence construction) and composition, including the writing process and strategies for writing. A key issue here is the balance suggested in the curriculum between transcription and composition. The fact that some countries require students to complete formal assessments of grammar, punctuation and spelling may shift the balance towards transcription, especially if compositional writing is assessed more informally, or not at all.

Teachers in classrooms implement writing curricula, in language classes and/or across the curriculum. Surveys of teachers described in this chapter suggest that, although generally confident or self-efficacious about teaching writing, teachers tend to overemphasise compositional skills, and underemphasise compositional writing, most clearly evident in the allocation of varying amounts of time to these elements. Where insufficient time is allocated to compositional writing, it is unlikely that key processes and strategies will be taught or reviewed, and this may ultimately impede the quality of children's writing.

The attained curriculum is often reflected in the performance of pupils on national assessments of writing. However, for various reasons, including the difficulty in assessing writing out of context, writing is typically not marked externally in such assessments. On the other hand, pupils are likely to be assessed more formally (for example, on computer-based tests) on grammar, punctuation and spelling. Where compositional writing is assessed and outcomes are gathered centrally, they indicate that large proportions of students have not reached expected levels of performance for their grade level. This is a worrying outcome, though below-par performance in writing cannot be attributed only to curriculum and teaching quality. Like reading, writing performance is also affected by students' characteristics such as gender and by their socioeconomic status. The challenge for schools and teachers is to ensure that all pupils write to the best of their ability, and that they enjoy engaging in writing and become lifelong writers.

Reflect, Connect, Act

1. Compare and contrast a writing curriculum in another country with your own national or regional curriculum. What similarities and differences can you identify? Are there any elements that should be added to either curriculum?
2. Explore your national writing curriculum. What is the balance between transcription and composition? Is this balance influenced by other factors, such as a national writing assessment?

Suggestion for Further Reading

Graham, S. (2019). Changing how writing is taught. *Review of Research in Education, 43(1)*, 277-303. https://doi.org/10.3102/0091732X18821125

Note

1 https://www.curriculumonline.ie/primary/curriculum-areas/primary-language/primary-language-toolkit/

5 Assessment of Writing

Assessment is a key element of writing instruction. The feedback children receive from assessment, and the feedback they generate and share among themselves through self- and peer-assessment, can have a significant effect on the quality of their writing, their self-efficacy in writing and their ability to self-regulate or manage their writing in the future (Graham et al., 2015; Philippakos & MacArthur, 2016; Lane et al., 2019). Assessment of writing should not be viewed as an end in itself and instead should be aligned with writing goals, curriculum and instructional methods (Graham, 2019). Furthermore, assessment should not be limited to evaluating completed texts, but should also include observations of children engaged in writing (Allott, 2019).

Reports on the effective teaching of writing (e.g., Bilton & Duff, 2021, see Chapter 2) recommend an approach to assessing writing whereby teachers identify pupils' strengths and weaknesses, and work to address both in the context of teaching writing. Hale (2017) underlines the value of working on students' writing strengths as well as their weaknesses and argues that strengths can be identified for even the weakest writers, providing a base on which to move forward.

If we assess a written text, it is relatively easy to identify convention errors (errors related to grammar, spelling and punctuation). However, there is a danger that if, as teachers, we focus only on these elements of writing in our assessments, children may receive the message that good writing is about adhering to conventions, and that compositional aspects are less important (Casey et al., 2016). This is similar to the argument about achieving a balance between transcription and composition in curriculum documents and in instruction (see Chapter 4).

This chapter begins by distinguishing between formative and summative assessment. Following this, the use of scoring rubrics as a tool for formative is discussed, an example of a scoring rubric is provided, and a commentary is presented for a set of texts scored with the rubric. Then formative assessment of other aspects of writing is discussed, including motivation to write. The final section of the chapter focuses on summative assessment of writing, following up on the last section in Chapter 4 (the achieved curriculum). The use of a writing rubric in whole-school planning is elaborated on in Chapter 12. After reading this chapter, you should be able to answer the following questions:

> **Reflect and Connect**
>
> 1. How can we assess children's writing?
> 2. Which aspects of children's writing should we assess?
> 3. How can we support children to assess their own writing?
> 4. Which forms of writing assessment lead to effective feedback for young writers?

Formative Assessment of Writing

Assessment of writing can be described as formative or summative. Formative assessment occurs on a day-to-day basis as the teacher and the pupils themselves generate assessment information and use it as a basis for planning teaching and learning (Kennedy & Shiel, 2019). Students' strengths can be highlighted, and weaknesses can be addressed through mini lessons, and/or through revision of written texts. Formative assessment may also be referred to as 'assessment for learning'. Examples of formative assessment include observing pupils as they engage in activities such as planning or revising their texts, asking them questions about what they have written or intend to write, asking them to tell you how they composed their texts, and applying marking schemes or scoring rubrics to completed written texts.

Summative assessment is typically used at the end of a period of study, such as the end of a school year or the end of a key stage. It involves the teacher and/or the students in arriving at an overall evaluation of a written text or a portfolio of texts. Or it may involve evaluating specific aspects of writing such as use of conventions, organisation or word choice. As noted in Chapter 4, summative assessment may occur in the context of a computer-based test of conventions, or it may focus on how these and other elements operate in children's written compositions. Summative assessment can also be implemented using a scoring rubric or rating scale. It may also be referred to as 'assessment of learning' as it usually takes place after learning has been completed, with less emphasis on providing the type of detailed feedback that is associated with formative assessment.

While formative assessment undoubtedly occurs during ongoing teaching and learning, with teachers asking questions or observing pupils, much of this may go undocumented. It is useful to keep records of what occurs, and this can be done by taking anecdotal notes – short reminders of what pupils have accomplished, or difficulties they encounter (see Table 5.1). A useful strategy is to focus on three or four pupils during any given lesson, rather than trying to document everyone's progress. Anecdotal notes can be referred to later as mini-lessons are planned.

In practice, formative and summative assessment may not always be mutually exclusive. For example, a scoring rubric (see below) could be used by the teacher or by students to assess a piece of writing across one or two dimensions. The outcomes can then be used by the teacher as a basis for planning instruction in specific aspects of writing where additional support is required. For example, a rubric on the organisation of expository texts might point to pupil strengths and/or needs in such areas as the internal structure of the text, the effective use of sequence and transition words, and the inclusion of appropriate introductory and

Table 5.1 Example of a teacher's anecdotal notes

Date	Note (Based On Observations, Discussion, Conferencing)	Next Steps
14/05	Jacques struggled to plan his story about ghosts. He was unable to complete a story map to help him to structure his writing. Writing vocabulary is limited.	Jacques needs individual work on structuring his stories. Perhaps a mini-lesson that includes the use of mentor texts on ghosts. This will also enhance his vocabulary.
14/05	Marleidi wrote three sentences in her story about ghosts. The sentences were complete and mainly accurate, but the effort left her with insufficient time to complete her story.	Provide Marleidi with some sentence starters to allow her to get her thoughts down on paper more quickly.
14/05	Mark did a good job revising his story on ghosts. After sharing his story with Ian and Monica, he made several word-level changes to create a scarier atmosphere, and then reread his story.	Encourage Mark to identify additional words in the Book of Ghost Stories that might enhance his story further.

Source: Authors.

final paragraphs. Low scores in one or more of these dimensions may lead to intervention by the teacher.

A rubric could also be used at the end of a term or school year to obtain an overall measure of a student's writing proficiency, which may then be reported to parents and/or recorded in the student's profile or record.

A distinction can sometimes be made between scoring rubrics that are analytic or feature-based (i.e., they allow for the assessment of different components of writing) and holistic (they allow for an overall measure of writing proficiency). In other cases, the same rubric can be used for analytic and holistic purposes. In general, analytic information is most useful when formative assessment is the goal, as such information is more likely to point to future learning needs.

Using Scoring Rubrics for Formative Assessment Purposes

According to Jonsson and Svingby (2007, p. 131), a rubric is 'a scoring tool for qualitative rating of authentic or complex pupil work. It includes criteria for rating important dimensions of performance, as well as standards of attainment for those criteria'.

In general, analytic scoring rubrics for writing focus on a number of key dimensions or traits that may also emphasised in corresponding curricula. Culham (2018) included the following traits in her rubric:

- *Ideas* – the central message (main idea) and the ideas that support it
- *Organisation* – the internal structure of a text, including creating the lead (opening), using sequence and transition words, structuring the body and ending with a sense of resolution.

- *Voice* – the tone of the text – the personal stamp of the writer that is achieved through an understanding of purpose and audience.
- *Word choice* – the specific vocabulary the writer uses to convey meaning and enlighten the reader. It includes using appropriate verbs, selecting striking words and phrases, and using language effectively.
- *Sentence fluency* – the flow of words through a text. It includes crafting well-built sentences, varying sentence patterns, and breaking the rules to create fluency.
- *Conventions* – the mechanical correctness of the text including correct us of conventions such as spelling, capitalisation, punctuation, paragraphing, and grammar and usage
- *Presentation* – the physical appearance of a piece. Elements include applying handwriting or word processing skills, and incorporating text features such as headings, page numbers and bullets.

In addition to these 'generic' elements, which are designed to be applicable to all texts, rubrics may provide genre-specific indicators. These rubrics focus on specific genres or modes of writing (see Chapter 3), such as narrative writing, expository/informational writing and persuasive/argumentative writing.

The Centre for Literacy in Primary Education (2015–2016) in the UK has developed a writing scale that is designed to show teachers what progress in writing is like. The scale allows teachers to place students at primary level into one of eight categories: beginning writer, early writer, developing writer, moderately fluent writer, fluent writer, experienced writer, independent writer and mature independent writer. Importantly, advice is provided on how to move each pupil on to the next level of writing proficiency.

A perceived need to assess multiple dimensions of writing across an entire class of students may seem overwhelming. However, it is not necessary to assess all dimensions of a text at the same time. If a school or class decides to focus on text organisation and word choice during a particular school term, then it would be appropriate to assess one or more of those elements and address other dimensions of the rubric (and corresponding curriculum) in subsequent terms.

Over time, pupils can be expected to identify the elements of effective writing for themselves, as they receive feedback from teachers and other pupils on the quality of their writing, and they observe examples of more- and less-effective writing in the texts they read. By becoming familiar with a scoring rubric and related writing samples, pupils can internalize the success criteria required for effective writing. McLean (2022) notes the importance of developing a metalanguage about writing between teachers and students, so that clear writing goals can be set, and consistent and effective feedback can be provided and acted upon.

In some schools, there may be value in developing a shared understanding of a scoring rubric. This can be done when groups of teachers come together to discuss the quality of one or more pieces of writing, and rank them based on the descriptive criteria in the rubric. The understanding of writing quality developed by the teachers can then be called on as they score writing samples of pupils in their own classrooms. Where writing scores are shared beyond the classroom, teachers may wish to adopt the following strategies, suggested by McLean (2022), to help reduce bias:

- Minimise the impact of handwriting bias when judging writing quality, by, for example, allowing pupils to use the writing modality in which they are most proficient (handwriting or typing).

Table 5.2 Components and subcomponents of the Write to Read writing rubric

Components	Subcomponents
Ideas	(a) main ideas; (b) details
Organisation and Genre	(a) paragraphs; (b) transitions and connectives; and (c) genre-specific structures
Word Choice	(a) choice at word level; (b) choice at sentence level; and (c) use of imagery and creative language
Voice	(a) awareness of an intended audience; (b) risk-taking and playfulness with language and punctuation; and (c) consideration of overall style and language register and
Conventions	(a) spelling; (b) capitalisation and punctuation; and (c) print concepts, grammar and usage.

Source: Authors

- De-identify writing samples prior to marking.
- Randomly order writing samples before marking.

The W2R Writing Rubric

Kennedy and Shiel (2022) developed a writing rubric as part of the Write to Read (W2R) Project – an initiative designed to raise literacy standards in urban disadvantaged schools. The rubric spans Junior Infants (four to five years of age) to Sixth Class (12 years of age).

A 'three-pronged approach' was adopted in developing the rubric (Banerjee et al., 2015), drawing on theoretical models of writing and research studies such as those described in Chapters 1 and 2, samples of children's writing across grade levels, and literacy coaches' professional knowledge. The rubric comprises 14 levels across five key components (ideas, organisation, word choice, voice and conventions), each of which is further broken down into subcomponents (Table 5.2). For example, voice is subdivided into audience, risk-taking (creativity or invention) and style. The sub-traits enable teachers to take a more in-depth look at and provide more detailed feedback on particular aspects of writing. The rubric also also includes genre-specific indicators as part of text organisation.

The full rubric and support materials (for example, word lists) are available at www.writetoread.ie Appendix A at the end of this volume includes indicators for one component, Word Choice, while Appendix B includes a class-level reporting template.

Annotated Sample 5.1: The Spoocy Cave by Harry (Narrative: Fiction)

Harry, Senior Infants (England & Wales: Year 1; Scotland: P2; US: Kindergarten):

> One day me and my cusins went to a spoocy cave. I was scerde but then I fayst mu firs (faced my fears) and we went in the cave. first we saw a bat, snacke, vanpier, zomby, witch, friy (furry) man, in visabl man, spider. An the monsters ran after us. We ran home but the monsters ran after us to but we were faster we opin the door cwicly (quickly) tene (then), We ran inside and locd all the doors and windos and all the monsters went away. The End.

The Spoocy Cave

[Student handwritten story titled "The spoocy cave" by Henry, accompanied by a drawing of monsters and a cave:]

> One day me and my cusins went to a spoocy cave. I was scerde but there I fayst my firs and we went in the cave. first we saw a bat, shieke, vanpier, zomby, vitch, fliy mon, invisabl man, spider. All the monsters ran after us. We ran home but the monsters ran after us to but we were faster we opin the door cwicsy tene We ran inside and locd all the doors and windos and all the monsters went away. The End

Conventions	Ideas	Organisation & Genre	Voice	Word Choice
Spelling: 4	Main Ideas: 5	Beginning/Middle/End: 5	Audience: 4	Word Level: 4
Capitals and Punctuation: 4	Details: 4	Connectives/Transitions: 5	Risk Taking: 4	Sentence Level: 5
Print Concepts, Grammar and Usage: 5		Genre: 4	Style: 4	Imagery and Creative Language Usage: 5

This fictional narrative text by Harry describes an adventure with his cousins, in which they encounter some dangerous monsters. Readers are referred to Chapter 7, where Harry's pre-writing plan for his narrative is laid out.

Harry's narrative text, The Spoocy Cave, demonstrates an emergent understanding of spelling. While several high-frequency words are correctly spelled, such as **cave, went, first, monsters, home, faster**), others are incorrect, but still represent strong approximations to the correct spellings (e.g., **spoocy, visabl, vanpier, opin, locd, snacke, windos**), meriting a 4 on this element of Conventions. Harry's use of capital letters and punctuation merits a 4. While at least half of the sentences include a capital letter at the start and a full stop at the end, others lack these elements, perhaps because his focus was on the story as he wrote. For print concepts, grammar and use, Harry's story merits a 5. This is because the spacing between words is consistent for the most part, and accuracy in verb tenses is beginning to emerge (e.g., **went, saw, ran**), though some relatively simple verbs are spelled incorrectly (e.g., **fayst** (faced), **locd** (locked).

The first element of Ideas, the main idea(s), merits a 5. This is because the main idea is represented in a text that is longer than five sentences and is also supported by the illustration. Details merit a 4, as there are several in the text, and they support the main idea, while the drawing provides additional detail.

The first element of Organization, beginning/middle/end, merits a 5, as these elements are present, but not fully developed. The text also merits a 5 on connectives and transitions. Connectives such as *but, then, first, an* (and), and *tene* (then) are used to good effect and create some coherence. Genre merits a 4, since Harry's story includes a basic setting, characters and one main event. A more complete description of characters and setting would have merited a 5.

The audience element of Voice merits a 4, as some awareness of the audience is present, with main ideas and details emerging, but with limited elaboration. Some risk-taking is evident with word choice (I *fayst mu firs*/I faced my fears) and the use of longer sentences, meriting a 4 on this element. A number of stylistic elements are evident (response to fear, list of creatures, use of adverbs such as faster and *cwicly*) to support the writer's purpose, meriting a 4 on Style.

On the first element of Word Choice – use of vocabulary at the word level – Harry uses adjectives and everyday verbs effectively, meriting a 4. Harry's sentence openers show some variety and have moved beyond patterned sentences often found in texts at this level, meriting a 5 on the sentence level element of Word Choice. Regarding imaginary and creative use of language, the use of the literary phrase *I fayst mu firs*/I faced my fears is indicative of a 5.

In addition to generating scores across the five dimensions of writing, the rubric can be used as a basis for planning further work. For example, in order to further improve word choice at the word and sentence levels, Harry could be supported to extend some of his sentences to make them more effective. He could be invited to suggest suitable adjectives to accompany his list of creatures – a blind bat, a slippery snake, etc. He could modify the sentence 'The monster ran after us' to provide the reader with more detail and heighten the reader's interest further.

Overall, it can be concluded that Harry's writing is good for his class level and shows clear signs of promise.

Annotated Sample 5.2: Running in the Yard by Tina (Persuasive letter)

Tina, Third Class (England: Year 4; Scotland & Northern Ireland: P5; US: Grade 3)

Dear Ms.,

I am very dissapointed and shocked that you are even considering banning fun running in the yard. Do you realise that you are dapring us of 2+ hours of fun running per week? Do you not see that obesity is growing bigger and bigger in ireland? It is on every tv and media outlet, this is an issue that is ongoing and we have to fight it your decision is adding to this issue.

The winters are getting fiercly cold so where are we supposed to sit on the cold, icy step frozen, stiff? Is that what you want for your pupils Absentees will increase The pupil numbers will get lower and lower that is even worse. We need our blood pumping I know you would do whatever you can to keep your pupils safe but we have to burn the energy off, When we get out of school we will nearly explode with the running we need.

76 *Teaching and Assessing Writing in the Primary School*

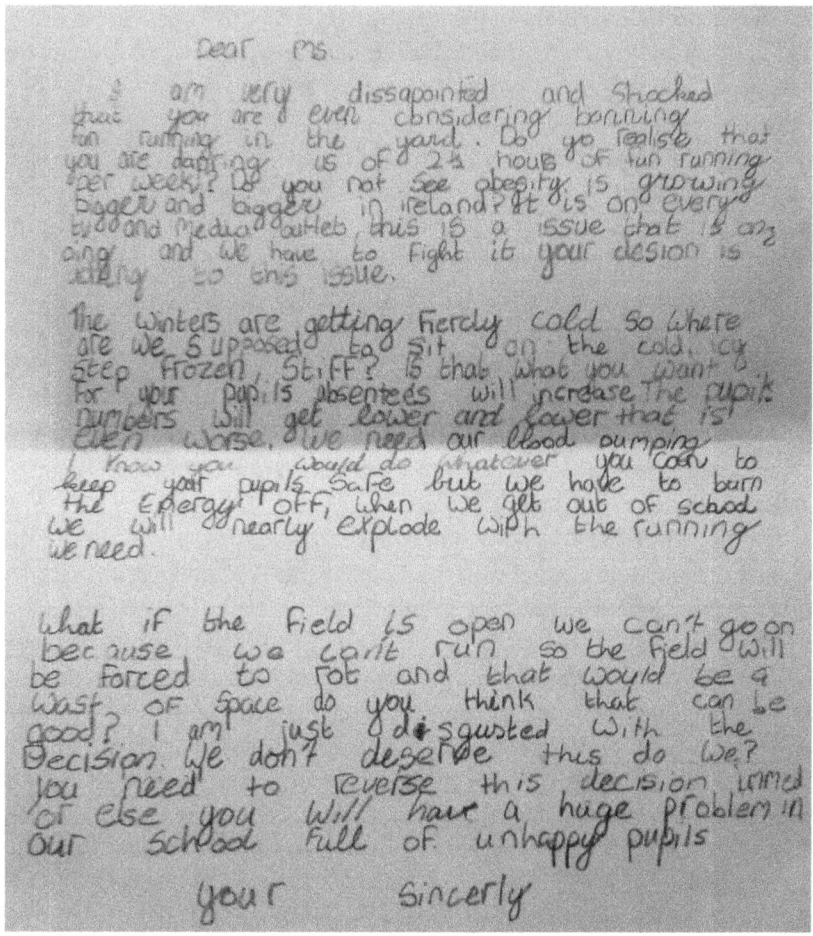

What if the field is open we can't go on because we can't run so the field will be forced to rot and that would be a wast of space do you think that can be good? I am just disgusted with the Decision. We don't deserve this do we? You need to reverse this decision immediately or else you will have a huge problem in our school full of unhappy pupils

Your sincerly,

Conventions	Ideas	Organisation & Genre	Voice	Word Choice
Spelling: 9	Main Ideas: 8	Paragraphs: 10	Audience: 8	Word Level: 8
Capitals and Punctuation: 5	Details: 9	Connectives/ Transitions: 8	Risk Taking: 8	Sentence Level: 8
Print Concepts, Grammar and Usage: 8		Genre: 9	Style: 10	Imagery and Creative Language Usage: 9

Tina's spelling (the first element of Conventions) is generally good, although there are a small number of errors that don't detract from meaning (*dissapointed*, *dapring* (depriving), *fiercly, wast*), meriting a score of 9 (Level 10 requires accurate spelling of words with common prefixes and suffixes). Capitalisation and punctuation merits a 5 because, while some sentences begin with a capital letter and end with a full stop, there are also examples of run-on sentences (e.g., *... that would be a wast of space do you think that can be good?*). Furthermore, the proper noun *Ireland* begins with a lower-case i. Greater attention to editing might help to improve punctuation. Grammar and Usage merit an 8 since there is noun-verb agreement on most sentences, the writer uses the appropriate verb tense for the genre (a mixture of tenses, in line with the persuasive intent of the letter), and there are several complex sentences (e.g., *I am very dissapointed and shocked that you are even considering banning fun running in the yard*) as well as simpler ones.

The first element of Ideas, main ideas, merits an 8. This is because the main ideas, broadly represented in paragraphs in a longer text, are linked to an over-arching idea (albeit an implicit one since no title is present): that children should be allowed to run for fun in the playground during lunchtime. However, each paragraph does not contribute to a unique main idea. Details merit a score of 9 since they are well-elaborated, in terms of contributing to their respective main ideas. This is most notable in paragraph 2, where the focus is on sitting around in the cold doing nothing, and the likely consequences of this. The point about unused playing fields in paragraph 3 is a little weaker since it is not unusual for playing fields to be closed down when they are deemed unplayable.

Turning to Organisation, paragraphing is quite strong, with an opening, development and conclusion evident across the text as a whole, and each paragraph generally remaining on topic. However, the flow between paragraphs could be strengthened. Paragraphing merits a score of 10. Relatively little explicit use is made of Connectives/Transitions between sentences or between paragraphs, though this does not detract from the overall coherence as paragraphs themselves are fairly self-contained and use other devices that might be expected to contribute to cohesion, such as anaphoric reference (e.g., *Do you not see that obesity is growing bigger and bigger in ireland?* **It** *is on every tv and media outlet,* **this** *is an issue that is ongoing*) and multiple rhetorical questions directed at the school principal, often in close proximity. This dimension merits an 8. Regarding genre, or the presence of key characteristics of persuasive writing, we see an effective if clunky opening sentence (*I am very dissapointed and shocked that you are even considering banning fun running in the yard*), and a reasonably effective closing statement. The organization of the text supports the writer's purpose, and some use of hyperbole is evident (e.g., *The winters are getting fiercly cold*). Although counter-arguments are not considered in any detail, it is acknowledged that the principal '*would do whatever [she] can to keep your pupils safe*'. The text is scored as 9 on genre.

Regarding Voice, it is evident that the writer is keenly aware of the audience (the school principal), that the text engages the reader, and that the language register (the formal letter) and syntax generally suit the writer's purpose (to persuade). There is some creative detail (e.g., linking the principal's decision to a possible increase in obesity, and to a lowering of pupil numbers). Audience merits an 8. Risks are taken in the text with regard to language (e.g., use of words like deprive) and more advanced punctuation (e.g., use of question marks,

78 *Teaching and Assessing Writing in the Primary School*

though these are sometimes omitted). Risk-taking also merits an 8. Turning to style, we can see that the purpose of the text and the writer's intentions emerge. There is a distinctive tone (disbelief, mixed with frustration), and the pace of the text is fairly evenly balanced across paragraphs, meriting a 10.

Word Choice at the word level encompasses the appropriate use of adjectives (e.g., *ongoing, dissappointed/disappointed, disgusted*), verbs (e.g., *dapring/depriving, fight, disgusted, deserve, reverse*), adverbs (e.g., *just, nearly*) and precise nouns (e.g., *obesity*)

> "Hi, I'm Jack Posavitz." I say. "Hi, Dean Sweeny It's a pleasure." he says in a raspy voice. He looks exhausted. It's no secret we all are. The Brazilian's keep running into our camp and shooting everyone, so now no one ever sleeps. I wish this war would end.
>
> "They should just give up. America is slightly bigger than Brazil, so the odds our against them." I say grumpily. "Ya, I know. How old are you?" He asks me. "24. You?" "I'm 25," he says.
>
> Everything that happens next happens so fast I have no time to react. The loud bang startles me, and I look to see Dean fall to the floor, dead; or at least I think he's dead. I can't tell because now a huge muscular arm has come out from behind me and has wrapped around my throat. The first thing that comes to mind is that I'M BEING CHOKED! The next thing I think is I DON'T WANT TO BE CHOKED!!!! Bang! Bang! Bang! Now Gun shots could be heard all over camp. I have to act fast or I will sufficate. I gather up all my strenghth and CRACK! I elbow him in the jaw so hard I think I broke it. He falls behind me.

in a consistent way that is appropriate to the genre. For example, *immediately* conveys a sense of urgency, while *deserve* builds on the idea of deprivation introduced earlier. Word choice at word level merits an 8. Word choice at the sentence level also merits an 8 as sentence openings show sensitivity to the language register of the genre (e.g., *I am very dissapointed and shocked, reverse this decision*), and the writer experiments with multi-clause sentences *(e.g., I know you would do whatever you can to keep your pupils safe but we have to burn the energy off)*, though not always successfully, since punctuation is problematic in places. Finally, imagery and creative language use merits a 9 since the writer sustains their use of grade-level nouns and verbs across the text, and, as noted earlier, uses hyperbole as a literary device.

Overall, this is a well-written piece of persuasive text though there is ample room for further development.

Annotated Sample 5.3: The War by Ken (Fiction)

Ken, Sixth Class (England: Year 7; Scotland & Northern Ireland: Year 8; US: Grade 6):

> "Hi, I'm Jack Posavitz", I say. "Hi, Dean Sweeney. It's a pleasure." he says in a raspy voice. He looks exhausted. It's no secret we all are. The Brazilian's keep running into our camp and shooting everyone, so now no one ever sleeps. I wish this war would end.
>
> "They should just give up. America is slightly bigger than Brazil, so the odds are against them," I say grumpily. "Ya, I know. How old are you?" he asks me. "24. You?" "I am 25," he says.
>
> Everything that happens next happens so fast that I have no time to react. The loud bang startles me, and I look to see Dean fall to the floor, dead; Or at least I think he's dead. I can't tell because now a huge muscular arm has come out from behind me and has wrapped around my throat. The first thing that comes to mind is that I AM BEING CHOKED!!!! Bang! Bang! Now Gun shots could be heard all over camp. I have to act fast or I will sufficate. I gather up all my strength and CRACK! I elbow him in the jaw so hard I think I broke it. He falls behind me, and I finally get a good look at him. A bald man with a long scar down his face from a battle long ago. Im surprised at my strength because not only is his jaw bloody and broken, I also knocked him out.
>
> I turn my attention back to Dean. A slight rise and fall of the chest. Alive. That's a good sign, but now I see the bullet hit him on the side of his stomach. "Hey," he says. "Hey," I say. "I'm going to get you to the medic." "Ah dont, I'm fine. I got a bullet vest on", he says. "But that doesn't mean it didn't hurt. Help me up". I get him on to his feet and he shoots the Brazilian soldier in the chest. We can tell it killed him because the bullet rips through his shirt and sinks deep into his chest.
>
> We both run back to camp, a small building where we keep our amo, and we eat dinner (Half a baked potato and a chicken leg). We got more amo for our AK47's, and we prepare for more fighting tomorrow.
>
> The End for now...

> and I finally get a good look at him. A bald man with a long scar down his face from a battle long ago. I'm surprised at my tstrenghth because not only is his jaw bloody and broken, I also knocked him out.
>
> I turn my attention back to Dean. A slight rise and fall of the chest. Alive. Thats a good sign, but now I see the bullet hit him on the side of his stomach. "Hey..." he says. "Hey", I say. "I'm gonna get you to the medic." "ah dont, I'm fine. I got a bullet vest on". He says. "But that dosn't mean it didn't hurt. Help me up". I get him on to his feet and he shoots the Brazilian soldier in the chest. We can tell it killed him because the bullet rips through his shirt and sinks deep into his chest.
>
> We both run back to camp, a small building where we keep our amo, and we eat dinner. (Half a baked potato and a chicken leg) We get more amo for our AK47's, and we prepare for more fighting tomorrow.
>
> The End for now...

Conventions	Ideas	Organisation & Genre	Voice	Word Choice
Spelling: 12	Main Ideas: 12	Paragraphs: 11	Audience: 11	Word Level: 12
Capitals and Punctuation: 10	Details: 11	Connectives/ Transitions: 11	Risk Taking: 11	Sentence Level: 13
Print Concepts, Grammar and Usage: 10		Genre: 12	Style: 12	Imagery and Creative Language Usage: 13

Conventions are generally strong in Ken's fiction text. Spelling merits a 12, with most words spelled correctly, including complex words such as **Brazilian, muscular** and **strength**. Suffocate is misspelled (**sufficate**) but is a very close approximation, while 'going to' is spelled **gonna**, reflecting an abbreviated version used in everyday speech. The abbreviation **amo** should read **ammo**. Capitals and punctuation merits 10, as Ken uses capital letters, punctuation marks (.!?), commas and quotation marks correctly for the most part in complex sentences. An exception is **Brazilian's** for Brazilians. Grammar and usage merits a 10 because verb tense and other elements, including adverbs (e.g., **grumpily, only, deep**) are appropriate to the genre.

Regarding Ideas, main ideas merits a 12, as the main ideas show a sense of originality and maturity, and the reader's attention is sustained through much of the text. Details merit an 11, since they contribute to the overall cohesion of the text and support the purpose of the writer. A small number of details are out of place – a slightly larger population in the US might not necessarily give it an advantage in a war, while details of what was eaten for lunch shortly after an armed struggle (**Half a baked potato and a chicken leg**) doesn't contribute to the overall picture. There might also be concern that Dean shot an adversary who had already been knocked out. Some of these issues can be addressed via discussion and feedback.

Turning to Organisation, paragraphing is strong and sustained, with most paragraphs more than 4-5 sentences in length, meriting an 11. There is a sense of flow across paragraphs, though, as noted earlier, some details seem to detract from the purpose of the text. Connectives/transitions also merit an 11. Although explicit links between paragraphs are not used, the writer achieves the same effect with back referencing (e.g., **I turn my attention back to Dean**). The introductory sentence in the third paragraph is especially strong (**Everything that happens next happens so fast that I have no time to react**) and sets the scene for the struggle that follows. The transition from narration to dialogue is smooth throughout. At this level, the W2R rubric allows for a consideration of the narrative genre across multiple dimensions, including character/protagonist/antagonist, setting and plot. On balance, genre (fictional narrative) merits a 12. There is a clear distinction between major characters (the narrator and Dean), and minor ones (the Brazilian fighter). The relationship between the narrator and Dean is sustained throughout. The text is too short to allow for evidence of character growth. The setting is especially strong as the mood and atmosphere are created through description and dialogue. For the most part, the setting is realistic, given the context (a war scene). The sequence is logical and the reader is carried by the sense of pace and urgency.

The first element of Voice, audience, merits an 11. Unique, creative and personalised details, appropriate to a narrative, hook the reader and are sustained throughout most of the text. The text does not merit a 12, as the final paragraph leaves a number of issues unresolved, although we are told that more may be on the way. Risk taking merits an 11. The writer shows awareness of apt and inventive use of language appropriate to the genre (**He looks exhausted. It's no secret we all are; Everything that happens next happens so fast that I have no time to react; I turn my attention back to Dean**). There is some evidence of punctuation being used to support language and elaborate on sentence structure (e.g., I AM BEING

CHOKED!!!!... CRACK!). Style merits a 12 as a unique style emerges that meets Ken's purpose and the reader's needs. A sustained tone, pace and momentum are maintained for the most part and the use of the present tense generally adds to the piece.

Turning to Word Choice, choice at the word level merits a 12. Ken uses descriptive language that draws on the senses in multiple parts of the text and involves the use of precise words (e.g., *raspy voice, sinks deep, I say grumpily, a slight rise and fall*), without overuse. Word Choice at the sentence level merits a 13. Here we see descriptive detail within complex sentences or phrases (e.g., *a huge muscular arm ... has wrapped around my throat; A bald man with a long scar down his face from a battle long ago*). Sentences vary in length to suit the flow of the text and the author's purpose. Imagery and creative language usage also merit a 13. There is judicious use of a wide range of literary phrases/figurative language across the text, which will linger in the reader's mind (e.g., *It's no secret we all are; The loud bang startles me...; Everything that happens next happens so fast...; at least I think he's dead; A slight rise and fall of the chest*).

Overall, this is a promising narrative text, and Ken demonstrates strong potential. Because his use of conventions and his word choice are strong, further instruction can focus on the craft elements of writing, including aspects of style. It would also be worth exploring more complex characterisation and motives.

Impact of Feedback on Writing Development

Timely formative assessment (e.g., teacher-pupil conferencing, written comments on students' writing, peer and self-assessment) can play a pivotal role in enhancing writing quality (Graham et al., 2015). A key component of this is the provision of adequate and appropriate feedback to pupils.

Graham et al. (2015) conducted a meta-analysis of the available research to examine whether formative writing assessments that are directly tied to classroom teaching and learning enhance the quality of students' writing. The research focused on studies involving children in Grades 1–8 that provided feedback about the quality of writing, or progress in learning specific writing skills and strategies. Across 25 studies, effect sizes for feedback about writing from adults (0.87), peers (0.58) and self (i.e., self-assessment) (0.62) were large, while they were small to medium for computers (0.38), and it was concluded that such assessments should be used more frequently by teachers. Studies that involved the provision of feedback by adults included teachers providing feedback to students on their progress in writing paragraphs, teachers giving feedback on progress on correct word sequence, spelling and total words written, and (trained) parents providing feedback to their child on their writing. The studies involving peer feedback included children giving feedback to their peers on writing quality and receiving feedback from peers, sometimes based on a rubric, or a learned strategy such as giving feedback on aspects such as clarity or completeness. The self-assessment studies included the use of a rubric to self-assess, and carrying out specific revision tactics such as substituting, adding, deleting or moving text to improve writing. The studies involving computer-based feedback were evaluations of commercially available programmes that provided students with feedback on summaries that they wrote, or on their writing more generally. The different sources of formative feedback are summarised in Box 5.1.

BOX 5.1 SOURCES OF FORMATIVE FEEDBACK TO CHILDREN ON THEIR WRITING

- Teachers (e.g., feedback on progress on different aspects of writing such as writing paragraphs, correct word sequence, word count)
- Parents (e.g., giving feedback on overall quality of writing, following training)
- Peers (e.g., feedback on writing quality, suggestions for further development; using a rubric as a basis for providing feedback; provision of feedback on specified aspects of writing such as unclear parts, gaps in content, adequacy of description)
- Self (e.g., review of own work, identifying strengths and challenges and implementing revisions)
- Technology/computers (e.g., feedback on specific aspects of writing such as completeness of summaries)

Adapted from Graham et al. (2015)

Peer feedback studies (e.g. Boscolo & Ascorti, 2004; Philippakos & MacArthur, 2016) show that students in receipt of feedback from their peers make more substantive revisions to their writing, resulting in improved quality. Success is contingent on modelling these feedback processes for students and engaging them in using relevant evaluation criteria. It is helpful 'for writers to discuss with peers what they have done, partly in order to get ideas from their peers and partly to see what they, the writers, say when they try to explain their thinking' (NCTE, 2016, p. 14). Providing feedback to a peer can sharpen students' understanding of the audience, as, when questioned, writers come to the realisation that the writing may require greater clarity or further elaboration. Students are more likely to be able to detect macro-level issues in another student's text than in their own but benchmarking a peer's work against criteria familiarises them with evaluation criteria and this can further enhance their own first drafts (Philippakos & McArthur, 2016).

Research in the Australian context that involved 59 teachers across six schools demonstrated a significant relationship between teacher ability to provide quality feedback and pupil writing achievement on standardised assessments of writing (Parr & Timperley, 2010). The quality of teacher feedback was linked to teachers' ability to ascertain where students were relative to desired achievement, the key characteristics of the desired level of achievement, and what specifically was required to close the achievement gap. A key conclusion in this study was that significant content and pedagogical (teaching) knowledge are required on the part of teachers to provide feedback that can be effective, especially deep knowledge of how written language works (Parr & Timperley, 2010).

Other Formative Assessments of Writing

Here, further strategies for assessing writing formatively are considered, including think-aloud, progress steps in writing, and writing conferences.

Think Alouds

Traga Philippakos and Moore (2020) recommend the use of think-aloud assessments to gain an understanding of students' thinking processes, their use of strategies and their attitudes towards particular tasks. They argue that such information can be used for diagnostic purposes by teachers, and to set instructional goals. They note, however, that students may benefit from training on how to engage effectively in thinking aloud and in making their ideas explicit to the teacher.

Portfolios

Traga-Philippakos and Moore also recommend the use of portfolios (including e-portfolios) – collections of pupil work gathered over time – to generate information for teachers and students about finished products and the processes used by students to arrive at those products.

A typical portfolio (whether paper or digital) may include:

- Samples of writing in different genres, completed in the course of a school year, including examples of drafts and independent work
- Reflections on written pieces as the writer identifies aspects on which they have done well, and ways in which they are working to improve their writing (thereby helping with metacognition).
- Samples of handwriting
- A rubric explaining to students how their writing is to be evaluated.

An advantage of digital portfolios is that, in addition to including completed multi-modal texts (see Chapter 3), they can include interviews with the child about their writing (e.g., beginning and end-of-year interviews). They can also be more accessible to parents and may facilitate peer feedback.

Portfolios have become more important in England in recent years, as they now form the basis of the end-of-key stage 2 writing assessment, and subsequent moderation of writing grades (see Cuff, 2019).

Progression Steps in Writing and Student-Facing Checklists

Progression steps in writing, sometimes called "learning paths", "learning trajectories", "learning progressions" or "progression continua", are increasingly a feature of curricula and writing assessments. In Ireland, for example, progression continua in writing are included in the primary language toolkit (see NCCA, n.d.). These are intended to support teachers in formatively assessing pupils' development across their primary school years. However, little research is available on how teachers use the continua, or on their effects on children's writing development.

Calkins et al. (2019) note the value of learning trajectories in supporting teachers to assess students' writing development and provide their students with relevant feedback. The authors argue that writing rubrics often incorporate learning trajectories, and hence facilitate the sequencing of instruction and assessment by teacher. However, they found that student-facing checklists based on trajectories can be more appropriate for supporting younger students to self-assess and set goals. They also emphasise the importance of making a range of exemplars (samples of pupil writing across different writing genres and different attainment levels) available to teachers and students to support them in interpreting learning trajectories and related tools (rubrics and checklists).

Writing Conferences

As noted in Chapter 10, writing conferences can play a key role in addressing children's needs in writing, especially when they based on students' assessed writing needs. However, conferences can also provide teachers with an opportunity to better understand why a child has structured their sentences or texts in a certain way, and how improvement can be brought about. Additional assessment information can be gathered, as the teacher interrogates the child's decisions as a writer, and evaluates aspects that require further development, whether they relate to planning for writing, the drafting of a text around a particular genre, the child's use of grammar and punctuation, the child's understanding of the writing process, or their motivation to write.

Assessing Self-Efficacy and Motivation to Write

Self-efficacy for writing can be assessed. For example, Pajares et al. (2007) developed a Writing Self-efficacy Scale which has been used in numerous studies. The scale has a two-factor structure – self-efficacy for basic writing skills, and self-efficacy for advanced composition skills – and correlates significantly with other attitudinal measures (e.g., writing self-concept) and with writing achievement, for students in Grades 4–11. While such instruments are useful in describing self-efficacy for writing in a general sense, it may also be the case that writers make multiple judgements about their self-efficacy in the course of a single writing task (Bruning & Kauffman, 2016), for example, when they receive an assignment, discuss ideas for writing with others, implement their writing plan and review their written texts.

Motivation to write can be assessed informally, by observing students as they engage in different aspects of the writing process. There are also child-friendly scales available. For example, Kear et al. (2000) have developed a 28-item scale that requires students to indicate how they feel about such activities as writing poetry for fun, writing a letter to share their opinion about a topic, and writing more in schools. Scores (between 1 and 4, ranging from a very unhappy Garfield to a very happy one) on each item are summed to obtain an overall raw score, which can then be converted to a grade-level percentile rank, allowing for comparisons with students at the same grade level, and between the same pupil over time. Information about attitudes towards writing can be useful in targeting children who otherwise might not have been identified as having negative attitudes or (one assumes), poor motivation to write well.

Parsons et al. (2023) have developed a writing engagement scale (see https://tinyurl.com/CopyWESForm). Students are asked to indicate their level of agreement with statements such as:

- When working on this writing assignment, I reviewed my writing and made changes to make it better (Cognitive engagement).

- When writing this assignment, I was interested in what I was writing (Affective engagement).
- I can think of at least one person who would want to read this writing (Social engagement).
- I tried hard to do well on this writing assignment (Behavioural engagement)

In addition to an overall engagement score, a profile of engagement can be generated, with students scoring on social engagement, affective engagement (interest and enthusiasm), cognitive engagement and behavioural engagement subscales. Information on subscale differences allows teachers to zero in on specific aspects of engagement. For example, a low score on social engagement might indicate a need to review strategies for working with peers during the writing process. This may, in turn, improve motivation and writing quality.

Summative Assessment of Writing

Many of the assessment procedures described in this chapter are designed for formative assessment purposes. Anecdotal notes, analytic scoring rubrics, writing portfolios, and scales with which to measure aspects of motivation and engagement are all intended to be used in classroom contexts by teachers seeking information to improve the quality of teaching and learning.

As noted earlier, another set of assessments, known as summative assessments, can be used to evaluate performance at the end of a programme or course of study. At the individual level, such assessments might include end-of-year grades for writing, perhaps based on a scoring rubric. At the system level, they may include national tests, such as the key stage tests in England or the NAPLAN assessment in Australia (see Chapter 4).

A key feature of summative assessments is that writing (composition) is completed independently by students. In England (gov.ie, 2024), teachers are provided with the following guidelines on what constitutes independent writing:

- Emerges from a text, topic, visit or curriculum experience in which pupils have had opportunities to discuss and rehearse what is to be written about.
- Enables pupils to use their own ideas and provides them with an element of choice – for example, writing from the perspective of a character they have chosen themselves.
- Has been edited, if required, by the pupil without the support of the teacher, although this may be in response to self, peer or group evaluation.
- Is produced by pupils who have, if required, sought out classroom resources, such as a dictionary or thesaurus, without being prompted to do so by the teacher.

The same guidance clarifies what constitutes non-independent writing, including writing that has been:

- Modelled or heavily scaffolded.
- Edited or re-written because of direct intervention by a teacher or other adult.
- Produced with the support of electronic aids that automatically provide correct spelling, synonyms, punctuation or predictive text.
- Supported by detailed success criteria that specifically direct pupils what to include, or where to include it, in their writing.

Assessment of Writing   87

As noted in Chapter 4, the outcomes of KS2 writing are reported with respect to three levels. The statements or criteria underpinning these levels are shown in Table 5.3.

A pupil's writing is expected to meet all of the statements within the standard at which they are judged to have attained, though teachers are permitted to use their discretion in the event that a particular weakness prevents an accurate judgement of the pupil's attainment being made.

Among the best-known summative assessments of writing is the National Assessment of Educational Progress (NAEP) in the United States. The NAEP writing assessment is based

Table 5.3 Key stage 2 standards for writing

Standard	Statements
Working towards the expected standard	The pupil can: write for a range of purposes • use paragraphs to organise ideas • in narratives, describe settings and characters • in non-narrative writing, use simple devices to structure the writing and support the reader (e.g. headings, sub-headings, bullet points) • use capital letters, full stops, question marks, commas for lists and apostrophes for contraction mostly correctly • spell correctly most words from the year 3/year 4 spelling list, and some words from the year 5/year 6 spelling list* • write legibly.
Working at the expected standard	The pupil can: write effectively for a range of purposes and audiences, selecting language that shows good awareness of the reader (e.g. the use of the first person in a diary; direct address in instructions and persuasive writing) • in narratives, describe settings, characters and atmosphere • integrate dialogue in narratives to convey character and advance the action • select vocabulary and grammatical structures that reflect what the writing requires, doing this mostly appropriately (e.g. using contracted forms in dialogues in narrative; using passive verbs to affect how information is presented; using modal verbs to suggest degrees of possibility) • use a range of devices to build cohesion (e.g. conjunctions, adverbials of time and place, pronouns, synonyms) within and across paragraphs • use verb tenses consistently and correctly throughout their writing • use the range of punctuation taught at key stage 2 mostly correctly (e.g. inverted commas and other punctuation to indicate direct speech) • spell correctly most words from the year 5/year 6 spelling list, and use a dictionary to check the spelling of uncommon or more ambitious vocabulary • maintain legibility in joined handwriting when writing at speed
Working at greater depth	The pupil can: write effectively for a range of purposes and audiences, selecting the appropriate form and drawing independently on what they have read as models for their own writing (e.g. literary language, characterisation, structure) • distinguish between the language of speech and writing and choose the appropriate register • exercise an assured and conscious control over levels of formality, particularly through manipulating grammar and vocabulary to achieve this • use the range of punctuation taught at key stage 2 correctly (e.g. semi-colons, dashes, colons, hyphens) and, when necessary, use such punctuation precisely to enhance meaning and avoid ambiguity. [There are no additional statements for spelling or handwriting]

Source: Standards and Testing Agency (2018, pp. 4-5)

on representative national samples of students and is designed to provide system-level information on standards in writing (i.e., it does not provide useful information at the individual pupil or school levels). In the past, NAEP writing was administered every four to five years in Grades 4, 8 and 12. Among the writing tasks assigned to students in earlier NAEP writing assessments were:

- Describe what lunchtime is like for you on a school day. Be sure to tell about your lunchtime so that someone who has never had lunch with you on a school day can understand where you have lunch and what lunchtime is like. (Informative writing, paper-based, 2002, https://www.nationsreportcard.gov/nqt/searchquestions).
- One morning a child looks out the window and discovers that a huge castle has appeared overnight. The child rushes outside to the castle and hears strange sounds coming from it. Someone is living in the castle! The castle door creaks open. The child goes in. Write a story about who the child meets and what happens inside the castle. (Narrative writing, paper-based, 1998, https://www.nationsreportcard.gov/nqt/searchquestions).
- Imagine that students at your school are going to select a new school mascot. A mascot is an animal or object used to represent a group. For example, many sports teams have mascots. Four choices are being considered as your school's mascot: Tigers, Rising Stars, Dolphins, and Rockets. You have been asked to choose one of the four mascots (pictured) and to support your choice to the school principal. Write a letter to your school principal, convincing him or her that your choice should be the school mascot. Be sure to include reasons and examples in your letter (Persuasive writing, computer-based pilot, NAEP, 2012).

NAEP writing texts are scored by trained markers, who are closely monitored to ensure that scoring is consistent or reliable from one rater to the next.

Much like national curriculum assessment in England, NAEP reports on the proportions of students at each level of proficiency (basic, proficient, advanced).

Starting in 2011, NAEP made the transition to computer-based assessment of writing. The outcomes of the 2017 NAEP assessment have yet to be published, because of the difficulty in looking at trends over time arising from a change from computer (PC) in 2011 to tablet plus keyboard in 2017. Although the change only related to Grades 8 and 12, results for Grade 4 have not been published either (NAEP, n.d.)

Conclusion

As noted in Chapter 2, a key characteristic of effective writing instruction is the implementation of formative assessment by teachers and/or pupils, and the provision of effective feedback. Effective writing instruction was characterised as being based on pupils' assessed needs. In Chapter 4, and again in this chapter, we also saw examples of summative assessments of writing, where the purpose is to inform school- or system-level policies on teaching writing.

A broad range of tools were identified as being compatible with formative assessment of pupils' writing. These included anecdotal notes, analytic scoring rubrics, think-alouds, portfolios, progression steps and checklists. These tools can support teachers and pupils to identify strengths and weaknesses, set goals for writing, and monitor progress over time. Chapter 10 in this volume looks at assessment processes in classroom settings, in the context of evaluating pupils' writing and providing pupils with tools to revise and edit their own writing. Chapter 11 looks at how an individual pupil progressed in writing over the course of six months, drawing on writing samples that they completed independently.

Summative assessment was referred to at the end of Chapter 4, in the context of the achieved curriculum in schools, and again in this chapter. It was noted that additional care is often exercised in the administration and scoring of summative assessments (compared with formative assessments), as such summative assessment is typically based on writing completed by the pupil without teacher help, and is scored by trained raters who do not know the pupil in question. An exception is the key stage 2 writing tests in England, which are scored by the pupil's own teacher, but may also be subject to external moderation, to ensure consistency in scoring.

This chapter marks the end of our overview of effective teaching and assessment of writing. Chapters 6-10 focus on teaching and assessing writing in classroom settings, while Chapters 11 and 12 refer to specialist topics - supporting diverse writers and school-level planning for writing.

Reflect, Connect, Act

Activity

Compare two writing samples (same grade level, genre and topic):

- Identify strengths and weaknesses (refer to key concepts presented in the chapter).
- Identify the broad stages of development (e.g., knowledge telling vs. knowledge transforming).
- Apply a rubric to the samples, and make specific suggestions for improvement.

Some assessment programmes (e.g., NAEP in the US, NAPLAN in Australia) require pupils to produce a written text based on a prompt (sometimes called on-demand writing), while others permit the use of already-completed writing, such as a text in a pupil's writing portfolio, as long as the work has been completed independently of the teacher. Which approach do you think is best? Why?

Suggestion for Further Reading

Hale, E. (2017). Academic praise in conferences: A key for motivating struggling writers. *Reading Teacher, 71*(6), 651-658. https://doi.org/10.1002/trtr.1664

6 Designing, Organising and Implementing a Writing Workshop

Drawing on the research explored in Part A, this chapter provides a framework for the structure and implementation of a daily Writing Workshop for children aged 4-12 years and how that structure can be adapted to accommodate a range of pedagogies, and whole class, small group and individual teaching balanced across a week. Each of these aspects is revisited and further elaborated in subsequent chapters.

> **Reflect and Connect**
>
> 1. What are some of the key differences between a writing workshop approach to writing and more traditional approaches?
> 2. How does a writing workshop facilitate the development of oral language, reading and writing?
> 3. Why is it important to consider the physical arrangement/design of the learning environment for writing (the classroom here)? How might it need to be adapted for 4-12 yr. olds?
> 4. What are some of the key conditions required for the successful implementation of an effective writing workshop? What are the common pitfalls?

The Building Blocks of a Successful Research-Informed Writing Workshop

There are many considerations to bear in mind when embarking on the design and implementation of a writing workshop approach to writing in your classroom. When key conditions are in place the workshop will be more effective and more likely to succeed in not only enhancing children's motivation and engagement to write but also in impacting positively on the quality of their writing.

Time and Choice

The first thing to think about is how time is used in your classroom on a daily and weekly basis. Consider how you currently teach writing. Do children have time to compose daily?

Do they have a choice over their writing topics within a given genre? Do they have a range of publishing options? If the answers are negative, begin by contemplating how you might find ways to give children a predictable protected daily block of time to write. What could you eliminate or reduce attention to?

As has been highlighted in earlier chapters, though the provision of sufficient time to write is a critical dimension for the success of any writing programme (National Commission on Writing US, 2003; Graham et al., 2012b), there is minimal research evidence to support this recommendation. This is largely due to the fact that not enough research has been conducted to establish if providing daily opportunities to write improves the quality of writing more than less frequent opportunities. However, without daily time to write, students are unlikely to develop writing to the level required for success in school and in life or to incubate ideas and bring them to life.

Writing is a highly personal complex and creative act and like any creative endeavour it needs time for ideas to percolate and develop. As Grainger and colleagues argue 'if children's writing is to demonstrate their creativity, individuality, voice and verve, then the seeds of their stories and other forms of writing need constant nurturing and support as well as time to evolve and reverberate' (2005, p. 2). Creativity is not like a tap that can be turned on at will. It is more likely to develop when a reliable daily time is built into the routine of classroom life. The provision of daily time to write confers a value on writing as an activity that is worth doing every day and it conveys subtle messages to children about what it means to be a writer.

The choice element is also critical; it is very difficult to write well on a topic for which you have little background knowledge or interest. In our work with schools, we have consistently found that choice is the most cited reason that children give for why they love to write:

> *I love stories, because I can make up whatever I want, and no one can say a thing!*
>
> (3rd class)

> *Because we can make up our own stuff and I really like making up stuff that teacher will let us.*
>
> (2nd class)

Graves (1994) suggests that when time and choice are predictable elements of classroom life, children engage more deeply and enter into what he calls 'a constant state of composition' (p. 104), experiencing what Csikszentmihalyi (1975) terms a 'flow' experience, a loss of awareness of time passing as they become absorbed in writing. He shares the words of Flannery O Connor (cited in Murray, 1990, p. 60) who scheduled daily writing time: 'many times I just sit for three hours with no ideas coming to me. But I know one thing, if an idea comes between 9 and 12, I am ready for it' (1994, p. 79). This highlights the unpredictability of writing; it doesn't come easy to most. But without time, it may not come at all! Ensuring the time is built into your routine at the same time daily, where possible, creates sub-conscious signals in the brain which begins to ruminate on writing ideas outside of writing time.

Children are more likely to invest in their writing when they have ownership over it. Though you may choose the genre, children should have choice and control over their individual topics. The combination of time and choice influences how children perceive the act of writing and the level of effort they put into honing their writing. Time allows children to ponder and consider their word choice and audience, as noted by this young writer:

And when you're writing it down, you get to like, take your time and figure out what's the perfect thing to say.

(4th class)

Choice can be balanced with prescribing writing topics from time to time. A good rule of thumb is for the teacher to allow choice 80-90% of the time. The other 10-20% of the time can be used for assessment purposes. At particular times, for example, after a unit of work on a genre or at a particular time of year, you may wish to check how students are applying what they are learning to independent writing and set a topic for everyone to work on for assessment purposes. This can provide evidence for how children at varying levels of writing competence and expertise approach the topic and the degree to which they transfer what they have learned from mini lessons taught into their texts.

How much time is another consideration. International surveys of writing practices among teachers indicate that students are not provided with sufficient time to write and in fact spend little time daily actually composing text (Cutler & Graham, 2008). Graham et al.'s meta-analysis (2012b/2018) recommended an hour a day balanced between explicit teaching to move the quality of the writing forward and time for children to write independently without interruption. An hour a day is a big ask in a primary school where time must be allocated to a wide range of other subjects and disciplines and time for literacy must also include attention to reading and oral language.

In the Irish context, evidence from the national assessments – typically conducted at five yearly intervals (Kavanagh et al., 2015) – indicated that on average, teachers of children in second class allocate 294 minutes weekly to literacy (oral, reading and writing) which equates to 58.8 minutes daily and a further 149 minutes are allocated to literacy across the curriculum. Though allocation of time is a contentious issue in Ireland (NCCA, 2005, 2008), time for writing can be enhanced by integrating writing with reading and embedding oral language within the timeframe. Not only is this a good use of time, but it has been found to be more effective than teaching each in isolation or separately. As noted by Graham et al., 2018, p. 279) 'literacy programs balancing reading and writing instruction can strengthen reading and writing and that the two skills can be learned together profitably'. Additionally, writing genres can be connected into a range of curricular areas (Graham et al., 2012b/2018). However, it is critical that the extra time does not compromise the integrity of the discipline so that every lesson does not become a literacy lesson and conversely that an over focus on literacy in the disciplines detracts from the study of literature and writing creativity. Furthermore, embedding the teaching of mechanical skills (grammar, spelling and punctuation) into children's authentic writing removes time spent completing skills in isolation in workbooks. Instead, they can be taught when children have demonstrated a need and a readiness for particular skills.

Finally, it is important to map the teaching of writing across a year and to consider the balance of time allocated to each genre, how genre may be linked into cross-disciplinary units of work and how returning to genres more than once in the year can build progression in writing and make meaningful links across genres (Table 6.1).

Table 6.1 A sample (not a prescription) yearly outline of genres across class levels

September	October	November	December
Fiction 1	Recount 1	Procedure Persuasive 1	Informational Writing 1
January	**February**	**March**	**April**
Poetry	Fiction 2	Persuasive 2	Informational Writing 2
May	**June**	**Gathering Samples for Assessment**	
Recount 2	Student choice	Beginning/end of year: September/June; Beginning/end of each genre study	

Table 6.2 A sample 90-minute block for literacy

Sample 90-minute structure: *early primary (4–6 years)*	*Sample 90-minute structure:* *middle and senior primary (7–12 years)*
Shared Reading (30 minutes): Comprehension, fluency, vocabulary, word-identification skills in context	**Reading Workshop** (35 minutes) comprehension, fluency, vocabulary, word-identification skills in context
Word work (30 minutes) phonics, spelling, tier 2/3 vocabulary	**Word work** (minutes) 20 minutes morphology, spelling, tier 2/3 vocabulary)
Shared writing (30 minutes) processes, craft and skills of writing	**Writing workshop** (35 minutes) processes, craft and skills of writing

It is clear that finding the time to devote to writing is a challenge but, in our view, one worth overcoming. In our work with whole schools, we have found that a 90-minute block for literacy works well and can accommodate both explicit teaching on a range of skills and strategies, along with independent time for children to engage in the higher-order processes required in reading and writing workshops. How the time is best used is an important consideration. It requires high levels of teacher expertise and up-to-date assessment data so that instruction can be tailored to children's assessed needs and stages of development (Table 6.2).

In the framework above, the word work becomes an important bridge between reading and writing. For example, within the reading workshop, children will be reading a wide range of 'texts' (fiction, poetry, informational, persuasive, procedural, narrative), be they in print or digital formats, and will encounter a wide range of vocabulary and sentence structures particular to the genre in question. As children are explicitly taught to notice these features of language, they can be guided to use them when creating their own 'texts' (print, multimodal, digital, spoken). In this way, the reciprocal relationships between the forms of language (Shanahan, 2016; Graham et al., 2018) can be signalled and harnessed to strengthen performance.

Structuring Writing Time

In a writing workshop in middle to senior primary classes, there are usually three phases to the lesson (Figure 6.1). The lesson may open with a mini-lesson (10–12 minutes) focused on a craft, process or skill of writing linked to features of a particular genre. It is followed by time for students to write independently on self-selected topics within the target genre study (20 minutes approximately), during which time teachers conference with children and provide feedback as children are engaged in the act of writing. The lesson typically concludes with a daily share session (5–10 minutes), in which children share their writing with peers and teachers.

Writing workshops apprentice children into the act of writing and support them in developing positive dispositions towards writing, motivation to write and opportunities to acquire a range of strategies and skills in developmentally appropriate and engaging ways. The motivational, socio-cultural, genre and apprenticeship models explored in earlier chapters (e.g., Vygotsky, 1978; Hayes & Flower, 1980; Halliday, 1985; Rogoff, 1990; Graham, 2018) come to life within the writing workshop structure.

Children in early primary grades can be inducted into the writing process through shared and interactive writing approaches (see Chapter 9) (e.g., McCarrier et al., 2000; Routman, 2004). Here, the teacher acts as a scribe for the children's ideas and demonstrates how to capture ideas on chart paper or on screen. Like their older peers, children are afforded control over the topic choice, discuss the topic with peers and teacher, and collaboratively compose. Teachers can demonstrate the processes (how to choose a topic, draft, revise, proofread), crafts (expression and word choice) and skills (grammar, spelling, punctuation) of writing:

- Concepts of print, e.g., left to right, spaces between words.
- Approximate spelling of unfamiliar words.
- How to use environmental print.
- How to combine ideas and elaborate on them.
- How to construct basic/focused sentences.
- How to add a description and build context

As children's skills and confidence develop, they can be invited to share the pen by coming up to write on the chart or interactive whiteboard (e.g., particular words or sounds that they are familiar with and can spell). Such collaborative writing opportunities are an important

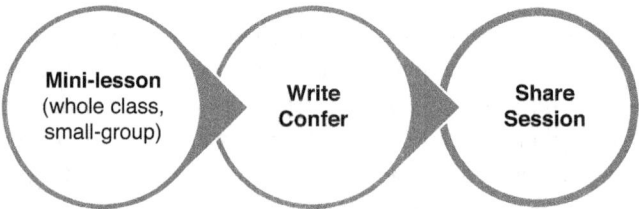

Figure 6.1 Structure of a writing workshop
Source: Authors' figure

precursor to the introduction of a writing workshop where children write independently. Children can transition into a writing workshop when they have some concepts of print, some sight vocabulary and some letter sound knowledge.

Mini Lessons: Powerful Pedagogies to Support Writers

Writing experiences in school should provide students with the opportunity to develop an understanding of the many purposes of writing (e.g., inform, persuade, narrate, explain, amuse, entertain, learn) as well as an understanding of writing genres (e.g., report, recount, fiction forms, poetry, persuasive forms, blog, email, text – see Chapter 3) and audience awareness (Graham et al., 2012b/2018; NCTE, 2016). Mini lessons are brief focused pre-planned lessons tailored to genre and children's assessed needs and stages of development. Mini lessons scaffold development in the processes, skills and craft of writing (Figure 6.2), 'writing is seen as an apprenticeship, and the teacher's job is to help the children develop the art of writing' (Kennedy, 2014, p. 112), Craft mini lessons focus on the literary, aesthetic and creative dimensions of writing and foster a 'word consciousness' (Graves & Watts-Taffe, 2002) and audience awareness amongst children. It is important that mini lessons are indeed mini so that there is sufficient time within the workshop for children to write independently.

Mini lessons can be conducted with a whole class or with a small group, depending on the purpose of the lesson. They should build incrementally from one lesson to the next. When the lesson content is a skill or a strategy that would benefit all children (e.g., craft or process-oriented), it should be taught whole class initially with follow-up small group work as needed. Process mini lessons can take place as needed; for example, at the start of a unit of work, children may need help choosing a topic on which to write, or after a number of weeks a process lesson on revision may be needed. The bulk of mini lessons across a week should focus on the craft of writing (see Figure 6.2 above). Conventions, on the other hand, can be taught in small groups when children demonstrate a readiness for the skill in their independent writing. Translating ideas into words, sentences and paragraphs is affected by

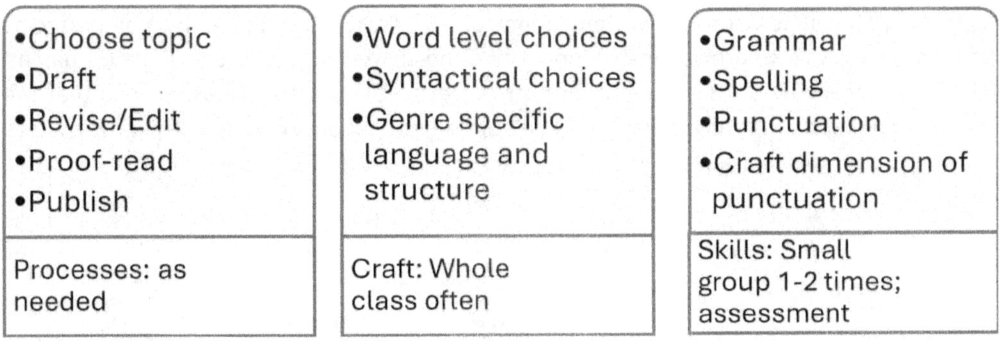

•Choose topic •Draft •Revise/Edit •Proof-read •Publish	•Word level choices •Syntactical choices •Genre specific language and structure	•Grammar •Spelling •Punctuation •Craft dimension of punctuation
Processes: as needed	Craft: Whole class often	Skills: Small group 1-2 times; assessment

Figure 6.2 Balancing attention to craft, process and convention mini lessons across a week, WC: whole class; SG: small group)

Source: Authors' figure

the degree of automaticity and fluency children have in relation to letter formation, phoneme-grapheme knowledge, orthography, high-frequency words and the capacity of their working memory. When these elements are less developed and not yet automatic, the act of capturing thoughts on paper is more demanding and there is less capacity available to engage in planning and revising writing as highlighted in Chapter 1 (Berninger & Swanson, 1994). It is essential that, within reading contexts (Table 6.2 above), systematic attention to phonics and word-identification strategies linked to spelling development occurs as part of the daily literacy block. Integrating reading and writing in this way will support developing writers in mastering the foundational skills that allow them to concentrate on the big ideas in their writing.

Writing workshop approaches have been criticised for the level of attention paid to conventions. Troia et al. (2009, p. 99) suggest that conventions rarely receive 'more than a passing nod' within the classroom, while Daffern et al. (2017, p. 84) argue 'one of the key challenges is to ensure instruction in spelling, grammar and punctuation are carefully balanced with other important aspects of written text creation, such as text structure, vocabulary usage and handwriting'. This is an important point as over-focusing on lower-level skills at the expense of creativity and expression can stymie students' writing and experimentation with new genres and crafts of writing and can also impact negatively students' sense of self-efficacy and quality of their writing. Balancing attention to the crafts, processes and skills in writing is key to a successful writing workshop. In getting started, consider how you currently balance attention to these dimensions. Do you prioritise one over another?

Mini Lesson Pedagogies

As mini lessons vary in purpose and content, there are varying ways to teach them. An effective approach for craft lessons is the *Gradual Release of Responsibility Model* (GRRM, Pearson & Gallagher, 1983; Fielding & Pearson, 1994) (Figure 6.3). While this model has its roots in research on reading comprehension, there is also strong support in the literature for using the model in relation to writing strategies (Graham et al., 2012b/2018). Graham and colleagues define writing strategies as a 'series of actions (mental, physical or both) that writers undertake to achieve their goals. Strategies are tools that can help students generate content and carry out components of the writing process' (p. 15). Overt modelling of strategies enables the teacher to provide instruction within the child's 'zone of proximal development' (Vygotsky, 1978, p. 87). The model brings strategies to a more conscious level so that the learner may better internalise them and call upon them when working independently (see Chapter 7, 8, 10 to see a sample lesson)

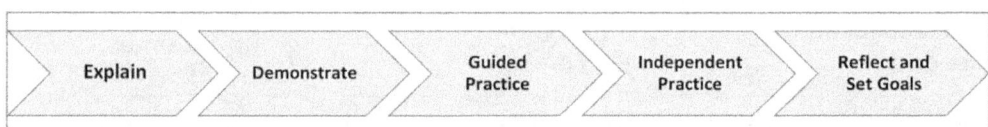

Figure 6.3 Steps in the gradual release of responsibility model
Source: Authors' figure

It is important to use **all** five steps of the GRRM (explain, demonstrate, guided practice, independent work, reflection and goal setting) in order to enhance the metacognitive dimensions of learning. The addition of the reflection and goal setting to the GRRM (Fielding & Pearson, 1994) further supports the metacognitive dimensions of the model, helping writers to become more aware of specific strategies and when and how to use them. In the field of reading, Paris et al.'s work (1994) suggests that metacognitively aware readers possess knowledge on three levels. The first of these is the *declarative level*, in which the learner is aware of a particular strategy and understands that using it can enhance comprehension. At the *procedural level*, the learner is aware of how to carry out the strategy. The third and most advanced level involves *conditional knowledge*, whereby the learner is aware of when and why one uses a strategy and chooses to activate its use in independent reading. This last level indicates that the learner has achieved self-regulation in using the strategy. Similarly, in writing, metacognitively aware writers can flexibly choose and effectively use a range of strategies for each component of the writing process. Though declarative and procedural levels of metacognition are highlighted in Berninger and Swanson's model (1994) discussed in Chapter 1, a notable omission is the conditional and highest level, which arguably is critical if writers are to value and internalise the strategies and know when and how to use them. Self-regulation supports writers in a multiplicity of ways (Harris & Graham, 1992; Troia et al., 2009), enabling them to:

> Attain greater awareness of their writing strengths and limitations and consequently be more strategic in their attempts to accomplish writing tasks; reflect on their writing capabilities; adequately manage paralyzing thoughts, feelings and behaviours and empower them to make adaptations to composing strategies when necessary.
>
> (Troia et al., 2009, p. 99)

A vital dimension of craft lessons is the use of high-quality 'mentor texts' in the genre under instruction (Fletcher & Portalupi, 1998). These are powerful models for children as they make visible the ways in which published authors have crafted words, phrases and sentences to create a particular mood, setting or complex character. Children can be supported to speculate on why the authors might have chosen particular words, sentences, paragraphs or text structures and encouraged to borrow such techniques when writing their own texts. Co-constructing anchor charts with children during the mini lessons (rather than preparing them ahead of time) captures key dimensions of learning and when displayed in the classroom serves as visual reminders to children to incorporate such techniques into their own writing (Figure 6.4). Craft mini lessons also offer opportunity for purposeful integration of and development of oral language, reading and writing skills (Figure 6.5).

The GRRM model can also be used when teaching higher-order writing processes (e.g., how to choose a topic, how to revise and edit, consider the author purpose and audience and explore publishing options). Rather than drawing on mentor texts as a model on this occasion, consider using a sample of your own writing to guide children through the process of revision. This can enable them to witness an adult grappling with wordsmithing to suit the purpose, audience, genre or text structure. Composing and thinking aloud about aspects of your writing is a compelling way for children to learn that writing is not perfect on the first attempt and that writers reflect carefully to refine writing before publishing.

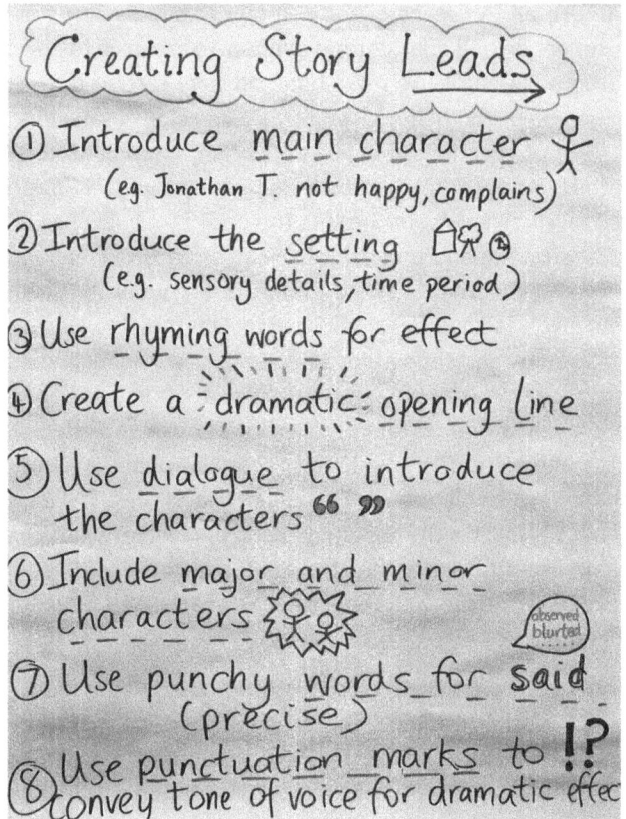

Figure 6.4 A sample craft anchor chart: Story leads

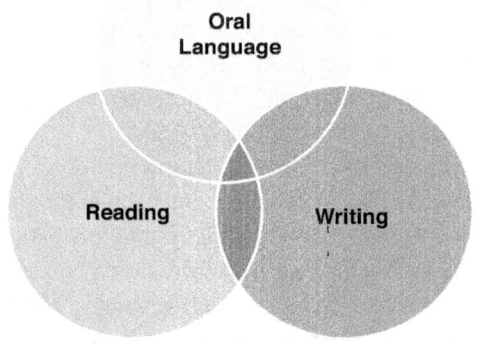

Figure 6.5 Mini lessons integrate oral language, reading and writing

Source: Authors' images

Small group mini lessons convened on the basis of formative assessment of children's independent writing are better served by a different approach. For many children, particularly those in upper primary, who continue to struggle with the mechanics of writing such as punctuation and spelling, adopting a *discovery* approach to skills is more effective. Graves (1994) terms these skills 'conventions' of writing and suggests presenting them to children as signposts that enable the reader to read the writing as the author intended. Encouraging them to speculate why the punctuation is placed in a particular part of a sentence supports children in developing an understanding of punctuation marks as purposeful. They begin to understand how they contribute to fluent reading; they also begin to internalise when and how to apply them to their own writing. They can begin to see punctuation as a craft of writing as well as a necessary skill when presenting published writing to an audience. This is a very different approach to the norm whereby children practise such skills in isolated workbook exercises. It is not surprising that many children are unable to transfer that learning to their own writing.

Supporting Oral Language in a Dialogic Writing Workshop

Talk permeates effective writing workshops and shared writing experiences. Though less widely researched than other aspects of writing, there is evidence that oral language is critical to writing development (Dockrell et al., 2015; Van der Heide, 2017). As has been outlined in Chapter 1, writing presents many contextualised opportunities for children to develop their expressive language skills and to gain confidence in their abilities to express their thinking as they discuss their writing topics, collaborate in the reading and writing of texts, work with peers to revise and edit a piece of work, share their writing product with the whole class in the share session through the Authors' Chair and provide constructive feedback to peers.

Providing such opportunities promotes a positive classroom experience and a stimulating affirming environment, key factors identified as contributing to the efficacy of writing workshop approaches to writing (Troia et al., 2009). Experiencing a responsive audience daily can be an empowering experience for the developing author. Students need to be taught explicitly how to listen for details, ask questions and state what they like about the piece of writing. The share session creates opportunities for teachers to model appropriate language structures in response to the writing and for children to develop their vocabulary and oral language (see Chapter 10). Feedback should increase in specificity and sophistication over time. When the right tone and climate of respect for each writer is established, share sessions have the potential to create an environment conducive to the formation of an engaged community of writers within classrooms.

Quick Review: Typical Structure of a Writing Workshop

- **Craft/Process Mini lesson** (explain, demonstrate through think-aloud, guided practice; begin the anchor chart in collaboration with the children)
- **Independent practice** (children **invited** to try the new technique while writing)
- **Share session** (listen, and respond with specific feedback)
- **Reflect + Set Goals** (refer to mini lesson and add to anchor chart)

100 Teaching and Assessing Writing in the Primary School

Embedding oral language throughout the workshop is key to an engaging and effective workshop. It requires a variety of teacher talk moves and expertise to optimise the power of talk to enhance writing quality and writer motivation and self-efficacy (see Chapter 10 for some guidance on how to do this).

Establishing Routines and Sourcing Essential Resources

In addition to balancing time for craft, process and skills lessons, it is worth spending some time in the first few weeks, negotiating with children about the management and organisation of the workshop and the physical environment and layout of the classroom itself. Establishing procedures and expectations for each phase of the workshop will not only support more effective implementation but will contribute to the building of a community of readers, writers and thinkers within the classroom. We find children respond well to being consulted on such matters and will readily contribute good ideas for the smooth running of the workshop and the best layout for the classroom. Look closely at the classroom design in Figure 6.6. Creating an enticing literacy environment immediately conveys to children and to visitors that literacy is a vibrant element of this classroom.

The literacy environment should include visual displays of children's work (Figure 6.7), anchor charts capturing important work taught in mini lessons (Figure 6.4), child-friendly shelving filled with browsing boxes of books filled with books matched to children's interests and stages of development, and a comfortable carpeted meeting place for children to come together and think and talk their way through books, mini lessons and a whole host of literacy strategies. It can be a place for some quiet reading where children can curl up with a good book during independent reading.

Figure 6.6 Designing classrooms for engaged readers and writers
Source: Watson (2014)

Figure 6.7 Visual displays of children's work.
Source: Write to Read

Figure 6.8 Knee to knee and eye to eye during the guided practice part of a mini lesson
Source: Write to Read

For whole class mini lessons, it is important for children to understand that, during the explanation and demonstration portion of the mini lessons, it's their job to turn on their 'listening ears' and to be ready to give feedback to you on what the focus of the mini lesson is and the kinds of thinking they heard you engage in. For the guided practice, establish

Table 6.3 A sample overview of a writing workshop across a week

Monday-Thursday (35--45 min)	Friday: 35-45 min
Whole class mini lesson 10-12 min: Craft/Process; Lessons build incrementally	**Small group mini lessons** (assessment) (spelling, punctuation, grammar)
Topic: Linked to genre/theme GRRM method Resources (mentor texts) Create anchor chart	Topic: based on assessed need Discovery method Group 1 (15 min); Group 2 (15 min) Create anchor charts: each group
Independent writing: 20 mins Pre-planned conferences with children *as they write*	Rest of class continues to work on their writing while you work with small groups (based on assessment)
Share session: 5-10 min: Note who shares	

routines such as think-pair-share and encourage children to go knee-to-knee and eye-to-eye with their partner to discuss what they noticed. They can be encouraged to discuss, interact and scaffold as needed.

It is important that they know on which days the workshop will begin with a whole class mini lesson and which days will be for small groups. In junior classes, small group mini lessons can be conducted on the carpet square or meeting area.

Materials for Writing

Writing workshop does not require a major investment in resources. To support your teaching, you will need large flip chart paper for shared and interactive writing sessions,

You will need lots of paper for children to write on and some folders for them to store their work. Consider what kind of paper is suitable for the children in your class. Paper shape, size, lined or unlined with assorted formats or layouts on the page, all convey varied expectations to children (see Figure 6.9a, 6.9b, 6.9c). In the early stages (Junior Infants/Senior Infants) or for children new to writing independently, unlined paper gives children free rein over how to organise their drawing and writing. Creating page layouts that vary in relation to the space allocated for drawing and writing can support emergent writers. Giving children autonomy over which paper to choose supports writer agency. Children in 2nd to 6th classes will enjoy writing on lined paper and owning a refill pad.

Table 6.4 Sections in a writing folder (upper primary)

Writing Ideas	A section where children jot ideas that occur to them for possible writing topics
Mini lessons: Craft	A section to keep a list of mini lessons and extracts from mentor texts exemplifying the craft
Mini lessons: Convention	A section to keep a list of small group mini lessons that focus on grammar, spelling and punctuation
Rough Drafts	All rough drafts of writing topics completed during a unit of work
Final Copy	A polished copy of one piece from each unit of work

Designing, Organising and Implementing a Writing Workshop 103

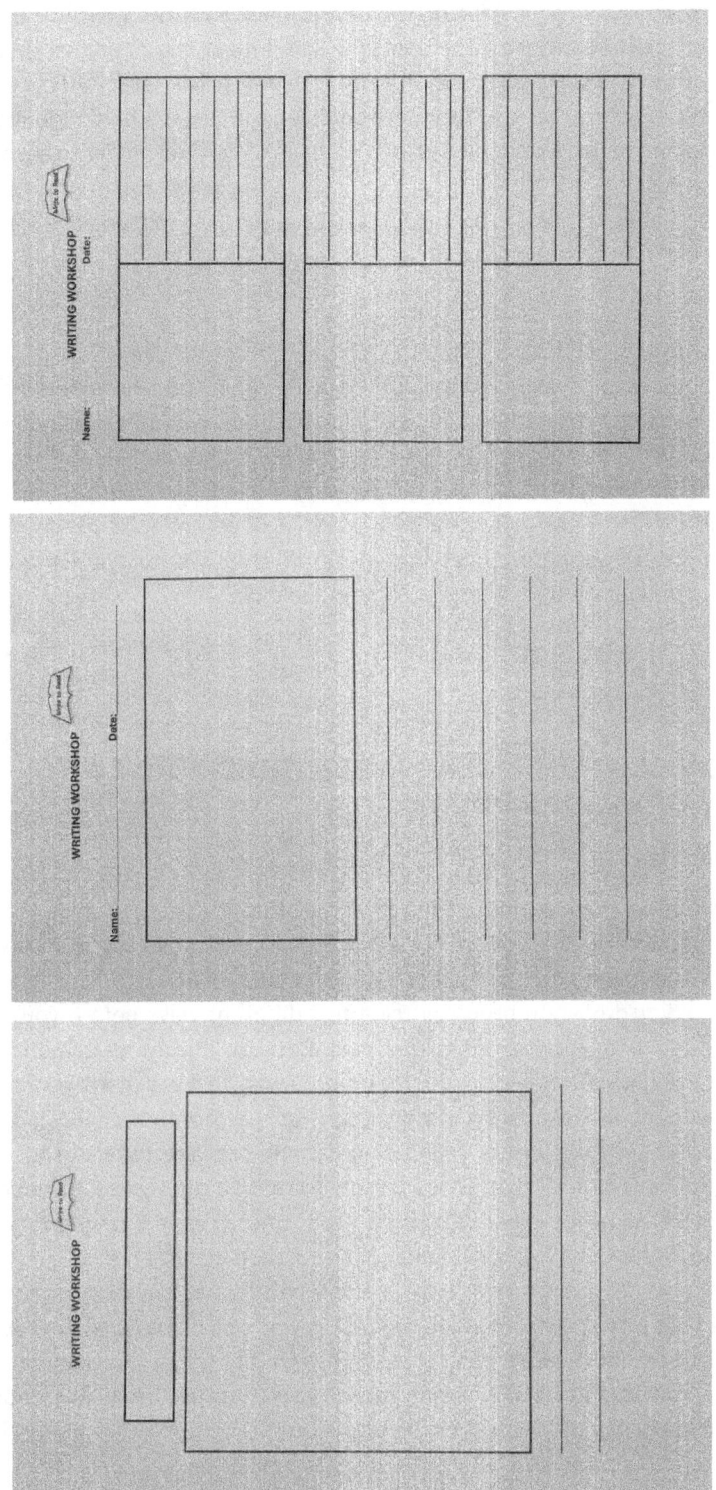

Figure 6.9a, 6.9b, 6.9c Sample paper layouts for writing in junior classes
Source: Write to Read

Supplying the youngest writers (four to seven-year-olds) with cardboard or plastic folders with pockets is helpful for storing their writing drafts, final copies and writing tools. At the end of a unit of work, a sample can be retained for comparison later in the year, and for handing on to the next year's teacher. The other samples can be sent home for sharing with parents. Children in 2nd to 6th classes are able to manage a two-ring binder to accommodate five sections (Table 6.4)

There is also the option of using e-portfolios (see Chapter 5) to manage children's writing and make it available to others (e.g., parents).

Conclusion

There are many things to consider when embarking on designing and implementing a writing workshop in your classroom. This chapter has provided an overview of the key concepts and the conditions you will need to put in place for the workshop to be successful. Chapter 12 contains several checklists which will support you in getting started. The advice from the teacher below is well-made. Putting the infrastructure in place is essential as children thrive on routine. The predictable routine provides the space for creativity to flourish and lays the foundations for an engaged community of writers to develop.

BOX 6.1 ADVICE FROM A CLASSROOM TEACHER NEW TO A WORKSHOP APPROACH

Source: Write to Read

I think you have to be quite patient at the start, because it does take a lot of time to get used to it, and it takes a lot of time to set it up for yourself, to see what way your reading groups and writing groups are going to work best for you.

Conferencing, you'd have to probably try a few different ways before you get the way that's going to work for your class that year. Because it's always going to take a different approach. Some classes can get it straight away, that teacher's conferencing there and I'm working independently. Others need more help with that.

But definitely at the start of the year, being patient, because I think I know sometimes we're quite hard on ourselves if one lesson doesn't go right and they're chatting and they're not getting their piece of writing produced because they didn't get that piece of reading discussion done, or reading done, or that kind of stuff.

It just takes time, definitely, to set it up. So don't be afraid at the start of the year to put a lot more time into the structural lessons of how it's going to work, how our folders are going to work, how our reading groups, that kind of thing. And sometimes you almost feel like you're not teaching during those times, because it's just management almost. But it'll really pay off the rest of the year.

Reflect, Connect, Act

1. Critically reflect on your current practice for writing. In what ways does it converge or diverge from the key conditions which the research on writing highlights is important for success?
2. Which areas of your practice would you prioritise for change? Why?
3. How does the layout and design of your classroom support or constrain the implementation of a writing workshop? What messages does it convey to children about what it means to be literate? What would you change/maintain? What opportunities are provided for student voice and agency to feed into the design of the room?

Suggestions for Further Reading

1. Atwell, N. (1998). *In the middle*. Boynton Cook.
2. Cremin, T., & Myhill, D. (2012). *Writing voices: Creating communities of writers*. Routledge.
3. Graves, D. H. (1994). *A fresh look at writing*. Heinemann Educational.
4. Wood Ray, K., & Glover, M. (2008). *Already ready: Nurturing writers in preschool and kindergarten*. Heinemann Educational.

7 Process Mini Lessons
Generating, Planning and Drafting Writing Ideas across Genres

This chapter focuses on getting children off to a good start with writing. Links are made with the models of writing development explored in Chapter 1 which highlight that planning for writing involves idea generation, organising ideas and setting author goals for the execution of the writing. Genre-specific strategies for supporting writers to generate ideas, plan and organise their first draft are presented.

> **Reflect and Connect**
> 1. Consider your writing history: How do you feel about writing? How would you rate your sense of self-efficacy for writing? Do you have a favourite genre?
> 2. Which features of strategy instruction are not always emphasised? How might this affect children's metacognition? (their understanding of why they are learning the strategy?)
> 3. In what ways might strategy instruction support or hinder children's writing development?
> 4. Why is it important to teach genre-specific planning and drafting strategies?
> 5. How can you support writers with idea generation?

I was amazed by the fact that the children are so keen to write. When they come up with their drafts…. I was amazed that they'd keep writing. I wasn't used to coming from that sort of a scenario. I would be used to where children would be saying, 'My hand is killing me', or this sort of stuff. They wouldn't be as keen to write as much.

(5th class teacher)

Writing is fun because you get to read it out to your whole class and you're allowed to make up stuff and all.

(1st class)

As the quote from the teacher above highlights, it is possible to create an engaged community of writers. That teacher was new to the *Write to Read* project and new to her school and was genuinely surprised that not only did children really want to write but that they enjoyed it! The second quote, by a writer in 1st Class, highlights that writing is a fun activity and that creativity, audience response and autonomy are key. This correlates with three of the key conditions for successful writing workshops highlighted in Chapter 6.

When children have regular predictable time to write, and agency over writing topics is a given, they are more likely to engage and invest in writing which in turn provides them with opportunities to discover their own *'voice'* (Graves, 1994). Creativity is nurtured as writers learn to look inward, drawing upon their own unique experiences for inspiration. As Grainger et al. (2005, p. 23) argue, children need time to 'talk, to read, to play, to imagine and inhabit, to dream, ponder and share ideas as well as to draft and reconstruct'.

All children can benefit from strategy instruction for each phase of the writing process. As discussed in Chapter 2, self-regulated strategy instruction has strong support in research (Harris et al., 2006; Graham et al., 2012). Emergent, developing and more advanced writers will need different supports when it comes to idea generation, planning and developing an initial draft. Children's needs will also vary according to the genre of focus. The first step is helping students to identify ideas to write about.

Generating Ideas

As highlighted in Chapter 1, planning for writing will be influenced by the writer's stage of development, knowledge of the genre, understanding of the audience, the degree of autonomy provided in the choice of topic and the quality of the child's background knowledge related to the particular topic (Hayes & Flower, 1980; Berninger & Swanson, 1994). As these dimensions are linked to a writer's memory, teaching children strategies for planning their writing will support them in sustaining their topic and adding relevant details to enhance quality. Though the theoretical models of writing explored in Chapter 1 highlight that motivation is important at each stage of the writing process (planning, translating, revising), getting the writer to write in the first place is key. General guidelines to build motivation include pupil choice of topic (Graves, 1983), connecting to pupils' personal interests, cultures and communities (Kelly et al., 2020), opportunities for children to observe the teacher as a writer (Cremin & Oliver, 2016), highlighting to writers that writing is purposeful and that writers consider their audience when setting goals for writing.

Supporting Writers to Choose Topics

For some children, ideas seem to come naturally and for others, it can be more challenging. In the following subsections, each of the nine strategies listed in column two (Table 7.1) are briefly discussed as options which writers can draw upon when they experience writer's block. Each of the strategies will need to be modelled explicitly for children (column three, Table 7.1).

Drawing, Play, Popular Culture and Reading as Inspiration for Writing

For very young children and emergent writers, ideas may be captured in drawings, which Moyles (1989) refers to as a type of intellectual play (Figure 7.1). Young children will use a range of semiotic tools to communicate their ideas (Dyson, 1993; Bodrova & Leong, 2006;

108 Teaching and Assessing Writing in the Primary School

Table 7.1 Supporting students in choosing writing topics across genres, setting goals and self-regulating their learning

Components of Writing Process	Writing Strategy	Classroom Application Model What, When, How: GRRM
Choosing topics • Choose writing topics and consider audience/purpose, theme	**Choosing topics** 1. Drawing, play, popular culture, reading 2. Creating lists of topics 3. Writing folder/writers' notebook 4. Considering why writers write (audience/purpose) 5. Personal artefacts 6. Imagining characters 7. Teacher as writer 8. Inquiry interests across curricula 9. Current events	**Choosing topics** • Develop an anchor chart: What to do when stuck for ideas. Over time add to the chart using the ten strategies listed in column 2 of this table. • Model how to use each of the strategies using the Gradual Release of Responsibility Model (see exemplar below) • Develop children's oral language/ academic language to discuss the value of the strategies
Set goals • Consider audience • Consider purpose	**Self-regulate** • Sentence stems for oral language development • Guiding questions to support oral language development	**Model reflecting/self-regulating** • How to check progress against goals • How to use a checklist • How to talk the plan through with a peer

Figure 7.1 Junior Infant drawing as inspiration for writing
Source: Write to Read

Wohlwend, 2011) while Vygotsky argued, '...make believe play, drawing and writing can be viewed as different moments in an essentially unified process of development of written language' (1978, p. 116).

As Scull et al. (2020, p. 240) note young children 'very often use a range of semiotic modes as they create texts that combine drawing, symbols, letters and words'. In Figures 7.2a-7.2c, we see an emergent writer's development over several months (January to March) in a class where children transitioned to the Writing Workshop in January after engaging in extensive shared and interactive writing in the preceding months (see Figure 7.2 below this child's June sample). Drawing is central to the communication of this young writer's ideas, and she enjoyed retelling her stories pointing to elements of the pictures and approximated words.

When asked about their inspiration for writing, we find children across primary often cite play with their friends or siblings as sources of inspiration:

> Well, at home, me and ___, my little sister like playing tons of games, the funnest games are always like the most randomist games, and she always makes me make them up. And then when I'm in school, probably the next day, when we're asked to write stories, I take from the games because usually they're like really good.
>
> (4th class)

Figure 7.2 a Junior Infant early January writing sample; b: Junior Infant late January writing sample and c: Junior Infant March writing sample

Source: Write to Read

110 *Teaching and Assessing Writing in the Primary School*

Figure 7.2 (Continued)

Children have also revealed that they draw on reading material and popular culture such as TV shows, movies and video games for inspiration:

> *Maybe like inspiration from movies and other books, or video games or something.*
>
> (5th class)

> *Sometimes it comes from things that I've done, things that I've played, things that I've watched.*
>
> (3rd class)

> *Well, one day I got an idea to write a book, I mean a story about the unicorns that came down to earth and turned into humans, because that night I'd watched the Equestrian Girls movie, where the ponies turn into girls.*
>
> (4th class)

Sourcing well-crafted animation and digital artefacts can provide writers with ideas from which to innovate. *The Present* (https://vimeo.com/152985022) offers many possibilities for writing: e.g., to tell the story from different perspectives (mother, father, siblings, friends); a prologue (how the boy lost his leg); continuation of the story (how has his life changed as a result of the puppy, what happens next). Similarly, The Piano (https://vimeo.com/57315645) an evocative piece can be used to tell the story from different perspectives.

Encouraging children to keep records of their leisure reading and an inventory of their writing drafts (Figures 7.3 and 7.4) are other ways to help children find writing topics. These lists can be stored in their writing folder (see Chapter 6). These activities will help you learn more about the children in your class as individuals, their personal taste in reading and their writing interests to date. In relation to reading, you could recommend other books by the same author, or others in a similar vein or recommend widening their choices. You could, for example, prompt children to add a sequel or prequel to a fictional piece.

My Reading List		
Title	Author	☆ ☆ ☆ ☆ ☆

Figure 7.3 Record of leisure reading

My Writing Topics		
Date	Draft Title	Published Title

Figure 7.4 Record of writing topics

Source: Authors' Figures, generated with MS Word icons

Creating Lists of Topics

In the early stages, children's writing may be in list form consisting of patterned sentences linked to everyday topics (Figures 7.5 and 7.6.) To assist them with topic selection, it is helpful to keep a display board with ideas for writing that children at this level can easily accomplish (see Figure 7.7) and to continuously add to it.

Children are fascinated by the natural world and enjoy writing about topics they are personally interested in (Figure 7.8). Creating lists linked to topics across the curriculum can be an entry point into report, procedural writing and explanatory writing. Nic Bishop, a naturalist, photographer and author of children's informational books, highlights how his interest in the natural world began in childhood and he starts his work by simply listing animals or insects that he is interested in learning more about: *First, I prepare a list of the animals that I want to photograph. Then I steadily check the list off. Some people think that I wander around and bump into my animal subjects in a sort of random fashion. (https://www.nicbishop.com)*

At first glance, the writing (Figure 7.8) appears to be a simple report, but on closer analysis, it contains many language and syntactical features typically found in a report (Box 7.1).

I can see big
Ben
I can see a car
I can see a shark
I can wok
I can dig

Figure 7.5 Junior Infant patterned list writing sample
Source: Write to Read

Process Mini Lessons 113

it was sunee.
i went to the Park
i so butrflie
it was p retee

Figure 7.6 Junior Infant list format writing sample
Source: Write to Read

Figure 7.7 Anchor chart Junior Infant writing ideas
Source: Write to Read

114 *Teaching and Assessing Writing in the Primary School*

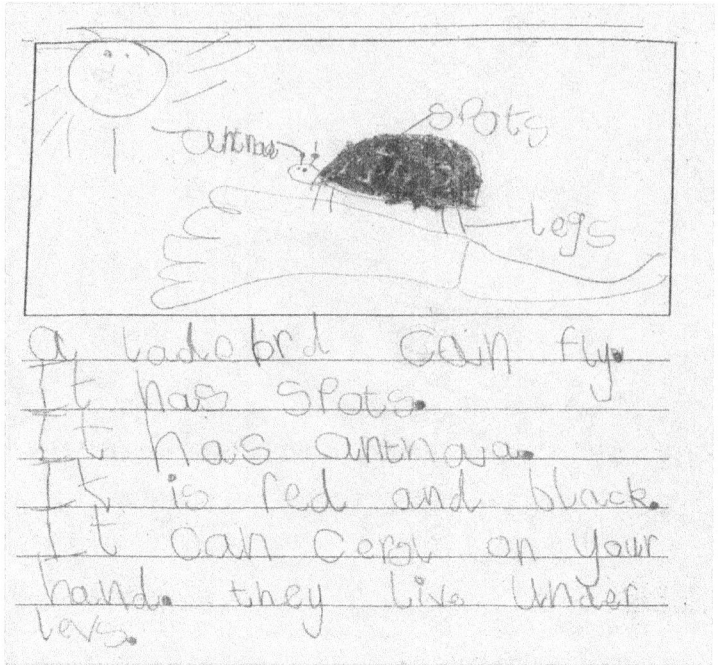

*A ladebrd can fly.
It has spots.
It has anthaa.
It is red and black.
It can cerol on your hand. they live under leves.*

Figure 7.8 Junior Infant ladybird report writing
Source: Write to Read

BOX 7.1

- Uses generic nouns
- Uses disciplinary vocabulary
- Uses present tense
- Labels/diagrams to illustrate
- Describes
- Gives facts

Maintaining a Writing Folder and Writer Notebook

Children can be encouraged to keep a *writing ideas* section in their writing folder (see Chapter 6) and as ideas pop into their heads, to jot them down quickly so they don't lose them. Predictable time, choice and daily mini lessons induct children into a writing life and they begin to take it seriously:

They're coming up with these ideas. They're more engaged and they'll be in the middle of writing and then stop to get their book because they remember a great idea. Whereas before, they would never have done that.

(3rd class, teacher)

We have found, in general, that most children have no problem coming up with ideas when they have free rein over topic choice. For some, having the opportunity to collaborate with a peer is an added incentive or support and can spill over into writing outside school as highlighted by these young writers who clearly have plans for bringing ideas to fruition:

Sometimes me and Sue work together with writing and doing our own book… then putting them together and it will be a longer book and more interesting. And then after that me and Mary are going to do a book together called "The Haunted House" and "The Haunted Boy and Girl".

(2nd class)

Yeah, my friend Cian and I write outside sometimes, and sometimes we read outside together and we write together, like we write about Christopher Columbus, like last week, and we work together.

(4th class)

Having children keep a **writer's notebook** is another way for them to keep in touch with emerging ideas and inspiration. Many writers keep notebooks to hand, so they can immediately capture a fleeting thought, a snippet of conversation, emotions, first-hand experiences or observations. When asked where his ideas come from, Jack Prelutsky, the much-loved American poet and first Children's Poet Laureate, responded: *Everywhere! Everything I see or hear can become a poem. Several toys in my studio have turned into poems. I remember things that happened when I was a kid … Or I write about things I like or don't like.* (https://www.poetryfoundation.org/articles/68683/a-childrens-what).

Likewise, Lucinda Jacob, an Irish poet finds poems in everyday events or remarks: a plastic bag in the gutter wants to become a balloon, and a gust of wind inspires a poem about flying grannies! (Box 7.2). It is important not to insist that all children keep a writing notebook, as not all writers utilise one. For a different perspective on writers' ideas notebook, tune in to popular children's authors Kate di Camillo and Katherine Paterson: (https://www.youtube.com/watch?v=GprltUiL-YQ).

BOX 7.2

Listen to Irish poet Lucinda Jacobs read three poems from her collection Hopscotch in the Sky and reveal the story behind each one (Figure 7.9): https://www.youtube.com/watch?v=ydH8GTOqzag

Source: Poetry Ireland

116 *Teaching and Assessing Writing in the Primary School*

Figure 7.9 Lucinda Jacobs Poet
Source: Poet

Figure 7.10 Hopscotch in the sky
Source: Little Island Press

Learning Why Writers Write

We write to fulfil many purposes in life: to create, amuse, imagine, inform, stay in touch, explain, understand, remember, learn, report, persuade, influence or discover new insights. Revealing these purposes to children is essential and gives them insider knowledge into the higher-order purposes of writing. Knowing that Kate di Camillo was stirred to write her first book *Because of Winn Dixie* upon experiencing homesickness following a move from a southern part of the US to Minnesota in the northwest, or, that R.J Palacio was moved to pen *Wonder* following a chance encounter with a child with a severe facial difference can help young writers develop a deeper appreciation of the writing process and how every encounter and experience is life can be a source of writing. Developing insights into why writers write can help children in moving beyond viewing writing as a school activity or task and in beginning to use it for their own purposes.

Graham and Harris (2019, p. 7) contend 'writing is a flexible, versatile, and powerful tool' which students can use to: 'aid in learning, improve reading comprehension, *understand themselves better, and communicate with others*.' It can prompt them to reflect more

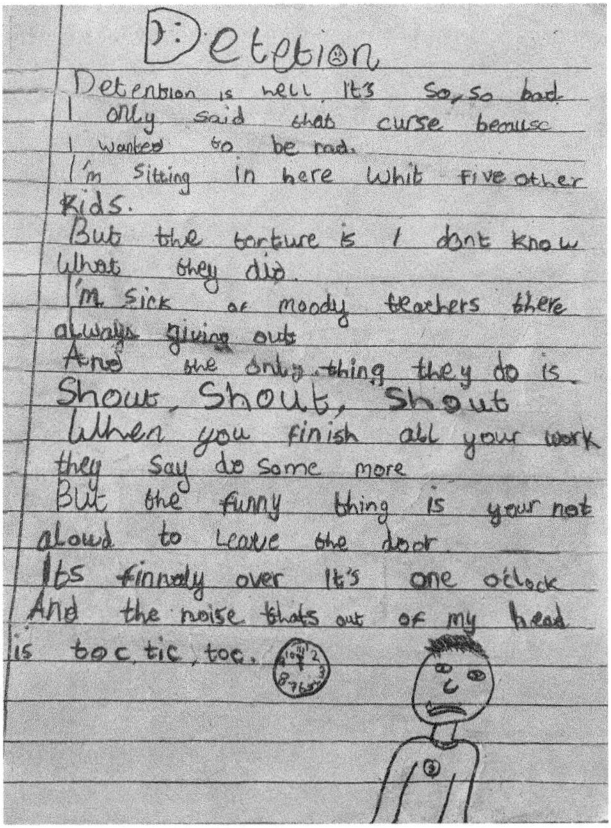
Detetion
Detention is well, It's so, so bad
I only said that curse becuse
I wanted to be rad.
I'm sitting in here whit five other
kids.
But the torture is I dont know
What they did.
I'm sick of moody teachers there
always giving out
And the only thing they do is
Shout, Shout, Shout
When you finish all your work
they say do some more
But the funny thing is your not
alowd to leave the door.
Its finnaly over It's one o'clock
And the noise thats out of my head
is toc tic, toc.

Detetion
Detention is, well, its so so bad
I only said that curse because
I wanted to be rad.
I'm sitting in here with five other kids
But the torture is I don't know what they did.
I'm sick of moody teachers, there always giving out
And the only thing they do is
Shout, Shout, Shout
When you finish all your work, they say do some more
But the funny thing is, you're not allowed to leave the door
It's finnaly over, its one o'clock
And the noise that's out of my head is tic toc tic toc.

Figure 7.11 Poem: detention (6th class)

Source: Write to Read

deeply on their own experiences, process emotions and lead them to discover ideas worth writing about. In Figure 7.11, we see a poem written spontaneously by a 6th-Class boy during a detention earned for a classroom outburst. Writing enabled him to process the event and communicate emotions that he found difficult to articulate orally.

Reflecting on Artefacts of Personal Relevance

Another useful activity to inspire young writers advocated by Graves (1994) is bringing personally meaningful artefacts into school, sharing orally the memories they evoke and creating an initial draft. It creates a sense of a writing community as both you and the children share aspects of your life through the writing workshop. Artefacts could include a favourite object, piece of jewellery, painting or sculpture, a photograph of a pet, a favourite place or important people or events in your life. Children can bring in their own artefacts and engage in a similar process.

118 *Teaching and Assessing Writing in the Primary School*

In sharing these photographs with children I might say a little about how I might use them to write: Figure 7.12 a memoir of my journey across the national parks on the west coast of America; Figure 7.13, perhaps a factual piece on common spiders or a fictional piece on the life of a spider inspired by Charlotte's web; Figure 7.14, a recount of the day our dog Bran went missing or a fictionalised piece about his adventures before he returned safely (see also Box 7. 6 below for an exemplar lesson on using familiar experiences as a way into writing).

Figure 7.12 Sequoia National Park, US

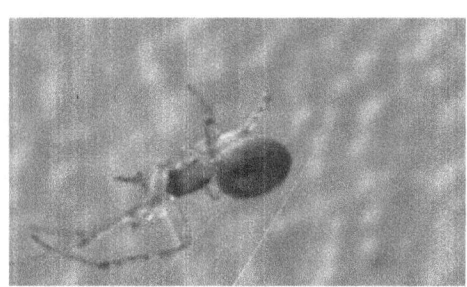

Figure 7.13 The spider living in the wing mirror of my car

Figure 7.14 Our dog Bran roaming the farm

Source: Authors Images'

Teacher as Writer

Writing alongside the children in the classroom and modelling your thought processes and choices as you write is a powerful way for children to see that writing doesn't come easy for most people, and that it evolves with effort. As noted in Chapter 2, Cremin et al.'s (2020) research on teachers as writers (teachers had participated in a writing workshop with authors outside of school) increased their self-efficacy for writing and pupils in their classes reported enhanced motivation to write and ownership of their writing. If you have never contemplated writing alongside children, it is worth taking a risk and experimenting with it. While it is relatively easy to do with young children, it is important to pitch it at the right level. One teacher who had initially demonstrated writing exciting stories for children (in First class), toned down the detail when she noticed that some children were intimidated thinking that the standard was unobtainable:

> ...I think then I started making the stories a little more ordinary because some of them were thinking 'Oh... I can't think of an exciting story like that'. So, I started making them like, just stories like how I was cooking the dinner or something, or how I was talking about my dog...

With older children it is important that they see you genuinely invested in composing your text, contemplating the characters and story elements and bringing them to life within the story. It is important to note, that writing in front of children is not a requirement, but it can impact positively on children's motivation, confidence, sense of ownership and skills as writers (Cremin et al., 2020).

Imagining Characters

Graves (1994) highlights several useful ways of developing characters including drawing on the drama techniques of 'conscience alley' or character in the role, and collaborative writing to encourage children to develop what he calls believable complex characters with needs and problems that speak to the human condition and will hook readers. This process should be modelled and can be supported by analysis of characters in reading material that children are exploring in class (see Chapter 8 for craft mini lessons). Creating planning templates can help children flesh out their characters before and during writing (see Figures 7.26 and 7.27 in section Teaching Writers to Plan and Draft Writing)

Many fiction writers begin with a character in mind and spend considerable time fleshing out character traits, thoughts dialect, personalities, actions and physical appearance. Brian Gallagher, author of many historical fiction novels for upper primary shares his approach to fiction writing and in particular the emphasis he places on character development (Box 7.3). In many of his books, chapters alternate between major characters to allow the story to unfold from their perspective.

BOX 7.3

I would do a lot of work/research before I start writing. I would draw up a really detailed CV for each character... But I also allow them to develop as the story unfolds. So, I usually plot about ten scenes at a time and as I'm writing those scenes, the characters hopefully come to life. I want the characters to reflect different sides of a situation, difficult situations are great for storytelling.

Listen to Brian discussing his writing process and how he developed the ideas for Resistance (Figures 7.15 and 7.16); link to Write to Read website: www.writetoread.ie

Source: Brian Gallagher and Mark O' Regan

Figure 7.15 Photo Brian Gallagher, Children's author

Source: Brian Gallagher

Figure 7.16 Cover of 'Resistance' authored by Brian Gallagher

Source: O'Brien Press

Tapping into Inquiry: Wonder Questions Linked to Interests and Curricula

Children in primary school are naturally inquisitive about the world and interested in learning more about it. They can learn a lot from the ways in which naturalists, historians and scientists who write books for children get started. Many of the award-winning authors

Table 7.2 Interesting non-fiction authors

Sy Mongomery, Naturalist/Scientist	https://symontgomery.com
Nic Bishop, Naturalist/Scientist	https://www.nicbishop.com
Seymour Simon, Scientist	https://www.seymoursimon.com
Husband/wife team: Steve Jenkins (Artist/Science interest) and Robin Page (Illustrator)	https://www.stevejenkinsbooks.com
Variety of non-fiction authors' blogs	https://inkrethink.blogspot.com/p/blog-page.html

have websites which showcase their writing processes from idea generation to publication (Table 7.2).

Aronson, a historian writing for both adults and children, sees his mission as inspiring young people to ask questions, to see themselves as detectives examining the clues that history left behind or as reporters telling the truth about the world today. As Aronson notes in an interview on Reading Rockets, his starting point for a new book revolves around a question: 'all of my books start with questions, and I hope they prompt readers to ask questions of their own' (https://www.readingrockets.org/people-and-organizations/marc-aronson).

Similarly, Sy Montgomery, who has been described as 'part naturalist, part poet, part Indiana Jones' opens her books by sharing key questions she researched to inform her books. Naturalists, scientists and historians will often spend considerable time in the field researching, photographing and carefully documenting phenomena from first-hand observations. As Nic Bishop, photographer and naturalist highlights: 'As a photographer, I have to spend five or six months in close contact with my animal subjects…Many of the details I write about – how a mother kangaroo cares for her joey…how a tarantula sheds its skin … do not come from other books. These are things I have been fortunate to witness' (source: www.nicbishop.com).

Inquiry approaches (see Chapter 3) are built into science, history and geography curricula in Ireland and in many countries and learning to ask relevant high-quality questions is a key dimension of such approaches. The entry point for children is in identifying interests and framing guiding questions that are investigable within the bounds of a classroom or a first-hand experience. Heard and McDonough's work (2009) on reading, writing and investigating with early primary grades highlights the importance of creating classroom environments that buzz with children's questions and provide as many first-hand and observational experiences as possible. These can be supplemented with high-quality video, audio and photography. In history quests, it is essential to have a stimulus to begin with. This could be a photograph of, for example, the aftermath of a busy, familiar street in a warzone, or a poem, a song or a story from the time period. There are numerous "ways in" to a topic but it should be well thought out to ensure that the children will be curious enough to want to find more. Children will need help initially in narrowing their questions and inquiry probes so they can zoom in on a particular sub-area of a larger topic to keep it manageable. Allowing them to work in small mixed-ability groupings will enhance motivation and provide peer support (Figure 7.17). Sometimes you can set up the groupings and at other points children should be given flexibility to choose their groups. Planning for choice in groupings is consistently cited by children as a key motivator and more importantly, that they can learn from peers (Box 7.4)

> **BOX 7.4 HISTORICAL INQUIRY**
>
> *I think it's better for us to do it ourself, because we're just listening to you and just, like, presuming it's correct and it could be a different, like, perspective to... It's like we have different sources to make sure that, like, one of them's right if the other one has them as well like, before we write (6th class, Write to Read)*
>
> *"I think that it, like, it has helped, because when we're doing our own piece, a piece that we really want to work on, let's say about Jim Larkin or something, and em, when we look it up, we can look into, like, deeper things and stuff, and find out more about him because we're thinking like historians... you can dig deeper into it." (6th class Write to Read)*
>
> Source: McEvoy, 2014.

Developing the questions 'is a way for students to bridge the cognitive gap between what they currently know and what they would like to know' (Rinehart & Kuhn, 2023, p. 68). Modelling how to develop 'small' questions from big questions and open exploratory or juicy questions is essential if children are to acquire the skill to do this themselves. You will need to guide children to jot notes on what they already know or think they know about a topic before they generate their questions.

This can be a quick write in bullet form with similar ideas/concepts grouped together It can be filling in the K (*What I know*), W (*What I Think I know and Want to Learn*) section of a KWLS chart (Ogle, 1986; Sippola, 1995). The LS (*What I Learned and Still Need to Learn*)

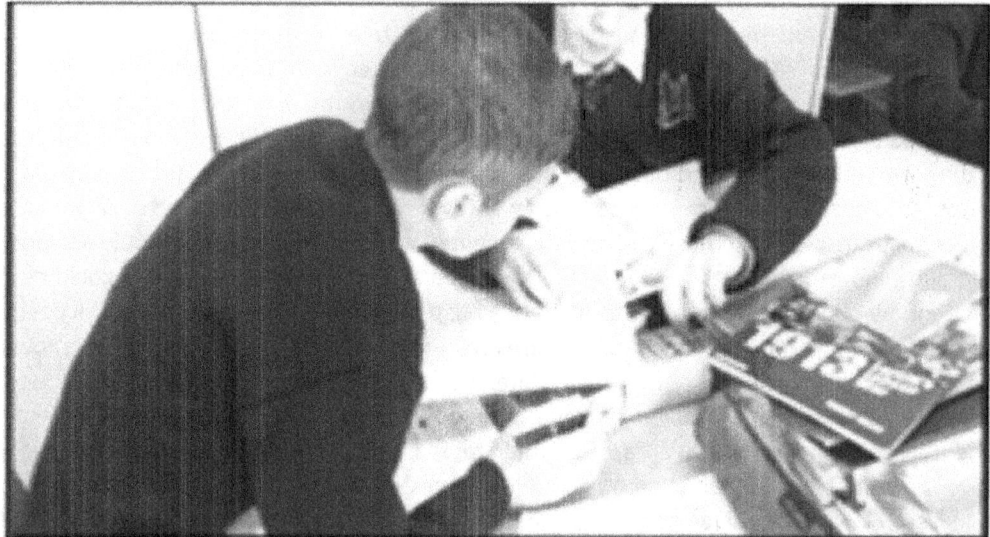

Figure 7.17 Mixed ability grouping in history

Source: McEvoy, 2014

sections can be filled in later. This process can be adapted for visual and audio-visual materials (see Figure 7.28 below). It can also be simplified to a two-column note frame (see Figure 7.29 below) where children can test out their current knowledge on their chosen topic and note connections or gaps.

Tuning in to Current Events

Current events can trigger inspiration for informational and persuasive writing, as children become aware of and discuss emotive and controversial local, national and global events and issues. Persuasive writing is a critical life skill and gives children agency and voice (see Chapter 3). As Crammond (1998, p. 230) argues: 'mastery of persuasive writing is important because it empowers children—it enables them to produce, evaluate, and act on the professional, ethical, and political discourse that is central to our democratic society'. It always proves popular with children in *Write to Read* partner schools who have enjoyed getting their teeth into a provocative issue (see Chapter 8 for examples of children's persuasive writing).

Using a range of stimuli across the many forms of persuasive writing (e.g., editorials, reviews, speeches, blogs, pamphlets, advertising, letters of complaint or advocacy) are ways to ignite children's interests. With very young children, providing opportunities to express opinions on topics is an entry point into persuasive writing. Using picture books such as *Red is Best, Winter is the Warmest Season, and I Wanna Iguana* as a stimulus, young children can be inducted into aspects of persuasive writing and learn how to give reasons for their opinions. Older children can generate lists of current events and topics that they are interested in researching and debating and develop the skills to reason both sides of an argument.

Box 7.5 shows some topics generated by a senior primary class. Engaging children in conversation during conferences and sharing sessions about how they come up with their topic choices and what they do if stuck demystifies the process and opens up possibilities for all children to learn from each other. Regularly updating visual displays on sources of writing ideas reminds writers that they have a range of options when writing. The next section looks at ways you can help children to plan and get started on a first draft.

BOX 7.5 PERSUASIVE WRITING TOPICS

- Climate change
- Vaping/smoking
- Uniforms
- Immigration
- Running on the school yard
- Zoos
- War
- Effects of TV viewing
- School on Saturday
- Learning a second language

Teaching Writers to Plan and Draft Writing

Importance of Genre-Specific Planning and Drafting Strategies

While it is important to demonstrate to children how to choose a topic and how to execute a plan for it, it is also important not to confine them to a rigid prewriting process, as planning is also an 'on-line' aspect of writing (Berninger & Swanson, 1994), occurring as the writing is in progress, as one idea sparks another as it makes its way onto the page. Indeed, Grainger et al. (2005, p. 15) suggest:

> *The nature of the final piece, however, will not always be known at the outset and the mental and practical activities through which the writing evolves need to remain open to the unexpected and be perceived as part of the creative process.*

Nevertheless, for children who struggle to come up with writing ideas and who have difficulties with text organisation, some direct instruction in choosing topics, pre-writing and planning activities with goal setting built in can alleviate problems and enhance writing quality (Graham et al., 2005; Saddler et al., 2005). While strategy instruction can benefit all writers, research highlights it is of most benefit to struggling writers (Graham & Perin, 2007). As noted in Chapter 2, De Smedt et al. (2019) found that explicit instruction affected motivation to write in unexpected and constraining ways. Explicit instruction can unintentionally convey to children that there is one right way to compose in a given genre and result in *more 'controlled motivation'*, highlighting the fine line between instruction to lift the quality of writing and the prescription of writing qualities.

Graham et al.'s meta-analysis (2012a, see Chapter 2) identified 7 single-subject studies in which planning and drafting strategies for story writing and persuasive writing were taught to struggling writers in second and third grade. An effect size of 0.80 (medium to large) was found for schematic structure, quality and length of compositions indicating the value of teaching such strategies to developing writers. In one study, Tracey et al. (2009) explored the effectiveness of explicitly teaching planning and drafting strategies for story writing to third graders in mainstream classes. The planning strategy involved three high level guidelines: (1) select a topic; (2) organise ideas into a plan; (3) upgrade the plan when writing. Children were explicitly taught story elements (*e.g., Who are the main characters? What do they want to do? Where does the story take place? What is the problem they face? How might the story end?*). Having knowledge of story grammar provided a scaffold for students to test out their ideas before writing. Children were also prompted to engage in self-talk as they organised preliminary ideas into a writing plan and as they worked on their initial draft. They were taught to set goals and monitor progress towards achieving them (ensuring story elements were present). To enhance children's self-efficacy, children were supported to compare their baseline writing sample with samples following instructions and guided to notice improvements and to attribute them to their personal effort and application of strategies. This helped them to see the value of the strategies they were learning.

As highlighted in Chapter 2, for children younger than second or third grade, planning and translating ideas onto the page are influenced by working memory as word-level encoding skills are not yet automatic and require such effort that there may not be a lot of capacity left to attend to the higher-order messages of the writing such as developing the ideas, structure, word choice and overall message. In the early stages, teaching transcription strategies are as important as craft dimensions of writing (Chapter 9). As noted in Chapter 2, strategies are powerful enablers of student success as when children have mastery over them, they can help children to self-regulate and persist with challenges encountered when writing independently.

Planning and Drafting Narrative Texts

Graphic organisers are useful for supporting writers in getting started with planning and creating a first draft and it is essential that they are scaffolded in using them appropriately. The numbered examples (Table 7.3, Column 2) can be modelled by drawing on each step of the gradual release of responsibility model (GRRM) (Fielding & Pearson, 1994) and are briefly discussed in the following sections.

Ensuring explicit attention to each one of the five steps within a lesson supports writers' metacognitive awareness. The choice of graphic organiser (see Table 7.3) should be influenced by children's stage of writing development and previous experiences in using organisers. These lessons can be facilitated in whole class mini lessons when a new organiser is introduced and reinforced in follow-up small group lessons for children who need it based on observational notes in class and reading children's writing.

Table 7.3 Generating narrative ideas with graphic organisers

Components of Writing Process	Writing Strategy	Classroom Application: GRRM Model What, When, How Using
Generating/Planning Ideas across Genres *Fiction/Sub-genre* • Fantasy? • Historical-Fiction? • Science-Fiction? • Realistic Fiction? • Adventure? • Detective? • Scary/humorous?	**Generating Ideas: Genre-Specific Graphic organisers** *Narrative samples* 1. Think, draw, label, write 2. 4-column story mountain 3. 5 Finger plan 4. Picture mapping 5. Story Map 6. Character profile/CV	**Generating Ideas: Modelling Genre-Specific Graphic Organiser** • Reflect and pick an idea • Test ideas by brainstorming ideas by populating a relevant graphic organiser or combination (e.g., draw a character and use a story map • Consider how many characters are needed: major/minor • Consider broad story structures: Beginning, Middle, End, Setting
Drafting • Create a first draft to match writer's ideas/goals	**Drafting** • Sentence and paragraph generation *Order/sequencing ideas* • Story structures • Lead/beginning, middle, end	**First Draft and Online Planning** • Get all ideas down on paper, write quickly, don't stop to check for correctness (*errors can be corrected when revising/editing/ publishing*) • Write on every second line to leave space for revising and editing • Use the graphic organiser to help remember ideas and structure **BUT** also allow ideas to unfold and deviate
Set goals • Consider audience • Consider purpose	**Self-regulate** • Sentence stems • Guiding questions	**Model Reflecting/Self-regulating** • How to check progress against goals • How to talk through a plan with peers • Model academic language register

Using the Think, Draw, Label, Write Strategy with Young Children

The following exemplar gives an entry-level lesson in a writing workshop with a class of 6–7-year-olds whose classroom experiences with independent writing were limited.

BOX 7.6 A SAMPLE INTRODUCTORY LESSON: GETTING STARTED ON NARRATIVE WRITING WITH FIRST GRADE (6–7-YEAR-OLDS): THINK, DRAW, LABEL, WRITE

Resources: books of varying genres, lyrics of your favourite musician; large chart paper; markers; and paper for children to write on

	Teacher Notes
Step 1 Explain (1–3 minutes) *There are all kinds of writers in the world! Another name for a writer is an author.* As you talk aloud show them lots of examples of different kinds of books/writing). *Some authors write picture books like this one* (show a familiar book), *and others write books that give us lots of information. Some of my favourites are…* (e.g., show a book about animals or famous people or places). *Others write poetry like my friend Lucinda who just won an award for her poetry book! Some write how-to books like recipe books; some write music and words for songs. My favourite singer is ___* (name one or one you know that they children will like). *I love the way he tells stories in his songs.* *You don't have to be famous to write! My mum writes every day. As long as I can remember, she writes up her diary every single day. She also loves to stay in touch with her brothers and sisters who live a long way away from her. She writes emails to them and posts messages online. I guess she passed that love of writing onto me! I love to write too!* *Authors write about what they know something about and things they are interested in. They think hard about their audience and who would like to read their writing. This year we are going to have the opportunity to write every day and learn lots of things about how writers write.* *Let me show you how I get started! Watch what I do to get going, and then you will have a chance to have a go* (Make sure the children are focused on watching you as you model).	*Step 1* The **Explain** step is specific and brief; it highlights to children the importance of what they are learning and provides concrete examples. Giving personal or memorable examples supports children in connecting with you and seeing themselves as potential writers. By showing them different kinds of writing genres, they begin to see that writing can be varied and fun.

(Continued)

Process Mini Lessons 127

Step 2: Demonstrate by Thinking Aloud (about 5-6 minutes)

Hmmmm what will I write about today? .....I could write about my weekend, I went to visit my friends down the country in their house by the lake... I could write about all the things I did with my friend Mary and her daughter Sue who came all the way from America to visit me a few weeks ago.... I could write about the honeybees who feed on my lavender bush right outside my back door, I love watching them but I don't know a lot about them though, so I don't think I could write much.... I know! I could write about the day my twin nephews played a trick on their Nana, my mum, when she was minding them!

Step 2

The **Thinking Aloud** step allows children 'see' the invisible processes in a writer's head and the choices they make when writing.

Show the children that you choose to write about something you know a lot about and which will be fun to write and fun for an audience to read.

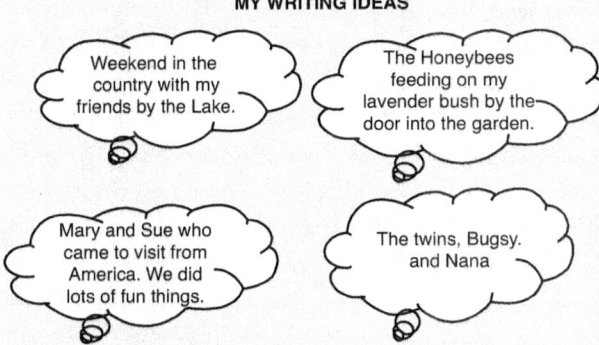

Figure 7.18 Trying out writing ideas
Source: Write to Read

Sketching, labelling and recording ideas is a **multilevel** activity which allows most children to participate. All children can draw, some can draw and label and some can draw, label and write.

Depending on the children's knowledge you could simplify by leaving out the terms **problem or solution** to simplify.

I could write about all of these things but today I think I am going to write about the twins. They are full of fun and always up to mischief (Figure 7.18). They have a hamster called Bugsy and Nana doesn't like Bugsy.....I think I could make up a story about that because there's lots I can write and I think all of you would like to hear it!

Next, *I am going to test my idea and draw some of the details I could add to my story to make it interesting. This is Bugsy (sketch the hamster and model how to label the picture by sounding out and writing the letters for each sound: B-u-g-s-y). Here are the twins Tom (T-o-m) and Shane. Shane begins with sh like shop and it has a magic e: Sh-a-n-e). They aren't identical, but they look alike. This is Bugsy's cage which is at the back of the*

Modelling spelling processes shows children how to draw on their knowledge to solve problems:
segmenting sounds/using tools such as the word wall to spell.

(Continued)

sitting room..cage sounds like a page, I know how to spell p-a-g-e, so I just need to change the first letter) and here's Nana (quick sketch and write N-a-n-a).

The **problem** is Nana doesn't like Bugsy.... Hmmmm, what could happen? I know! Maybe they take Bugsy out of the cage and creep up behind Nana sitting in the armchair and pop him on her head! Nana screams and hops up out of the chair, poor Bugsy goes flying into the air! Hmmmm what could be the **solution?** The twin's Mum arrives home, hears the commotion, comes running into the sitting room, scolds the boys and grounds them for a week!

Now I will write my first sentence....Nana sat down to have a little rest after lunch (how do I spell down? /D/-ow for /ow/, then n; 'little' that's up on the word wall; 'after' that's also up on the word wall) lunch /l/ /un/ /ch/ (as you write, exaggerate how to sound out easily encodable words; show how you use analogy to spell a word that sounds like one you do know; use the alphabetised word wall as a tool)

Ok everyone what did you notice about how I got started? (Listen to the children's responses and build from there)

The lesson above was the first lesson I taught to several First-grade classes (six to seven-year-olds) who were participating in a small-scale research literacy project in one junior primary school (four to eight-year-olds). In this school in most of the classes, writing time consisted of structured activities such as copying Our News from the co-constructed chart or writing based on a response to text read in groups during literacy time. The following comment highlights typical practice:

> Writing based on like Our News, and whatever sight word we'd be doing, like 'it is' or whatever, just putting them into sentences. Or like the cloze procedure, just a paragraph with a few words missing that they have to fill in the right words. But it's all based on the reader, so they can read everything. They wouldn't be able to write anything creative. You know, they can just about write very simple stuff.
>
> (1st class teacher)

Needless to say, given the children's classroom experience with writing I was a little nervous about teaching the lesson! But I needn't have worried. Children sat quietly and observed me at work. When I asked them what the first thing I did was, they responded: 'you drew your picture!' I replied: 'are you sure?' It took a few minutes for the penny to drop but eventually one child exclaimed: *you thinked first!"* I explained *'yes I did,' because writers don't always pick the first idea they think of. They choose their best one and think about their audience"*. This active listening helps children to see the purpose of demonstrations and concretises the lessons we hope they will take from the demonstrations.

Modelling strategies for transcription (getting ideas onto the page) by sounding out and matching sound to graphemes, using analogy and using the word wall was also key to building these young writers' confidence and encouraged them to have a go and take risks. It can be especially challenging for high-achieving children, who are used to getting everything right and may be reluctant to take a risk as highlighted by this teacher:

> *The two really that I've noticed it the most in would be two that were lacking with confidence in their writing. They were probably up there in the top in other areas but when it came to their writing they really lacked confidence. So, they've come on loads.*
>
> (Senior Infant Teacher)

Exploring the spelling subcomponent of the Conventions Component of the *Write to Read* rubric will give you insights into expectations for emergent writers (see www.writetoread.ie) connect also to Chapter 9 for some mini-lesson ideas on moving children along the spelling continuum). The next steps of the lesson are highlighted below.

BOX 7.6 CONTINUED

Step 3: Guided Practice (2-3 minutes)

Close your eyes for a couple of minutes and have a think about what you might like to write about.....then turn and talk to the person beside you and tell them all of your ideas (As children share ideas, circulate, listen in and affirm their efforts; after a couple of minutes invite a few children to share their ideas with the whole class (Figure 7.19).

Figure 7.19 Children turn and talk with a partner to share ideas
Source: Write to Read

I am hearing some great ideas here, I can't wait to read these ideas. Before you start your own writing, let's remind ourselves of what we learned about writers today. What will we write on our chart? (co-construct an anchor chart with the children) (Figure 7.20).

Teacher Notes

Step 3
Guided Practice
Provides a verbal rehearsal and takes the fear out of the blank page so writers can begin to think about their topic; anchor charts are visible reminders of learning and support writers in applying new techniques.

(Continued)

Figure 7.20 Anchor chart: Getting started on writing in junior classes

Source: Write to Read

Step 4: Independent Writing (about 10-15 minutes)
Pass out some paper to the children and ask them to think, draw, label and write. As they engage, work your way around the room and take notes: notice who begins right away and who is hesitant (i.e., engage in formative assessment). You will know your children, so choose who to conference with and take some notes. Choose a method that works well for you. We have found that using a large roll of labels is versatile. Notice who might need some help with sounding out (note who only has the beginning sound, end sound or dominant sounds) and using the word wall. Scaffold as needed.

Step 5: Share, Reflect and Set Goals (about 5-7 minutes)
Affirm all writers and ask them to turn to the person beside them, show their writing and say one thing about what they wrote: their drawing, labels or writing. Then invite 2-3 children to read their work aloud. Encourage children to listen and respond. Model how to give feedback: *I really like your drawing, especially the…*(name something specific). Then conclude with reflecting on what was learnt and setting a goal for the next day: *Writers, today we learned that writers begin by thinking, drawing, labelling and writing ideas. They think about their audience and choose their best ideas.* Encourage children to orally reflect on what was easy, what was hard and to recall strategies for writing: *What was easy today? What was hard? What did you learn? What is your goal for tomorrow?*

Step 4
Independent writing time is an excellent formative assessment opportunity. It will help you notice specific aspects of writing that children require further support in. It will help you plan different kinds of mini lessons (craft, process and skill) linked to children's actual needs.

Step 5
Reflect and set goals strengthens learner's *metacognitive awareness* (Chapter 1) and links back to the explanation in **Step 1**.

Once children in our study realised that they would be writing daily and that their choices would be taken seriously, they entered into a 'constant state of composition' (Graves, 1994,

p. 104), pondering their selection of topics both inside and outside of school. Interview data revealed that they had internalised key messages from mini lessons on idea generation:

> *I think deep in my brain...I think all the while during my life. When I just get the best one, the best one for my story, I'll go yeah, I'll use that.*
>
> (1st class)

> *I'd think which one was the best. Like which one is really important. Like if I got my dog, if I was going to the shop or if like some morning if my sister wasn't well cause she was in hospital, I'd write about my sister. That's the most important thing.*
>
> (2nd class)

Placing the emphasis clearly on the communicative aspect of writing demonstrates to children that writing is primarily about capturing one's thoughts on paper in a first draft and not on the accuracy of conventions. Thus, children whose phoneme-grapheme knowledge is not well established can draw a picture and describe it in the share session. Those who are more advanced can also label and, in the case of the most advanced writers, can write connected text, albeit with invented spelling. Considering the layout of the paper you provide to young children to write on can also support them as emergent writers, as paper design conveys certain expectations for writing (see Chapter 6).

Very soon into the process, as children gain confidence and some fluency in writing, we have found that they gravitate towards writing first and the drawing comes after. You may also find that there are more details in the drawing than appear on the page. This can be highlighted to children during conferencing, or the share session and they can be encouraged to add more detail. Depending on their stage of development, more specifics could be added to pictures/labels/writing.

Adapting Narrative Graphic Organisers to Children' Stage of Development

The exemplar lesson above can be extended upwards to present a higher cognitive challenge or downwards to make it simpler. To make it simpler, leave out reference to the problem and solution and model one strategy for spelling. To stretch it, use a four-column grid and model how planning can be extended to include story elements such as characters, setting and plot (problem and solution). The writer (Figure 7.21) creates a credible plan and clearly demonstrates an understanding of an imaginative narrative structure.

Children in Junior Infants on the other hand will do little preplanning of stories and writing will be more spontaneous (Figure 7.22). This is an end-of-year Junior Infant (5-yr.-old) writing sample. We see a character, the Monster, conjured from the child's imagination and it is clearly described to match the drawing: he has an X across his middle, two heads, three feet and simple adjectives are used to describe his features. Though sentences are simple, openings are beginning to show variation and logical invented spelling approximations are used. It is clear that drawing is integral to the communicative process. The *Write to Read* rubric (Chapter 4) honours the authorial role played by drawing in children's writing. It recognises that young children 'very often use a range of semiotic modes as they create texts that combine drawing, symbols, letters and words' (Scull et al., 2020, p. 240). Were this piece to be scored on the *Write to Read* rubric it would achieve scores that are reasonable for the end of the first year of school. The writer could be encouraged to talk about the character in a conference with the teacher and nudged to add more details to the drawings (Figure 7.22).

132 *Teaching and Assessing Writing in the Primary School*

Figure 7.21 Four column fiction writing plan Senior Infants
Source: Write to Read

My Monster (title written by teacher)
This is a munstr with a ex.
Look aT The munstrs 2 heds.
I see his 3 PheeT.
I see The munsTr.
I like the green heds.
Look at The Big pingk feet.

Figure 7.22 Junior infants imaginative writing sample June: My Monster
Source: Write to Read

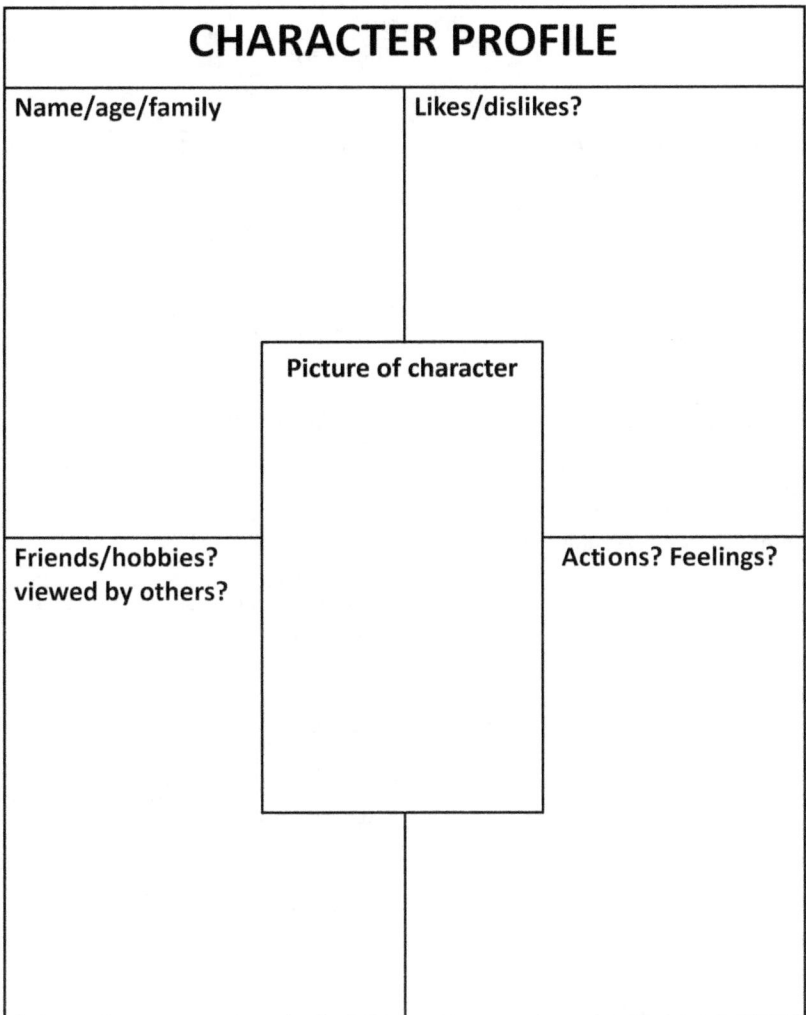

Figure 7.23 Template for a basic character profile
Source: Authors' own

As noted earlier, when characterisation is strong, readers learn to walk a mile in the moccasins of the characters contemplating how they would react in similar circumstances. Children will need substantial support to create characters that are believable, more complex and which build empathy. As noted earlier, authors spend a lot of time developing characters and know more about them than will ever make its way into a book. Figures 7.23 and 7.24 are ways into helping children think more deeply about characters, their motives and actions.

Creating an interesting setting and plot for characters to take shape can be supported by **picture mapping** (drawing the story in sequence or comic strip style and adding captions). Older children can be introduced to more complex graphic organisers to scaffold their thinking and elaboration of their topics. The **five-finger recount plan (**Figure 7.25**)** encourages writers to consider how to start their writing, extend the middle to include three events and to consider how to end it.

Character CV	
Location	Time period
Physical appearance/age	Favourite food and drinks
Favourite clothing	Favourite food/beverage
Favourite sport	Interests/hobbies
Siblings	Home/bedroom
How the character is viewed by other characters major/minor	Friends
How the character feels in particular situations	How the character acts in particular situations
How the character speaks: dialogue	Motives
Favourite places for holidays	Likes/dislikes
Favourite books/movies	Anything else?

Figure 7.24 A more complex character curriculum vitae

Source: Authors figures

Graphic organisers can be enhanced to build children's oral language by, for example, referring to characters as protagonists/antagonists/major/minor; the setting could include attention to place, geographic location, time; the problem/solution could include reference to build up/rising action, tension, climax/resolution (Figure 7.26). Furthermore, more advanced terminology can be introduced to children as they gain proficiency with basic story grammar, e.g., protagonist, antagonist, villain, major/minor. As one teacher noted:

> I had a girl come in in second class with a reading response she did at home, who came in and started 'the protagonist in my story'…one of them found it in a book and it came

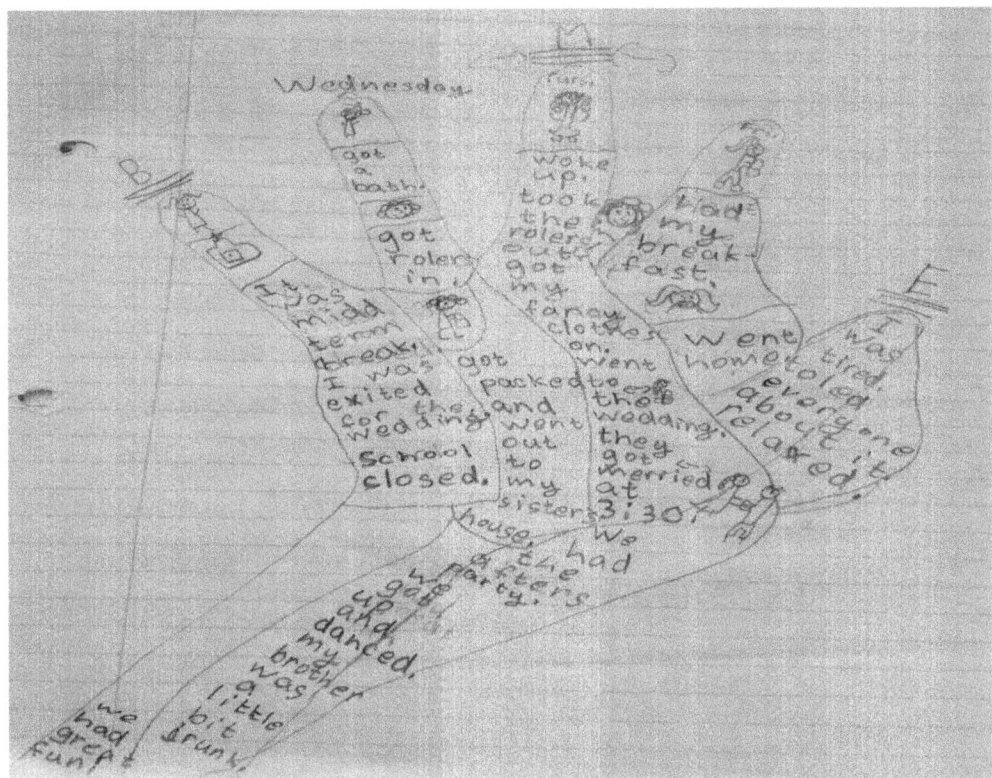

Figure 7.25 A five-finger plan for recount writing (2nd class)

up as one of the 'wow words and they picked it for the week. It's a simple word when you think of it, the main character, and I'm kind of going probably two years ago, would I even know what protagonist was, probably not, but they're using it!

(Teacher 2nd class)

Teaching Researching, Planning and Drafting of Informational Texts

As noted above, in writing informational, persuasive or disciplinary texts children may need opportunities to engage in inquiry-focused lessons so that they can develop authentic questions and acquire the processes and research skills needed to investigate, source and 'analyse immediate, concrete data to help them develop ideas and content for a particular writing task' (Graham & Perin, 2007, p. 19). Honouring children's choices in non-fiction and inquiry processes allows them to take on the mantle of the expert, as they acquire new knowledge that other children may not have and establish themselves as the classroom expert on a particular topic. choosing topics and planning when writing in a range of genre (see Table 7.4).

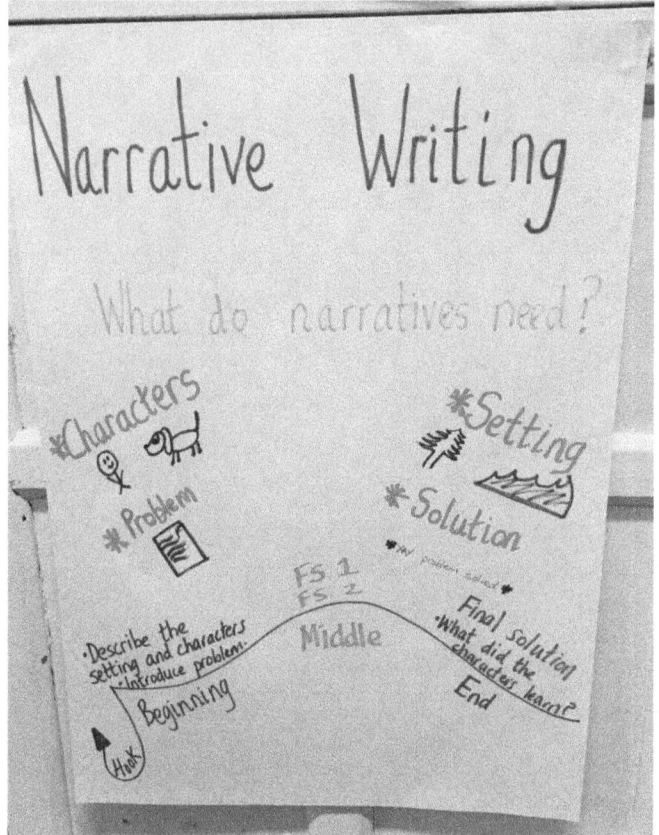

Figure 7.26 Anchor chart for planning narrative writing in senior classes
Source: Write to Read

Links with Reading

Researching requires high levels of reading comprehension, which Goldman and colleagues (2016) have captured in their model of reading comprehension across multiple texts. They extend Kintsch's (1998) reading comprehension construction integration model to address the further challenges posed when key concepts are investigated across multiple texts. They propose the addition of three levels to the Kintsch model: the task model, the integrated model and the intertext model. The task model guides the other two levels as it supports the reader in holding their goals for reading (and in this case writing) central and in selecting appropriate strategies to succeed in accomplishing these goals. The integrated model highlights the need to establish a global understanding of the phenomena across texts and to create inferences and interrelations. Finally, the intertext model highlights the need to adopt a critical stance on text (Who created it? When? For what purpose? From what perspective?) and to detect and resolve conflicting or contradictory information. Just as we expect journalists and the wider media to fact check what they are reporting, so too do children need to learn to do so prior to writing their drafts.

Table 7.4 Generating writing ideas for informational genre with graphic organisers

Components of Writing Process	Writing Strategy	Classroom Application: GRRM Model What, When, How Using
Generating Ideas/ Planning Informational *Informational Genre* • Report • Persuasive • Procedural • Recount/Historical *Link to Inquiry/Discipline* • Draw on prior knowledge • Take notes/ research *Link with reading comprehension*	**Generating Ideas/Panning** Informational Specific Graphic Organiser *Sample Informational* • Key questions: big/small • KWL • Concept map • Bubble map • 2/3 Column notes • Venn Diagram • Outlining ideas • Digital organisers: e.g., Popplet • Convince me template *Order/sequencing ideas* • Main ideas/supporting details • Compare/Contrast • Cause/Effect • Chronological • Mixed sequence	**Generating Ideas: Genre-Specific Graphic Organiser** • Informational: Generate authentic questions: big/small • Use a graphic organiser: Test the topic on paper: *do I have enough prior knowledge to write about this topic?* • What research might I need to do? **Planning Sequencing Ideas** • Research using reliable sources (print/ digital) and record sources • Identify multiple sources for reliability • Take notes: bullet point key nouns and verbs related to interesting/ surprising/ puzzling/confusing/missing information • Synthesise ideas across sources • Put ideas in a possible sequence by numbering each (print) or cutting and pasting or moving ideas around (digital) (e.g., Popplet) • Record quotes: page numbers/source
Set Goals • Consider audience • Consider purpose	**Self-regulate** • Sentence stems • Guiding questions	**Model Reflecting/Self-regulating** • How to check progress against goals • How to use a checklist • How to talk the plan through with peers

Adopting a critical lens (see Figure 7.35, end of chapter), highlights for children that texts are not neutral and that they should be cognisant of an author's level of expertise, the language used to convince or persuade, and the possibility that language may convey bias or a particular perspective. As Roche (2015, p. 15) emphasises, critical thinking 'means thinking for yourself. It is the opposite of receiving information passively. It means looking at something from all sides and weighing up the evidence before adopting a particular stance'. Analysis of multiple perspectives interrogates and 'disrupts the normal' dominant discourse (Leland et al., 2005, p. 264). Furthermore, when students engage in critical literacy from a young age they are prepared 'to make informed decisions regarding issues such as power and control; to engage in the practice of democratic citizenship and develop an ability to think and act ethically' (Vasquez et al., 2019). Such skills are critical in contributing to making the world a more equitable and socially just place. The implications of these dimensions of reading are just as important in the context of writing. Students can be guided to research their informational topic carefully with a critical stance and to consider their own point of view when writing up their research and in deciding on the most effective presentation mode (print, multimodal,

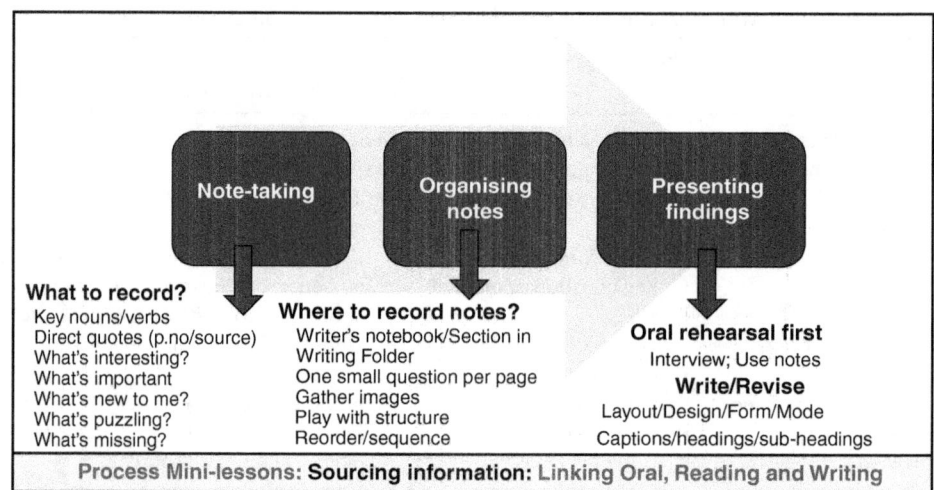

Figure 7.27 Overview of notetaking and drafting steps for informational writing
Source: Authors' figure

digital). As Aronson and Zarnowski (2015, p. 11) highlight: 'All non-fiction is a conversation with sources and readers, and as teachers, we are inviting children to join in the discussion'.

Students will require support in researching their topics and in selecting and accessing a range of print and digital sources. Given the rise of fake news and reporting, children should be taught to check the reliability of their research by using more than one source and websites that are recognised as reliable and up-to-date. In digital reading environments, the interactions between the reader and the text are more fluid, opportunistic and dynamic. The reader needs to be more effortful and purposeful and reader choice and control are heightened (Cho et al., 2018; Dwyer et al., 2022). Consequently, children will need particular guidance on how to take notes and stay focused while researching on the internet (see Dwyer, 2020 for a teacher-friendly classroom guide to the internet inquiry cycle). Reliable note-taking is a skill in and of itself (see Figure 7.27) and critical to accurate reporting and a variety of methods should be modelled using each of the steps of the gradual release of responsibility model.

Strategies for Taking Notes

When students have selected their inquiry focus (a big question and some smaller questions, they should be taught how to take effective notes in response to their questions. Figure 7.27 provides a brief overview of the process. It is helpful to have students write one 'small' question per page/section in their notebook and to record notes pertaining to that question on the same page. This ensures all of the information related to a particular question is in one place. As children will be using multiple sources throughout the inquiry process, they will need to reference each source as they take notes and later cross reference, evaluate and synthesise information across sources (print, digital, visual, audio, primary and secondary). They should note Tier 3 (disciplinary, domain-specific terminology) vocabulary (Beck et al., 2008) and carefully examine the graphics, photos, videos captions, charts and tables they

Identify Image Source: From where? Perspective? Bias?			Write to Read
K: What we observe	**W:** What we think we know / What we want to learn	**LS:** What did we Learn? What do we Still need to learn?	Language needed by children to express thoughts and ideas Tier2/3
People Who is there? Who is absent?	*Why* do you think they are doing this? *How* do you think they are feeling: what *clues* do you have?		
Objects/Places What can you hear?	What objects/places can you identify?		
Action: what are the people doing?	*When* do you think the picture was taken? *Who* might have taken it and *why*?		
	Other questions this photo raises? Anything missing?		
	Where could you find the answer?		

Figure 7.28 Using KWLS to take notes from images

Source: Authors' figure generated in MS Word using MS Word icons

encounter. They will need some strategies to guide them in looking and listening closely to notice important, surprising, interesting or puzzling information.

Figure 7.28 gives some ways to approach it with a photograph. Listening is a more complex skill and so after a recording or video has been seen/heard in its entirety, it will need to be replayed a few times and paused regularly to allow children to augment their notes. Rosenblatt's (1978) transactional reader response theory is a useful framework to adopt when considering links between reading and writing. Rosenblatt suggests that students can be guided to respond to written texts by adopting an efferent and aesthetic stance. An efferent stance entails reading to acquire information while an aesthetic stance requires the reader to take a step back and respond to the literary quality of the text and how it makes the reader feel or engage with the text. The aesthetic stance is highlighted as a key element of craft (see Chapter 9).

Graves (1989, 1994) suggests that students should be taught to record only concrete nouns and active verbs. If longer excerpts are copied from a text, students should learn to reference them appropriately (Graves, 1994). Limiting note taking to key words and phrases means students will then have to generate their own sentences and are more likely to imbue their writing with their own voice and style rather than relying on the source. In this way, they create their own unique author voice while learning the norms of writing within the discipline.

The process of note-taking will need to be modelled multiple times and children will need lots of guided practice with it. As with narrative writing, begin with note taking strategies that are relatively easy for children to grasp and gradually increase the level and complexity of the strategies. Some examples can be seen in Figures 7.29, 7.30 and 7.31). Two-column notes

Testing my interest and knowledge in the topic	
What I know or think I know	What I need to find out

Figure 7.29 2-Column note taking

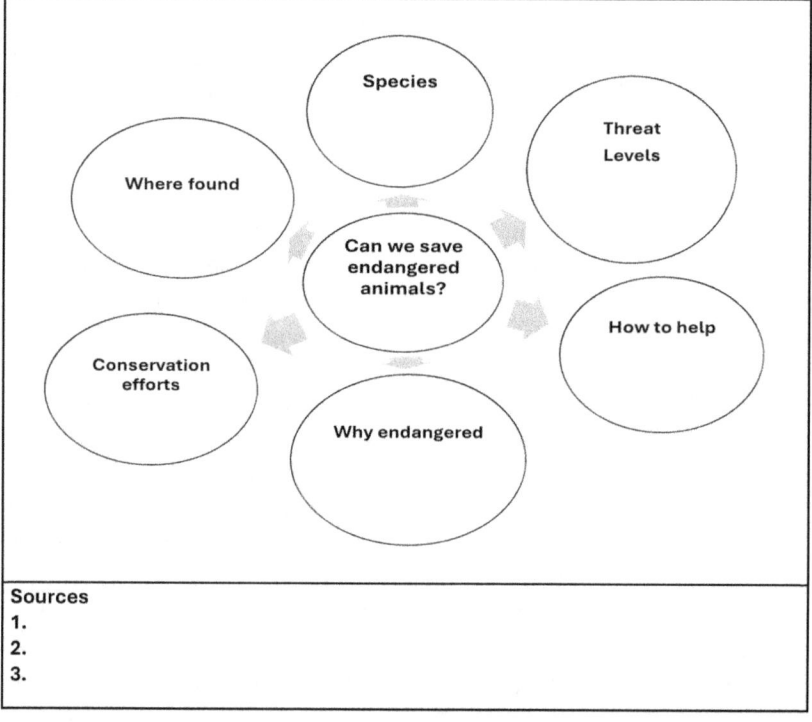

Figure 7.30 Bubble map note taking

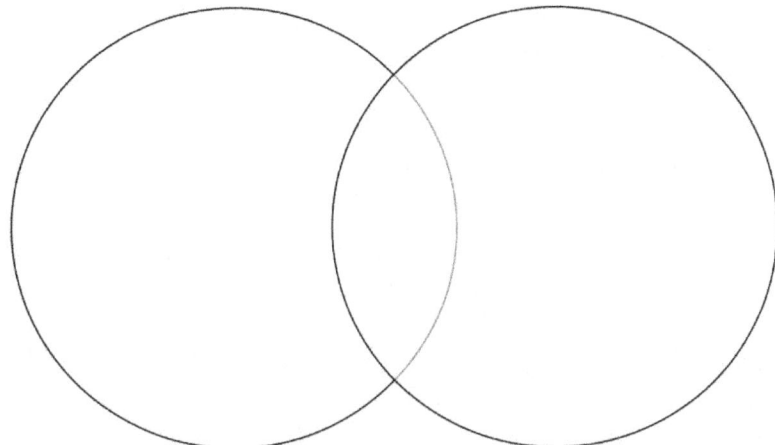

Figure 7.31 Venn diagram for recording compare and contrast notes
Source: Authors' figure generated in MS Word using MS Word icons

are a versatile tool and can be adapted to three or four columns and to a variety of writer purposes. For example, if children want to align their information across three different sources, they write the inquiry question at the top of the page. Next, they record notes in each column (column one, source one and so on).

The two-column note can also be used to:

- Create a quick summary of key points (column one); writer connections, further questions, thoughts) in column two.
- What I know/ What the source makes me think/wonder about
- What's interesting/What's important?

The bubble graphic is a simple way to record key ideas from one source (in no particular order; the bubbles can be numbered later) and the key question is written in the centre. The bubble can be enlarged to accommodate more information. The Venn diagram is useful for recording comparisons and contrasts (e.g., as in the sample: differences between killer whales and blue whales). Teaching children to undertake a simple outline of a text (Figure 7.32) helps them to attain a macro-level overview of the text or chapter and signals the big ideas to be noted. Under each heading quick write notes can be added to capture the key ideas in that subsection and/or it can be used in conjunction with the four-door organiser (Figure 7.33)

Persuasive writing will require a different kind of graphic organiser (Figure 7.34) signalling to writers that when they have strong supporting evidence for their perspectives (facts, statistics, examples) that their argument will be more powerful and likely to be actioned and taken seriously. Graphic organizers should be adapted to children's stage of development and experience with writing.

142 *Teaching and Assessing Writing in the Primary School*

**Chapter 7 Process Mini-lessons:
Generating, Planning and Drafting Writing Ideas across Genres**

Introduction
Generating Ideas
Supporting Writers to Choose Topics Across Genres
    Drawing and Play as Inspiration for Writing
    Creating Lists of Topics
    Drawing Inspiration from Leisure Reading and Popular Culture
    Maintaining a Writing Folder and Writer Notebook
    Learning Why Writers Write
    Mining the Everyday
    Reflecting on Artefacts of Personal Relevance
    Imagining Characters
    Teacher as Writer
    Tapping into Inquiry and Wonder Questions Linked to Interests and Curricula
    Tuning in to Current Events

Teaching Writers to Plan and Draft Writing Across Genre
Importance of Genre-Specific Planning and Drafting Strategies
Planning and Drafting Narrative Texts
    Exemplar lesson: Using the Think, Draw, Label, Write Strategy with Young Children
    Adapting Narrative Graphic Organisers to Children' Stage of Development
Researching, Planning and Drafting Informational Texts
    Links with Reading
    Strategies for Taking Notes

Figure 7.32 Informal outlining: An outline of Chapter 7

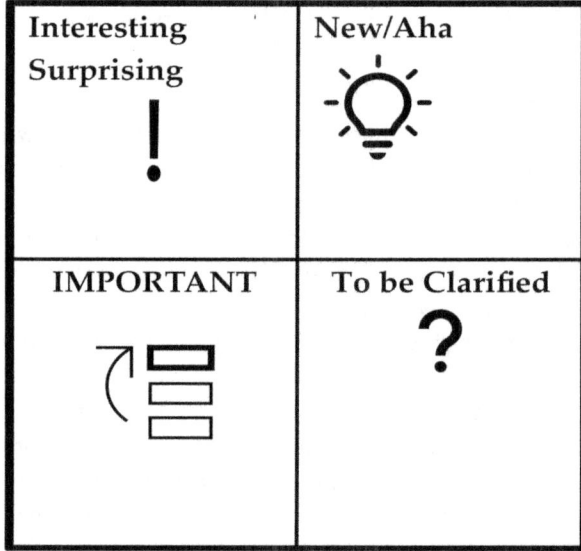

Figure 7.33 Four doors note taking

Source: Authors' figure generated in MS Word using MS Word icons

CONVINCE ME		
Purpose	Audience	
Introduction to Argument		
Reason 1 • Facts • Examples • Evidence • Statistics	Reason 2 • Facts • Examples • Evidence • Statistics	Reason 3 • Facts • Examples • Evidence • Statistics
Counter-Argument 1 • Facts • Examples • Evidence • Statistics	Counter-Argument 2 • Facts • Examples • Evidence • Statistics	Counter-Argument 3 • Facts • Examples • Evidence • Statistics
Conclusion Restate/Summarise your key argument		

Figure 7.34 Note-taking template for persuasive writing
Source: Authors' figure

While it is important to stress to children that the graphic organisers are key to helping them organise their inquiry questions, notes and ideas, it is equally important to stress that the outlines, notes and plans must be flexible enough to allow for unexpected ideas that pop up which will need to be added and worked on. When children have gathered ideas and located information from one source, it is a good idea to guide them to take a step back and to interrogate the source, drawing on reading comprehension strategies (if known to them) such as determining importance, asking questions and evaluating, which are summarised in the anchor chart (Figure 7.35; exemplar reading comprehension lessons can be found on the Write to Read website).

The anchor chart can be used to guide children in taking their thinking a little deeper. They can then apply the same thinking to each of their sources. They should consult a least three sources. They will then need to synthesise the findings and consider an appropriate sequence and structure. A verbal rehearsal of the findings with a peer prior to writing is an engaging and valuable opportunity for children to discover how well they understand their topic and are able to make it comprehensible to peers. Answering peers' questions may prompt them to revisit sources and identify any gaps and consider what to keep and what to omit.

Write to Read

My 'Big' Inquiry Question(s) ?

My 'Small' Inquiry Questions ?

Determine Importance

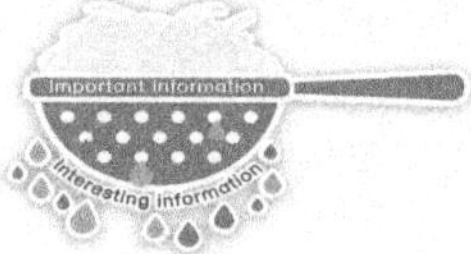

For *each* source Identify and record:
- the important facts
- the interesting facts
- surprising information
- puzzling or confusing information

Ask Questions

For *each* source dig a little deeper:
- What are the key concepts/big ideas?
- How does this information align with other sources?
- What is the evidence base for claims?
- What is missing?

Evaluate

Evaluate each source for:
- Accuracy; check other sources for consistency
- Currency: recent/old
- Author expertise
- Author perspective
- Bias/stereotypical views

Synthesise

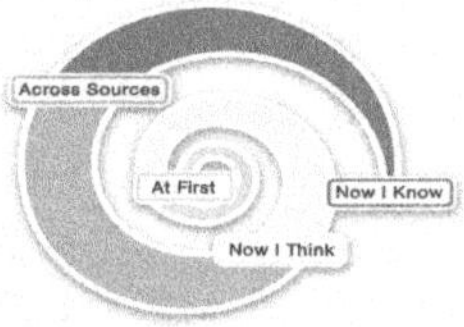

- What have you learned across sources?
- Consider the best structure to present your writing
- Craft the headings/subheadings in an outline

Sources
1.
2.
3.

Figure 7.35 Anchor chart interrogating sources

Source: Write to Read

Reflect, Connect, Act

1. Observe children as they begin a new piece of writing:
   - What strategies do they utilise to help them in planning and getting started?
   - Notice who plans overtly, who doesn't (some may plan in their heads)?
   - Do strategies vary across learners with varying proficiency in writing?
   - Do children have a range of strategies for planning and do they adjust them to suit the genre? Who is ready for further development in planning?

Suggestions for Further Reading

1. Graham, S., Harris, K. R., & Mason, L. (2005). Improving the writing performance, knowledge, and self-efficacy of struggling young writers: The effects of self-regulated strategy development. *Contemporary Educational Psychology, 30(2)*, 207–241. https://doi.org/10.1016/j.cedpsych.2004.08.001
2. Kervin, L., & Mantei, J. (2016). Digital writing practices: a close look at one grade three author, *Literacy, 50(3)*. https://doi.org/10.1111/lit.12084
3. Tracey, B., Reid, R., & Graham, S. (2009). Teaching young students strategies for planning and drafting stories: The impact of self-regulated strategy development. *Journal of Educational Research, 102(5)*, 323–331. https://doi.org/10.3200/JOER.102.5.323-332

8 Craft Mini Lessons
Developing and Enhancing Writing Quality across Genres

This chapter focuses on mini lessons to support children to write with clarity and originality. It outlines the critical role of high-quality mentor texts to support the development of craft mini lessons across a range of genres. Reference is made to the reciprocal nature of the forms of language and the value of the *Write to Read* analytic writing rubric as a formative assessment tool for enhancing the quality of children's writing across genres.

> **Reflect, Connect**
>
> 1   Why is teacher knowledge about language and writing genres critical for the development of craft lessons?
> 2   In what ways can the models of writing development in Chapter 1 support teachers' planning for the craft dimensions of writing?
> 3   In what ways, can craft lessons support children in developing links between oral language, reading and writing?
> 4   How can the analytic *Write to Read* rubric support teaching, planning and assessment of craft dimensions of writing?

Prioritising Craft Mini Lessons

As Grainger et al. (2005, p. 2) argue 'if children's writing is to demonstrate their creativity, individuality, voice and verve, then the seeds of their stories and other forms of writing need constant nurturing and support as well as time to evolve and reverberate.' Craft mini lessons are at the heart of the writing workshop and are a critical part of supporting children to find their 'voice', which Graves (1994, p. 227) has suggested is the 'imprint of the self on the writing'. In a similar vein, Springsteen observes, writing is a 'single fingerprint.... all the filmmakers we love, all the songwriters we love, they put their fingerprint on your imagination, in your heart. And on your soul' (Springsteen in Burger, 2013, p. 350). It is what draws us back time and again to our favourite writers, musicians and film makers as they explore the universal themes central to the human condition. It is their individual tone, style and word choice that strike a chord in us.

Our work with schools has shown us that as children engage with a range of genres over the year, they discover which ones they enjoy most and begin to favour some genres over others. The variety and choice offered seem to be particularly important for children who are less motivated to write as noted by teachers:

When you tell them that they have choice they cheer! The love to choose their genre… when they find their niche and interest in writing, they write pages!

(4th class teacher)

There are lots of little things along the way that strike you…when you saw Peter suddenly beginning to write out of being so resistant and Paul so into…. we did poetry very briefly for about a week or two and what he wrote! I think they will benefit, for the rest of their lives regardless of how it goes. Cause all of them have come out with a sense that they are authors.

(2nd class, teacher)

Craft mini lessons are critical to enhancing the quality and range of children's writing, expanding the sophistication of their writing vocabulary, text organisation and genre knowledge. Such lessons put the emphasis firmly on the authorial dimensions of writing, communicating to children that content and form take precedence over secretarial dimensions. They open up a host of possibilities for children and scaffold them in acquiring a repertoire of strategies for creating compelling engaging texts across a range of genres. As Rosenblatt (1988, p. 7) argues these 'verbal elements, actually, often serve as cues to the reader to adopt an aesthetic stance'.

Influence of Quality Literature on Word Consciousness across Genres

Teacher 'content and pedagogical content knowledge' (Shulman, 1987) related to genres, craft features and language registers is essential to planning a broad series of craft lessons. Each genre requires a carefully curated pool of mentor 'texts' (print, digital and multimodal) which can serve as models for developing writers if used effectively in mini lessons. Craft mini lessons (Pytash & Morgan, 2014) explore how published authors have conceptualised the organisation of the text and crafted words, phrases and sentences so that readers can empathise, connect, visualise, infer, question, predict or synthesise. These are concepts students encounter in relation to reading comprehension and can be guided to transfer into writing.

Mentor texts should represent engaging high-level exemplars of specific techniques you would like children to learn and transfer into their writing. When selecting texts for a word choice mini lesson, it should be at grade level and contain sufficiently challenging vocabulary and apt, inventive use of language in the context of the target genre. This is key if children are to continue to intensify vocabulary growth and develop a deep appreciation of language as they progress through primary school. It is helpful if children are already familiar with the chosen text as it will free them up to concentrate on the aesthetic dimensions rather than on striving to understand a text for the first time. It will support them in making deeper connections to the author's choice of words for the context.

If the focus is on informational text structure or theme, choose texts written by authors in a discipline (e.g., historians/naturalists/scientists) (see Table 7.2, Chapter 7 for some of our favourites) who are as passionate about crafting the text as they are about their subject (Box 8.1).

> ### BOX 8.1 CRAFT IN NON-FICTION
>
> Too much nonfiction has basically serviceable prose. In other words, in the mind of the author, what matters is the content. So, they're basically getting you to the content in an okay way. They're sort of adding the bricks and then you have a wall. I think an author who pauses to really look at why is it this word and that word, why is it the cadence of that sentence against this sentence? The care of how the author crafts a sentence…I think of my books really more as symphonies, as compositions, and I really try to feel the unfolding of the melody.
>
> (Aronson, Reading Rockets. no date)
>
> **Watch and listen:** https://www.readingrockets.org/people-and-organizations/marc-aronson

Teacher knowledge of current literature (e.g., Wooten & Cullinan, 2018; Gamble, 2019) and how to select developmentally appropriate and genre-specific mentor texts (Pytash & Morgan, 2014; Laminack, 2017) for mini lessons is critical to a successful writing workshop and will also inform the development of vibrant school and classroom libraries which entice children to read. However, Cremin et al. (2024, p. 835) have highlighted that primary teachers tend to rely on a 'narrow repertoire' of texts and their own preferences for reading when choosing literature for the classroom. In choosing texts for the classroom Miller (2021) advocates that texts chosen should offer 'a stimulating and satisfying aesthetic, imaginative, intellectual or emotional experience that goes beyond the banal and the obvious, and develops or challenges the reader's inner life, sense of self, or understanding of and engagement with the world'. Keeping up to date with newly published books for children across a range of genres is essential (see Chapter 12) though often a challenge highlighted by teachers in our partner schools. However, teachers have recognised the value of investing in mentor texts and noted that not only were children more interested in the mini lesson when they knew the text selected was written by a published author but also more likely to use the craft in their writing:

> *I really think from showing, I do a good bit, say just to put up on the visualiser. You know, from the real books, that's huge, because then it's not, you know, from a workbook or something they go, oh, this is a real author and I'm a real author by writing this.*
>
> (5th class)

> *We got a lot of nonfiction books last year, which were brilliant for the report-writing. exciting nonfiction books, the -and -, all those ones. And the difference in the reports that they wrote from January to May was staggering. Just by taking a different approach to it.*
>
> (4th)

Creating a timeline of major book awards and regularly reviewing the winning books for fiction, poetry, nonfiction and illustration is a good start (see Chapter 12). Through direct instruction using each step of the Gradual Release of Responsibility Model (GRRM, Fielding & Pearson, 1994) (see exemplar in Box 8.2), across genres techniques to emulate from authors can be highlighted in craft mini lessons and children supported to speculate why authors might have chosen particular words to create a mood, setting or believable character, or ponder why a particular report or argument linger in the mind long after reading. Making these dimensions visible to students through visual displays, anchor charts and a good writers' checklist is an important first step in raising children's awareness of the features of highly engaging and effective writing.

Developing Word Choice Craft Mini Lessons across Genres

As noted in Chapters 7 and 10, as writers engage in the act of writing, they are continuously making choices through 'online planning' and 'online revising' (Berninger & Swanson, 1994). Focusing on word-level choices initially makes the process more manageable for emergent and developing writers and moves them forward along a trajectory from *knowledge telling* towards *knowledge transforming* (see Chapter 1, Bereiter & Scardamalia, 1987). Guiding them to discuss and consider an author's word choice puts a focus on the literary, aesthetic and creative dimensions of writing. It provides valuable opportunities to integrate the teaching of the forms of language (oral language, reading and writing) into each lesson. Rather than teaching them in isolation or separately, this capitalises on the interconnections between them, which research indicates is important for overall literacy development (Graham et al., 2018). Reading and writing connections are forged when children adopt both efferent and aesthetic stances while reading (Rosenblatt, 1988).

It is helpful if children are also reading in the genre in which they are learning to write. During the reading workshop students should be encouraged to notice when words have been used in interesting ways in texts they are reading, to record these in vocabulary notebooks and to utilise these words in appropriate ways in their personal writing. Adopting the stance of first the reader and then the writer helps children to value the precision and apt use of language (Hansen, 1987; Graves, 1994; Barrs, 2000). As Calkins (2000, p. 360) notes 'good readers the world over pause as they read, to gasp, weep, imagine and remember'. Considering how the author stirred these emotions fosters a 'word consciousness' amongst children and creates a positive disposition toward noticing and acquiring new words (Graves & Watts-Taffe, 2002). Over time children will internalise mini lessons and naturally notice words and phrases that appeal to them, as highlighted by a writer in 5th class: '*Sometimes authors have really cool lines that mean things, but he doesn't say it. Like, the boy was sad, once an author said, 'The boy felt like a burst balloon'*'.

Word choice is linked with vocabulary knowledge in reading. Biemiller (2005) reported that children in the lowest quartile in reading in 5th grade have vocabularies similar to the 2nd-grade median. Word-level craft mini lessons provide fruitful avenues for children at the primary level to expand vocabulary knowledge, experiment with and play with language (Naumann et al., 2011) and to contemplate the precision and impact of their word choice when writing. This is particularly critical for children in disadvantaged contexts who need every opportunity to push the boundaries of oral and written language (Kennedy & Shiel, 2022).

Olinghouse and Wilson (2013) in a study investigating the diversity and maturity of vocabulary (word choice) in primary-level compositions in story, persuasive and informational writing have highlighted that semantic knowledge is fundamental to supporting writers to 'render(s) into linguistic form ideas, experiences, and sensory images that are stored in long-term memory... without vocabulary such things cannot be expressed' (p. 46). Children can learn the nuances of word choice and how to adjust the tone of the writing to resonate with their intended purpose and audience, e.g., writing a letter of complaint to a manufacturer for a faulty product (see Figure 8.9) will be different to a science report on an experiment or a recount of a recent school trip or a fantasy story from their imagination.

A useful way to categorise words is to use Beck et al.'s (2008) three tiers. Tier One represents words that most children already know (e.g., table, door, sister) when they come to school (but may need to be taught explicitly to children learning English as an additional language). Tier Two words (Figure 8.1) are more mature words for concepts already known to children (e.g., ancient for old; prosperous for rich) and appear often in texts. Tier Three words are uncommon words typically associated with a specific discipline or domain of knowledge (e.g., carnivore, cumulus). Priority should be given to the instruction of Tier 2 words, given their high utility and importance for understanding the increasingly challenging texts that children encounter as they progress through school. They are critical to enhancing writing quality.

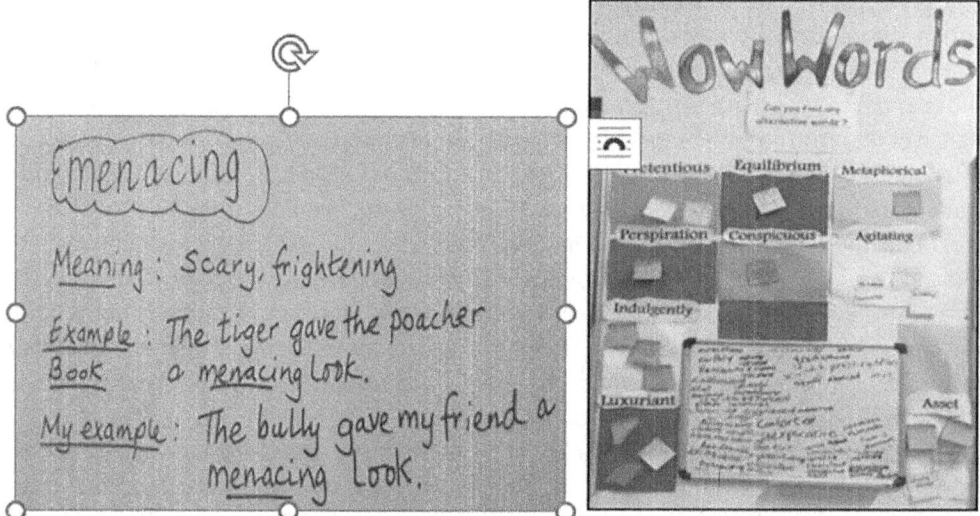

Figure 8.1 Examples of Tier Two vocabulary instruction
Source: Write to Read

Using the Write-to-Read Rubric to Guide Planning for Word Choice

In our work with schools, we have put a significant emphasis on building children's lexical knowledge across oral language, reading and writing. It is reflected particularly in the **Word Choice** and **Voice** components of the *Write to Read Rubric* (see Chapter 5). Both have three subcomponents (word choice: *word-level, sentence-level, imagery and creative language use*; voice: *audience, risk-taking and style*). Consulting the rubric will provide you with some useful starting points. These components reference a variety of *word-level* descriptive language and poetic devices which can be successfully integrated across genres for effect (Table 8.1). The rubric also recognises that writing can be powerful without undue or unnecessary description, so writers are not penalised for a sparer style of writing. Examples of language included across the 14 levels of the rubric are drawn from the actual writing samples of children participating in the *Write to Read* initiative. Teachers have valued these practical grade-level examples of vocabulary and highlighted that they have been useful reference points in signalling levels of sophistication and maturity in language across levels and stretched their expectations for children:

> I think that's one of the biggest impacts the rubric has had on me. It's kind of heightened my expectations even further allowing me to push the boundaries and in turn to heighten the children's expectations and to kind of push them more… I've seen a huge leap in the descriptive language overall.
>
> (6th class)

Sentence-level mini lessons can focus on developing descriptions across sections of the text. These kinds of mini lessons develop children's awareness of how to add detail and colour to their writing by, for example, moving from simple patterned sentences to a variety of sentence openers; clustering descriptive detail around several sentences to stretch moments providing the reader with a sense of being present in the text; and varying the syntactic complexity of sentences for effect by including short sentences and sentences with one or more clauses. As Myhill et al. (2012) emphasise, grammar can act as a 'design tool' and as part of a 'repertoire for shaping text: the possibilities of short sentences for impact, varying sentence lengths to create textual rhythm, and altering the syntactic structure of sentences to shift focus' (p. 157). These sentence-level techniques can bring life and energy to the writing regardless of genre. Mentor texts can explore the textual rhythms of a variety of authors to demonstrate to children that these techniques are authorial choices which signal the author voice and are not prescriptive elements to be added to every piece of writing. As Fletcher

Table 8.1 Dimensions of word choice related to word-level, sentence-level, imagery and creative language use across genres

Adjectives	Onomatopoeia
Alliteration	Simile
Verbs	Metaphor
Adverbs	Personification
Precise nouns; Disciplinary tier 3 vocabulary	Hyperbole
Rhyme	Irony
Repetition	Assonance

(1993, p. 32) so aptly put it: 'the writer's real pleasure comes not from using an exotic word but from using the right word'.

The *imagery and creative language usage* mini lessons, move beyond the single word level (nouns, adjectives, verbs) to more advanced elements such as similes, metaphors and alliteration which can help children appreciate the power of apt language to stir readers' emotions and convey the writer's intentions more vividly. As Rosenblatt (1988, p. 7) highlights:

> The aesthetic reader experiences, savors, the qualities of the structured ideas, situations, scenes, personalities, emotions, called forth, participating in the tensions, conflicts, and resolutions as they unfold. This lived-through meaning is felt to correspond to the text. This meaning evoked during the aesthetic transaction constitutes "the literary work," the poem, story, or play. This evocation, and not the text, is the object of the reader's "response" and "interpretation" both during and after the reading event.

Children can be taught to transfer skills learned from narrative and fictional writing (see Chapter 12 for a monthly plan) to non-fiction genres to avoid the trap of 'serviceable prose'. As one of our teachers noted:

> Nonfiction, people approach it as a boring kind of genre they kind of, they just think it's information overload. Non-fiction needs to be brought to life, it needs this impact.... It can be aesthetically pleasing as well because the language you know, it's what draws you in. So, therefore if the language is descriptive and is visual, it kind of really jumps off the page and brings things to life.
>
> (6th class)

Children can be guided to use poetic devices in memorable ways to capture a character or setting in fiction or convey complex information in non-fiction in ways relevant to their intended audience and genre (see Box 8.2, exemplar lesson).

Teachers in our partner schools have acknowledged that the rubric has prompted them to transfer these techniques across genres:

> There were certain areas which I wouldn't have focussed on at all prior to seeing the rubric. Like a good example of that was imagery, you know, poetic devices, it's something that I wouldn't have done outside of the poetry genre...It really opened my eyes and it's something that I latched onto quite early.... and I've seen huge progress with the children's ability as writers.
>
> (6th class teacher)

Word choice and voice are related as writers consider their audience. The next section explores how children can be supported to infuse their writing with a sense of their own voice.

Developing *'Voice'*: Craft Mini Lessons across Genres

Definitions of voice vary in the literature on writing and are contested. In one research study on voice, O'Halloran and Schleppegrell (2016) designed an intervention focused on infusing 'voice' into argumentative writing in science with 2nd and 4th-grade students. They note that historically, 'voice' has been characterised as an expression of the personality and

BOX 8.2 A SAMPLE CRAFT LESSON: SIMILES

Using Similes in Non-Fiction Writing: 3rd/4th class (eight to ten-year-olds)
Link with Science Curriculum
Mentor text: *Frogs* by Nic Bishop
Resources: large chart paper; markers; writing paper for children

Step 1: Explain (1-3 minutes)
There are all kinds of non-fiction writers in the world. Just like fiction writers, these authors think about who might read their book and they think carefully about their word choice. When we were working on our stories and poems, we learned about how powerful a simile can be to create a memorable picture in the reader's mind. We can also use this technique in our non-fiction writing. Similes can help us remember important information. Let's see how Nic Bishop, one of our favourite non-fiction authors, uses similes to help us learn about the many varieties of frog in the world.

Step 2: Demonstrate by Thinking Aloud (about 5-6 minutes)
Children should sit on a carpet square and be close enough to see the book (wonderful photographs) as you read aloud the opening page (5):
< >
Frogs are found on
every continent
except Antarctica.
They live in ponds, rivers, forests and fields. Some even live in sand dunes.
The biggest, the Goliath frog from Africa is as heavy as a newborn baby.
Imagine a frog as heavy as a new baby! I held my nephew when he was born and he was heavy! He was more than 6lbs! I didn't know frogs could get to be that size! that's a very clever simile that Nic Bishop used…by comparing the Goliath frog to a new baby, I can visualise how big and heavy the frog is! That will stick in my head and I will be able to remember the Goliath frog. Let's see if Nic Bishop uses any other similes.

Teacher Notes
Choose a familiar text/author where possible.

Step 1: Explain
Notice that the lesson begins with a **statement** rather than asking who can remember what a simile is. Connect to what children have already learned in fiction and how it can transfer to non-fiction. Briefly state the focus of today's lesson and how similes help to enhance writing in this genre.

Step 2: Demonstrate
Craft a think aloud in your own words to explain how the simile helps the reader to visualise and remember the size of the frogs. Ask children to notice what you did in your think-aloud. The Thinking aloud step allows children 'see' the invisible processes in a writer's head and the choices they make when writing.

(Continued)

Continue reading page 5 aloud:

One of the smallest, the gold frog from South America could sit on the tip of your little finger. But, big or small, frogs are always easy to recognise. Almost all have long back legs, a large head, big eyes, damp stretchy skin and no tails.

Ah, I see Nic Bishop has used another clever comparison! I can visualise how small the gold frog is. Imagine how tiny it must be to fit on the tip of my finger!

So, what have we learned about writing today? Authors use unusual comparisons to help the reader visualise and remember facts. Let's see if Nic Bishop uses any more unusual comparisons in his book.

Step 2: Guided Practice

Turn to page 23 and read the caption under the photo. Ask the children to turn and talk to the person beside them and identify and discuss the simile:

This toad from the Amazon looks just like a dead leaf on the rainforest floor.

Listen in as children discuss and invite one or two children to share their thoughts. *Yes, you are right...the frog looks just like a dead leaf, he is almost the same colour, you can hardly see him in the photo, so that's another great comparison that Nic Bishop used. Now listen as I read page 23 and see if you can spot the simile on this page. Turn and talk to your partner.*

The simile is in the middle of the page: '**Its eyes sink into its head for protection, and special see through "eyelids", called** *nicitating membranes* **cover them like safety goggles**'.

After children have identified the simile and shared their responses to it, begin to co-construct the anchor chart. It might go something like this: *How will we start our anchor chart? What do we notice about similes? How does the author signal the comparison (uses words like/as)? Why does the author use a comparison? When might you use one in your writing?* Take the children's suggestions and scaffold as needed.

Step 3: Guided Practice

In pairs, children should read p.23 identify the simile and explain why it was a good comparison.

Talking about the images they have in their head and co-constructing the anchor chart with you will help children to understand the purpose of a simile, when to use it and how it brings writing alive.

(Continued)

Step 4: Independent Writing (20 minutes) *Before you start writing today, read over your writing from yesterday and see if you can spot where you might be able to use a simile to create a picture in your mind and when you continue on writing, use a simile wherever you think it will bring your writing alive.* **Step 5: Share Session/Reflect and Set Goals (5-8 minutes)** Affirm all writers and ask them to turn to the person beside them, show their writing and say one thing about what they wrote. Invite 2-3 children to share their writing with the whole class. Model feedback and be specific in relation to aspects of writing that you noticed as children read their work aloud. If a simile was used, praise children for applying the technique to their writing. Then conclude by reflecting on what was learned: *Writers, today we learned that writers often use similes to signal a comparison between two things that are very different from each other. It helps the reader to visualise and remember important facts.* Encourage children to orally reflect on what was easy, and what was hard and to set a goal for the next day: *What was easy today? What was hard? What did you learn? What is your goal for tomorrow?*	***Step 4: Independent Writing*** As the children write, conference with four or five children. Focus on their strengths and what they are trying to accomplish in their text rather than on errors. ***Step 5: Share, Reflect, Set Goals*** If children used a simile in their writing encourage them to add it to the anchor chart. Concluding the lesson this way strengthens learner's metacognitive awareness and links back to the explanation in Step 1.

individuality of a writer and distinguishable in tone, mood or style, but they argue for more nuanced definitions of 'voice' so writers are 'apprenticed into disciplinary discourses' and also taught to write in ways valued by the disciplines.

While teaching children to write in a way that hooks and engages the reader is important, it is equally important to guide them to notice and utilise disciplinary language so that they build domain-specific terminology and concepts. Thus, there is a delicate balance to be struck between literary and disciplinary language in creating informational texts, bearing in mind the audience for whom the text is intended. Consider the examples (Table 8.2), both of which seek to inform the reader about seals.

In reading the first text with an 'efferent stance', we learn facts about seals, including a domain-specific definition, where they live and their physical characteristics. In reading the same text with an 'aesthetic stance', we can notice the author's choice of words and sentence structure. While there is some description, there is little 'voice' or evidence of passion about the subject. The second text, on the other hand, connects with the reader through a range of literary devices. It opens by speaking directly to the reader. Apt verbs such *as flumping* enable the reader to visualise the seal on land while shoot and slip enable us to visualise the seal moving in the water. Precise adjectives *fat sunbather, sleek, smooth, pointed at both ends* enable us to visualise what a seal looks like. The author also appeals to our senses describing what the seal sees and hears within his dark habitat (*seaweed forest, gloom*). The use of

Table 8.2 Authorial examples of non-fiction writing

There are several species of seal including the gray seal, harbour seal, harp seal, hooded seal and ring seal. All seals have similar physical characteristics. They have whiskers which detect vibrations in the water and help them sense the approach of dangerous prey. Though you can't really see their ears, they hear very well above and below water. Seals use their flippers to propel their streamlined bodies through the sea. Seals consume a wide variety of fish and crustaceans while swimming. Though they eat at sea, they are semiaquatic and spend time on the shoreline. Their bodies store food in the form of blubber under their skin. This protects and insulates them in the cold water.	*See what a seal can do* (Butterworth, 2014) Adapted If you are down by the sea one day you might spot a seal, lying about like a fat sunbather or flumping along the sand…seal spends most of his time in the sea…His body is just the right shape to shoot through the water: sleek, smooth and pointed at both ends…Seal slips through the seaweed forest-big eyes searching the gloom. His sharp ears hear dolphins whistle and a ferry-boat's engine chugging… he has two fur coats that keep him waterproof and a thick layer of fat under his skin that wraps around him like a duvet.

a simile: a *thick layer of fat under his skin that wraps around him like a duvet* enables us to conjure up an image of plumpness, comfort and protection. Possible mini lessons that these two texts could be used for include: figurative language, active precise verbs or imagery, apt adjectives or domain-specific vocabulary. The first text contains a discipline-specific word *'blubber'*, while the second refers to it as a thick layer of fat. Guiding children to make comparisons between the two types of texts broadens their understanding of audience and purpose. It offers possibilities for authorial decisions around how best to combine form, genre and content in ways that hook the reader. Including punctuation in voice as a craft technique heightens children's awareness of it as a design technique which can be used for creative emphasis. It is also linked to the syntactical complexity of sentences highlighted above in relation to the Word Choice component. This dual emphasis gives writers a deeper appreciation of the role of punctuation in writing and its contribution to a text's flow. It is important to notice if children are not experimenting with or using a wide range of punctuation in their writing and to begin with mini lessons on craft dimensions rather than on accuracy which can be addressed within small group skills mini lessons and guided by the Conventions' component of the rubric (see Chapter 9). As one teacher noted:

> It's important to have people thinking about punctuation… in second grade, they should be using more than a capital letter and a full stop…. to show people that it moves on. There is a sophistication around that too… to embed it in the Writing Workshop.
>
> (4th class teacher)

Using the Write to Read Rubric to Guide Planning for Voice

The *voice* component of the rubric draws together many of the other craft dimensions of writing which work together to establish writer identity and writer expression. The sub-components (a) language choice for an intended audience; (b) evidence of risk-taking/playfulness with language and punctuation; and (c) consideration of overall style and language register) were created to broaden conceptions of voice which can be subjective and nebulous to pin down. Teachers have highlighted that the rubric provides an academic language register and framework for how to approach these more unique dimensions of writing which can be difficult to concretise in planning and to teach explicitly. As one teacher noted in feedback to us on the development of the rubric:

> *Even things like voice. I probably would not have thought twice about voice or taking risks or style or creating imagery. I wouldn't have thought of it in that level of detail. And I might have struggled in mini lessons to make them really specific.*
>
> (4th class teacher)

When children experience an effective and engaging writing workshop where they feel part of the writing community (see Chapter 6) they will quickly pick up on key messages on apt use of language and will begin to apply mini lessons to their writing. In Figures 8.2a-8.2e, we can see a text written by a child in Senior Infants (six years approx.) in one of our partner schools at the end of a unit on fiction writing. The teacher read fiction aloud to children daily. They also engaged in shared reading and small group reading activities and had experienced a writing workshop approach to writing development since Junior Infants (the first year of primary school). Upon analysing the writing sample, though it is incomplete and loses momentum by page 4, it exudes *voice* and we can see the transfer of many craft elements from mini lessons to writing (see Figure 8.2a,b,c,d,e). There are many ways that teachers could respond to this young writer to harness the potential of the story through further development and elaboration.

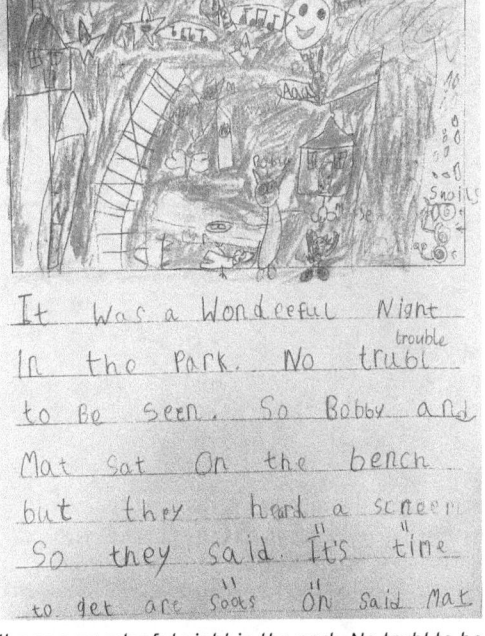

It was a wondeeful night in the park. No trubl to be seen. So Bobby and Mat sat on the bench but they herd a screem so they said its time to get are soots on said Mat.

So they went into ther tiny house's. Mat swooped in-to the night and Bobby ran into the night but when they got there there it was catastrophe there was a man falling off. A ladder and a bunny falling off a thee and a cat with red boots.

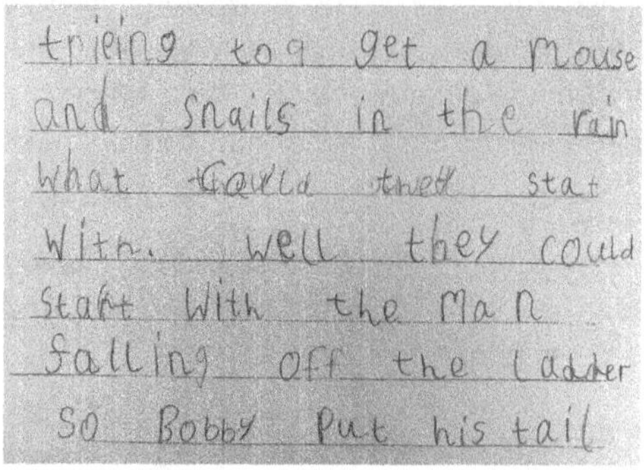

trieing to get a mouse and snails in the rain. What could they stat with. Well they could start with the man falling off the ladder so Bobby put his tail

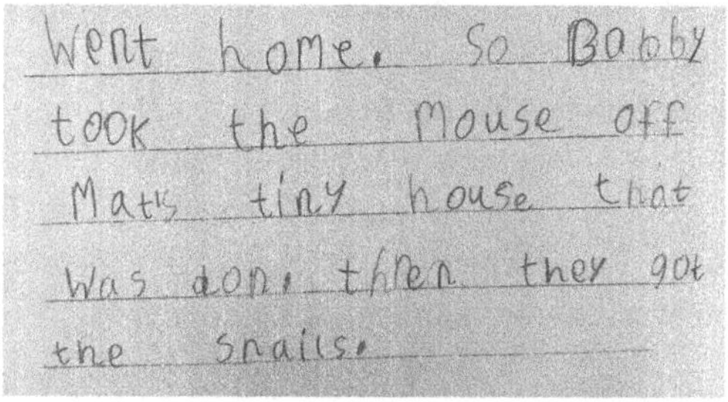

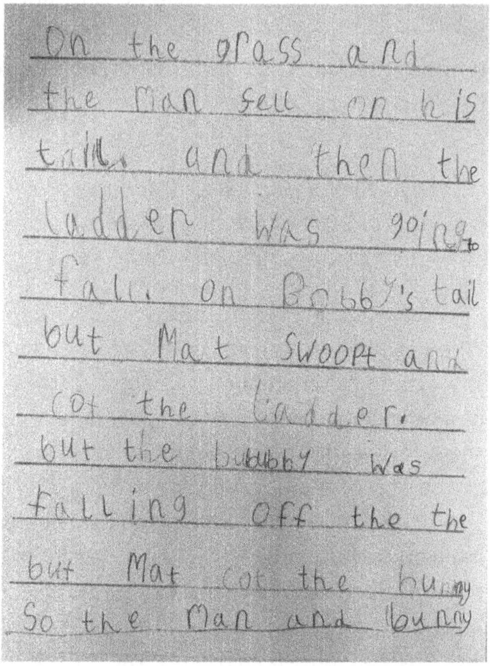

on the grass and the man fell on his tail and then the ladder was going to fall. on Bobby's tail but Mat swoopt and cot the ladder. but the bubby was falling off the thee but Mat cot the bunny so the man and bunny

went home. So Bobby took the mouse off Mat's tiny house that was don. then they got the snails.

Figure 8.2a–8.2e: Fiction writing, end of senior infants All pages typed as written
Source: Write to Read

Table 8.3 Evidence of mini lesson transfer to fiction writing

A literary lead highlighting setting	It was a wondeeful night in the park.
Literary language	No truble to be seen.
Two major characters described	Bobby, Mat
Minor characters	Bunny, man
Ambitious vocabulary	Swooped, catastrophe
Sentence openers show variety	Though several sentences begin with So, others show variation
Connectives	But, so (overused), and, when
Dialogue between characters signal information about the characters	Reader can infer that: Characters are small in stature as they live in 'tiny houses' Characters are superheroes who come to the aid of others One character is a flying vertebrate ('swooped into the night')
Action/Plot	Several events in the middle
Adjectives for effect	Tiny houses; Red boots
Rhetorical question	What could they start with?
Experimentation with punctuation	Speech marks: "its time to get are soots on" Possessives used correctly: Mat's house, Bobby's tail; used incorrectly in a plural: house's

The sample of writing in Figure 8.3 was completed by a pupil in Senior Infants towards the end of the school year after a field trip to the Zoo, where the Zookeeper had given a talk to the children about the rhinoceros while visiting the rhino habitat. The next day, the pupil was observed writing this text by one of our research and professional development team who happened to be present. She reported that the child wrote quickly without stopping, embodying what Graves (1994) suggests for writers embarking on a first draft: write quickly, change nothing and let all ideas in, as the first flurry of ideas onto the page tend to capture key nuggets of what a writer has envisioned in their mind's eye. While the language and sentence structure might be finessed subsequently, the freedom and spontaneity in a first draft is a useful starting point.

In looking carefully at the sample, we can clearly sense the enthusiasm of this young writer for the subject. It is clear the writer has not stopped to erase words perceived to be incorrectly spelled but has quickly put an X through them. In our work with schools, we have suggested banning erasers during writing workshops so children begin to focus on the fluency of their ideas and begin to regard their text as a draft and not the finished product. This writer has transferred many non-fiction craft mini lessons into this draft writing (see Table 8.3). It calls to mind Graves (1994, p. 219) who observed:

> Until a writer discovers a subject and decides what interests him, the nouns will often be thin and colourless, and the verbs lifeless and imprecise. Until I discover what my subject is and have some conviction about it, how can I have verbs that will march across the page with force and energy

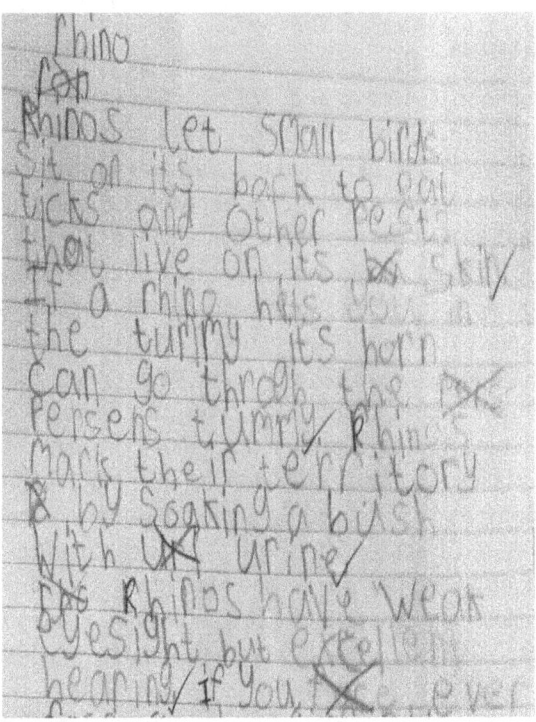

Rhinos let small birds sit on its back to eat ticks and other pests that live on its skin. If a rhino hits you in the tummy its horn can go throgh the persens tummy. Rhinos mark their territory by soaking a bush with urine. Rhinos have weak eyesight but excellent hearing. If you ever face a charging rhino throw a rock to side and itll change course and head for the thud. Rhino's skin is bumpy and lumpy. A rhinos horn is made of the same stuff as your hair and nails. Black rhino's have a hooke'd upper lip that they use for plucking leaves off bushes and trees. Rhino's are smelly animals.
(typed as written)

Figure 8.3 Informational writing, *Rhino* end of senior infants
Source: Write to Read

Table 8.3 Evidence of mini lesson transfer to non-fiction/informational writing

Use of generic noun (refers to a class of things/animals rather than a specific one)	Rhinos
Use of present tense	Rhinos are smelly animals
Describes/provides interesting facts	A range of facts are presented
Adjectives	Small birds, hooked upper lip
Apt verbs	Plucking, soak
Uses connectives	But
Varied sentence openers	Though several sentences begin with Rhinos there is variation across the text
Disciplinary language	Rhinos mark their territory by soaking bush with urine
Rhyme	Bumpy/lumpy
Experimentation with punctuation	Apostrophe: Rhino's; hooke'd

The precision of the word choice and sentence structure indicates the kind of excitement, conviction and expertise highlighted by Graves in the quote above. When predictable time, choice of topic and high-quality teaching converge year after year, such experiences can set young children up with a sense of achievement and self-efficacy and set them on an upward trajectory in building their writing skills as they progress through primary school.

Text Structure as Craft Across Genres

As Rijlaarsdam et al. (2006, p. 208) highlight, speakers and writers 'must represent a text as not merely a neutral collection of words, but an intentionally arranged selection, intended to communicate a more or less subjective perspective of a state of a world'. Craft lessons on text structures are integral to supporting children in moving beyond word choice to building an appropriate interesting, thought-provoking and innovative framework for their text. For informational texts, the key to this is not only good quality content and expertise on a topic but also linguistic knowledge to create flow, rhythm and fluency within texts, which signal critical information to the reader within and across paragraphs. Several researchers (e.g., Saddler et al., 2004; Graham et al., 2012; de Smedt & Van Keer, 2017) have explored the potential of sentence combining as a strategy given that it has been repeatedly identified as important in teaching students to construct more complex and sophisticated sentences; however, these studies have been critiqued, as very few examine whether the overall quality of written composition is improved. Students may improve their ability to combine sentences, but this may not transfer into more sophisticated writing. However, when sentence combining is taught by drawing on a range of grade-level connectives and transitional phrases, it can bring internal cohesion to a text, and when combined with a language register suited to genre and author purpose, it can create a satisfying 'text' experience for the reader.

Signifying Text Structure

As with all craft lessons, quality literature can be used to help writers develop flow and fluency in their texts. Children in the upper primary may find this challenging (de Smedt & Van Keer, 2017) and will need multiple opportunities to enhance their skills in this regard. In relation to non-fiction writing, children can be guided to choose an organisational structure that suits their purpose e.g., cause/effect, compare/contrast, chronological and/or combinations of these. For naturalist Nic Bishop, selecting the right text structure is particularly important and he spends considerable time pondering the best configuration for his book before he begins writing: *I begin by jotting down all the facts I want to include in the book. At first, they are in no particular order. But over a few weeks I rework everything several times. I like to pay particular attention to the overall structure of the book so that it is informative and yet simple to read in a linear fashion.*

Using appropriate transitions and connectives signals the structure and highlights important information to the reader (see Table 8.4).

Craft mini lessons of this nature can focus on highlighting the transitional words and phrases in context and discussing how the language contributes to cohesion, flow and signal the comparisons. In the text below, similarities and differences between turtles and tortoises are highlighted:

> Though, frogs and toads share some similarities, there are also key differences which can help you differentiate between them. They are both amphibians, meaning they can **survive** on land and in water. However, the frog is more comfortable in water than on land. Frogs have **smooth, sleek** skin which always looks **moist** even when they are out of the water. Toads on the other hand, have skin that looks **bumpy and lumpy** and **wart-like** and it is nearly always dry. Another difference is in the length of their legs. Frogs' legs are longer than their head and body **combined**, while a toad's legs are **short**. Frogs are **agile** and travel by **leaping** from place to place. By contrast, toads are **squat** creatures who crawl rather than jump.
>
> (Authors' text)

Attention could also be drawn to other word-level crafts that the authors have employed alongside the transitional phrases: alliteration (smooth sleek), precise verbs (survive, leaping,

Table 8.4 Sample transitions and connectives signalling compare/contrast

Compare	Contrast	Other Phrases
• Both	• Instead of	• For instance,
• Too	• Another difference	• For example,
• Also	• But	• In particular,
• Another	• However	• Therefore,
• Have in common	• On the other hand	• Moreover,
• Share the same	• By contrast	• Furthermore,
• By comparison	• Differences include	• As a result,
• Similarly		• Usually,

crawl, combined), precise adjectives (moist, bump, lumpy, wart-like, short, agile, squat). Have a second mentor text on hand (e.g., Frogs, Nic Bishop, 2008, p. 6) and during the guided practice part of the mini lesson, ask students to identify the structure and add any new phrases to the anchor chart. Students can also be encouraged to use such phrases and high-level vocabulary in oral presentations and discussions.

Crafting an Engaging Lead

The opening page(s) of a text are recognised as critically important and may determine whether or not a potential reader will continue to read or leave the text aside. Story leads can be explored using as wide a range of fiction and writing styles as possible, linked to student interest and stage of development. It is best to explore leads as a theme across a week using the gradual releases of responsibility model to identify techniques (view 2nd class video: crafting story leads: www.writetoread.ie).

Leads are important in fiction, but they are just as critical in disciplinary and informational texts. As Heard (2013, p.60) argues 'a lead is a doorway into writing. The first sentence or paragraph in any piece of writing needs to invite the reader in and capture the reader's attention'. Aronson, a historian who enjoys writing for children and adolescents as well as adults, has this to say about openings:

BOX 8.3 SAMPLE MINI LESSON ON STORY LEADS (3RD/4TH CLASSES)	Teacher Notes
	Resources
	Pick two texts with different story lead techniques for contrast.
Resources: *The Christmas Miracle of Jonathan Twomey:* E. Wojciechowski; Illustrator P.J. Lynch; *Charlotte's Web:* E.B. White Anchor chart paper	
Step 1: Explain (1-3 minutes) *Today writers we are going to learn a new technique that writers use. Authors use many different techniques when writing the first page of their story. They know how important that first page is and try to write in a way that draws the reader in, into wanting to read on to find out what happens next. The first page of a story is called a story lead. Today we are going to examine some leads and explore some of the techniques that the authors used to hook us in. This will help us with our own writing.*	**Step 1: Explain** Notice that the lesson begins with a statement rather than asking who knows what a story lead is. Briefly state the focus of today's mini lesson and how crafting an engaging story lead will hook the reader to read on.

(Continued)

Step 2: Demonstrate by Thinking Aloud (about 5-6 minutes)

Read the opening page aloud and then share your thinking.

The author introduces us to the main character Jonathan Toomey whose name is also in the title. We find out a few important things about Jonathan. We find out that Jonathan is not happy: he rarely smiles or laughs; he gives out/complains all the time: about the noise the children make when playing, the birds' singing annoys him and the church bells are too loud. These details make me wonder why he is always angry. What happened to make him feel like this?

Another thing I notice is that the author tells us about the setting: where the story takes place: it happens in a village. I think from the picture it happened a long time ago: the buildings and the way the people are dressed are clues.

Another thing I notice is that the author uses rhyming words: gloomy/Toomey; She also uses lots of 'ing' words in the same sentence: I can get a picture of him in my mind walking around: mumbling and grumbling, muttering and sputtering, grumping and griping. So that's three things the author did: I am going to add them to my anchor chart on how to do a good story lead:

> **Creating Good Story Leads**
> 1. Introduce the main character and give some details (e.g., name in the title; not happy, doesn't smile, complains: makes us wonder why?
> 2. Introduce the setting (time period/place)
> 3. Use rhyming words for effect: describe character actions.

Say to the class: *Did you see what I did? I read the page and looked at the pictures and then I really thought about the words and what the author was doing. Now you can have a go. Read the opening page of Charlotte's Web with your partner and discuss what techniques the author used to get us hooked on the story. Be ready to share what we should add to the Story Leads chart.*

Step 2: Demonstrate

Craft a think-aloud in your own words to verbalise the techniques the authors are using to engage the reader.

Ask children to notice what you did in your think-aloud.

The thinking-aloud step allows children 'see' the invisible processes in a writer's head and consider the choices they make when writing.

(Continued)

Step 3: Guided Practice (5 minutes)
In pairs children read and discuss the opening page. They should notice:

- the dramatic opening line: "Where's papa going with that axe?"
- dialogue between two characters: Fern a major character and her mother, Mrs. Arable a minor character.
- dialogue reveals that Fern and her mother react very differently to the news that Mr. Arable is on his way to kill the runt of the pig litter; the author uses strong words instead of said (replied, continued, shrieked) and punctuation for effect (?!)
- setting is introduced: hog-house and farm; the time period is not modern: (papa, pitcher of cream on the table, axe)

As the children work in pairs, circulate and scaffold their efforts. Take contributions and add to the anchor chart:

Creating Good Story Leads

1. Create a dramatic opening line
2. Use dialogue to introduce characters
3. Include major/minor characters
4. Use punchy words for said and punctuation marks (!?) to convey tone of voice for dramatic effect

---

Step 4: Independent Writing (20 minutes)
Invite students to think about their story lead if they are about to begin a new story or if they are revising a story to consider revising it using one of the techniques: but remember, it is an invitation to students not an order!

Step 5: Share session Reflect/Set Goals (about 5-7 minutes)
Have three to four children share their writing. If they changed their story lead, incorporating one or more of the techniques explored in the mini lesson, praise children for their efforts in applying new knowledge. Reflect on what has been learned about story leads. How do story leads enhance writing? Why is it important to think about story leads? What was easy? What was hard? Set a goal for the next session. Children should make a copy of the ideas on the chart and put them into the mini-lesson section of the folder

---

Step 3: Guided Practice
In pairs, children should read the opening page and identify the techniques the author used and say why they think it a good lead. Add their ideas to the anchor chart.

See Figure 6.4: Anchor chart: Creating Story Leads

Step 4: Independent Writing
As the children write, conference with four or five children. Focus on their strengths and what they are trying to accomplish in their text rather than on errors.

Step 5: Share, reflect, set goals
Naming and describing what was learned, why it was learned and how it enhances a piece of writing builds children's metacognition. Metacognition is awareness: knowing about strategies, how they work and when and why the strategy is useful.

(Continued)

Formative Assessment Opportunities throughout the Workshop	Assess children's level of meta-cognition:
After the think-aloud, can children describe what they saw you do? • During guided practice can children apply what they saw you model? Note who can and who is unsure. Do you need to conduct another think-aloud or convene a small group to reinforce the message? • Take brief notes as you conference with children. • During the share session, ask who began a new story today and if they used any of the techniques on the anchor chart. Ask if anyone revised their lead before continuing and invite them to share. • As children reflect and set goals, take notes on who is able to name, give examples of and explain the purpose of the mini lesson on leads.	**Declarative** *(can name the strategy)* **Procedural** *(can give some examples)* **Conditional level** *(can name it, give examples, say how it enhances writing and **why** an author chose that technique to open the book)* Use the assessment notes to plan follow-up lessons
Follow-up Work Across the Week On subsequent days, begin the mini lesson by reviewing the anchor chart and briefly discussing the importance of a good lead. Provide time for children to work in pairs: or mixed-ability groups and to read the first page of their library book. Challenge them to add to the anchor chart. Ask children how many techniques an author used in the story lead. Why might the author have selected a particular technique? Why is it effective?	Continue to build the range of techniques across the week. Steer children toward the understanding that a good lead draws on several techniques at once and sets the tone for the piece.

When I wrote my biography of Robert Kennedy, one of the challenges I had is Robert Kennedy was so defined by his place in the family that I did not feel I could begin the book with 'Robert Fitzgerald Kennedy was born on...' because that would be as if he was an individual. So, the way I wrote that first page, he is not mentioned until the very last word on the first page. The page is about his brothers...because you need to feel how overwhelmed he was by the family that surrounded him.

(Aronson, interview, no date: www.readingrockets.org)

As children have been introduced to the concept of a good lead in fiction, they can build on that knowledge to consider how non-fiction authors also attend to the opening page of their book. One way to do that is to gather a range of good quality non-fiction books and through pair work ask children to consider how the non-fiction book opens. How is it similar/different from a fictional piece? A Venn diagram can be utilised to capture their discoveries. Leads are also genre-specific (see Box 8.4): a lead in a persuasive text will differ from an informational text. Consider how the writers (Figure 8.9 and Figure 8.11a/8.11b) hooked the reader.

> ### BOX 8.4 LEADS IN PERSUASIVE WRITING
>
> - A rhetorical question
> - Powerful emotive language
> - Use a personal pronoun
> - A focused statement of the issue

Of course, as noted earlier, for this to be effective, the informational texts must attend to craft as well as content. Ask children to experiment with a number of different leads for their piece before settling on one and choose a lead that sets the tone for their text. In the extract from a report on Hurricane Katrina below (Figure 8.4), the writer (a child for whom English is an additional language) opens in narrative form conveying a sense of a New Orleans on a typical day with music wafting through the air before introducing a sense of foreboding. Though perhaps the word choice is somewhat exaggerated and needs refining for impact, the writer has succeeded in painting a scene:

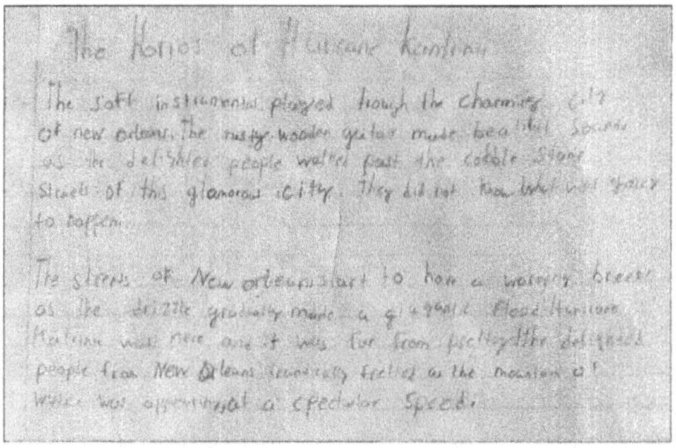

The Horros of Hurricane Kantrina
The soft instrumental played trough the charming city of new orleans. The rusty wooden guitar made beautiful sounds as the delighted people walked past the cobblestone streets of this glamorous city. They did not know what was going to happen.
The streets of New orleans start to have a worrying breeze as the drizzle gradually made a gigantic flood. Hurricane Katrina was here and it was far from pretty.
the delighted people from New Orleans frantically fretted as the mountain of water was appearing at a spectacular speed.
(typed as written)

Figure 8.4 A lead that paints a scene: *The Horros of Hurricane Katrina* (6th class pupil)
Source: Write to Read

Craft Mini Lessons 167

For a more sophisticated example (Figure 8.5), see below. In this example, the writer draws the reader in with a variety of literary devices: setting the scene, creating mystery, alliteration (*swirling shoal*); descriptive detail (*worried eyes, small, lonely turtle, you'd mistake for a bottle top*); vivid verbs: *saunter*; similes (*shell as soft as cotton, eats like a ravenous beast, as big as dinner plate*). Yet this writer also presents important facts about the young turtle and how it grows and develops. Disciplinary sentence construction such as writing in the present tense is also employed. Leads are also genre-specific (see Box 8.4)

Using the Write to Read Rubric to Guide Planning for Text Structure

The importance of text structure is captured in the *Write to Read* rubric within the *Organisation* component. Like *word choice and voice*, it contains several sub-components to break down the process for assessment and planning purposes. The first subcomponent **Overall Structure** highlights the development of the beginning, middle and end in narratives; introduction, development and conclusion in other genres and as text increases in length and complexity, the development of paragraphs and sections within a text. Second, it provides guidance on expanding children's repertoire of **Transitions and Connectives** to generate flow, rhythm and sentence complexity sensitive to the needs of the particular genre. For example, transitions in informational text will differ considerably from narrative text. In narrative text, pace and rhythm may be achieved through a balance of dialogue and descriptive text whereas in non-fiction it may be achieved through headings and subheadings or transitional phrases which signal structures such as cause and effect, compare and contrast or chronology. Like the *Word Choice* components, we have also included examples of increasingly more mature transitions and connectives as prompts when considering these kinds

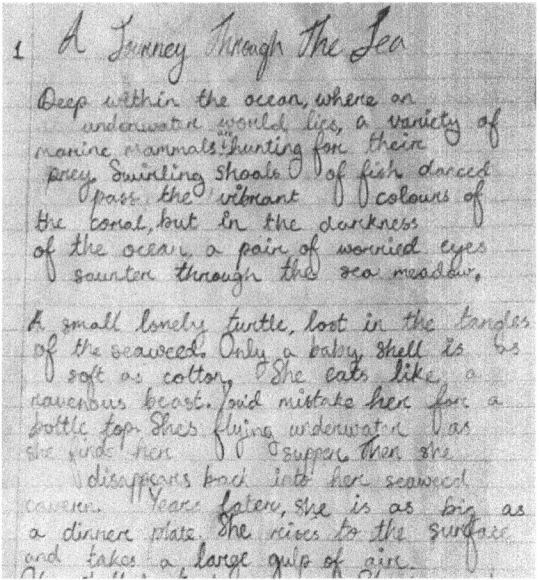

A Journey Through the Sea
Deep within the ocean, where an underwater world lies, a variety of marine mammals are hunting for their prey. Swirling shoals of fish dance past the vibrant colours of the coral, but in the darkness of the ocean, a pair of worried eyes saunter through the sea meadow. A small lonely turtle, lost in the tangles of the seaweed. Only a baby, shell is as soft as cotton. She eats like a ravenous beast. You'd mistake her for a bottle top. She's flying underwater as she finds her supper. Then she disappears back into her seaweed cavern. Years later she is as big as a dinner plate. She rises to the surface and takes a gulp of air.
(Typed as written)

Figure 8.5 A lead that paints a scene: *A journey through the sea* (6th Class)
Source: Write to Read

of craft mini lessons (see Chapter 5). As highlighted above, good quality mentor texts are essential to these lessons to avoid constrained formulaic templates, which have been identified as a limitation of genre study (Derewianka, 2015).

Using the Write-to-Read Rubric to Enhance Genre Knowledge

Key features of genre-specific structures are highlighted in the rubric under **Narrative (Fiction), Persuasive, Report, Recount and Procedural.** As noted in Chapter 3 there are several critiques of genre study which should be borne in mind when planning a unit of work in a particular genre. While genre knowledge is important, teaching it requires a thoughtful and creative approach to avoid children following the features like a recipe in a 'lockstep manner' which can result in a formulaic text that over-emphasises elements of genre at the expense of creativity (Kennedy & Shiel, 2019). This is less likely to happen if children are choosing their own inquiries and topics when engaging in writing informational genres and they have had sufficient time to plan and research their topics (see Chapter 7).

A traditional genre approach involves extensive teacher modelling and collaborative writing often resulting in insufficient time for children to write independently in the genre. Adopting a writing workshop approach to genre study ensures that children write in the genre from day one of a unit of work and are apprenticed into the genre through mini lessons which build their repertoire of techniques from one unit to the next and from year to year. Furthermore, Derewianka (2015) argues attention should be given to subgenres such as historical recounts (under the broad umbrella of recounts), rather than focusing only on major genres (see Chapter 3).

BOX 8.5 SUB-GENRES OF PERSUASIVE WRITING

- Opinion
- Advertising: brochures, travel, products
- Emails/Letters e.g. complaint
- Debates
- Reviews: books, movies, products
- Blogs
- Speeches
- Political pamphlets
- Editorials
- Imaginative: Fiction

Subgenres provide many more nuanced ways in to the language, tone and structure of writing within a genre (Box 8.5). In addition to exploring mentor texts, children can be guided to analyse videos of orators giving speeches (Box 8.6). In persuasive writing, speeches and debates require as much attention to oral delivery-conscious of body language, gesture and eye contact – as to the content, tone and structure, while a letter of complaint (Figure 8.9) will differ from an advertisement enticing you to buy a product or travel to a particular destination (Figure 8.11a/ 8.11b).

BOX 8.6 GRETA THUNBERG SPEECH	Read, watch and analyse
https://www.theguardian.com/environment/2019/apr/23/greta-thunberg-full-speech-to-mps-you-did-not-act-in-time	

An easy introduction to persuasive writing with young children is to begin with opinion pieces whereby children state what they think, believe or prefer (Figures 8.7 and 8.8) and can be scaffolded to provide evidence for their views (Figure 8.6). Children learn to listen to other points of view and how to present their own viewpoints in a constructive manner providing an early induction to critical life skills.

As noted in Chapter 7, if persuasive writing is to be effective, it must be founded on solid research and inquiry. In an age of misinformation and disinformation, persuasive writing teaches children to question what they read, fact-check across multiple sources and check that the sources they themselves are using are reliable. Learning how to research teaches children that when they write persuasively, it must present an accurate, current and unbiased text. In the persuasive sample (Figure 8.9), a letter of complaint to a sports manufacturer, the writer conducts research to support the complaint and uses a range of persuasive crafts (at times highly exaggerated) to convey dissatisfaction.

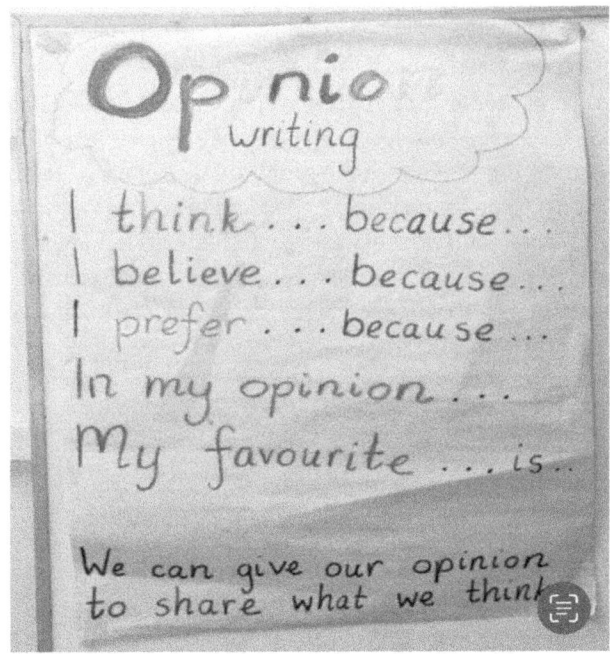

Figure 8.6 Anchor chart: Persuasive Writing with Junior/Senior Infants

Source: Write to Read

170 Teaching and Assessing Writing in the Primary School

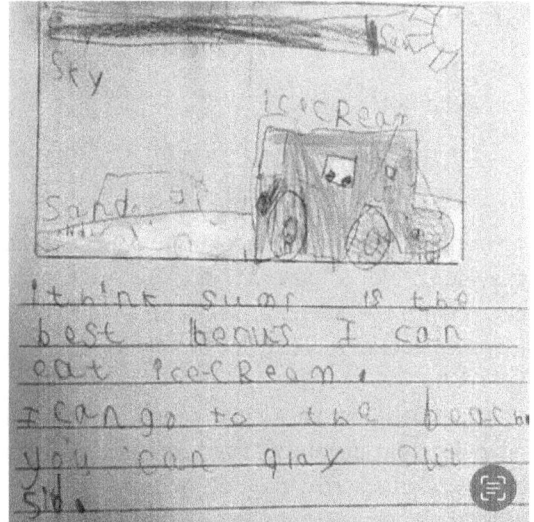

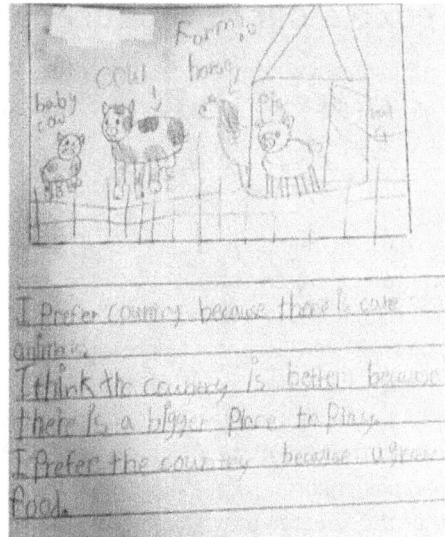

Figure 8.7 Opinion writing, Junior Infants
I think sumr is the
best becus I can
eat ice-cream.
I can go to the beach.
you can play out
sid.

Figure 8.8 Opinion writing, Senior Infants
I prefer country because there is cute
animals.
I think the country is better because
there is a bigger place to play.
I prefer the country because u grow
food.

More recently, the field of literacy has shifted from a content or generic genre approach to informational writing to a more disciplinary focus (see Shanahan, 2019 for a discussion). Ippolito et al. (2019, p. 16) argue that "age-appropriate disciplinary literacy ways of thinking and working can … begin to be taught in age-appropriate ways as early as kindergarten". In this perspective, writers are not taught generic genre features but are inducted into thinking, reading, talking and writing like historians, scientists, mathematicians, artists or musicians. They begin to see literacy as a social practice and to appreciate the nuances between different disciplines.

The writing will also be mediated by consideration of the intended audience (e.g., the age and expertise of a six-year-old will differ from that of an upper primary or post-primary pupil). These are all important variables to bring to children's attention when generating ideas, planning, drafting and revising their texts. Nic Bishop, an award-winning naturalist writing for children highlights his process when creating a new book:

> I begin by jotting down all the facts I want to include in the book. At first, they are in no particular order. But over a few weeks I rework everything several times. I like to pay particular attention to the overall structure of the book, so that it is informative and yet simple to read in a linear fashion.

(Nic Bishop, https://www.nicbishop.com/)

To whom it may concern,

I am flabbergasted and utterly bemused by the fact that your worldwide organisation think it's acceptable to sell a faulty product.

I am writing to complain about the Nike air Huarache which clearly has a manufactori. fault. Since the re-establishment of the Nike air Huarache, I have been considering buying a pair but fellow classmates have informed me about the fault. The fault in question is that the plastic on the back continuously snaps.

Recently I investigated how many students in the senior end of our school had purchased the Nike air Huarache. In the senior end of our school, 45 pairs have been purchased, out of the 45, 33 have broken meaning that a staggering 73% are faulty! This is a shocking statistic on your behalf and you must rectify this fault immediately. In 6th class alone 19 students have purchased 30 pairs, In 5th class 10 students have purchased 10 pairs and in 3 & 4th class 4 students have purchased 5 pairs making it a net spend of €4860.

I am afraid that we'll have no other alternative but to stop purchasing this product if you don't fix the fault. I'll have you know that I'm 12 years of age. Do you think that if you keep producing faulty goods I'll be purchasing this product in ten years? Do you not think that we have started looking at your competitors? Already 5 students have purchased the Adidas ZX flux.

This exodus will continue unless you do something rapidly.

While I wish to stay loyal to all your Nike based products as i've done throughout the years, you need to understand that I expect quality when you produce shoes like these.

Please clean up your act or I will be forced to stop purchasing your products.

With Anticipation,

Figure 8.9 Persuasive writing: A letter of complaint (6th class)

Source: Write to Read

172 *Teaching and Assessing Writing in the Primary School*

In the sample below (Figures 8.10a and 8.10b), we can see that the writer (6th class) chose an effective structure for a report on a night in the life of a bat. Told in a circular chronological sequence in narrative form, it traces the bat's journey from dusk to dawn and back to dusk, with the final sentence echoing the title. Table 8.5 provides an analysis of the disciplinary and aesthetic qualities evidenced in the text.

> **The Life Of A Bat**
>
> Deep within the dark depths of the forest, The forest creatures rest their eyes and fall asleep, but as these animals drift it is just morning for some. The deafening silence of the night is soon brocken by natures nocturnal nemisis. Wings flap at furios speed as mother bat awakes from her slumber.
>
> She is upside down as uasual, her toenails gripping from the crunchy crooked branch. Her weary eyes open, her pixie ears twitch. She shakes her furry, fuzzy har, and unfolds her paper thin wings that reveal her bones.
>
> She unhooks her toes and drops into A freefall. The sky around her is a pitch black blanket of dark with A sharp icy wind which flows into her face. Her webbed wings slowly begin to flap, bat is flying.
>
> She glides though the misty air, all is silent. Through towering trees, over beautiful bushes, under gargantuan gates... She swoops untouched. Bat floats through the air like a fish in the water. She doesn't see, she can hear were she's going, anyways exellent ears are more usefull than eyes in the dark
>
> Bat howls as she flies, louder than a firework, higher than A squeel. She echoes her voice around like A torch. listening hard, she can hear the snap of A twig, the blow of A leaf. A fat, jucy moth hovers beneath hear, He is unaware that shes there.

Figure 8.10a and Figure 8.10b Report writing: *Life of a Bat*, p.1 and p.2, 6th class
Source: Write to Read

> She dives down as quick as can be, resembling a polar bear plunging through ice, searching for it's prey. She grabs it in her mouth, but it's slippery, slimy body slides out. She goes in. Her razer sharp teeth catching the tip of the wing. She bites hard and the moths wings come trickling down like raindrops. Soon the moth is gobbled down her petite stomach.
>
> Hunting time has run out. Her nocturnal necessities requires her to return to comfortable cavern. She returns home were her fifty battlings are waiting impaitently for their dinner. She grips her toes once again on the branch, as her babys scrap and scuffle to get onto her fur. As her baby is wrapped in her old leather wings they suck on her milk.
>
> Outside were birds chirp and people are awakening for their day, She rests through the blinding sunlight, ready for her next sleeping session. When she awakes she will reaper the process all over again. This is the life of a bat.

Figure 8.10a and Figure 8.10b Continued

Table 8.5 Evidence of mini lesson transfer to non-fiction/informational writing Figures 8.10a and 8.10b

Craft of Writing	Mini lessons Evidenced in the Sample
Lead Painting a scene	• Deep within the dark depths of the forest, the forest creatures rest their eyes and fall asleep bust as these animals drift, it is just morning for some
Alliteration/literary phrase to create a sense of time, habitat	• Deep within the dark depths of the forest • Nature's nocturnal nemesis • Crunchy crooked branch • Slippery slimy body slides out as she goes in • Her nocturnal necessities require her to return to her comfortable cavern

(Continued)

Table 8.5 (Continued)

Craft of Writing	Mini lessons Evidenced in the Sample
Present tense	• The forest creatures rest their eyes and fall asleep but as these animals drift it just morning for some • Multiple examples throughout the text
Precise Adjective	• Deafening silence • Paper thin wings • Pitch black blanket of darkness • Sharp icy wind • Petite stomach
Adjectives and Verbs for effect	• Wings flap at furious speed • Her weary eyes open • Shakes her furry fuzzy hair • A fat juicy moth hovers beneath her, he is unaware that she's there • Her razor-sharp teeth catching the tip of the wing • As her baby is wrapped on her old leather wings they suck on her milk • She rests through the blinding sunlight ready for her next sleeping session
Precise noun	• Awakes from her slumber • Pixie ears twitch
Precise verb	• Reveal her bones • Unhooks her toes and drops into a freefall • She glides through the misty air, all is silent • Gobbled • Grips her toes once again on the branch as her babies scrap and scuffle to get on her ear • Birds chirp
Adverb	• Waiting impatiently
Commas in elaborated sentence	• Through towering trees, over beautiful bushes, under gargantuan gates, she swoops untouched • She can hear the snap of a twig, the blow of a leaf
Simile	• Bat floats through the air like a fish in the water • Bat howls as she flies, louder than a firework, higher than a squeal • She echoes her voice around like a torch, listening hard • She dives down as quick as can be resembling a polar bear plunging through ice searching for its prey • She bites hard and the moth's wings come trickling down like raindrops
Structure	• Begins at night and takes us through Bat's journey from dusk to dawn; each paragraph gives us new information and helps us visualise her journey while giving us plenty of information on the life of a bat
Final sentences allude to the title	• She will repeat the process all over again. This is the life of a bat

Informational writing can also link well with persuasive writing. As children engage in inquiry across the curriculum, they may decide to present their findings as a factual report or to write their report using a different genre form (see Chapter 10) as can be seen in Figures 8.11a/8.11b. This young writer presents her report in the form of a persuasive narrative, seeking to entice tourists to choose France as their next destination.

> **Fantastic France**
>
> Bonjour you terrific tourists. Would you like to visit the most magnifique country in the world?
>
> Come to France, it is the most popular tourist destination in Europe. France welcomes some 89 million visitors annually. Why don't you be the next?
>
> French love eating out. French like a lot of food. Here are some foods french like to eat:
> macarons, macarons are these dilicious sweet cookies filled with butter cream.
>
> Next are crepes. Crepes can be sweet or thay can be savoury. thay are often filled with hot chocolate sause. Or somtimes thay can be filled with fruit. Delicious!
> Next is croissants. Croissants are typically used for a delicous Breakfast, but can also be eaten & filled with ham and cheese for a more filling meal later during the day.
>
> P.1

Figure 8.11a and Figure 8.11b Persuasive writing: *Fantastic France*, p.1 and 2, 2nd class
Source: Write to Read

French also eat snails. The French word for snails is escargot. thay usually eat them with garlick butter to get that mouth-watering scrumptious taste.

Paris is the Copital City of France. It is also one the most popular tourist destinations in the world. known as the City of love for its romantic setting, you can see some of the best landmarks the world has to offer. The world' Famous Eiffel tower is an iron tower. It was construced from 1887 to 1889. It is 324 metres tall, about the same height as an 81-story building. You can visit the Eiffel tower and go right to the top, and see the spectacular and stunning view.

The second greatest sight to see is the palace of Versailles use to be the main palace for the royal famly. The palace is huge & some of the furniture was made of solit silver it truly is magnique! So what are you waiting for? Book France as your holiday destination. You will not be disappointed! À bientôt!

P. 2

Figure 8.11a and Figure 8.11b Continued

While the sample above (Figures 8.11a and 8.11b) shows evidence of excellent research, writer 'voice' and passion for the topic, it could have been further developed into a multimodal ensemble complemented with photos and inclusion of some headings and subheadings.

Reflect, Connect, Act

1. Identify the craft techniques used in Figure 8.9 and Figure 8.11a/8.11b What do these children know about the art of persuasion when writing? What craft mini lessons might the teacher have taught?
2. Examine a writing sample of a high-, middle- and lower-achieving writer in your class for a genre of your choice. Examine the writing for evidence of 'word consciousness' and structure). How would you rate:
    - The level and precision of descriptive language? Is it at, below or above expectations for this class level?
    - The level and quality of the transitions and connectives linking ideas within and across paragraphs?
    - The range of structural and organisational features of the writing? Suitability for the genre?
    - Are children using the full range of literary and poetic devices? Are there any gaps?
3. How might you use this assessment data to plan craft lessons to meet children's needs?

Suggestions for Further Reading

1. https://ncte.org/statement/role-of-nonfiction-literature-k-12/print/
2. https://www.slj.com/story/nonfiction-as-mentor-text-style-on-common-core
3. Dalton, B. (2014). Level up with multimodal composition in social studies. *The Reading Teacher, 68(4)*, 296-302.

9 Conventions Mini Lessons
Developing Accuracy in Writing across Genres

This chapter focuses on how conventions (spelling, grammar and punctuation) can be developed in parallel with the craft dimensions of writing. Drawing on relevant research, it outlines methodologies and assessment tools to support differentiated classroom instruction in these secretarial skills.

> **Reflect and Connect**
> 1. Why is there a need to balance attention between lower- and higher-order writing skills?
> 2. Consider the research presented in Chapter 2. How can our understanding of what is involved in developing spelling, punctuation and grammar be incorporated into the writing process?

I have like a column for what we've been working on that day or week and then I also have like an additional comment for anything I notice...that helps me plan the next lessons or like small group work on something that's not clicking, just because they might need a different approach to it.

(Junior Infant teacher)

Balancing Attention to Constrained and Unconstrained Skills

The teacher in the quote above is clearly invested in formative assessment practices and has procedures in place to capture valuable data on the secretarial aspects of children's writing that require further attention. We can infer that she keeps records of children's mastery of specific learning outcomes and is attuned to the need for a variety of approaches and small group work when particular children have not fully grasped new concepts. Rather than a one-size-fits-all whole class lesson with everyone learning the same skill at the same time, such responsive assessment means that children receive timely differentiated instruction when they have demonstrated both a need and a readiness for a particular skill, process or craft.

Some researchers (e.g., Troia et al., 2009, p. 99) have criticised writing workshop and process-based approaches for variability in attention to spelling and other transcription skills (e.g., handwriting, keyboarding) which they argue rarely receive 'more than a passing nod' within workshop classrooms and as a result, writing quality is adversely affected. Other researchers highlight the need for a better instructional and assessment balance between lower- and higher-level processes of writing, particularly in the early years, as mechanical aspects are often over-emphasised and over-assessed in these classrooms (e.g., Casey et al., 2016; Daffern et al., 2017). Paris (2005) argues for parallel attention to what he terms the 'constrained skills' (e.g., phonics, decoding, encoding/spelling, handwriting) and 'unconstrained skills' (e.g. vocabulary, comprehension, writing expression across genres), as the latter continue to grow and develop across the life span, contributing to enhanced reading and writing achievement.

While Chapters 7 and 8 have focused on the development of unconstrained skills and processes, in this chapter we explore how the research on conventions (see Chapter 2) can be harnessed to inform the teaching and assessment of these dimensions of writing. In our work with schools, early constrained literacy skills are addressed in multiple ways: both in context (e.g. shared reading, shared and interactive writing, reading and writing workshop) and out of context in discrete word work sessions. This is necessary to ensure explicit systematic sequential structured attention to alphabetics which can then be reinforced through authentic application within contexts such as sentences and longer texts. Drawing on a range of research (e.g. NICHHD, NRP, 2000; Torgerson et al., 2019; ILA, 2020) we work with teachers to ensure parallel attention to stages of phonological awareness, phonics and spelling while bearing in mind that 'programs that focus too much on the teaching of letter-sounds relations and not enough on putting them to use are unlikely to be very effective' (NRP, 2000, pp. 2–96). *Write to Read* coaches, who themselves are practising classroom teachers who also support partner schools, have been able to lead by example and demonstrate to teachers with examples from their own classrooms how they balance attention to skill development. In the example below, the coach illustrates how analysis of writing samples combined with conferencing notes and the *Write to Read Writing Rubric* supports her planning:

> *I'm sitting down with the samples, and I just started anecdotal notes today beside my conferencing notes...So, I can really see like conventions, high frequency, you know basic punctuation that you'd kind of expect to be there at this stage isn't there, and then I also want to draw in a craft as well alongside it... the ideas piece seems to be pretty good, but the word choice is weak.*
>
> (Write to Read Coach)

Such powerful examples have been pivotal in convincing teachers that a dual focus is possible, and that such instructional density ensures children's writing progresses along multiple dimensions at the same time.

Supporting Development of Conventions in the Context of Writing

There are a number of approaches to supporting children's writing development in the early stages, prior to introducing the writing workshop, where important work can be done on developing children's understanding of writing conventions. These approaches include shared writing and interactive writing.

Shared Writing

A shared writing approach is an engaging way to induct children into a writing life and to promote writing as a creative social purposeful act. In shared writing, the children choose what they would like to write about (the topic) and the teacher acts as their scribe. The topic can be imaginative or linked to particular genres or integrated across the curriculum. As has been highlighted in Chapters 2 and 6, offering a choice of topic is key to motivation. In shared writing, the teacher and children discuss the topic and they work together to communicate ideas in writing. The teacher records the children's writing ideas on a chart or interactive screen by modelling aspects of the writing process such as:

- Concepts of print, e.g., left to right, spaces between words, punctuation.
- Approximate spelling of unfamiliar words by segmenting syllables, stretching sounds and matching letters to phonemes.
- How to use the alphabetised word wall for spelling words.
- How to use environmental print in the room for spelling words.
- How to combine ideas and elaborate on them while writing.
- How to add description, build context and choose precise apt words.
- How to revise ideas and word choice.
- How to proofread.
- How to publish and present writing.

Shared writing is a valuable way for teachers to model all aspects of the writing process and to explicitly teach key concepts. After the chart has been constructed, it can be read aloud and utilised to reinforce key concepts, vocabulary, high-frequency words and phonics (Figure 9.1). Children are invited up to the chart to identify high-frequency words (box around them) and to circle particular sounds or parts of words that they have learned. Noticing these in print is a beneficial activity that supports young writers in reviewing known concepts in a meaningful context.

Interactive Writing

Interactive writing (see McCarrier & Pinnell, 2000; Williams, 2018) builds on the concept of shared writing as the teacher and children *share the pen*. It can be used to teach key features of particular genres in authentic ways and to encourage children to be more precise in their word choice. In relation to using and consolidating conventions, children are invited to participate in the physical act of writing on the chart (Figure 9.2a/9.2b). Calling on children to

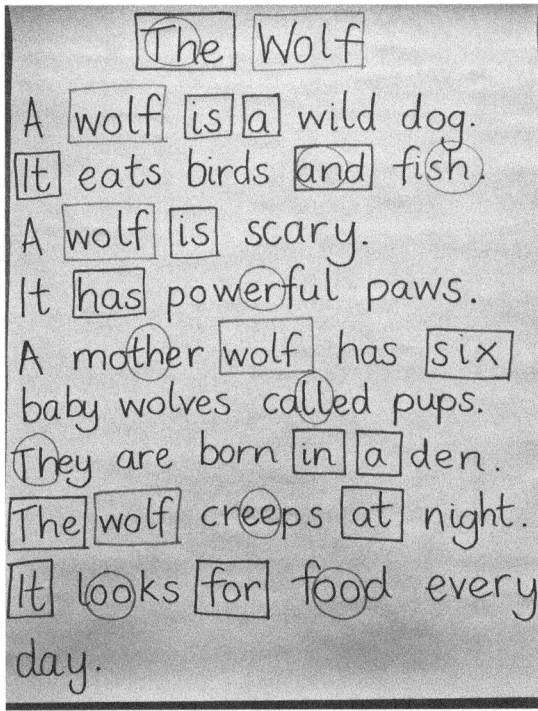

Figure 9.1 Shared writing chart: *The wolf*, Junior Infants, Key words boxed letter patterns circled

Source: Roche, 2017- Junior Infants, Key words boxed; letter patterns circled

write particular words or sounds that they are familiar with and can spell, supports them in applying their knowledge in a real context.

It is also an opportunity for teachers to model invented spelling of words that are ambitious and show children that not all words need to be spelled correctly on a rough draft and can be checked later by using our writing tools e.g. environmental print in the classroom and alphabetised word wall (see Figures 9.3 and 9.4).

Collaborative writing opportunities are essential precursors to the introduction of a writing workshop where children will write independently. These experiences scaffold children into the writing process and show them that what I think I can say, what I say can be written and read back by others (see Chapter 12 for a monthly plan for shared and interactive writing in a Junior Infant class).

Transitioning to Writing Workshop

Children can begin to write their own texts independently after they have experienced extensive shared and interactive writing lessons and have knowledge of some letter-sound relationships and high-frequency words along with an understanding that the written word is a communicative act. Prior to joining the *Write to Read* project, children in partner schools

182 Teaching and Assessing Writing in the Primary School

Figure 9.2a, 9.2b Teacher and child sharing the pen: Interactive report writing Senior Infants
Source: Write to Read images

Conventions Mini Lessons 183

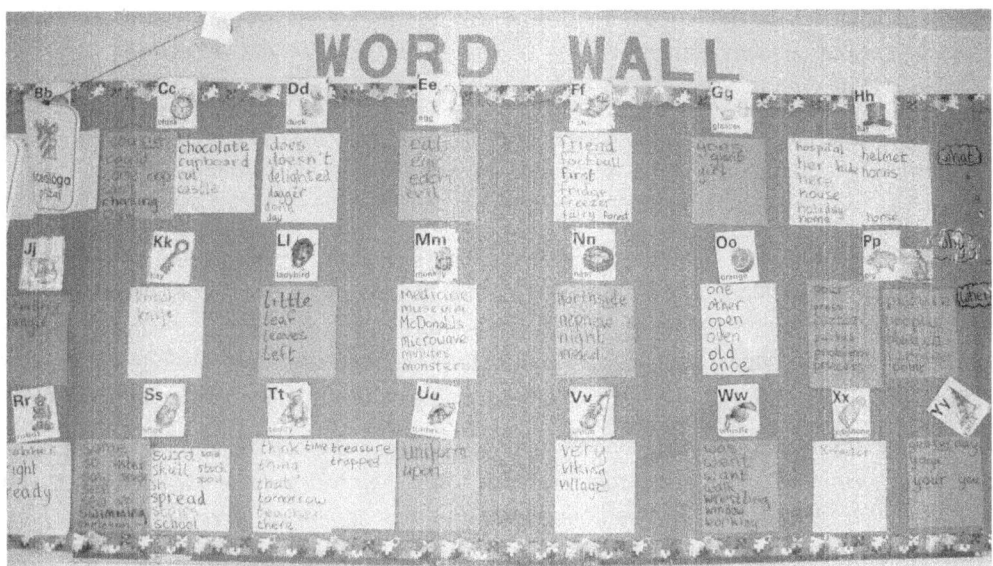

Figure 9.3 Alphabetised word wall
Source: Write to Read images

Figure 9.4 Using environmental print as an aid to spelling during independent writing
Source: Write to Read images

were not expected to write independently and writing was mainly on teacher directed topics, which one of our coaches highlighted was not motivating for teachers or children:

> *Some of the teachers were saying like it was painful, like they were trying to drag it out of them and it was a lot of patterned sentences they'd write, I like, I like, I like and it wasn't really genre-focussed and it wasn't really focussed on a writing process.*
>
> (Write to Read coach)

The *Write to Read* rubric (Chapter 5) helped teachers see that children could write if drawing and invented spelling were viewed as part of a continuum of writing development, that children could write independently, and that they were captivated by the process of inventing ideas to put on paper. Once teachers accepted this, they used the rubric to establish a baseline for each child and began to use the data gathered to plan responsive mini lessons:

> *For the rubric, one week we kind of focussed on like mark making and seeing who was using their letter sound knowledge, who was using their tricky words and then some who were like – working towards sentence formation and some that were legible . . . where someone other than the child or you could decipher it without their help.*
>
> (Junior Infants teacher)

In our partner schools, some teachers introduce children to independent writing in January of Junior Infants (reception year). Others have approached it much earlier, towards the end of the second month of school, but doing so in developmentally appropriate ways:

> *So, you start off basically with teaching them how to draw a good picture, and then that leads on to labelling the things in the picture, which leads on to writing a sentence about the picture.... then you work on developing their sentences after that.*
>
> (Junior Infants, Teacher)

In an interview at the end of the school year, the same teacher highlighted the growth in children's writing and how the daily experiences can enhance writer confidence and enjoyment of writing and establish positive dispositions towards writing:

> *Now, every child is able to make a good stab at writing sentences, most importantly for me as an infant teacher, their willingness to write... it does, I think, make an impact on how they view it as they get into the older classes... in junior infants, when they hear it or see it on the timetable they're like, "Yeah! It's writing workshop," which is lovely, as opposed to "Oh, it's writing."*

As has been highlighted in Chapters 7 and 8, minilessons are at the heart of the writing workshop. These young writers will need continued reinforcement and modelling in mini lessons (see exemplar lesson, Chapter 7, Box 7.6) that demonstrate how to:

- Choose topics of personal significance and brainstorm ideas.
- Draw ideas and label elements of the picture (focus on segmenting at the word level).
- Write sentences related to the picture (acquire concepts of print, use writing tools for support, construct sentences).

- Add to and refine ideas.
- Consider word choice and select interesting and apt vocabulary.
- Proofread and revise writing (may include conventions),
- Present writing to an audience and respond to peers in share sessions.

Teachers have found it beneficial to retain a focus on shared and interactive writing for two days a week as children transition into writing independently in a writing workshop on the other three days (see Chapter 12, Box 12.12). On the shared/interactive writing days, the mini lessons are embedded in the co-construction of the chart and on subsequent days, mini lessons can further build on the content as children write individually on topics of their own choice. In the sections which follow, the role of spelling, phonics and grammar in writing is explored and ways to support them both in and out of authentic contexts are presented.

The Role of Spelling and Transcription in a Writing Workshop

Graves observed that 'spelling more than any other aspect in the school curriculum, is used to mark social status...Indeed, spelling and handwriting marked the educated person. "He can spell and has a good hand" was a high compliment' (1994, p. 255). Almost 30 years later, Putman (2017) in a review of research on spelling, draws attention to the prevailing view that 'the ability to spell correctly is an essential trait of literate people' and referencing Moats (2005) notes that 'making anything beyond a few minor spelling errors is equated with ignorance and incompetence' (p. 24). On the other hand, Graves also put the role of spelling in perspective when he remarked 'I am fond of quoting Harold Rosen: *Any idiot can tell a genius how to spell a word*' (1994, p. 256). How then should children be taught to spell well? How should spelling be assessed in the primary classroom? How can spelling development be supported in the context of a writing workshop?

Putting strategies in place to help children with the mechanical aspects of writing is essential in order to free them up to concentrate on the content of their writing and to mitigate negative effects that gaps in such skills can have on children's confidence and sense of self-efficacy as writers (Snowling, 2000). Such gaps have been found to constrain writers' word choice (see Chapter 2) as students are less likely to choose ambitious words they can't spell (Graham et al., 2012b/2018; Lowe & Bormann, 2012). Thus, there is a delicate balance to be negotiated between fostering creativity in writing and explicitly supporting skill work.

Spelling Development, Assessment and Pedagogy

The English language has a deep or opaque orthography and has been influenced by other languages such as Latin, Greek and French (Dombey, 2006). As such, it has been viewed traditionally as a primarily irregular language with limited regular phoneme-grapheme correspondence, making it a more challenging language for learners to master compared with languages with shallower orthographies (e.g., Spanish, Finnish) (Barnes et al., 2017). Consequently, traditional approaches to spelling development have emphasised rote memorisation of word lists and weekly spelling tests. However, despite its deep orthography, research in the 1960s (Hanna et al., 1965) revealed that English is a logical rule-based language system (albeit with many rules to master), and spelling is about 84% predictable, indicating that phonology, orthography and etymology could be usefully deployed in the service of spelling acquisition. Memorisation is useful for mastery of the remaining 16% of words that are irregular or are exceptions to rules. Children can be taught memorisation strategies to support the retention of these words.

Despite such research findings, the current practice of the Friday test continues to proliferate in classrooms. Putman (2017, p. 25) referred to the weekly test 'as Friday test, Monday miss,' and highlighted research (e.g., Templeton & Morris, 2000; Abbott, 2001) which found 'that students often learned to spell the words correctly for the tests but failed to retain or generalize this knowledge to writing or other language activities'. This research highlights the importance of a multifaceted approach to decoding, encoding and transcribing which includes ample opportunities for children to apply strategies in authentic reading and writing contexts.

> **KEY POINT**
>
> Phonics instruction in the early stages of literacy development is essentially spelling instruction.

As highlighted in Chapter 2, there is ample evidence that the process of *writing* words and the process of *reading* words draw upon the same underlying base of word knowledge (Ehri, 2005; Ehri, 2020). The more pupils know about the structure of words – including their spellings – the more efficient and fluent their reading will be (Gentry, 2000), aligning with Templeton and Morris's view (1999, p. 103) that spelling knowledge is the 'engine that drives efficient reading and writing'.

Historically, research has highlighted that writing is an important approach to beginning reading (Montessori, 1912/1964; Chomsky, 1979; Read, 1975) while Huxford (2006) argues that early phonics instruction is essentially spelling in the early stages of development. This argument is borne out by the early research base. Liberman et al.'s work in the 70s has shown that phonemic segmentation (required for spelling) is necessary for the development of phonemic blending (required for reading) while Frith's model of literacy development (1985) suggests that segmentation is in fact a precursor to phonemic blending.

> **KEY POINT**
>
> Supporting young children with opportunities to spell inventively plays a causal role in later reading development.

Emergent writers use a range of semiotic tools to communicate their ideas (Dyson, 1993; Scull et al., 2020). Moyles (1989) refers to their use as intellectual play. The imagination, creativity and thinking capacities of emergent writers outstrip their transcription skills initially but provision of invented spelling opportunities within authentic writing contexts supports writer agency and assists early writers in capturing their thoughts in written form. More recently,

Ouellette and Sénéchal (2017) have demonstrated that providing such experiences to young writers plays a causal role in later proficient reading development. They argue that invented spelling 'is a highly analytical and engaging process' (p. 86), is instrumental in supporting children in acquiring the alphabetic principle, and results in later higher reading achievement scores, compared to children who learn to spell in the traditional, conventional manner. Such opportunities align with a writing workshop philosophy.

> **KEY POINT**
>
> Supporting young children with opportunities to spell inventively plays a causal role in later reading development.

Reference has been made to a wide range of research in Chapter 2 including stage models of spelling including those of Gentry (2000) and Bear et al. (2012) and triple word form theory (e.g. Berninger et al., 2010; Garcia et al., 2010), which posits that spelling development occurs in more complex ways than represented in stage models and that young writers can draw on and integrate knowledge from each domain (phonology, orthography, morphology) from the outset of learning to spell. Gentry conceptualised spelling as developing across five broad stages or phases. While each stage is distinct in nature, children's writing may exhibit characteristics of more than one stage at a time (Table 9.1).

Bear et al. (2012) use different terminology to describe their five stages and highlight the age ranges at which such development typically occurs (Table 9.2). Knowledge of these stages can assist teachers in identifying which stage children are largely operating in and moving learners up from one stage to the next. Bear et al. (2012) have developed three spelling inventories (Primary: K-3rd grade; Elementary: 3rd-5th grade; Upper Level: 5th to secondary school; all available online) which can be used to assess children's stage of development and to provide differentiated small group instruction along the continuum

Table 9.1 Gentry's (2000) stages of spelling development

Precommunicative	Demonstrates no knowledge of letter-sound correspondences, spelling efforts appear to be a random string of letters, numbers, scribbles
Semi-phonetic	Partial phonetic representation, with one, two or three letters selected to represent the whole word
Phonetic	Dominant sound features of the word are represented and almost all is decodable without the child's help
Transitional	Vowels occur in every syllable; vowel digraphs and inflectional endings appear; there is evidence of moving from phonological to morphological and visual spelling
Correct	Evidence of extended knowledge of word structure including accurate spelling of prefixes, suffixes, contractions and compound words, ability to distinguish homonyms; English orthographic system firmly established

Source: Summarised from Gentry (2000)

Table 9.2 Bear et al.'s (2012) stages of spelling development

Stage of Development	Age Range	Example
Stage 1 *Emergent Spelling*	3-5-year-olds	Scribble, strings and letter-like forms; No phoneme association to mark making
Stage 2 *Letter Name Alphabetic Spelling*	5-7-year-olds	Represents phonemes in words with letters; short vowels, blends, digraphs in evidence
Stage 3 *Within Word Pattern Spelling*	7-9-year-olds	Long vowel sounds appear, may confuse meat/meet
Stage 4 *Syllables and Affixes Spelling*	9-11-year-olds	Uses knowledge of one-syllable words to spell multi-syllabic words; uses inflectional endings
Stage 5 *Derivational Relations Spelling*	11-14-year-olds	Learn to use Greek/Latin roots; Notices words similar in meaning have similar spelling: nation

Source: Summarised from Putman (2017)

(a range of interactive word sorts and activities) as presented in their *Words Their Way* programme.

While the stage models of the spelling process include attention to the key domains of phonology, orthography, morphology and etymology, their disadvantage lies in the linear nature of the models which implies that development occurs sequentially and at particular ages; this may convey to teachers that instructional content in the upper stages should be left until later. We also do not know under what pedagogical conditions the writing samples used in developing the stage models were derived from. Based on their synthesis of the research and *triple word form* theory, Daffern et al. (2015) developed the *Components of Spelling Test* (CoST) and have established its reliability and validity as a spelling assessment tool which teachers may find helpful to use alongside the stage model assessments as they analyse the quality of spellings in children's writing.

We have incorporated the findings from this body of research into the development of the **Conventions** component (*Spelling, Punctuation, Grammar*) of the *Write to Read* rubric (see Chapter 5). Exploring this component can also assist in planning for conventions, enhance teacher content knowledge and raise their expectations around when particular aspects should typically be mastered. Our research has shown that writing development is influenced by the 'affordances of classrooms which can either constrain and hinder it or propel it forward' (Kennedy & Shiel, 2022, p. 127) and that when classroom instruction (in and out of context) is optimised, the range and accuracy of conventions appearing in children's writing can occur much earlier than the stage models indicate.

Alphabetics: Integrating Phonemic Awareness, Phonics, Spelling and Handwriting

Given the influence of foundational literacy skills on writing quality, it is critical that students develop phonological awareness and master the alphabetic principle (e.g., how the 26 graphemes and 44 phonemes map onto each other and combine to spell individual words). Research (ILA, 2020) indicates that although phonological awareness progresses from large concrete linguistic units (e.g., words, syllables, onset/rimes) to smaller, more abstract ones (e.g., phonemes), these phases overlap and 'phoneme-level awareness is not only achievable for most 4- and 5-year-olds without prior syllable-level instruction but also seems to proceed more smoothly when children do not need to overcome a learned focus on syllable units' (Ukrainetz et al., 2011, p. 6). Not all children will need the same level or duration of instruction and so assessment should play a key role in determining children's particular needs (Cunningham & Cunningham, 2002; Ehri & Nunes, 2002). Instruction in phonemic awareness is most effective when combined with letter manipulation, at which point it functions as an entry into phonics.

An entry point into segmentation for emergent writers and children who exhibit difficulty with hearing and isolating the sounds of the language is the use of Elkonin Boxes (see Bodrova & Leong, 2006 for a discussion). These are versatile tools which support children in learning how to segment sounds, initially without letters, and might be expected to support children in later reading and invented spelling (Figure 9.5). Children are taught to say each word, articulate each individual sound, and, as they make the sound, to slide a counter into a box. In the example below, the word shop has four letters but three sounds. Children are given lots of practice in segmenting sounds in familiar words: beginning with 2 sounds, three sounds and gradually increasing in complexity. When children can isolate and articulate the sounds without help, they can be challenged to match magnetic letters to the sounds or write the letters. When adding letters to the challenge, it is important that the words are chosen carefully to match letters and sounds that have already been taught explicitly.

Difficulties can arise when children do not integrate knowledge of letter names, sound and shape. Research highlights the important role of handwriting (see Chapters 2 and 11) in linking letter names and sounds and has been found to be even more effective than tracing or passively viewing a letter (Fancher et al., 2018). The physical act of writing on paper facilitates motor memory for the shape and feel of the letter. Adopting a multisensory approach (VAKT: visual, auditory, tactile and kinaesthetic, see Figure 9.6) can help

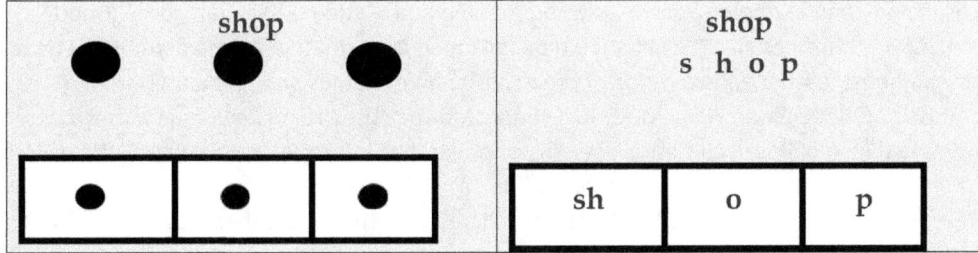

Figure 9.5 Using Elkonin boxes to support phonemic awareness

students to internalise and consolidate this knowledge (Fernald, 1943 cited in Kennedy et al., 2012)

In addition to segmenting when writing independently, children need to be able to blend sounds to decode unfamiliar words when reading. Blending sounds can cause a particular difficulty for some children. When stuck on a word, children often resort to sounding the letters individually and then are unable to create the word by blending the individual sounds together. Orton's pioneering research in the early 20th century with children with dyslexia highlighted:

> *In these cases, examination has revealed the fact that while the teaching of the phonetic equivalents may have been fairly complete, the next and most cardinal step, that of teaching the blending of the letter sounds in the exact sequence in which they occur in the word, had not been attempted, or had been poorly carried out. It is this process of synthesising the word as a spoken unit from its constituent sounds that often makes much more difficulty for the strephosymbolic[1] child than do the static reversals and letter confusions.*
>
> (1937, p. 162)

Recent experimental research (Gonzalez-Frey & Ehri, 2021) conducted with kindergarten children ranging in age from 5.6 to 5.8 years reported superior results for decoding (using non-words) when children were taught to use a connected phonation (mmmaaaaaffff) approach rather than a segmented phonation (/m/a/f/) approach. The researchers highlighted that problems are created when children are taught by 'segmented phonation, a procedure used frequently in synthetic phonics programs' (p. 284) and 'error analysis suggested that breaking between phonemes caused students to forget initial phonemes during blending'. They argue that decoding instruction could be made more effective by teaching connected phonation first with continuants (consonant sounds which are easy to hold (e.g., m, n, f) and then transitioning to stop consonants which are more difficult to hold (e.g., b, d). Though promising, they highlight the need for further research through studies that adapt the approach for use in classrooms.

It is essential that alphabetic knowledge is taught in a logical sequence moving from simple to more complex concepts (e.g., from simple CVC words to CCVC/CCVCC (initial and final consonant blends with short vowel sounds); consonant digraphs with short and long vowels (CVe, vowel digraphs, diphthongs, r-controlled vowels), syllable division, spelling rules, morphemes and Greek and Latin roots. Such instruction teaches children to draw on orthography, morphology and etymology of words when reading and writing unfamiliar words (Goodwin & Ahn, 2013; Daffern et al., 2015). It should be informed by formative assessment as needs will vary amongst learners and a range of organisational groupings should be utilised.

Bussis (1985, cited in Hall, 2006) has suggested that the brain is a unique pattern detector so teaching children to notice patterns and use that information to decode and encode makes sense. However, not all children find it easy to work with patterns, particularly children with reading difficulties, and research highlights that a synthetic approach (where, for example, sounds are blended to form words) may work better for them (see Chapter 11,

BOX 9.1 EXAMPLE: MAKING AND BREAKING

(adapted from Cunningham & Hall, 1994)

Reviewing and Consolidating Letter Sound Relationships: t, p, i, n, s

Materials: a set of alphabet letters for each child, small whiteboards, mini whiteboard markers, flashcards of the target words, chart paper

As you call the word, children make the word; After everyone makes the word, invite one child to write it on the whiteboard and ask another child to select the word card from your table and place it on the chart paper.

- Make me the two-letter word: is
- Change one letter and make: in
- Change one letter and make: it
- Add one letter and make: sit
- Change one letter and make sip
- Change one letter and make sin
- Add one letter and make spin
- Rearrange the letters and make snip
- Add one letter and make snips
- Rearrange the letters and make spins
- Change one letter and make spits

Ask children to categorise the words on the chart paper in a variety of ways:

- Put two/three/four/five letter words in columns; then read them aloud in pairs
- Words beginning/ending with: i, n, s, p, t
- Words with two consonants: start/end (consonant blends)

As children learn more letters and sounds, increase the complexity and range of the letters, sounds and patterns. Using the letters: r, g, i, s, p, n

- In
- Pin/pig/rig/rip
- rips/nips/spin/snip/pins
- ping/sing/rings/rings
- ringing/singing/pinging
- Challenge: Use all letters to make a word (Spring)

Box 11.1; synthetic phonics exemplar lesson). The making and breaking activities presented in the exemplar below (Box 9.1) support children in noticing patterns and also in blending and segmenting sounds to form words.

Children should also be taught to progressively read, write and spell the most frequently occurring words in the language. As May (1994) points out almost half of everything we read is made up of the 100 most frequent words in the English language (1994) and argues that a key 'teaching goal is to have children recognise these words through visual memory within one second' (p. 110). Many of these are the abstract 'anchor words' (Clay, 2002) within sentences which readers and writers need to be able to rely on recognising instantly when reading or creating text, ensuring that only unfamiliar words have to be decoded and encoded.

Typically, high frequency words are taught alongside phonics in a structured manner. Traditionally the emphasis has been on recall of the words, rather than on simultaneously learning to spell and write them. There are several word lists available (e.g. 220 Dolch list compiled by E. Dolch, 1936; Fry List, 1984). These words are organised according to the frequency with which they are found in early reading materials. However, frequency is not to be confused with decodability. May (1994) reported that 'three quarters of the 100 most frequent words in the English language have regular spellings and (citing Fry, 1984, p. 22) that these words make up about 50% of all written material' (p. 110). Take, for example, the first 20 words on the Dolch word list: many of these words are phonetically regular (e.g., a, and, I, it, in, that, for, on but, had) and so do not need to be memorised. Those that are more irregular (particularly for emergent readers) can be taught as part of word study lessons. Using a multisensory approach, highlighting the tricky part, identifying the target words in context and consolidating through games and pair or group activities (Figure 9.8) supports young children in mastering the words. Some practical examples drawing on the research base are offered next (Box 9.2).

As young children are engaged in writing independently during a writing workshop, they can be supported in this process by providing some scaffolds (e.g., such as taping a laminated simple black and white alphabet with a picture and image of the letter onto each desk (Figure 9.9) and a list of the current set of irregular words that the class is working on (Table 9.3). Having these tools in close proximity to children as they write helps to minimise interruption to their thought processes as they can quickly check initial letter-sound relationships, the form of the letter and the spelling of important 'anchor words'.

As children develop confidence and automaticity these visual scaffolds can be removed. Small-group mini lessons can be conducted with children who continue to experience difficulties with spelling and basic conventions of print. Based on formative assessment data, children can be grouped according to need, for example:

- Children who are not consistently using finger spaces between words.
- Children who only write one sound to represent a word.
- Children who have beginning and end sounds but not the other dominant sounds.
- Inserting vowels (short/long).
- Spelling inflectional endings (e.g. hop/hopping; looked).

Introducing independent writing at such an early stage was a new departure for many teachers in our partner schools. It was a leap of faith which teachers felt was worth taking, raised their expectations for children's writing and brought many benefits:

> I would not have attempted to ask my Junior Infants (4-5yrs) to write or label stories as they are doing or to the level of which they are writing at! This is feeding into their phonics and sounds and moving them on at a great rate.
>
> (Junior Infant teacher)

BOX 9.2 TEACHING CHILDREN TO READ, WRITE AND SPELL HIGH-FREQUENCY WORDS

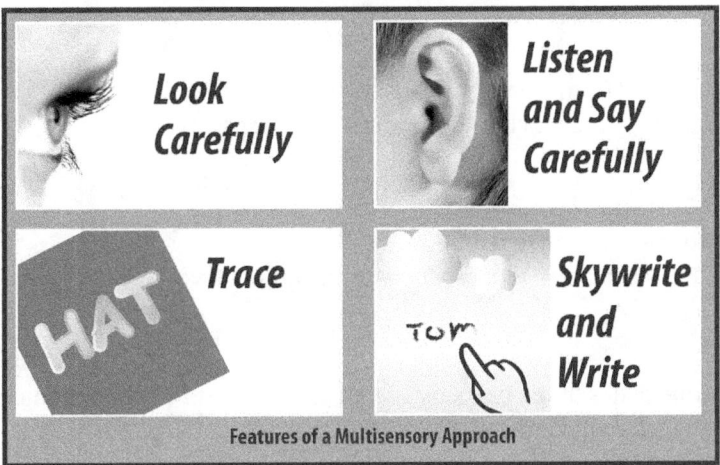

Figure 9.6 Features of a Multisensory Approach
Source: Write to Read

Example: Irregular Target Word: 'Said'

Visual/Auditory

- Show and read aloud a sentence from the big book or a poem/rhyme that children are familiar with. Underline or highlight the word.
- Hold up a flashcard: Look at the word out of context: say it aloud.

Visual

- Examine the distinguishing features e.g. four letters, two vowels; circle the ai.

Auditory

- Discuss the tricky bit (ai doesn't sound like A it sounds like /e/; how could we remember the word?
- Chant the letters in the word in sequence.

Tactile

- Trace in salt/sand tray.

Kinaesthetic

- Make the word with magnetic letters.
- Skywrite the word.

Visual

- Look closely at the word again and take a mental photo of it; close your eyes; can you see it in your mind?; open your eyes and check.

Write It

- Write the word from memory on paper.
- Write it with your eyes closed (shuts out other senses).

Visual

- Check to see if you were right.
- Check if you used the word in your writing and see if you spelled it correctly.

Finally

- Read some pages of the big book: match post-it notes to the word on the page.
- Chant the letters in order.
- Add word to the alphabetised word wall.

Follow-Up Activities

Revise Words Often

- Call the word **(auditory)**.
- Invite a child to find it on the word wall **(visual)**.
- Class chants the letters in the word **(auditory)**.
- Child puts it in a sentence **(auditory)**.
- Class writes it in the air/on paper from memory **(kinaesthetic)**.
- Check if correct (pairs) **(visual)**.
- Extension activity: make a word that rhymes/with the same onset.

Games to Consolidate

- Snap.
- Word bingo.
- Memory.
- Fish for words.
- Word dice.
- Jump it out on an alphabet mat.

Regular Maintenance and Assessment

Regular Assessment: Check children can read, write and spell the words (Figure 9.7).

Independent Peer Pair Work: One child reads the words aloud; the other writes the words. Check if correct. Swop roles.

List 1			
the			
to			
and			
he			
a			
I			
you			
it			
of			
in			
was			
said			
his			
that			
she			
for			
on			
they			
but			
had			

Figure 9.7 Checklist Dolch List 1
Source: Write to Read

Figure 9.8 Pair work: Children reviewing sight vocabulary.
Source: Write to Read

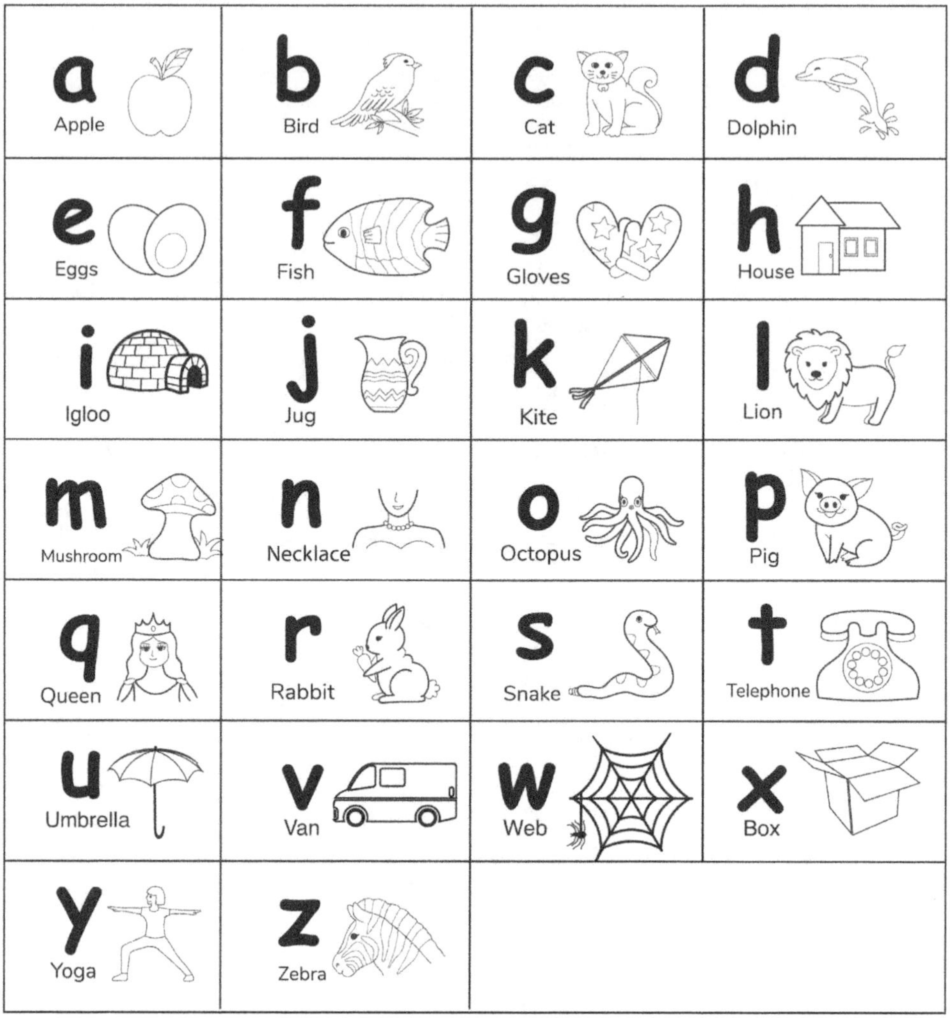

Figure 9.9 Desktop alphabet to support young writers

Source: Write to Read

Table 9.3 Irregular words Dolch List 1

of	said	you
the	they	
to	was	

At this point, children are aware that there is one way to spell a word, and many are perfectionists who do not like to take risks. It is vital that they are given a consistent message on how to approach spelling an unknown word and reassurance that incorrect spelling can be addressed after all ideas are captured on the page. As one teacher remarked:

Then it's a big leap to not be certain how to spell everything, to say, 'Give it your best guess. Make your sounds. What do you think comes next? What little words can you find hidden in that, that might help to you?' To be brave enough to do that, it can be a challenging for the children to say, 'Everything doesn't have to be right. It just has to be your best guess today'. This idea that... your letters don't all have to be perfect, you're spelling doesn't have to be perfect. The only thing you have to do is keep writing. That's the thing. We can fix up as we go along but you just need to keep writing. I think that's a great positive.

(Senior Infant Teacher)

Drawing on experiences with the making and breaking activities outlined earlier, children can be encouraged to use analogy (see Chapter 7, Box 7.6) when trying to spell words in their own writing (e.g. I can spell *cat*, so I can spell *mat, fat, flat*). They can also be taught to use visual and morphemic strategies alongside phonology for ambitious words. Such strategy work supports writer independence, promotes a 'growth mindset' (Dweck, 2007) and builds children's sense of self efficacy and confidence. They are also more likely to persist in the face of a challenge, as noted by one child:

Well, I think I've changed by...I always give up when I am stuck on a word, but now I use all my tools.... The hardest thing I would think is when you get stuck on a word because you think, oh I won't be able to get this done. But if you use all your tools, then you will get it.

(2nd class)

Providing laminated 'have-a-go' cards (Table 9.4) nurtures 'brave spelling' efforts (Schrodt et al., 2020) as children begin to use their knowledge to solve spelling issues and only look for teacher help after other attempts have been made. A variation on have-a-go cards is instigating an alphabetised individual spelling notebook (Figure 9.10) which children can keep on their desks while writing and consult to check the spelling of words they have previously worked on:

We have have-a-go notebooks....So it has the whole alphabet in it, and then if you're stuck on a word you just write it the way you think it's written, you bring it up, and then she

Figure 9.10 Personal spelling notebook assistance when writing
Source: Write to Read

Table 9.4 Sample have-a-go-card

My Have-a-Go Card

1. Say the word slowly. Do I have all the sounds/parts?	2. Does it look and sound right?	3. **Ask a friend** for help (if needed)	4. **Check with teacher** (which parts are correct; give the correct spelling)

Source: Write to Read

> *fixes it. But it's on the right letter page. You can look back if you wrote that word already and spell it the right way.*
>
> (2nd class)

Ensuring children develop strong transcription skills (handwriting fluency and spelling) is important as research (Kent & Wanzek, 2016) indicates that relative to all component skills examined, the quality of writing was most strongly correlated with transcription and reading achievement..

Addressing Grammar and Punctuation

There are conflicting findings on the role of grammar in writing pedagogy and its potential to impact writing quality (see Chapter 2). Myhill and Watson's (2014) review of the literature explored the question: Does explicit knowledge of grammar support writing development and attainment in writing? The answer lies in how it is conceptualised and presented in curricula, the extent to which it is taught in isolation and 'as an arbiter of accuracy' (Myhill & Watson, 2014, p. 45) or within the context of authentic writing where it can be utilised as a 'design tool' for communicating. Previous early meta-analyses (cited in Graham et al., 2012a) concluded that grammar teaching in isolation has little or no effect on students' writing (Hillocks, 1986) or a negative effect on it (Braddock et al., 1963). In another meta-analysis, Graham and Perin (2007) found negative associations between writing quality and a focus on traditional grammar instruction, concluding that it was: 'unlikely to help improve the quality of student writing. Such findings raise serious questions about some educators' enthusiasm for traditional grammar instruction as a focus of writing instruction for adolescents (p. 21). In contrast, Slavin et al. (2019) and several studies reviewed in Myhill and Watson (2014) (e.g., Fearn & Farnan, 2007; Jones et al., 2013) highlighted its value when it is conceptualised more broadly and taught in the context of children's writing.

Other research indicates that students who do well on worksheets and workbook pages focused on skills such as grammar and punctuation may not transfer these skills to authentic meaningful independent writing contexts (Graves, 1994; Graham, 1999). In the Irish context, grammar and punctuation are often taught in the context of workbooks and skill and drill worksheets rather than in the context of children's writing, indicating that the role of grammar is under-utilised as a craft technique.

As highlighted in Chapters 2 and 8, grammar can be presented as a 'design tool' (Myhill et al., 2012) and children can be taught to write more elaborated and syntactically complex sentences that infuse their writing with rhythm and texture. As sentences grow in complexity, punctuation plays a key role in determining how to read the sentence. Punctuation is a constrained skill, as there are only so many punctuation marks in the English language and children should progressively learn to apply them purposefully and accurately in their writing (Figure 9.11). Some aspects of punctuation mostly appear in informational texts and are best taught in that context.

Graves (1994) suggests demonstrating to children that punctuation marks are essentially signposts that enable the reader to read the writing as the author intended. When children begin to see punctuation marks as purposeful, they also begin to internalise when and how to apply them to their own writing. Varied use of punctuation provides evidence of experimentation and risk taking and of the writer's understanding of the potential of punctuation to bring their writing to life. As such, punctuation is best presented as a craft dimension of writing initially and accuracy can be addressed in the revision and editing processes. When approached in this way, experimentation and accuracy in first drafts begin to improve as children gain greater control over conventions. The punctuation subcomponent of the Conventions component of the *Write to Read* rubric rewards both experimentation and accuracy and highlights when specific aspects should be mastered. These are important when considering whole school approaches to writing (see Chapter 12).

Resolving particular issues with skills such as spelling, punctuation and grammar is best addressed in small groups using children's writing as the context. Keeping assessment records of children's use of conventions is essential if mini lessons are to be timely and useful. This formative assessment data can be gathered in conferences, share sessions, and when reading over children's writing. Groups should be formed based on need and no more than 5-6 children in the group. This means that children who are not yet ready for the skill,

Table 9.5 Punctuation as signposts

Punctuation Marks: Signposts to Author Intent and Fluency		
Capital letters Capital letters+ full stops Exclamation marks Question marks Quotation marks in dialogue Commas in dialogue Comma in a list Commas in elaborated sentences	Apostrophe in contractions (speech) Apostrophe in singular possessive Apostrophe in plural possessive Colon Semi-colon Ellipsis Ampersand Hyphen Brackets	 Punctuation = signposts from the author about how to interpret the text. Link with fluency.

Figure 9.11 Punctuation as signpost

Source: Write to Read
Created with MS Word icons

or who have already mastered it, can continue to work without interruption on their writing and time is used well. We have found designating one day of the week for small group work provides a predictable routine and children adapt to the different structure and expectations for group and independent writing (Box 9.3).

> **BOX 9.3 CONSIDERATIONS WHEN PLANNING SMALL GROUP LESSONS**
>
> - Be aware of the expectations for each class level.
> - Check curriculum documents and classroom textbooks.
> - Make a list of punctuation conventions.
> - Examine children's writing for evidence of punctuation.
> - Note who is/not experimenting with punctuation.
> - Group children who are not using punctuation correctly.
> - Differentiate teaching: use one day to do small group mini lessons while the rest of the class continues with their writing.
> - Focus on authors as mentors: highlight how authors of children's books use punctuation.
> - Choose one day of the week for small group work: See sample organisation below.
>
> | Wednesday: Group 1 (15 min) | Wednesday: Group 2 (15 min) |
> |---|---|
> | **Punctuation mini lesson:** Colon John, Mary, Susan, Brian, | **Punctuation:** Commas in complex sentences Joanne, Martin, Conor, Emma, Grace, |
> | **Mentor text:** *Elephants*, S. Simon, p. 20; children's writing. | **Mentor text:** *Resistance*, B. Gallagher p. 10; children's writing. |
> | Discovery Approach (see Chapter 6; Box 9.4) Children apply what they have learned to their own writing and support each other in fixing up errors. As they do so, call the second small group to another table. | Check back with group 1 while group 2 works on correcting their writing; As group 1 return to their desk, check in with group 2 to see how well they were able to correct comma usage in complex sentences. |

Rather than using the gradual release of responsibility model (see Chapters 7, 8, 12), in line with Graves's (1994) recommendation to have children hypothesise about the function of punctuation marks, we have found adopting a discovery approach is effective. A small group convention lesson on punctuation is offered next (Box 9.4) as an example.

> **BOX 9.4 SMALL GROUP SKILLS LESSON: SPEECH MARKS: 5TH CLASS**
>
> **Resources:** *Friend or Foe* by Brian Gallagher, p. 72; children's writing folders and writing samples; anchor chart paper, copy of the extract for children, coloured pens/pencils
>
> **Teacher Notes**
> Pick any text with a variety of speech punctuation and text layout.

(Continued)

Conventions Mini Lessons

Call the small group (four to six children) to the area of the classroom where you conduct small group lessons. Remind the rest of the class that they must continue writing quietly and not disturb you as you work with the small group.	Children should be selected based on assessment notes: a demonstrated need/ readiness for the skill.
Step 1: Explain (1-2 minutes) *Writers, we have been learning about how dialogue in a story reveals character traits. We can learn lots about characters from what they say and how they interact with others. We can infer how they might be thinking or feeling. I am delighted that you all have been including lots of dialogue in your stories. Today we are going to focus on how to signal the dialogue and ensure the punctuation helps the reader to follow it.*	Briefly state the focus of today's mini lesson and connect it to earlier mini lessons.
Step 2: Discovery Approach (8-10 minutes) *Open your copy of Friend or Foe by Brian Gallagher, one of our favourite authors and which we are currently reading in class and turn to p. 72.* *Before we read it, how could we tell that there is a lot of dialogue on this page? What conventions does the author utilise to signal this to the reader?* Children should notice that the text is indented each time a person speaks and another replies (Figure 9.12).	Always begin with a correct sample: e.g., a piece of text with correct usage of speech conventions.
'I have details of the annual gala,' said the captain, a well-built man in his early forties who had a deep voice and a strong Dublin accent. 'It's going to be held this year on November the twelfth, in Iveagh Baths. So what are we going to do?' 'Swim in it?' whispered Ben, and Jack realised that Ben had been infected by Joan's giddiness. Jack wanted to laugh, but he kept his face serious as the captain looked down at the club members. 'We're going to win it!' said the captain. 'This is a chance for you all to prove yourselves. It's been seven years since we last won the cup, and it's high time we took it back. There'll be teams competing on every level, so I want to see you all training hard between now and November. OK?' 'OK!' answered the members, and Jack felt a tingle of excitement. *Maybe I could get on a team*, he thought to himself. He was at *Figure 9.12* Extract *Friend or Foe* by Brian Gallagher, p. 72	It is important to set the tone for the small group. Adopting a questioning diWscovery approach helps children to speculate/ hypothesise about punctuation and its purpose in the context.
Invite a child to come up to the IWB/visualiser and point out one convention in the first segment. Highlight it with a marker/	Encourage them to see conventions as signposts or tools to serve author intent and as signposts for the reader to guide oral reading fluency.

(Continued)

pen. Children may notice the quotation marks only (e.g., the captain speaking to the children). *Why are the quotation marks placed in those particular spots?* Discuss how the author or publisher may at times use single or double quotation marks but that consistency in their usage is important.

Do you notice any other punctuation that is part of what the captain said? They should notice the question mark at the end of the sentence. Children can then mark these on their own copy. Have a child come up and circle the commas and full stops in a segment of the conversation. *How do they help us read the dialogue? What would happen if the quotation marks, commas, full stop and question mark were not there? What tone of voice do you think the captain used? What helped you read it in that way?*

Proceed in the same manner with the next piece of dialogue on the page. *What else do you notice about speech conventions?* Children should notice a new paragraph begins as each person replies. Ask children to read to the end of the page and to highlight any other punctuation associated with the dialogue. They should notice that an exclamation mark has been used instead of a comma in two places. *Why did the author use an exclamation mark there? How did the author know to put it there? What tone of voice should it be read in? The word OK is used twice towards the end of the extract. Would the author want us to read OK in the same tone of voice in both sentences? Can you explain why?*

They should also notice that 'whispered, answered' are apt choices of words in this context.

Let's create our anchor chart so we can remember how to use speech conventions accurately when we create dialogue in our stories. How could we remember? What is the tricky bit? What will we include?

> **Anchor Chart: Speech Conventions**
> - "Use" 'or ' to show the beginning and end of what the person says.
> - Use a comma, to indicate who the speaker is. It could be at the start, middle, or end of the dialogue
> - Use ? and ! marks for effect.
> - Indent and go to a new line when someone replies.

Having a copy of the extract ensures children are actively involved in marking up the text and can use it as a visual reminder later.

It is important to draw attention to all aspects of punctuation in the discussion so that children don't just focus on the quotation marks.

Co-construction of the anchor chart is critical. Children are more likely to remember what they have learned if they have created the wording and examples. This also builds their metacognitive awareness.

It is important that children immediately apply what they have learned in the context of their own writing rather than completing a skill and drill worksheet on isolated sentences.

(Continued)

Step 3: Independent Practice (8-10 minutes) Ask children to take out their last piece of writing and check it for speech conventions using the extract and anchor chart as a guide. Ask them to rewrite the dialogue on a separate piece of paper going to a new paragraph each time a speaker replies. Ask them to swap papers with a partner to check they have followed conventions correctly. While the children are applying what they have learned to their writing, watch them as they work and scaffold and coach as necessary. Do a quick review: *What did we learn today? What can we do when we are not sure where to put speech marks? How will we remember how to use speech conventions in our writing? What is our goal for tomorrow? (e.g., read my piece of writing aloud to myself and check if I have remembered to put in correct punctuation and go to a new line when someone speaks).* **Share Session (5 minutes)** Children who have been writing independently can be invited to share their writing.	Observe the small group as they work independently or alternatively call another small group and work on another skill for a further 15 mins. Review what has been learned in the small group lesson, discuss strategies for remembering and set some goals.
Assessment Read over the work later: Who has been able to apply the new learning to their writing? Who is still having trouble? What is the specific problem? How can you follow up? Record this information in your assessment folder. Continue to monitor application over the coming weeks. Schedule another mini lesson if required. This text (p. 72, Gallagher) could also be reused as a craft lesson to explore how to build authentic believable characters (see Chapters 7 and 8)	Reuse the text for a craft lesson.

On occasion, an alternative and fun way to engage children in learning about punctuation is to draw on the Convention Game as outlined by Graves (1994). This is a playful interactive and collaborative game which can showcase to children the range of punctuation that their peers are using in their writing and can encourage a spirit of experimentation. Through peer collaboration and accountability, children can learn productively from each other as all members must be able to explain the convention and answer the key questions.

BOX 9.5 CONVENTION GAME

Materials: writing folders, fiction, non-fiction books

Teams of three: Mixed-ability

Preparation: Decide which punctuation marks you will focus on. Prepare 5–6 sentences derived from books in the classroom which exemplify the punctuation in context. Consider children's age and stage of development as you plan.

Playing the Game

- Write a sentence on the board that shows a particular convention and underline it.
- As soon as soon as the target punctuation is underlined, children have to:
    - Find the target punctuation in their own writing folder.
    - Find the target punctuation in a book.
- Once found, the whole group must work together to answer the following questions:
    - How does this convention help the *meaning* of the sentence?
    - How does this convention help *readers*?
    - Teach each other: when **all** members of the group can answer **both** questions, they put their hands up.
- Note which teams raise their hands first, second, third. When there are three groups with their hands up, stop and discuss.
- Ask **any** member of the group for the answer and call on the other two groups to explain as well.
- Award points as follows:
    - 1 point if the convention is found in the writing folder.
    - 1 point if it is used correctly in the context of the writing in the folder.
    - 1 point if found in a book.
    - 1 point for each question answered correctly.
- Repeat a number of times. The highest-scoring team wins. Commend children who had experimented with the convention in their own writing.

Source: Summarised from Graves (1994)

As the year progresses and children's skills develop, it is important to 'up the ante' (Pressley et al., 2001), communicate high expectations and hold children accountable for correctly spelling words that are on the word wall and for accuracy in punctuation marks that have been taught. As mini lessons build, you should find that skills and conventions improve on first-draft pieces, indicating that children have begun to internalise them. Developing checklists of skills taught and providing copies of mentor texts used in mini lessons supports writers in reviewing their writing for accuracy (see Chapter 10).

Analysis of Writing Samples to Inform Teaching of Conventions

Children's writing samples provide a window into their worlds and a visible manifestation of their knowledge of conventions (see also Chapter 11 for further discussion of conventions in relation to addressing the needs of struggling writers; Chapter 12 for a whole school approach to assessment and planning). When writing independently, children must fall back on their own resources to capture their ideas on the page. Careful analysis can provide valuable insights into children's writing craft and voice, as well as phonemic, phonic, morphological, orthographical, grammar and punctuation knowledge, which can be harnessed to inform next steps. One can feel the energy and enthusiasm of the young writer (Figure 9.13) whose words appear to fly off the page as she quickly sketches and recounts some details of her cousins' visit. It is a first draft, and she has hardly paused for breath, having crossed out words and letters rather than stopping to erase them, and there is only one instance of a full stop. Many children of this age have trouble knowing when a sentence is finished and where to place the full stop. She provides some interesting details of the visit and likely draws on environmental print to correctly spell the adjective 'delicious'. While there are many strengths, there are several conventions that could be targeted to enhance accuracy (Table 9.6).

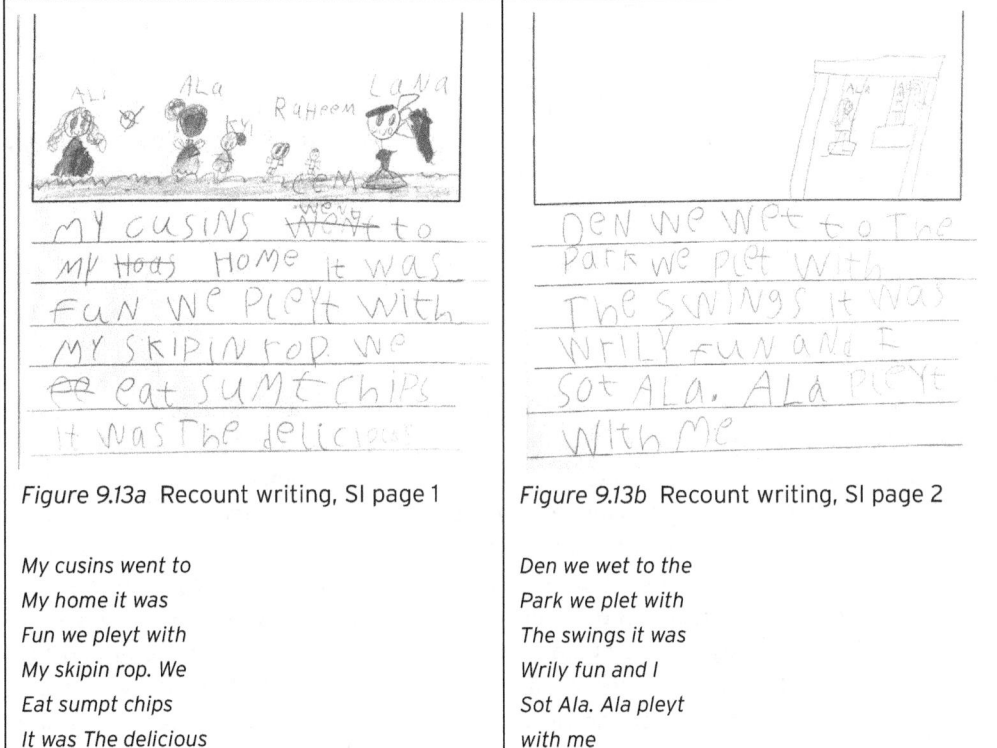

Figure 9.13a Recount writing, SI page 1

My cusins went to
My home it was
Fun we pleyt with
My skipin rop. We
Eat sumpt chips
It was The delicious

Figure 9.13b Recount writing, SI page 2

Den we wet to the
Park we plet with
The swings it was
Wrily fun and I
Sot Ala. Ala pleyt
with me

Table 9.6 Analysis of writing sample Figure 9.13a/9.13b

Analysis of Conventions (based on Figure 9.13)

Conventions	Used Correctly	Approximated
High-Frequency Words	My, went, was, with, to, the, we, and, me, it	Wnt (went), sot (saw), sumt (some), den (then)
Phoneme-Grapheme Knowledge	Home, chips, park, swing, fun	Rop (rope), wrily (really)
Morphology	Chip(s), swing(s), wri(ly)	Skippin (skipping), pleyt/plet (played)
Ambitious Words	Delicious *(environmental print)*	Cusins
Capitalisation and Punctuation	Capitals used at the start of a name	Capital letters randomly interspersed throughout
Grammar/Articulation		sot (saw), sumt (some),

Mini Lessons for Conventions

This writer would benefit from a small-group mini lesson on:

- Concept of sentence and how to use capital letters and full stops to indicate a sentence
- Inflectional ending: ed (sounds like /d/, /t/, /ed/)
- Long a sound (ay/ai/ey); reading and spelling words with these patterns
- Multisensory approach for high-frequency words: went, saw, some, then
- Some daily practice for letter formation

It is essential to keep records of formative assessment data derived from conferencing, sharing sessions and reading over children's work. These will inform the grouping and scope and sequence of the small-group mini lessons. These are explored further in Chapter 10.

Conclusion

Research at the primary level highlights an over-emphasis on grammar, handwriting and spelling skills and insufficient attention to the writing processes and crafts of writing. Nevertheless, these skills play a key role in writing development and, given that children who struggle with these skills will have fewer cognitive resources available to devote to the higher-order dimensions and processes of writing (Berninger et al., 1992 cited in McMaster et al., 2018), it is essential that they are taught explicitly in developmentally appropriate ways.

Research has established the magnitude of the effect of transcription skills on variation in writing output and quality. According to Graham et al. (1997) it explains two-thirds of the differences in writing fluency and up to 40% of the differences in writing quality in upper-elementary and early secondary school students. More recently, an Australian study (Daffern et al., 2017) examining the influence of grammar, spelling and punctuation on the writing quality of four cohorts of students in upper primary (years 3, 4, 5, 6) found that 'between approximately 24% and 43% of the variance in written composition was explained by the three language convention measures and that spelling was the main predictor of written quality'.

Clearly, the capacity to write well with accurate grammar, spelling and punctuation 'remains a fundamental part of being a literate writer' (Patino et al., 2020, p. 494). Addressing punctuation and grammar skills in the context of children's writing holds much promise for enhancing writing quality while a combination of explicit teaching both in and out of context is required to systematically address phonics, orthography and morphology. No single practice on its own is sufficient for success; rather, it is how teachers enact research-informed practices in combination in response to children's assessed needs in the moment-by-moment interactions in the cultural and social context of classrooms that supports development. As Hall and Harding (2003, p. 42) posit, it is a 'complex interaction of many components; an intelligent weaving together of a lot of skills instruction combined with voluminous reading and writing'.

Reflect, Connect, Act

1. Reflect on how time for mini lessons is used in your classroom. How well do you balance attention to conventions and the craft of writing? Why?
2. Examine a writing sample of a high, middle and lower-achieving writer in your class for a genre of your choice. Examine the writing for accuracy of conventions. How would you rate:
   - The accuracy of the spelling? What kinds of spelling errors do you notice? Is there a pattern? (draw on the Write to Read rubric if you wish).
   - The range and accuracy of the punctuation? Are children experimenting with punctuation? Is punctuation used to build sentence sophistication and support author intent? What particular difficulties do you notice?
   - The accuracy of the sentence constructions? Are they generally grammatically correct? What particular difficulties do you notice at the different writing levels?

Suggestions for Further Reading

Daffern, T., Mackenzie, N. M., & Hemmings, B. (2015). The development of a spelling assessment tool informed by Triple Word Form Theory. *Australian Journal of Language and Literacy, 38*, 72–82. https://doi.org/10.1007/BF03651958

Myhill, D., & Watson, A. (2014). The role of grammar in the writing curriculum: A review of the literature. *Child Language Teaching and Therapy, 30(1)*, 41–62. https://doi.org/10.1177/0265659013514070

Ouellette, G., & Sénéchal, M. (2017). Invented spelling in kindergarten as a predictor of reading and spelling in Grade 1: A new pathway to literacy, or just the same road, less known? *Developmental Psychology, 53(1)*, 77–88. https://doi.org/10.1037/dev0000179

Note

1. Strephosymbolic: meaning twisted symbols representing the reversals of letters characteristic of the writing of learners with dyslexia

10 Process Mini Lessons
Evaluating, Revising and Publishing Writing across Genres

This chapter makes distinctions between strategies to support writers in first evaluating their writing, then revising it based on this evaluation and choosing the most appropriate form for publication. Links to the developmental models explored in Chapter 1 highlight how the models can support revision, while assessment explored in Chapter 5 is drawn on to illustrate peer and teacher feedback processes. It begins by emphasising the critical role played by oral language in enhancing children's writing development.

> **Reflect and Connect**
>
> 1 Should everything a child writes be revised? Why/why not?
> 2 What stages of development do children go through as they develop their writing/revision skills? (Look back to Chapter 1). In what ways can this knowledge help you support children in revising their writing?

Nurturing the Social Context: Classroom Talk to Support Writing Development

Writing has 'a complex relationship to talk' (NCTE, 2016), indicating that being able to engage in authorial conversations requires a certain level of oracy as well as knowledge of writing craft and genre if conversations are to benefit writing quality and support writers to transform ideas onto the page. Oracy has been defined as 'our ability to communicate effectively using spoken language. It is the ability to speak eloquently, articulate ideas and thoughts, influence through talking, listen to others and have the confidence to express your views' (APPG, 2021, p. 2). In the context of writing, craft mini lessons give children a common language which they can draw on to frame responses to peers' writing. Drawing on 'accountable talk' moves (Hampton & Resnick, 2009) teachers can set the tone for interactions by modelling how to identify specific craft techniques and highlight how they enhance the writing, how to seek clarification, question authors, infer the 'big ideas' in the writing, and provoke reflection.

Like writing, talk varies according to each discipline's structure, goals, ways of thinking and learning, vocabulary and texts. Van der Heide adopting genre theory (see Chapter 3) and a socio-cultural lens (2017, p. 342) contends that 'learning to write should be a social process in which students learn to make the writing moves of a genre by talking about writing with others and through trying out and hearing talk moves in conversation'. The ways in which teachers are able to structure talk and provide opportunities for students to converse meaningfully within writing workshops are pivotal, as talk moves act as a verbal rehearsal for writing moves.

Successful writing workshops provide multiple opportunities for teachers and children to connect with each other daily through the social fabric of the workshop (share sessions, conferencing, peer collaboration and peer assessment). These opportunities have the potential to influence children's understandings of what it means to be a real writer and can shape their attitudes towards writing as a pleasurable and worthwhile activity in and outside school, ultimately laying the foundations for the habit of life-long writing to be established.

Writing workshops that provide such experiences are rooted in socio-cultural perspectives on learning and cognitive apprenticeship models (Vygotsky, 1978; Rogoff, 1990) which recognise the critical role of interaction in shaping the construction of knowledge and higher-order thinking through participation within the writing community. Scaffolding such interactions in the share session and when conferencing supports writers in developing insider knowledge of writer techniques, and the language to articulate their thinking and responses to both their own and peers' writing (see Tables 10.1 and 10.2).

Scaffolding Interaction in the Share Session

Experiencing a responsive and appreciative audience daily can be an empowering experience for the author. It is a powerful motivator for children as they gauge the reaction of the audience to their choice of topic and to their words (Kennedy, 2014; Kennedy & Shiel, 2024). Children feel affirmed when the audience laughs spontaneously at a funny bit or a peer points out something specific they liked in the writing. Similarly, when a peer asks a pertinent question, it clues the writer into potential confusions or omissions in the current draft of the writing and can lead them to add further detail.

If this part of the workshop is to be successful, writers must feel assured that their work will be taken seriously and that responses to it will be appreciative and constructive. Given that writing is such a personal act, the share session can empower and build confidence, or if not managed well, impact negatively on a writer's self-efficacy. As one teacher noted:

> *I suppose the share session has really worked well in that their confidence has really grown and they have a purpose to their writing.*
>
> (4th class)

The first step is to teach children to actively listen to the writer. Listening closely does not come naturally to many children. With young children (and older children who are not used to participating in a plenary session), we have found it helpful to spend time teaching

210 *Teaching and Assessing Writing in the Primary School*

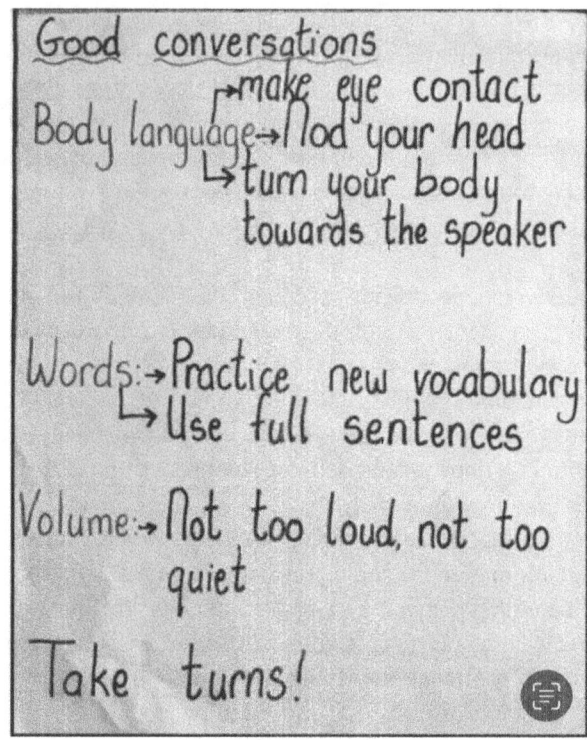

Figure 10.1 How to be a good speaker and listener
Source: Write to Read

the nuances of what is involved in demonstrating to others that you are actually listening (Figure 10.1) to them. As one second class teacher shared:

> *I suppose just to the say to them, if you were up there talking, would you like everybody to be chatting and then daydreaming when you're talking. No, you wouldn't. Then, the whole thing to explain that you just don't learn stuff from me you can learn things from listening to other children as well. And they do kind of realize that now, so there's kind of quality stuff going on here when other people are talking. And I suppose even the physical things like move your chair over and look at them. You need to teach them that, as they are quite young at the same time, and it is a hard skill to listen. Even the physical aspect, turn your chair which is the first step and then are you actually listening to what is going on? Or even have you a question ready now for the speaker when they are finished? Or even I used to get the speaker just to scan the room as well and maybe just don't start talking until everybody is looking at you.*
>
> (2nd class teacher)

Furthermore, the author must also take some responsibility to read their work aloud in an authoritative and engaging manner. When children read their texts aloud dysfluently, peer attention plummets and the value of the share session is seriously diminished (Figure 10.2).

Process Mini Lessons 211

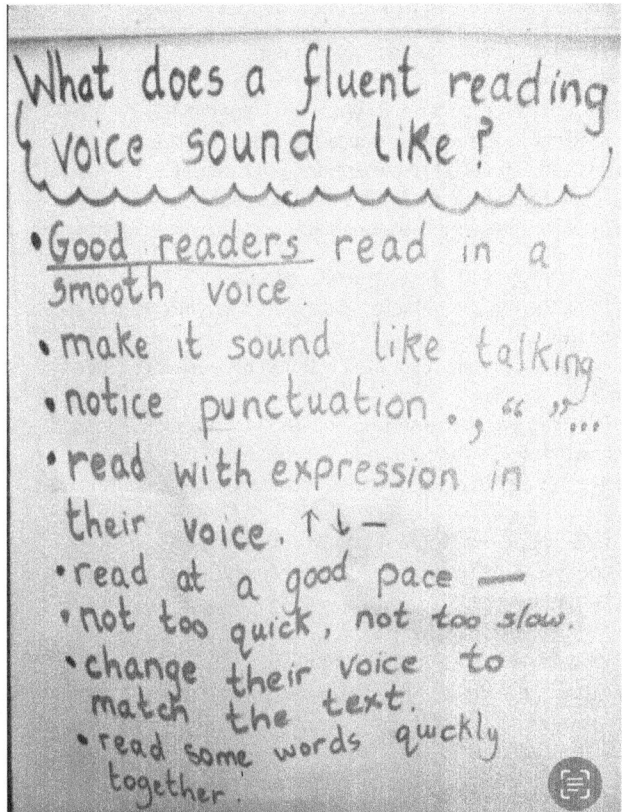

How to read your writing aloud:
Scan the room
Wait for everyone to look up
Wait for everyone to be quiet
Make eye contact as you speak
Use all of your reading fluency tools

Figure 10.2 Anchor chart fluency junior class
Source: Write to Read

It is often in orally sharing their texts, that children begin to realise the importance of conventions such as punctuation and spelling in guiding their oral reading. They can be taught to draw on the fluency tools they have learned during reading instructional time to ensure that listeners can hear them and enjoy listening to their 'performance'. These skills can be role-played and should be explicitly modelled.

As children grow in confidence, they can be supported to share their writing with a wider audience than the classroom, further enhancing their sense of self-efficacy:

> It's incredible. Their confidence, their self-esteem in writing. They see themselves as writers. They see themselves as readers…the share sessions at the end, they will get up and share in front of assemblies, never mind the class, whereas before they wouldn't have had the opportunity to do that.
>
> (3rd class teacher)

Once students have grasped the basics of effective speaking and listening, model for them how they can show interest in authors by identifying specific details, asking questions, stating what they liked about the text and indicating why. Oral feedback should increase in

Table 10.1 Sample sentence stems for responses to narrative writing in the share session

Praise for the writer's: word choice; literary and aesthetic language use **Model using exact words that children used in their text**	You used a precise (adjective: name it)...so I could see ....in my mind's eye The precise verb (name it) you used helped me... I really liked the simile-----because I could picture... I noticed you used the metaphor---- to describe.. The bit that stuck in my mind was....because... The lead was memorable because...
Praise for the writer's: text structures	I empathised with the character because... I think the minor character you created was interesting because.... That (event) really resonated with me because it reminded me of... I felt like I was in the setting because you did such a great job showing.... I like the way the plot unfolded....it was gripping, exciting, sad, funny The prologue was a great way to start the piece. I could feel the tension building because... I laughed at the bit.... I was sad when.... The dialogue was really authentic...
Asking for clarification	I was wondering why: the character acted that way? It ended that way? I was puzzled by... Could you clarify, I was a bit confused when... Could you tell us more about? Did you consider....

sophistication as children progress through primary grades. They should be able to notice specific examples of craft mini lessons in their peers' writing and respond using appropriate academic language structures (Table 10.1).

It is important to model language and sentence structures that attend to the particular features and text structures of each genre, that the level of language reflects children's stage of development and increases incrementally from one year to the next. Creating anchor charts will scaffold children's language usage and they can be encouraged to continue adding to the chart (Table 10.2).

With limited time available in primary classes, one way to increase participation in senior classes – where children tend to write longer pieces – is to invite them to choose a section or portion of the text for sharing. This can ignite children's curiosity and generate lots of questions for authors as peers wonder what preceded the part read aloud, what followed and why the particular portion was selected in the first place. It has the added advantage that with shorter pieces it is easier for writers to sustain oral fluency and for listeners to sustain active attention. It promotes greater reflexivity as authors justify their choices.

Though it might be tempting to omit or neglect the share session due to time constraints, try not to do so, as it can be a powerful motivator for children. As children witness the

Table 10.2 Sample sentence stems across genres for responses in the share session

Praise for the writer's: word choice; literary and aesthetic language use text structures	You had some really interesting facts...I did not know that ... You used interesting tier 3 language: I had never heard the word *nictitating* before I was very surprised when you reported that.... Your report made me feel like doing something about ... Straightaway I picked up on the structure because you used great transitional phrases that signalled the (compare/contrast; cause/effect; chronology)... I liked the way you created the lead...I felt like I was in New Orleans on the day of the hurricane.... You used hyberbole/slogan/catchphrase/repetition to great effect in your speech/letter Your arguments were very convincing The counter arguments were interesting, and you did a great job disparaging them The adjectives/verbs/similes were very effective I could visualise the.....
Asking for clarification	Why did you choose this topic? What kind of sources did you use? How do you know they were reliable? How did you fact-check?
Review the writing samples in Chapters 5, 8 and this chapter	What specific examples of craft would you draw attention to?

individuality and creativity of their peers, it influences their thinking and spurs them on to further hone their own writing. When it forms a predictable part of the daily routine and a sense of community develops, many children look forward to it and are eager to share. For others, it can be a nerve-wracking or intimidating experience, if the right tone is not struck. Participation in the share session should always be voluntary, given that writing is such a personal act. Consider the responses of this focus group (6th class children) when their opinion was sought on share session participation:

CHILD 1: I personally don't really like reading out my work because I feel like it's more sort of my work, I kind of like it private. But I remember when I did do it, I was really nervous at first but the whole thing is, when you actually start getting into the reading, and sort of giving your work to the class, it's actually really nice to see people appreciate it and sort of like tell you maybe how you could make it even better for more people to appreciate

CHILD 2: It's a good idea but I never do it because I'm too nervous that people won't like my work.

CHILD 3: ...I remember last year, I was too scared to get up because I had a different style to everyone else. But this year, it's kind of more like, I know what to do, I know what to write about and all that.

CHILD 1: As you do everything you sort of get more of a feel for yourself as a writer, like, you're not really relying on what other people are saying, you're more

	sort of doing what you think is the best way to do it.... you sort of become more confident in your style.
INTERVIEWER:	What do you mean by writing style?
CHILD 1:	Well, it's hard to describe a writing style, each individual author sort of has a different feeling in their writing, like, it's almost like you can read one piece and say, oh that's by JK Rowling, or that's by Michael Morpurgo or whatever. Because they sort of have this way of expressing the characters through the writing.

Also, bear in mind that children are sometimes more comfortable sharing particular genres over others, as indicated by this child:

> I would prefer reading out poems and factual writing, like reports, because it's not as personal feeling, because it's just more fact. And I also prefer reading out recounts because even though everything is the same, everyone's going to write about the same thing, it's very interesting to see how people have a different take on it .... are different at telling the story.
>
> (6th class)

Keeping a tally of share session participants from week to week (Figure 10.3), will help you to notice who readily volunteers, who is shy and who might need some encouragement. On occasion, the plenary share can be replaced with self-chosen small groups where children read each other's texts silently and respond orally, providing less public ways for children to receive peer feedback.

Positive interactions during conferences as children are engaged in the act of writing can also build their confidence to talk about their writing ideas, to recognise the worth of their writing and increase their willingness to share publicly in the share session. As with the share session, it is important to keep a tally of conferences across a week in addition to developing a system for recording conference data as indicated in the reflection above. An efficient way to record the frequency is to alphabetise children's names so you can easily tick off the names of those with whom you conference and those that share weekly (Figure 10.3).

Scaffolding Talk in the Writing Conference

As highlighted in (Chapters 2 and 6) research advocates responding to the writer as s/he is engaged in the act of writing (Graves, 1994; Calkins, 2000). This is a daily occurrence in an effective writing workshop. Through preplanned conferences (based on assessment and reading of children's work), either individually or in small groups, children and teachers can focus meaningfully on the writer concerns. According to Graves (1994), the hallmark of a good conference is 80% child talk and 20% teacher talk whereby the teacher nudges details from the writer, seeks to understand what the writer is attempting to capture and scaffolds them in doing so. The key is to respond to the *writer* and to resist the urge to 'fix' the secretarial errors that may jump out on the page. This is in direct contrast to more traditional approaches whereby teachers respond to the product and correct it after it is completed.

Conference Tally: Date Mar 11th-Mar 15th 2024					
Pupil	Mon	Tues	Wed	Thurs	Fri
1. AB		✓			
2. CB	✓				
3. EB					✓
4. FC	✓				
5. GC				✓	
6. ED		✓			
7. HD					✓
8. EF	✓				
9. MF					✓
10. SF		✓			
11. SG	✓				
12. EH				✓	
13. IK				✓	
14. MK				✓	
15. JL			✓		
16. JM	✓				
17. SMcD			✓		
18. RMcN					✓
19. JN			✓		
20. JOR			✓		
21. SOM		✓			
22. CT			✓		
23. SS					✓
24. JT				✓	
25. MT	✓				

Share Session Tally: Date Mar 11th-Mar 15th 2024					
Pupil	Mon	Tues	Wed	Thurs	Fri
1. AB	✓				
2. CB		✓			
3. EB			✓		
4. FC	✓				
5. GC			✓		
6. ED		✓			
7. HD				✓	
8. EF	✓				
9. MF					✓
10. SF		✓			
11. SG	✓				
12. EH				✓	
13. IK				✓	
14. MK				✓	
15. JL			✓		
16. JM	✓				
17. SMcD					✓
18. RMcN					✓
19. JN					✓
20. JOR				✓	
21. SOM		✓			
22. CT					✓
23. SS					✓
24. JT				✓	
25. MT	✓				

Figure 10.3 Keep a daily tally of participation in share sessions and conferences
Source: Write to Read

While a writing workshop is a multilevel activity, in that writers can work at their own pace and level, having personal time with the teacher is key to supporting writer growth, particularly with younger writers who are still finding their writing wings and do not yet have automaticity over transcription. In some of our partner schools, teachers have found it beneficial to have the learning support teacher in the room during independent writing time, so that children receive timely feedback and scaffolding:

> *My learning support teacher, I've organized so he's in class at that time. So, we're both there to conference because they're young. At the start we weren't doing that… they came on loads when all got a chance to conference a lot.*
>
> (2nd class teacher)

Such support allows for targeted scaffolding and is helpful when there is wide variation in writer development. However, it is also important that children have time to formulate their ideas and work unaided. An adult always on hand to prompt and spell a word or remind a child to include punctuation, removes the need for children to develop that awareness themselves and to use their tools to persist in the face of a challenge.

Conferences are an opportunity for you to connect with writers on a personal level and when combined with other formative assessment data (e.g. reading over the writing prior to the conference, share session notes, benchmarking on the *Write to Read* rubric) can assist you in bringing a sharper focus and purpose to conferences. As one teacher noted, conferences help you *'kind of build a picture of them as a writer, things that they're achieving, things that they're struggling with'*. They are also an opportunity to see how children are integrating mini lessons into their writing, to build their oral language skills, to prompt them to consider the aesthetics of language and text structures. Integrating explicit attention to the decontextualised academic language register relevant to each genre provides students with further practice in acquiring and using such language (e.g. proposition, corroborating evidence, counterclaim) in authentic interactions.

We have found it helpful to begin the conference by asking the writer to tell you a bit about the writing so far or to ask an open-ended question such as: how is the writing going today? Reading quickly over the writing on the page, it is also a good idea to find something to praise:

- Great title, intriguing, it didn't give the story away!
- I love the opening sentence, it really made me want to read on…
- I really like that you have included ideas from yesterday's mini lesson on adjectives, your use of the word…is perfect there.

Reacting to the writer, responding to their ideas and prompting them to disclose or elaborate more orally can help writers see how they can embellish text or add details for clarity or emphasis. Showing such interest conveys to authors that their ideas are valued and respected. Conferences should also be an opportunity for children to highlight for you the parts that they are pleased with and parts where they would welcome some advice (Figure 10.4).

Addressing one aspect for development during a conference is more effective than drawing attention to multiple dimensions that you might spot need support. Conferences should leave children feeling good about their writing and with a sense of direction as to how they might further develop and enhance it. Such feeding back and feeding forward are a hallmark of effective teachers of writing (Gadd & Parr, 2017).

Learning how to manage conferences and how to converse with writers of different ages and stages of development takes practice and comes with experience and lots of reflection on how well conferences are working in reality for both you and the children. The account shared below (Box 10.1) illuminates one teacher's journey towards effective conferencing from tentative beginnings.

Teacher might say…	Writer might say…
* Tell me about your writing	* Can you help me with this please?
* Why did you choose this topic?	* I'm really proud of this, can I show you?
* What are you finding tricky?	* I'm finding ____ difficult
* What are you planning to do next?	* This is my favourite part.

Figure 10.4 Sample anchor chart: oral language conference prompts

Source: Write to Read

BOX: 10.1 A TEACHER'S PERSPECTIVE ON CONFERENCING

Roisin O Shea has taught in DEIS schools for all of her career as a classroom or learning support teacher. She is a *Write to Read* coach and has supported schools and teachers to align their literacy practice with research. She is currently a principal of a DEIS school.

Overheard in the classroom: 'I like it when she conferences with me because I get to do all the talking. It's better than answering questions!'

Little did this child know that I was struggling with the conferencing aspect of the writing workshop. Mini lessons, sharing, feedback, setting goals, reflecting – these I felt I could plan for and support adequately in the classroom. How could I plan for the type of comment or questions that could stump me? That I would not have an answer for? Anyone who has spent any time in a classroom or working with children knows those type of questions!

I had knowledge of the theory and on the surface, I knew what conferencing with children about their writing involved. I had done the readings, discussed things with the mentor working with our school and then did more readings for good measure. We spend the largest proportion of time in writing workshop on the children writing and conferencing so I knew the importance of it. Still, I was struggling to make it work or even to understand what conferencing could look like in my classroom. Something had to change.

In everything I had read and heard about conferencing, its importance as a source of valuable assessment information and the importance of having systems in place to capture this information were emphasised. In reflecting on my struggle and trying to make conferencing with the children more natural, I realised that I was focusing my attention on capturing all of this precious data and I was missing out on real, valuable and genuine conversations with enthusiastic young writers. I pared back the note-taking! Gone was the printed template to fill with details of our conversations and replaced with an address label. This 9 X 3.5 cm rectangle of paper helped me to focus on the child rather than the notes and the genuine interaction filled with reactions, questions and conversations about writing. I intentionally noticed if they were using the skills from the mini lessons. I learned about their preferences, their styles, tools they were using in their writing and where, they, as writers were placing their emphasis and importance. Ironically by using a smaller physical record of the conference I was gaining a better picture of the children as writers.

As the term went on, I noticed that some children would talk for hours about their writing but it was the quieter children that I worried about. These were the children who gave the shortest answers, there was nothing they were struggling with (or so they told me!). The writing folder stayed firmly closed while we both sat in uncomfortable silence waiting for the conference to be over. It was time to give the children a wider range of tools to speak about or improve their talk about their writing.

During mini lessons, we focused on phrases, vocabulary, sentence stems and made anchor charts. We worked on conversation skills; tone of voice, body language, eye contact (where appropriate). We watched video clips from well-known authors speaking about their work. As a class, we made decisions about classroom systems and procedures that made conferencing time valuable for everyone. This time and effort helped to strengthen our classroom community and climate, built trust and helped to develop the confidence of the community of young writers.

Lastly, the children (and myself) realised that the teacher doesn't always have the answers but that's ok – real authors don't always have the answer straight away either!

The rest of the class must learn to respect each other's time and space and not to interrupt as you engage in conferences. You can set the tone in September and ensure children learn to self-regulate, manage time, work independently and problem solve when they encounter difficulties. They can be encouraged to add suggestions to the anchor chart (see Figure 10.5).

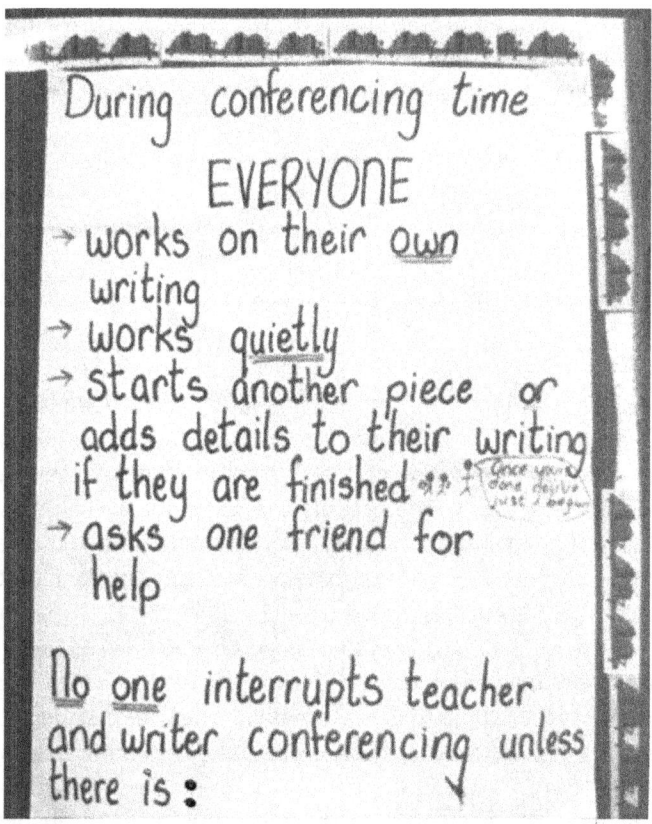

Figure 10.5 Anchor chart: Expectations during conferencing time
Source: Write to Read

Cultivating an engaged collaborative community of writers conveys to children that there are many teachers in the room, and that they may seek help from each other when warranted. Teachers have noted:

> *There's a working noise, it's not a silent classroom, whereas English before...They would have been just working away quietly, getting through the workbook, whereas now they're busy and they're choosing what they're writing. They're working away. They're talking about their work to other kids. They're helping each other. I'm not just up at my desk or whatever waiting for them to finish or helping probably just the weak child. You help all the kids now... like you do little mini-lesson groups and it's more productive. There's more going on. There's learning going on, whereas before I don't know how much learning was...*
>
> (3rd class teacher)

Table 10.3 provides a brief summary of the key elements of scaffolding social interaction and writer response in the context of the Author's Chair and conferencing within writing workshops.

Teaching Writers to Evaluate Writing

While share sessions and conferencing play a key role in assisting children in discerning and evaluating the strengths and weaknesses of their writing, evaluation can also be promoted more formally by drawing on checklists and rubrics linked to mini lessons (see Table 10.7). Highlighting to children that their favourite authors critically evaluate their word choice and add and delete sentences and paragraphs as they continuously work towards shaping the words on the page, to create the original intention seen in their mind's eye, gives them insights into the purposes of writing. As highlighted in Chapter 1, such revision may occur in the moment as children compose while writing, and after writing as they read back over it. Reflecting on the intended audience is important if writers are to adjust their language register, sharpen their writing and convey their intentions to readers. Reflection requires the ability to detect 'dissonances between the author's intended meaning and the text produced' (Philippakos & MacArthur, 2016, p. 419). Evaluating and revising do not come naturally (de Smedt & Van Keer, 2017) and typically require repeated explicit demonstrations, particularly for struggling and inexperienced writers. Before writers can be expected to revise, learning how to evaluate the strengths and weaknesses of their work is a critical first step and should focus on helping them to self-assess how well they have acted on the mini lesson content and realised their ambitions. As highlighted in earlier chapters, mini lessons are at the heart of the writing workshop and as children's repertoire of writing techniques grows, they begin to write with greater clarity and originality. Mini lessons teach children to consider their word choice, sentence structure, genre structures, leads and conclusions. As one teacher remarked to us in adopting a writing workshop:

> *Now, you're actually teaching writing. When I look back to myself, my teaching here even before Write to Read came in, I mean I was probably guilty of you know, I taught sixth class for two years, going 'here, write an essay' but never actually telling them how to write a good one or how to make it better.*
>
> (Teacher 2nd class)

Table 10.3 Summary of key dimensions of effective share session and conferencing

Components of Writing Process	Writing Strategy	Classroom Application Teacher Models What, When How Using GRRM
Sharing and Responding Communicating with peers and teachers; giving and receiving feedback	**Peer sharing** Facilitate feedback in pairs, small groups or through the Authors' Chair Create anchor charts with sentence starters for the academic language register	**Positive environment:** Create a community of writers through a daily interactive share session Teach students to listen carefully to each other Establish trust and tone of classroom **Modelling how to respond to writers:** Show writers you are listening through your body language (e.g., eye contact, nodding) Model academic language (specific to the genre) and responsive feedback Co-construct anchor charts with children Teach students to respond sensitively to each other's writing **Use a structured format:** Begin by commenting on an aspect of the writing that you like and say why Notice specific elements of writing (imagery, word choice, character, structure, argument, etc.) Ask questions to clarify (enables the writer to understand that the reader needs more information) Offer constructive suggestions to the writer
	Conferences Individual and small-group feedback	Focus on the *writer*; not the writing! Resist the urge to correct errors. Encourage children to drive the conference direction: 80% child talk Employ wait time; give children time to express their thinking, questions, challenges Ask genuine open-ended questions: <ul><li>How is the writing going today?</li><li>Can you tell me about your piece so far?</li><li>What is your goal with this piece?</li><li>What are you trying to achieve?</li><li>What is going well for you?</li><li>What is not going so well?</li><li>What strategies have you tried?</li><li>What will you write next?</li></ul>

Table 10.4 Things I know about the craft of writing

12/9/24	Use Adjectives to Help Readers Visualise Characters
	Mr. Gum was a <u>fierce old</u> man with a <u>red beard</u> and <u>two bloodshot eyes</u>...(mentor text) Jack wore stripy green and blue socks and a short-sleeved t-shirt. (Child sample)
-/-/-	

Table 10.5 My skill mini lessons

10//12/24	Use a Full Stop at the End of a Sentence to Show the End of an Idea
	The duck did the work. The farmer stayed all day in bed. (mentor text) I cycled to the shop to buy sweets. I bought some for my little sister too.
-/-/-	

Providing children with templates to keep a record of mini lessons (one for craft (Table 10.4 and one for skills Table 10.5) creates a concrete reminder of the lessons taught. These can be placed at the start of the mini lesson section of the writing folder (see Chapter 6). Keeping a master list and retaining a copy of the mentor text extract used to teach the craft or convention will help you build a bank of authentic texts that can be used again and also shared with other colleagues. On the template, children should include the date, a key phrase to signal the content and a sample sentence from the mentor text. Additionally, creating a personal example helps writers to transfer what they have learned in the mini lesson to their own writing. This can be done just before they begin writing independently or added at the end of the workshop during the reflect and set goals part (what did I learn today? Did I try it in my writing? Choose an example from my writing; if not, set a goal).

As the year enfolds, the lists grow and are a visible reminder to children of all the writing techniques, skills and strategies that they have learned. Providing them with a copy of the mentor text used in the mini lesson allows children to mark up the text during guided practice and it can be used for further reference (Table 10.5).

Scaffolding Peer and Self-Assessment

Towards the end of a genre unit, mini lesson lists can be used to collaboratively generate child friendly checklists and rubrics based on the broad categories highlighted in Table 10.6. Reflecting on the learning from mini lessons paves the way for children to adopt an evaluative stance, to begin to engage in peer and self-assessment by identifying which techniques they have succeeded in transferring into their writing and to identify future goals. As the year progresses, greater precision and sophistication in language (word, sentence and discourse levels) and complexity of genre features should be expected.

Rubrics which break key dimensions of new strategies or processes into smaller steps can help children better comprehend the steps needed to apply the techniques to their writing,

Table 10.6 Peer and self-assessment strategies to promote reflection

Components of Writing Process	Writing Strategy	Classroom Application Teacher Models What, When How Using GRRM
Evaluating Rereading text with a critical eye: examining if the 'text' matches one's intentions **and** meets goals	**Self-evaluation** **Peer evaluation** Noting strengths and areas for revision at: • Word level • Sentence level • Discourse level Review craft anchor charts Review mini lesson list Create checklists	**Sample Questions to Ask** *Focus on quality of writing: Did I:* • Use apt precise words? • Use an appropriate level of vocabulary? • Vary my sentence structures? • Vary the complexity of my sentences? • Use a range of connectives and transitions to create flow and coherence? • Use an appropriate language register for the genre? • Use a range of craft mini lessons suitable to the genre? • Consider the audience? • Engage the reader? *Focus on ideas/clarity:* • Are my ideas clear? • Does the writing make sense? • Are my ideas in a sequence? • Is the structure relevant to the genre: e.g., beginning, middle, end? • Are there any gaps or confusions? • Does the writing capture the ideas I had in my mind's eye?
	Self-monitoring **Self-regulation**	***Did I meet my goals for this draft? If not, what do I need to change?*** • Identify priorities • Keep a written record of goals • Keep a checklist of goals achieved

articulate their understanding and consider the degree to which they are transferring techniques to their writing. Table 10.7 presents one example constructed by a classroom teacher and *Write to Read* coach who were working on showing young children (five to six years.) how to elaborate ideas and show details in their writing. It specifically addresses oral language and links the mini lesson to self-assessment, pair work and listening and feeding back in the share session.

When approached in this way such specificity clarifies the meaning and intent of learning goals, communicates high expectations and sets the children up to be successful. Figure 10.6 shows how a child in that class identified details in the writing (circled) and articulated a growing awareness of audience response and feedback which prompted further reflection.

Process Mini Lessons 223

Table 10.7 Sample rubric for adding details to writing, senior infant class

My Rubric: Adding Details	☆	☆☆	☆☆☆
I can put **details** in my writing			
I can **circle** details in my writing ⬭			
I can **talk** about my details with my partner 💬 💬			
I can **listen** for details when my partner shares 👂			
I can **say** what I think about my partner's details 💬			

Source: Authors, icons Microsoft Word

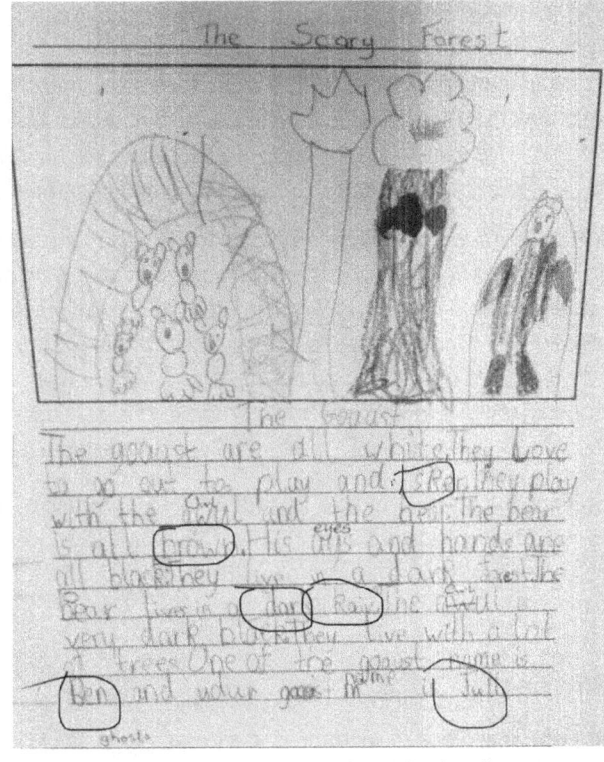

Figure 10.6 The Scary Forest, Senior Infant writer
Source: Write to Read

Senior Infant Writer response to peer and self-assessment. Response captured by Write to Read coach in class.
I didn't pick the part saying the ghosts were all white because people know the ghosts are white, so that wouldn't have been good. If the ghosts were a funny colour like pink then that would've been good. But I did pick their names at the end because they're funny names for ghosts and it tells you more about them. I did say lots about the ghosts and I showed that they like to have fun because they play but they are a little naughty too because they like to scare. That's why I put the star on that word…
____ said he picked the bit with the owl being very dark black because he liked that part. I think I would put the star there instead because it is better… I did pick a different one but I would change the next time.

In using rubrics, there is also a danger that mini lessons can become formulaic and viewed as a prescribed list of rules and features that must be included in 'good' writing, limiting children's deeper understanding of their purpose. In the UK, the inclusion of success criteria for writing quality has been criticised for its emphasis on criteria linked to 'grammatical complexity and ostentatious vocabulary' which it is argued results in writing that is 'inflated and unconvincing' (Barrs, 2019, p.18). Similarly, others have sounded a word of caution on explicit teaching, hypothesising that it may unintentionally constrain students' writing resulting in more 'controlled motivation' as children make their writing conform with features identified in lessons (de Smedt et al., 2019). Thus, there is a fine line between direct instruction which prescribes writing qualities and direct instruction that builds children's repertoires of techniques which they can employ to further develop their writer voice.

To safeguard against these unintended consequences, in our work with schools, we have emphasised the importance of presenting mini lessons as invitations to experiment with in writing rather than as prescriptions (see Chapter 8). The goal is for children to internalise and flexibly use techniques to fulfil their authorial intentions when composing and to be able to explain their choices and articulate how they enhance their text. Drawing on each step of the gradual release of responsibility model throughout craft mini lessons supports writers in developing their metacognitive awareness to the conditional level indicating that they not only can name the technique and give an example but more importantly can discern when to apply it and articulate why they employed it in their writing.

Encouraging children to compare their current writing with earlier samples using their checklists and rubrics affirms for them how they are growing as writers. As one Junior Infant teacher noted: *'when they compare it they're like, I was such a baby in September but now I'm so big and I'm doing such a great job'*. It is also reassuring for teachers to examine samples:

> *We went back in the folder, took out a recount that he did early in the year and were comparing the two... I was doing it to give the boy a boost and I myself was going 'oh my goodness', it was just unbelievable how he'd come on... but the difference in what they can write now at the end of the year! We're looking at a recount and adding extra things like 'is it boring? Have you used adjectives? Are you building tension?' Whereas at the start of the year it would have been just, is it in chronological order, in the past tense.*
>
> (2nd class teacher)

Keeping examples of work from one year to the next is also key to building progression in writing across a school (see Chapter 12). Once children have identified strengths and weaknesses in their writing, the next step is to encourage them to follow through and act on the feedback by revising parts that are not as strong as they could be.

Teaching Writers to Revise Writing

It is important not to insist on revision of every piece of writing, as it is not a good use of time given that not everything that is written is worth revising (Graves, 1994). Rather, revision and proofreading for publication should occur at regular intervals (at the end of a unit of work) and children should have control over which piece they will polish up and correct, but only after the processes of critique and evaluation have been modelled and completed.

Revision requires the writer to stand back, adopt a reader stance and consider the audience's reaction. It requires high levels of reflection, awareness of the craft dimensions of writing, of genre and a willingness to explore alternatives. It is linked to the writer's content knowledge of their topic and passion for it. As Graves (1994, p.219) notes:

> Until a writer discovers a subject and decides what interests him, the nouns will often be thin and colourless, and the verbs lifeless and imprecise. Until I discover what my subject is and have some conviction about it, how can I have verbs that will march across the page with force and energy?

It is interesting that Graves in the quote above focuses on the precision of language at the *word* level. This is in line with research that highlights the capacity to revise at the word level develops before revision at the sentence or whole text level (Berninger & Swanson, 1994) indicating a developmental pathway.

Drawing on reader response theory (Rosenblatt, 1978) and guiding children to read their own creations (print, multimodal, digital) with both an efferent and an aesthetic stance can pave the way for students to begin to consider their audience and engage in actual revision. Studies (e.g., Boscolo & Ascorti, 2004; Philippakos & MacArthur, 2016) have found that students make more substantive revisions to their writing resulting in improved quality when opportunities for reciprocal peer-review and support are provided.

It is helpful 'for writers to discuss with peers what they have done, partly in order to get ideas from their peers and partly to see what they, the writers, say when they try to explain their thinking' (NCTE, 2016, p.14). Providing feedback to a peer can sharpen students' understanding of audience, as when questioned, writers come to the realisation that the writing may require greater clarity or further elaboration. Though students are more likely to be able to detect macro-level issues in another student's text than in their own, responding to a peer's work can prompt children to further enhance their own first drafts (Philippakos & MacArthur, 2016).

As mini lessons accumulate, and students develop their knowledge of the various crafts they can employ to enhance their writing (ideas, word choice, sentence structure, leads, text and genre structure) they can be guided to consider alternatives at word, sentence and discourse levels. Drawing on Bereiter and Scardamalia's (1987) model (see Chapter 1), revision strategies can also focus on moving children from merely knowledge telling (a characteristic of less-skilled writers) to knowledge transforming (a characteristic of more-skilled writers). Modelling how to add further detail to elaborate and clarify, remove redundant detail and to reorder or sequence by moving sections around scaffolds children in doing so independently.

Encouraging students to write on every second line when composing allows space for revision at the word level and sentence levels to occur on a first draft. This can include highlighting, adding, deleting and honing word choice to capture the author's vision and intentions for the writing. This is a good entry point for primary school students and teachers can explicitly model through thinking aloud how they make choices to replace words, include transitions and connectives across sentences in their own compositions in order to hone, clarify and polish the writing.

Cremin and Oliver (2016) have pointed to the value of teachers sharing their writing with students. They examined teachers' attitudes to writing, their sense of themselves as writers and the potential impact of teacher writing on pedagogy and student outcomes in writing. Acknowledging that while the research is not strong (it has not been widely researched) teachers can be explicit role models for children when they write alongside them in the classroom. This is more likely to occur when teachers have a strong sense of self-efficacy and a positive attitude towards writing which research indicates enables them to better engage struggling writers and enhance their writing quality (Graham & Harris, 2002, cited in Graham et al., 2021). Such teachers are more likely to possess a growth mindset and are better able communicate to learners that improvement occurs with sufficient effort (Ekholm et al., 2018). Demonstrating how you approach revision makes visible for children, the invisible-in-the-head thinking processes and choices writers make as they reflect on their text and strive to bring it in line with the original ideas conjured in the mind's eye. In modelling the process, draw on the evaluation checklists which have been used by children to consider the strengths and areas for improvement (see sample checklist Table 10.8 (see Chapter 12 for the unit of work it is based on). This checklist could also be adapted to a four-point rubric and children could be encouraged to consider to what degree they have included these craft features in their writing.

Table 10.8 Sample checklist for evaluating informational writing: 6th class

Craft Checklist: Informational Writing	✓	x
Hooks for the Reader: An Engaging Lead		
Emotive lead		
Setting scene lead		
Question lead		
Surprising fact lead		
Word Choice		
Alliteration: Adjectives/verbs		
Tier 3 (terms specific to my topic e.g. amphibian/nictitating)		
Paint a scene		
Facts into scenes		
Similes		
Metaphors		
Drawing on the senses to show not tell		
Commas in elaborated sentences to show not tell		
Direct quotes for effect: referencing		
Organisation		
Crafting engaging headings/subheadings		
Transitional phrases to match structure (compare/contrast; cause/effect; chronological)		
Transitions to create flow		

BOX 10.2 A SAMPLE STRUCTURE FOR A REVISION LESSON

Materials: Craft evaluation checklist (based on mini lessons taught during the unit of work). A sample of your writing that you have selected for revision that is long enough to allow you to model how to enhance the draft using aspects of the checklist; colouring pencils to highlight.

Explain

Good morning writers, today we are going to focus on revising our chosen piece for publication. We have chosen the piece we are most proud of from our unit of work on informational writing. Yesterday we used our checklist to identify which mini lessons we had managed to incorporate into our writing. Now today, let's work on revising and polishing it for publication.

Demonstrate/Independent Practice

1. *Let's begin by identifying and highlighting in yellow the sentences that we really like. We don't want to lose these in the revision! I'm highlighting these because....* Give a reason and ask children to also highlight what they really like in their own rough draft.
2. *Next, I am going to think about my lead. I have opened with a surprising fact to jump into the piece. I am happy with that so I think I will leave it be.* Ask children to read over their lead and decide whether to retain or rework it. If they want to rework it, ask them to circle it and mark it No. 1 to remind themselves to revise it later, as it will take too long now.
3. *Let's look at word choice now. I have used an interesting adjective here, but I think I'll add another for effect as alliteration will create a better image; This verb here is a bit basic...I think it could be more precise to show how the ___ moves.* Model how to X it out and replace it with a more precise verb. Ask children to do the same with a couple of paragraphs of their own.
4. *In this paragraph here, I think I could include a simile....it would be more powerful than an adjective and will help the reader visualise. Here's another spot where I can add one.* Show children how to make an insertion using the caret symbol: ^. Think out loud and write the similes. Ask them to follow suit.
5. *In these two paragraphs, I have tried to paint a scene. I think could do a better job by drawing on the senses...I could describe sounds, smells, sights. I haven't room to rework this on my draft, so I am going to put a circle around these two paragraphs, and I will number them No.2, I will draft this on a separate page.* Ask children to see if there are sections of text that they would like to strengthen, circle them and number them for revision on a separate sheet of paper.

6. *Looking at my draft now I can see that some of my sentences are very short. I could add a connective and join these two together.* Insert a connective using the caret symbol^. *In this one here, I could add some details and use a comma to separate out the ideas/details.* Insert some details and say how they help the sentence to show not tell. Ask children to do the same.

7. *I am comparing and contrasting ___ with ___ in this piece. Next, I am going to check if I have used transitional words that clue the reader into the structure. The anchor chart will help me out...* Identify a couple of places where transitional phrases could be employed to bring greater internal coherence to the piece. Ask children to think about their structure and to consider if transitional phrases are used effectively (cause/effect, explanation, chronology).

8. *Lastly, I am going to check the flow between sections. Actually, I have lots of paragraphs, but I notice I haven't any headings in yet! Headings are important so the reader can see at a glance what the overall structure of the piece is. This section here is mostly about.....* Insert and create an engaging heading; Ask children to do the same. *I notice this section is a bit short and could do with more facts. I will go back to my notes and see what else I could include. I am going to mark it No.3. This paragraph maybe belongs earlier/later. I am going to move it up/down.* Circle it and use the change location symbol (Figure 10.7) to show where to put it

9. *So, everyone, do you see how we have used our checklist to help us to revise our writing? Let's create an anchor chart to help us remember how to do this in the future.*

How to Revise and Edit

1. Identify the parts I like, strong colourful words, phrases, descriptions, sentences (keep these)
2. Identify weak, boring language; consider alternatives (my wow words)
3. Consider figurative language instead of adjectives/verbs
4. Identify any confusing parts and reword
5. Identify where information is needed by the reader and insert details
6. Check the sequence and move things around to get a better flow;
7. Check the mini lessons list
8. Finally: Does what is written on the page match my intention? Is this my best effort?

Now spend some time reading and revising. Take out another sheet of paper and revise the lead, sections that you numbered. Don't forget to put the same number on the new sheet so you can use it when you publish. You can work in pairs or on your own (Table 10.9).

Table 10.9 Summary of revision strategies

Components of Writing Process	Writing Strategy	Classroom Application Teacher Models What, When, How Using GRRM
Revising/Editing Cognitive activity where the writer makes conscious decisions to revise and reorder text to make it more effective and engaging	Rework text at the: • Word level • Sentence level • Discourse level Polish writing Create anchor charts for each craft element Utilise self-evaluation, peer and teacher feedback Choose the most effective form/genre to communicate ideas (e.g. a poem, a report, a narrative)	NOT EVERYTHING should be revised. ***Revising Word Level (How precise is my word choice?)*** • Replace overused words with more apt choices; Promote ambitious word choice • Use precise verbs and nouns • adjectives/adverbs where necessary • Use imagery (similes/metaphors) and sensory detail where appropriate • Use a combination of tier 2 (sophisticated descriptive language) AND tier 3 (domain-specific) vocabulary in informational/persuasive texts. ***Revising Sentence Level*** • Refine level of connectives and transitions between sentences (varying according to genre and class level expectations) • Vary sentence length for pace • Introduce elaborated clauses to extend sentences • Rework order and precision of sentences within paragraphs ***Revising Discourse/Text Level*** • Rework the sequence/chronology of the overall text to ensure coherence/flow • Consider more elaborate or sophisticated structural forms to engage the reader (e.g. cause/effect; compare/contrast; time twists; foreshadowing) • Identify where further detail is warranted and add it (number new insertions in text; write new text on a separate page; numbering facilitates the writer in remembering where to find new information) • Delete redundant detail • Clarify any confusing parts

Teaching Writers Proofreading Strategies

As with any process of writing, teaching proofreading strategies to students is essential. Research-supported strategies such as COPS (Graham & Harris, 2005) support students in identifying surface-level errors in their writing (Table 10.10). As students in older classes tend to write longer texts, it is useful to devote some time daily towards the end of each writing workshop to proofreading, e.g., in the last 2-3 minutes prior to the share session, students can be directed to stop and reread what they have written so far that day and to fix up any errors they notice using editing symbols (Figure 10.7) and a coloured pen (green is better than red: Kennedy, 2014). This keeps the task manageable for students as if it is left until they are publishing a text, it can be a more onerous task and one not relished by children at the primary level.

As with all processes of writing putting peer support mechanisms in place for final proofing prior to publication is effective in making children pause and check accuracy. Again, the tone and spirit in which this is enacted is key:

> *Sometimes, I will put a spell on them and they are the teachers so they will swap their work and they'll give their partners two stars and a wish. Now, what they give is very much neat handwriting or it's quite basic stuff, but they just love the idea of checking over. And you will notice as well, they check their work a lot more because before they are handing over to someone else; they don't want to get mistakes back.*
>
> (1st class teacher)

Similar to the revision process, children may not notice their own inaccuracies but may pick up on them in other children's work. How these are pointed out has to be handled sensitively and modelled for children.

Table 10.10 Proofreading strategies and practical classroom application

Components of Writing Process	Writing Strategy	Classroom Application Teacher models What, When, How Using GRRM
Proofreading	**Prepare text for publication** • Identify surface features interfering with meaning • Clean text for grammar, spelling, punctuation and sentence combining	**Proofreading symbols** • a carat for missing words: ^ • Delete extra words: / • Circle spelling for checking: • New paragraph ¶ • Underline grammar/syntax for checking **COPS strategy (Graham & Harris):** • **C**apitalise first word in sentence and proper nouns • Check **o**verall appearance of paper • Use commas/end **p**unctuation correctly • Check **s**pellings and correct

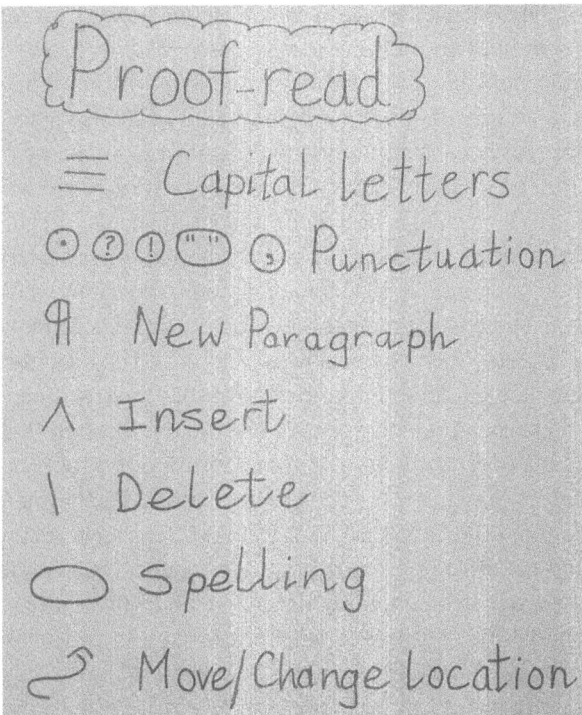

Figure 10.7 Anchor chart: Proofreading symbols
Source: Write to Read

Publishing Writing

Recent reviews of research of the impact of digital tools on writing (Williams & Beam, 2019; Dwyer et al., 2022) show that they support students' composing processes and writing skills. Dwyer et al. (2022, p. 6 citing Colwell & Hutchison, 2015) report five positive findings for primary-aged children engaging in digital writing:

a) students write for more authentic purposes;
b) the inclusion of oral language activities using digital recording devices supports students' idea development and writing;
c) students have increased opportunities to interact and collaborate with peers, critically evaluate each other's work, and consider multiple perspectives;
d) students are encouraged to think about traditional content in new ways;
e) digital tools provide insight into students' reading behaviours and comprehension.

As highlighted by NCTE (2016, p. 15) using 'technologies such as voice recording apps on smartphones and audio editing tools…students create podcasts, videos, or other multimedia work in which they share their writing through oral production' (NCTE, 2016, p.15) benefitting their oral language development and an appreciation of the differences between speaking and writing.

The final step in the writing process is deciding on how to present the writing (see Table 10.11). Using the evaluation and revision process, children can be guided to use their revisions to develop a final copy. This can be as simple as writing it out in their best handwriting or typing it up on a tablet or computer. Students can also learn that there are several options open to them in considering the best genre/mode for their text (Graham et al., 2012b/2018) e.g., might the theme of climate change be best represented in a traditional written report or a multimodal ensemble with audio and visual links or might it be just as powerfully conveyed in poetic form? Using a writing workshop approach Smith (2014) and Dalton (2014/2015) found that 'students were highly engaged in designing multimodal pieces that would appeal to a peer audience and reveal their unique talents as multimodal storytellers' (cited in Dalton, 2014, p.296). Such options invite children to consider design, layout, imagery and audio and to choose a digital tool that best presents their writing (infographics, multimodal PowerPoint digital posters and ebooks). Technology used in this way demonstrates how digital tools can support them as writers and in using the tools children learn how to use the new technologies effectively for their own purposes. Furthermore, a significant finding highlighted by Dalton (2014/2015) was that training children in small groups on different aspects of design and technology promoted student agency, independence and collaboration: 'perhaps the most valuable lesson we learned came from students when we employed a cascading expert model. This positioned students as experts and allowed us to spread the workload to reach more students (p.302).

Providing children with opportunities to present their writing in a different genre form further develops their appreciation of author's voice and how the genre can be harnessed in the service of their writing intentions. One strategy that has worked well for teachers is teaching children how to develop a found poem (see Box 10.3) from their polished writing piece. Found

Table 10.11 Publishing and sharing writing

Components of Writing Process	Writing Strategy	Classroom Application Teacher models what, when, how using GRRM
Publishing Presenting a written oral, multimodal or digital text to an audience	Public sharing Celebrate the work	NOT EVERYTHING a student revises should be published. Students should have autonomy over text selected for publication and form of publication: • Present a range of publishing options: Print, digital, multimodal • Binding techniques for book making • A range of digital tools (audio, video) • Celebrations (e.g. a poetry café/school assemblies/sharing in other classes • Display in the classroom

poems take 'existing texts and refashion them, reorder them, and present them as poems. The literary equivalent of a collage, decisions of form, such as where to break a line, are left to the poet' (https://poets.org/glossary/found-poem). It is important to model the process of creating a found poem. See Figure 10.8 to view a child's efforts to publish their writing in more than one form.

> **BOX 10.3 HOW TO CREATE A FOUND POEM**
> - Choose an award winning descriptive informational narrative text (see Chapter 8 for suggestions)
> - Think aloud and pick out words and phrases that reflect the soul and kernel of the topic.
> - Collect about eight-ten key words or phrases.
> - Make sure you write the exact words (quotes).
> - Then put them into an interesting and meaningful order.
> - Decide on the line breaks.
> - That becomes your poem!

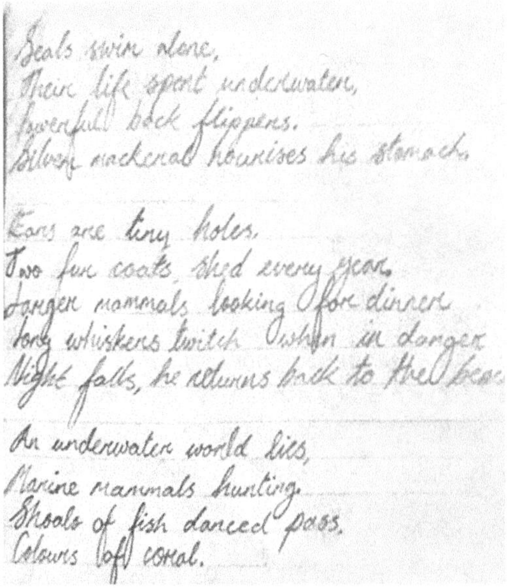

Seals swim alone,
Their life spent underwater,
Powerful back flippers,
Silver mackerel nourishes his stomach.
Ears are tiny holes,
Two fur coats shed every year,
Larger mammals looking for dinner,
Long whiskers twitch when in danger,
Night falls, he returns back to the beach.
An underwater world lies,
Marine mammals hunting,
Shoals of fish danced past,
Colours of coral.

Figure 10.8 A poem developed from a narrative report (see Chapter 8 for an extract of the narrative form)

Source: Write to Read
(see Chapter 8 for an extract of of this 6th class writer's narrative form)

Finally, consider providing an external audience for children to celebrate and present their work. Poetry cafes, publication on school website and displays in hallways (see Chapter 6, Figure 6.6) are significant motivators for children and build their confidence and sense of self-efficacy.

Reflect, Connect, Act

1 Share a piece of your own writing with the children. Using the gradual release of responsibility model, demonstrate for children how you would evaluate your writing: e.g. identifying lines, sections you like, sections that are strong and words, sentences and paragraphs which could be honed with stronger, more apt vocabulary and/or further elaborated and clarified. Develop an anchor chart with the children. Observe children as they engage in evaluating a piece of text of their choice and document how children negotiate the process.

2 Repeat the process and demonstrate how you would use the evaluation to revise your writing. Draw on a checklist of strategies previously taught in craft mini lessons to model the process.

3 Compare the writing product (before and after revision) of a high, middle and lower-achieving writer in your class for a genre of your choice. At what stage of development are children: are they revising at the word level only? The sentence level or discourse level? Are they knowledge telling only or knowledge transforming?

4 Consider mini lessons in which children have successfully integrated new strategies and techniques into their writing. Which children need further scaffolding to transfer the strategies they have learned? Which genre features have children demonstrated in their writing and which aspects could be further enhanced in a further study of the genre later in the year? Make notes to inform your future planning.

Suggestions for Further Reading

1 Graham, S., Bollinger, A., Booth Olson, C., D'Aoust, C., MacArthur, C., McCutchen, D., & Olinghouse, N. (2012b/2018). *Teaching elementary school students to be effective writers: A practice guide* (NCEE 2012-4058). Washington, DC: National Center for Education Evaluation and Regional Assistance, Institute of Education Sciences, U.S. Department of Education. Retrieved from http://ies.ed.gov/ncee/wwc/publications_reviews.aspx#pubsearch.

2 Philippakos, Z. A., & MacArthur, C. A. (2016). The effects of giving feedback on the persuasive writing of fourth- and fifth-grade students. *Reading Research Quarterly, 51*(4), 419-433. https://doi.org.dcu.idm.oclc.org/10.1002/rrq.149

3 De Smedt, F., & Van Keer, H. (2018). Fostering writing in upper primary grades: A study into the distinct and combined impact of explicit instruction and peer assistance. *Reading and Writing, 31*(2), 325-354. https://doi.org/10.1007/s11145-017-9787-4

11 Addressing the Needs of Diverse Writers

As outlined in earlier chapters, writing is a complex process, involving co-ordination of multiple sources of knowledge, including topic knowledge, knowledge about text genres and text structures, metacognitive knowledge, and knowledge about grammar, punctuation and spelling. Writers should be able to engage in the writing process and co-ordinate or regulate sources of knowledge, motivational and memory processes as they compose text. They must be motivated to write. Given the above, it is not surprising that national assessments of writing point to a significant number of children who struggle to meet grade-level expectations in writing.

This chapter addresses the writing needs of diverse learners including children with learning difficulties, children for whom English is a Second Language and children in socio-economically disadvantaged contexts. A cluster of interventions is proposed to address varying needs among these diverse learners, with modifications as needed, recognising that some children may belong to multiple at-risk groups. After reading this chapter, you should be able to answer the following questions:

> **Reflect and Connect**
>
> 1. What difficulties can students experience in learning to write?
> 2. How can we distinguish between development differences and learning difficulties, as they relate to children's development as writers?
> 3. How can we support the writing development of children in different at-risk groups?
> 4. What instructional adaptations may be needed?
> 5. How can we evaluate the effectiveness of interventions for at-risk writers?

There are a number of areas in which differences between pupils may arise, including planning (linked to students' generation of ideas), translating ideas into grammatical strings (linked to writers' linguistic experience and knowledge at the word, sentence and discourse levels), and transcription (including handwriting/keyboarding and spelling), which might be expected to become more fluent and automatic over time. Variation in one or more of these

DOI: 10.4324/9781003303510-11

areas may constitute a difference or a difficulty.[1] Children with writing difficulties may not have access to writing as a learning tool, a vehicle for self-expression and self-reflection, or a skill required in society.

Three groups of children who may experience writing difficulties are identified in this chapter: (i) children with special education needs, including those with learning difficulties in such areas as transcription skills, sentence- and discourse-level skills, and motivation (Gillespie Rouse, 2019); (ii) children for whom English is a second or additional language, who may need additional support in developing ideas for writing, as well as support in developing language through writing; and (iii) children in socio- economically disadvantaged contexts, who may need support in identifying the functional uses of language in the range of ways that the school (or curriculum) demands (Halliday, 1978, 1985) or may need to extend their academic language and content knowledge, including language structures associated with different genres.

Examples of modified environments for children with difficulties are described (e.g., Pasquarella, 2019), and specific strategies that can be deployed when working with at-risk writers are outlined (e.g., self-regulated strategy development; self-evaluation of writing, meta-cognition as it relates to writing, direct instruction of text structures, technology supports, and specific interventions/programmes). The need to evaluate the impact of interventions is stressed.

Children with Special Needs in Writing and Struggling Writers

Gillespie Rouse (2019) notes that, while a strong body of research has focused on addressing the needs of children with learning difficulties in writing, the same strategies are appropriate for other groups, including those with autism spectrum disorders (ASD), emotional and behavioural disorders and speech and language difficulties, as well as those whose difficulties may not have been diagnosed but who still struggle with writing. Collectively, these students can be referred to as struggling writers. That said, Gillespie Rouse acknowledges that instruction and adaptations for students with ASD and those with intellectual difficulties may need to be more intensive than for others with writing difficulties.

Pupils with writing difficulties can struggle with a number of aspects of writing. In considering these, it is important to note that younger (less mature) writers may also demonstrate some of the same difficulties, even though they may be developing along an expected trajectory. Areas of potential difficulty for struggling writers include:

- *Transcription* – difficulties with handwriting/keyboarding or spelling can impact in negative ways on other aspects of writing such as content, meaning and organisation as an inordinate amount of attention is allocated to basic processes; children who struggle with handwriting or typing (for example, writing slowly, letter by letter) or spelling often produce writing that is difficult to read (without their help) and characterised by many spelling errors. These children may not be able to write for sustained periods of time. Moreover, their difficulties with transcription may mask other aspects of their writing in assessment contexts, leading to low scores on dimensions such as ideas and organisation.
- *Translating ideas into sentences* – struggling writers may experience difficulty as they translate ideas into words, and link those words in grammatically correct sentences.

Struggling writers tend to produce sentences that are shorter and less syntactically complete than other writers and lack variety. According to Saddler (2013), constructing a sentence is linguistically and cognitively demanding, requiring the same level of processing as planning and organising a full written text. Fayol (2016) describes the linguistic skills involved in sentence construction as including consideration of lexical, syntactical, punctuation and rhetorical choices, while also ensuring that the sentence makes sense within the context of the text being written. When difficulties with transcription and sentence construction co-exist, children may not write fluently, with writing speed half that of non-struggling writers.

- *Composing skills* – according to Graham et al. (2013), instead of approaching writing as a process requiring intentional goal setting, planning, multiple drafts and reflection on audience, organisation and progress towards goals, children with writing difficulties view writing as a process of content generation, translating an idea into a sentence, which then becomes the basis for the next sentence, and so on (the knowledge-telling approach described by Bereiter and Scardamalia (1987), which is also characteristic of younger writers). Texts produced by struggling writers may contain fewer elaborations, details or connections between ideas, and may fail to meet the needs of intended audiences. Gillespie Rouse (2019) also points out that struggling writers may have difficulties with revising and editing. When they reread texts to improve them, they are more likely to make 'surface-level' edits, such as correcting spelling and punctuation, rather than substantive revisions to a text. According to Graham and Harris (2005), pupils with writing difficulties lack the strategies for planning, writing and revising, the procedural ('how to') knowledge to implement strategies, and the ability to self-regulate strategies needed to produce good quality writing. Students with learning difficulties may also lack genre knowledge and associated text structures, and so there may be significant gaps in the structure of their writing.
- *Motivation and Engagement* – struggling writers or writers with learning difficulties may lack the motivation to engage in and complete writing tasks (Gillespie & Rouse, 2019). They may also lack the knowledge of why writing is important or personally relevant to them. According to Graham and Harris (2005), struggling writers may also have difficulty sustaining effort during writing tasks, though they may overestimate their writing abilities (i.e., they may have high self-efficacy as writers). This may lead struggling writers to underestimate the effort they need to put into their writing. Another viewpoint is that children with writing difficulties doubt that their efforts impact on their writing performance, causing them to allocate less effort to writing, because they believe that writing performance is outside their control, and under the influence of external factors (Troia et al., 2012).

Gillespie Rouse (2019) recommends evidence-based strategy instruction for children with writing difficulties. In the case of handwriting, she recommends:

- Providing explicit instruction on how to form letters, with several letters that include common features introduced at the same time (e.g., c, d and g all contain backward strokes). Teacher modelling is recommended for forming letters, as well as time for guided and independent practice.

- Using visual cues (e.g., a dot) to indicate where to begin and numbered arrows showing the correct sequence of strokes required to form each letter. Visual cues should be available as scaffolds during guided practice, and removed for independent practice.
- Using cover-and-copy activities, as pupils examine a properly-formed letter, then cover the letter and copy it from memory.
- Integrating handwriting practice with writing extended text, as children apply handwriting skills. One suggested activity is to write words and sentences that include the newly learned letters for a specific period of time such as 2 minutes. Another is to use the new letters in writing a longer text.

Gillespie Rouse also advises that, although keyboarding may be introduced as an accommodation for children with writing difficulties, it should not replace handwriting instruction and should be accompanied by explicit instruction in how to keyboard and use other software features such as spell check or grammar check.

A number of evidence-based strategies can also be deployed with children who have spelling difficulties. Identified by Graham (2019), McMaster et al. (2018) and Williams et al. (2017), they include:

- Providing explicit instruction in letter-sound correspondences and in spelling syllable patterns, meaning patterns (morphemes) and irregular words.
- Teaching pupils to use self-correction strategies when studying spelling words (e.g., cover-copy-compare, where the pupil looks at the spelling word, covers it, writes the word from memory, and compares the written word to the target word).
- Distributing spelling practice over time, by limiting the number of words that pupils are expected to learn in a given session.
- Providing immediate error correction. This is evident in computer programs that provide immediate feedback when a student misspells a target word.
- Enabling pupils to apply new spelling knowledge in sentence writing and in longer texts to support writing fluency.

For children with learning difficulties, a multi-sensory approach is often recommended for teaching reading and spelling. An example is provided in Box 11.1.

BOX 11.1 TEACHING ALPHABETICS: COMBINING SYNTHETIC, ANALYTIC AND MULTISENSORY APPROACHES TO TEACH PHONEME-GRAPHEME RELATIONSHIPS

Example (adapted from Montgomery, 2000) **Materials:** objects for particular sounds, puppet, big book or rhyme, chart paper for modelling, handwriting sheet for practice, crayons, letter cards, picture cards	The array of materials is designed to support active learning. The first part of the lesson involves the revision of previously learned sounds.

Introduction

Good morning readers, today we are going to learn a new letter and its sound and how to write it. We have learned four so far. Let's see what we can remember. Have the four picture-letter cards ready. Flash the cards quickly in any order. Children name the object in the picture and say the initial sound:

- table /t/
- sock /s/
- igloo /i/
- nest /n/

Ensure they clip the consonant sounds and do not tack on a vowel sound as they articulate each one. Do this a couple of times and observe if children are articulating correctly.

Source: *Write to Read*

Next use the plain letter cards. Flash the cards quickly. Emphasis should be on automaticity and accuracy. Children have to remember the object (without the picture clue this time), name it, and say the sound. For example: when you flash the following plain letter cards: t, s, i, n, the children say:

- table /t/
- sock /s/
- igloo /i/
- nest /n/

Skywriting can help children to remember how to write the letters.

The multi-sensory approach involves auditory, visual, kinaesthetic and tactile elements.

The teacher plays a key role as they model letter formation.

(Continued)

| t | s | i | n |

Let's see if we can remember how to write the letters. Name each letter and have children stand up and, using their large motor muscles, skywrite the letter as you model. Next, call the sound, and on their whiteboard ask children to name and write the letter that makes the sound. Check for accuracy as children hold up their whiteboards.

Multisensory Introduction to a new letter/sound: p
Auditory

Feely bag of objects (e.g., pen, pencil, paper, pasta, potato, pepper); Invite children to reach in and pull out an object and identify it; Emphasise the beginning sound. When all objects have been identified repeat the sound and show the picture-letter card.

Visual

Hold up the plain letter card, and name it: this is the letter p. p says /p/ as in pig, potato, pasta, pen, paper, pencil; Make sure the children articulate it correctly without tacking on any sounds.

| t | s | i | n |

(Continued)

Read a sentence from context e.g., a big book: *The Pig in the Pond* or a rhyme; circle the letter p every time it occurs: Where is it placed: beginning, middle or end of the word?

Kinaesthetic

Model how to write p using large motor muscles: emphasise the beginning and endpoint.

Tactile

Children trace it in a sand tray/or over sandpaper letters.

Writing on paper

- replicate the handwriting page on large format chart paper and model tracing over the letter with chunky crayons
- using crayons children trace over the model 3 times, saying a rhyme that emphasises the beginning and end point
- in the box to the right, model writing the letter independently; children follow suit
- model writing the letter three times (one very good formation, one not so good and one very messy) on the first of three lines on the paper and think out loud: '*I think this is my best one because I started in the right place, I stayed in between the lines and I angled the curve*'; children follow suit and complete three times on each of the three lines, they write the letter three times on each line and put a star above the letter they think is formed the best
- finally, have children turn over the page and write the letter from memory with their eyes closed

Trace the letter 3 times with a crayon	Try writing it here on your own

- using the cards to review letter names and sounds; use the puppet to make some errors and ask children to correct the errors

(Continued)

Practice blending sounds using letters known to the children • begin with CVC words initially: have 4-5 words ready on flashcards and model how to blend sounds to make the words e.g. tip, sip, tin, nip, sit **Practice segmenting, spelling orally and in writing** • Call 4-5 words with the target letter/sound relationships: beginning with CVC • Children say the word orally first, finger tap it, then write it • Show the words on cards and in pairs; children check over what they wrote to see if they were right: encourage them to put a check mark over all letters that are correct.	
Assessment Take anecdotal notes on which children: • are fluently able to name, sound and write the letter • are not accurately articulating the sound • cannot write the letter from memory (have to look at the picture/plain letter cards for support) • form letters incorrectly (e.g., beginning/end point, reversals) • need support with blending CVC words • need support with segmenting sounds and writing	Short anecdotal notes help the teacher to recall what the child has learned, and what needs to be reinforced.
Follow up work • Review the letters/sounds before introducing new concepts • Initiate some small group work to support children identified as needing further reinforcement (e.g. Elkonin boxes for segmentation) • To increase the challenge: move beyond CVC words progressing to CCVC (spin; snip); CVCC (tips/tint); CCVCC (stint) for both reading and spelling • Continue to add new sounds/letters/concepts each week (2-3)	

Chapter 2 provided a number of suggestions for teaching sentence construction to pupils. Further evidence-based strategies for improving sentence structure have been suggested by Datchuk and Kubina (2013), Datchuk et al. (2015); Furey et al. (2017), Saddler and Graham (2005) and Scott Sheldon et al. (1998). These are generally presented to older learners (those from Grade 2 onwards) and include:

- Providing learners with direct instruction in constructing simple and more complex sentences that include subjects/verbs, infinitives, prepositional phrases, adjectives and coordinating conjunctions, with attention to capital letters and punctuation as well. Pupils should then be held accountable for applying the sentence-construction techniques they have learned to their own writing.
- Providing learners with picture-word prompts (a picture and set of associated words) during initial instruction so that they are supported in generating the sentence, without having to worry about content as well.
- Engaging learners in sentence combining, so they learn about syntactical choices for their writing as they combine simple sentences into more complex ones and decide which combinations work best. As with sentence construction, parts of speech and grammar can be taught in the context of sentence combining.
- Situating grammar instruction in an authentic writing context, where learners consider the effect of different grammatical choices on their writing.
- Applying knowledge of sentence structure to revising and editing – learners can discuss how to improve sentences in the text they have written, drawing on their knowledge of sentence construction and grammar.

In addition to instruction in transcription and sentence construction, struggling writers may need support with compositional aspects of writing. The following are among the specific interventions that have been recommended for the improvement of compositional writing:

- Provide instruction to increase knowledge of the writing process (planning, writing, revising, self-regulating) and knowledge of different writing genres (Graham & Harris, 2005; Graham & Perin, 2007). Chapter 2 provides a set of mnemonics that can be taught to children with writing difficulties to support them in remembering the steps in key writing strategies.
- Teach self-regulated strategy development (SRSD). As outlined in Chapter 2, this includes six stages that should be implemented in sequence, with the pace and content of instruction tailored to learners' individual needs:
    - Develop background knowledge about the topic
    - Describe the strategy, as well as its purpose and benefits
    - Model the strategy (the teacher models how to use the strategy)
    - Memorise the strategy (the student memorises the steps in the strategy and accompanying mnemonic)
    - Support acquisition of the strategy (the teacher may scaffold student acquisition of the strategy)
    - Promote independent use of the strategy.

- Provide instruction on the various text structures (see Chapter 3 for details on structures underpinning narrative texts, informational texts, persuasive text, recount, etc.). Text structures such as sequencing ideas can be taught using the gradual release of responsibility model (GRRM) (Chapter 8) or Derewianka's (2015) key stages of genre study (Chapter 3).
- Emphasise self-regulation of writing by including the following student-level activities, recommended by Graham and Perin (2007):
  - Goal-setting activities (e.g., clarifying the purpose of writing)
  - Self-monitoring (self-assessment and self-recording)
  - Self-reinforcement
  - Self-instructions/self-statements
- Use schematics, diagrams or frames, such as those introduced in Chapter 3 in the context of genre study, to help pupils plan and structure their writing.

The writing motivation of struggling writers can also be addressed, as necessary. While motivation to write can be expected to increase as students engage in instructional activities and successfully compose texts, Gillespie Rouse (2019) suggests incorporating the following activities into ongoing teaching and learning to further enhance motivation to write:

- Provide instruction on why learning to write is important and why writing skills are valuable (e.g., writing to a local newspaper or contributing to a blog) and give students a choice of relevant writing topics.
- Set high expectations for students' writing while also scaffolding writing instruction. The provision of positive feedback (see Chapter 5) throughout instruction is also important in increasing student effort.
- Establish a positive classroom climate for writing, where students are willing to take risks and persist with challenging tasks. In this regard, teachers might share their own challenges with writing with their students.
- Help students to establish goals for their writing (e.g., number of genre elements to be included in a story; aspects of revision to focus on).
- Monitor children's writing performance, and show students how to self-monitor.

BOX 11.2 DYSGRAPHIA

According to the International Dyslexia Association (IDA) (n.d.),

> Dysgraphia is the condition of impaired letter writing by hand, that is, disabled handwriting. Impaired handwriting can interfere with learning to spell words in writing and speed of writing text. Children with dysgraphia may have impaired handwriting, impaired spelling (without reading problems), or both.

The IDA attributes dysgraphia to impaired orthographic coding, or 'the ability to store written words in working memory while the letters in the word are analysed or the ability to create a permanent memory of written words linked to their pronunciation and meaning'. They note that, while children with dysgraphia do not have a primary developmental motor disorder (an alternative cause of poor handwriting), they may 'have difficulty planning sequential finger movements such as the touching of the thumb to successive fingers on the same hand without visual feedback'. Hence, children with dysgraphia may have difficulty with one or other of orthographic coding and planning sequential finger movements, or both.

The IDA note that dysgraphia may co-occur with attention deficit hyperactivity disorder (ADHD), dyslexia (impaired reading) and with oral and written language disability or selective language impairment. The Association recommends explicit teaching in handwriting, spelling and composition for children with dysgraphia (see, for example, https://dyslexiaida.org/understanding-dysgraphia/). Some of the strategies and instructional adaptations described in this chapter may also be relevant.

Lavan and Talcott (2020) provide an overview of special intervention programmes that have been researched in the United Kingdom, and have been found to improve the handwriting, spelling and composition of writers with learning difficulties at both primary and secondary levels.

In many cases, the needs of students with learning and other difficulties can be addressed by making adaptations to existing instructional strategies. In a study by Troia and Graham (2017), the most frequent adaptations made by teachers in Grades 3-8 related to: extra time in which to complete assignments; feedback on problem areas; individualised instruction; conferencing; time to practice keyboard skills and strategies; sentence writing instruction; and peer assistance. Adaptions made least often included: self-regulated instruction; technology to aid writing; handwriting instruction; composition to aid dictation; and homework to reinforce skills/strategies. Homework was also considered by teachers to be the least effective adaptation, although they reported that it required a large amount of effort on their part.

Supporting Learners of English as an Additional Language as Writers

A key feature of the educational environment in many countries is the increase in children for whom English is an additional language. In England, the proportion of such children in public primary schools increased from 18.0% in 2015/2016 to 20.2% in 2022/2023 (Clark, 2023). It might be noted that such students are not evenly distributed across schools. A study by Strand et al. (2015) found that almost one-quarter of schools had fewer than 1% of EAL students, over half (54%) had less than 5%, while 8.5% (1 in 12) had a majority of students with EAL. In Ireland, the 2016 census found that 13% of the primary school population spoke a language other than English or Irish at home (Oireachtas Library & Research Service, 2020) and the proportion is likely to have increased since then. Children for whom English is an additional language have to learn the language of instruction, as well as content knowledge and academic skills such as writing.

Pasquarella (2019) notes that EALs are a diverse group, and that their cultural background, language exposure and school experiences should be considered when planning inclusive instruction in literacy. For example, a child's culture may impact on their view of writing, their understanding of the functions of writing, and how they see themselves as writers. Children who can already write in their native language may be at an advantage when writing in English. They may already understand the purpose of writing, and have linguistic and non-linguistic resources that they can use as they write in English. They can be supported to apply the knowledge about writing acquired in the first language to writing in the second language.

In England, the Department for Education (2020) issued a report showing a strong association between English language proficiency and performance in writing among students with EAL at the end of Key Stages 1 and 2. Considering EAL students at different levels of assessed proficiency, just 22% of students categorised by their schools as New to English achieved the expected standard in writing at KS1, compared to 46% of Early Acquisition students, 67% of those Developing Competence, 83% of those deemed to be Competent and 89% of those deemed to be Fluent. Furthermore, fewer EAL students at KS1 were found to have achieved the expected standard in writing, compared to reading, mathematics and science at each level of language proficiency. By KS2, writing was marginally ahead of reading for EAL students at each level of language proficiency.

Before considering specific strategies for supporting the writing development of EAL students, it is worth noting some general principles for teaching EALs students proposed by Liu et al. (2017). These are offered in the spirit of inclusion and reflect the adaptations that can be made to accommodate EAL students. They also have clear relevance for teaching writing:

- Using bilingual resources and strategies for specific teaching purposes – for example, dictionaries and online translation tools can be used to translate students' ideas in the native language into English and vice versa.
- Employing multimodal aids to reduce the language demands in learning – for example, multimodal 'tools' such as pictorial science dictionaries, video clips and pictures and cartoons can be drawn upon to support students' learning.
- Simplifying tasks to cater to individual needs and contexts – for example, teachers may modify and simplify their English input by speaking more slowly and reducing the use of colloquialisms.
- Using the home language for academic and social purposes – for example, teachers may wish to support children in developing literacy (including aspects of writing) in their home language and in English.
- Making cultural and contextual references to create resonance and rapport – different heritages and cultures can be celebrated.
- Combining mainstreaming with individual-focused support to ensure that no one is left behind.
- 'Buddying' or pairing to provide peer support for learning and social integration.
- Using dialogic tasks for effective content and language integration – including pair and share and collaborative learning, allowing EAL students to interact with their English-speaking peers in communicative contexts.
- Using flexible and continuous assessment to promote learning.

Addressing the Needs of Diverse Writers 247

One approach educators have taken to addressing the language needs of EAL students in the broader context of literacy development is to integrate oral language, reading and writing (see Chapter 10). Carlson (n.d.) recommends the following sequence in structuring writing activities for students with EAL:

- **Start with speaking** the vocabulary, sentence structures and ideas students will need to complete a writing task. In this way, students will better understand the content they will need to draw on as they write.
- **Follow with reading**, by providing students with reading practice on texts similar to what they are expected to write. This encapsulates the idea of mentor texts (Chapters 8, 9).
- **Finish with writing** – After students have engaged with speaking and reading, they are better prepared to move on to the writing stage.

Pasquarella (2019) recommends providing language support to students with EAL in order to increase their command of language, and their confidence in using it, with expected transfer to reading and writing. A key element of language support involves teaching academic vocabulary. This can involve direct instruction of keywords (6–8 per day), with student-friendly definitions provided. This can be extended so that students use the target vocabulary in sentences and paragraphs, thereby supporting transfer. Pasquarella recommends explicit instruction about morphological awareness so students can construct and understand morphologically complex words. There can be a focus on words with inflectional endings (e.g., *-s, -ing, -ed*), derivations (words with prefixes such as *un-* or *sub-*, and suffixes such as *-ness, -ly*) and compounds (e.g., *tombstone*). Instructional activities based on morphemes might be expected to improve sentence construction (grammar), spelling and vocabulary in writing, particularly if opportunities for transfer to writing are provided.

A number of proposals have been put forward on ways in which instruction should be modified to address the needs of students with EAL (e.g., Pasquarella, 2019; Bhowmik & Kim, 2021; Carlson, n.d., Lu & Kim, 2021). These include:

- Use diaries and journals to promote writing fluency and self-expression. Dialogue journals allow students to maintain ongoing communication with teachers or peers, enabling students to build writing fluency. Dialogue journals also provide teachers with a way to provide feedback and praise
- Engage in joint construction of text, with the teacher and EAL learners writing together (shared writing). Learners can contribute orally to the writing, and act as scribes together with the teacher to write the text. Oracy strategies (e.g., prompting words or phrases) can be used and students can be encouraged to use word banks to identify words.
- Ensure that EAL learners have opportunities to write in disciplines across the curriculum so that they become familiar with the multiple purposes of writing.
- Engage EAL students in collaborative writing, including computer-assisted writing.
- Incorporate a word wall. This can be a bulletin board or a folder that will help students remember and apply vocabulary words. Visuals and realia can help to connect to EAL students' prior knowledge. Word walls can be constructed ahead of students engaging in particular writing tasks.
- Provide EAL learners with opportunities to engage in self-assessment. Identify and

discuss a specific aspect of spelling or grammar that students struggle with and let students examine their own work to see if they can correct their errors. This can be done in pairs or small groups where students share papers. Over time, students can be taught how to use correction or editing symbols for inserting full stops and deleting words or letters.
- Provide EAL students with sentence stems and frames as forms of scaffolding to support sentence construction. A sentence stem may include the beginning part of the sentence, and students are required to complete the sentence (e.g., I think that... I notice that..., I agree with... because...). They can be used as prompts to get children to begin writing. A sentence frame provides a deeper scaffold and may include the entire sentence (e.g., The main idea of the text is _____. I know this is the main idea because _____). Some newcomer students may need access to essay or whole text frames, which may include a number of pre-written paragraphs.
- Teach grammatical structure. Students with EAL may need explicit grammar instruction and opportunities to learn and apply grammar in context.
- Use graphic organizers/writing frames. These often include a number of boxes and prompts for the type of information needed to write in a particular genre. The graphic organizer or frame can act as a planning tool for subsequent writing (see Chapters 3 and 7 for examples). However, if overused, writing frames may lead to formulaic writing.
- Provide opportunities for students to substitute words in completed paragraphs or longer texts. Students can go through the text and substitute words to improve the text or make it their own. To provide a bit more structure, teachers can underline those areas of the text where they want students to change the wording. Ultimately, students can revise their own texts in this way.
- Leverage technology. Assistive technology, like word prediction and spell-checks, can help students to identify words with which to complete a sentence and identify possible errors. Software that provides definitions of words allows students to identify the meanings of words and their pronunciation, thus building spelling, speaking and vocabulary skills.
- Integrate formative assessment into the teaching of language and of writing. Enabling students to participate in self- and peer-revision processes can result in more conscientious and focused writers.
- Provide opportunities for creative writing (e.g., tweets about a current event or a book that has been read; fictional advertisements for books or films).

Educational Disadvantage and Writing Development

How disadvantaged students are identified differs by country. In England, disadvantaged students are ordinarily defined as those registered as eligible for free school meals at any point in the past six years, children looked after by a local authority or who have left local authority care. In Ireland, schools are categorised as disadvantaged or non-disadvantaged, depending on the average level of poverty in the areas in which the school's students live. Hence, rather than referring to students as disadvantaged, they may be referred to as attending disadvantaged schools.

Data on student writing performance shows that, on average, disadvantaged students perform less well on literacy tasks, including writing. In their report on Key Stage 2 performance in England, gov.uk (2023) reported that, in 2023, 58% of disadvantaged students achieved the expected level (for their age) on teacher-assessed writing, compared to 77% of students not known to be disadvantaged. While these percentages represented an improvement since 2022 (55% and 75% respectively), they are well behind pre-Covid-19 percentages (e.g., 68% and 83% respectively in 2019). Moreover, the size of the gap has increased – 19% more non-disadvantaged students achieved the expected standard in 2023, compared to 15% in 2019.

In considering the performance of disadvantaged students, it is worth bearing in mind that such students may present with a range of other difficulties besides disadvantage. For example, they may include children for whom English is an additional language, children with general learning difficulties, and children with a range of other difficulties including dyslexic difficulties, dysgraphia and autism. Hence, any instruction designed to alleviate performance gaps will need to be tailored to the needs of the students involved, bearing in mind that some disadvantaged students may be dealing with multiple challenges.

Many of the instructional strategies presented in this report, and in this chapter in particular, are relevant to addressing the writing needs of children in disadvantaged circumstances. Key principles for teaching writing to struggling writers, including disadvantaged students, identified by Graham et al. (2015) include:

- Establishing writing routines that create a pleasant and motivating writing environment.
- Implementing a process-based approach to writing (planning, drafting, revising, editing, publishing).
- Creating routines that ensure that students compose regularly (daily, if possible).
- Implementing instructional routines in which students compose together (collaborative writing).
- Establishing goals for students' writing.
- Providing frequent feedback.
- Teaching handwriting, spelling and typing.
- Teaching sentence construction and sentence combining.

According to Slavin et al. (2019), key features of effective programmes also include supporting students to assess their own and others' drafts to generate feedback (peer assessment), building students' motivation and enjoyment of writing and providing extensive professional development to teachers. Unlike reading literacy, there are few studies that directly address the teaching of writing to low-SES children, though inferences on what is likely to work can be drawn from meta-analyses on writing instruction more generally (e.g., Graham et al., 2012). While Puzio et al. (2020) reported a good average effect size of 0.96 for writing studies based on differentiation to address the needs of lower-achieving students, their analysis was based on a small number of studies.

A useful distinction to make in considering interventions to improve the writing of disadvantaged students is that between provision at the individual student level, and provision at the whole-school level. Where just a few students in a class live in disadvantaged circumstances, it may be sufficient to differentiate instruction for any struggling writers among them, using the suggestions provided by Graham et al. (2015) and others. On the other hand, where large proportions of students in a school are disadvantaged, and there are many struggling writers, it is preferable to implement a school-wide approach to modifying the teaching of writing to address student needs. This idea is further developed in Chapter 12 in the context of school-level planning for writing.

Box 11.3 provides a description of how principles of effective writing instruction were implemented by teachers of pupils in the Second class in one of the disadvantaged schools for which the author was responsible as part of the Write to Read Project. The text was written by Anne Marie Roche, one of the W2R coaches, who provided professional development to teachers in the school on a regular basis.

In the remainder of this section, we track the writing of Filip, a pupil in Second grade in the school. Figure 11.1 shows Filip's attempts at writing in September, the beginning of the school year. Here, we see evidence of a Think-Draw-Label-Write approach, where just some elements of the drawing are recognisable without Filip's input. We can see the initial letters in brother (b), and computer (c) are recorded. There is also a 'g' for nugget. The sentence at the right side of the figure was dictated by Filip to his teacher. Applying the W2R scoring rubric (Chapter 5), we can say that this piece of writing merits Level 1 or Level 2 across most dimensions of the rubric, because Filip is only beginning to present his ideas through pictures, and his drawings may not be understandable without his own input. Furthermore, he has not written any complete words (his teacher supplied *me, computer, brother* and *mum*).

BOX 11.3 ADDRESSING THE WRITING NEEDS OF CHILDREN IN SECOND CLASS IN A DISADVANTAGED SCHOOL

By Anne Marie Roche, Teacher and Write to Read Coach

Working across different schools, we support teams to evaluate and develop their literacy approaches to learning and assessment. Professional development is tailored to a school's individual needs and interventions are planned in collaboration with school management and teachers. The intervention, detailed below, took place in an urban school designated as disadvantaged, with a population of over 50% of students for whom English was an additional language.

Background

This senior boys' school (2nd to 6th Classes) identified the need for a whole school approach to literacy development, based on a balanced literacy framework. However, it was understood that several students might not have had the prerequisite experiences needed to participate effectively in classrooms where the Write to Read framework was being implemented. Children entered the school in 2nd Class, aged seven to eight years. Many transferred from local junior schools; others attended school for the first time or had limited formal school experience.

During year 3 of this school's implementation of a whole school workshop approach, teachers addressed ongoing concerns regarding progress in the 2nd classes specifically.

Children in these classes presented with little formal experience of writing. Teachers discussed issues with motivation and engagement, a reluctance to write unaided and little experience of a genre approach. Teachers also expressed concern about their ability to effectively differentiate to ensure all children were suitably challenged with meaningful learning activities which aligned with the whole school approach. One classroom teacher stated that she "didn't know where to start". It was identified as an overwhelming learning setting.

Steps

- A team gathered to formulate a plan with the support of school management and the Write to Read coach.
- Challenges were identified and documented.
- A thorough assessment approach was agreed upon to inform the intervention – the analysis of a writing sample per child (using the W2R rubric), phonics, high-frequency words, and accuracy and fluency in oral reading.
- Input on these assessment approaches was provided by the coach.
- Assessments were conducted by the literacy team in the school (by class and special education teachers).
- The team gathered to analyse and discuss their findings.
- A plan was formulated with four teachers assigned to support (2 mainstream class teachers and two special education teachers).
- Resources were sourced, with advice from the W2R coach (see below).

The Intervention

- This intervention was completed across the daily 90-minute literacy block, during which writing, reading and word work were taught.
- Shared writing mini-lessons and a writing workshop were employed to introduce genres and demonstrate the targeted areas for writing development. This included the introduction of a *Think-Draw-Label-Write-Add-Detail* approach for those assessed as performing at the very early stages of the W2R rubric and those with little expressive language. Children chose writing content from the start and teachers modelled how to select writing topics, and plan and write around those topics. A daily share session was implemented.
- High-quality fiction and non-fiction reading resources were sourced. Teachers also targeted specific reading outcomes through the shared reading of poetry weekly. This allowed for whole-class emphasis on the early literacy skills including concepts of print, which were absent from children's writing.
- Children were grouped for the targeted explicit teaching of phonics/spelling and high-frequency words. Whole class vocabulary and oral language work are featured daily.

Implementation, Monitoring and Evaluation

- Teachers met regularly and shared practice and feedback.
- Teachers requested support and addressed any concerns they had with the Write to Read coach on a regular basis.
- Assessments were conducted to monitor progress to support dynamic groupings (grouping based on students' needs, with groups changing, based on assessment outcomes).
- Students' writing samples were analysed over time using the W2R rubric.
- Teachers recorded conferencing notes and used these to plan writing mini lessons.

Findings

- Motivation and engagement increased very quickly for the children. Teachers observed that the combination of shared writing and a writing workshop approach increased the pace of learning. Children were less fearful of the pencil and blank sheets of paper. Writing samples demonstrated shifts of several levels in the W2R rubric over the course of 6 months for some, in tandem with exposure to a wide range of genres.
- Teachers discussed the benefits of such finely tuned differentiation. They felt they were finally meeting the needs of all students including those achieving at and above grade level. This intervention enhanced in a meaningful way the support that children for whom English was an additional language received.
- Although teachers acknowledged that there was a very specific structure and increased preparation time for their explicit teaching, they were much happier and felt "they finally had a grasp on how to help these kids" and the "extra work was worth it".
- Progress was evident in writing samples. Children whose writing was assessed at Level 1 on the W2R rubric began blending through attempts at labels in drawing, then moving on the simple sentences using new known words. Writing samples collected across the school year showed that many children were composing class-level narratives and attempting to use genre features explored during craft mini lessons in the third school term. Children used their developing literacy skills across the different workshops.
- Some children found the composing elements more difficult, particularly those in receipt of receptive and expressive language support. They tended to rely on the teacher's shared writing or something related to a text they had been exposed to when composing in the early stages. Later, as confidence increased, they self-selected their topics. Drawing featured as an entry point for these children.

Reflections

- The teachers' drive to succeed and willingness to adopt new approaches were central to the success of the intervention, which led to an improvement in outcomes over time.

- Teachers were enabled to meet during school time and a culture of teachers working together with a shared vision was evident.
- The importance of high-quality assessment approaches was highlighted. Teachers in this setting were familiar with common assessment approaches but reported that meeting together to discuss and analyse these assessments led to the greatest shift in their thinking and practice.
- Mini lessons were powerful in progressing writing.
- Children responded very positively to mentor texts including shared readings of poetry.
- Students responded positively to increased agency in their own learning between the workshops.
- Routine and consistency were viewed as critical.
- The team noted an increase in expectations for children's writing, with scope for all children to be challenged.

This intervention highlights how schools can create a culture for teachers to work together to improve learner outcomes underpinned by effective assessment practice and research-informed pedagogy. Critical reflection on the part of teachers led to a learning environment where students were self-motivated to engage in, extend and become active agents in their learning.

I played on my computer (dictated to the teacher)

Figure 11.1 Filip's writing sample – September

254 *Teaching and Assessing Writing in the Primary School*

Filip's second sample, completed in November, shows some improvement. Again using the Think Draw Label Write approach, he presents a detailed drawing, a complete word (shop) added as a label (Figure 11.2). The main idea is still a little unclear, and requires his input, indicating a Level 2 on that dimension on the rubric. Filip is beginning to attempt detailed drawing, with the word 'shop' added as a label. Filip has produced some patterned sentences (I in taxs car; I in the shop) although punctuation is lacking. He has progressed to Level 3 on the spelling dimension of the rubric, because phonetic spellings are emerging (e.g., sait to said), and some high-frequency words are spelled correctly (e.g., shop, man, we, kill). There is also some degree of audience awareness beginning to emerge, as Filip includes some details in his text, though important information is still missing.

Filip's third sample, produced in January, has a stronger focus on writing over drawing (Figure 11.3). The main idea is present but not always clear to the reader, meriting a Level 3 on the rubric. It is also unclear how details contribute to the main idea, suggesting a Level 2 for details. Filip is drawing on a broader range of vocabulary and continues to combine correct spelling of some high frequency words (*among, crew, but, your, best* and *impostor*) with phonetic spelling of other words (e.g., *and* for *end*, *sus* for *says*), meriting a Level 3 on the spelling element of the rubric. There is evidence of increased risk with word choice (e.g., crewmate, impostor) and sense of audience continues to emerge. Capital letters are not used, except for children's names, and punctuation is also missing.

Filip's fourth sample, produced in February (Figure 11.4), shows further development. In this case, the main idea (a fight between XBox Skeleton and a Human), and basic details around this main idea are provided (They were in the big house; a knife was used during the fight; the Human missed Skeleton; then Skeleton got the upper hand). This merits a Level 4 on main ideas, and a Level 4 on details. With regard to Organisation, a basic beginning,

I (in) a taxs car (taxi car). *I in the shop. the man sait (said) you t (too) we kill.*

Figure 11.2 Filip's writing sample – November

Addressing the Needs of Diverse Writers 255

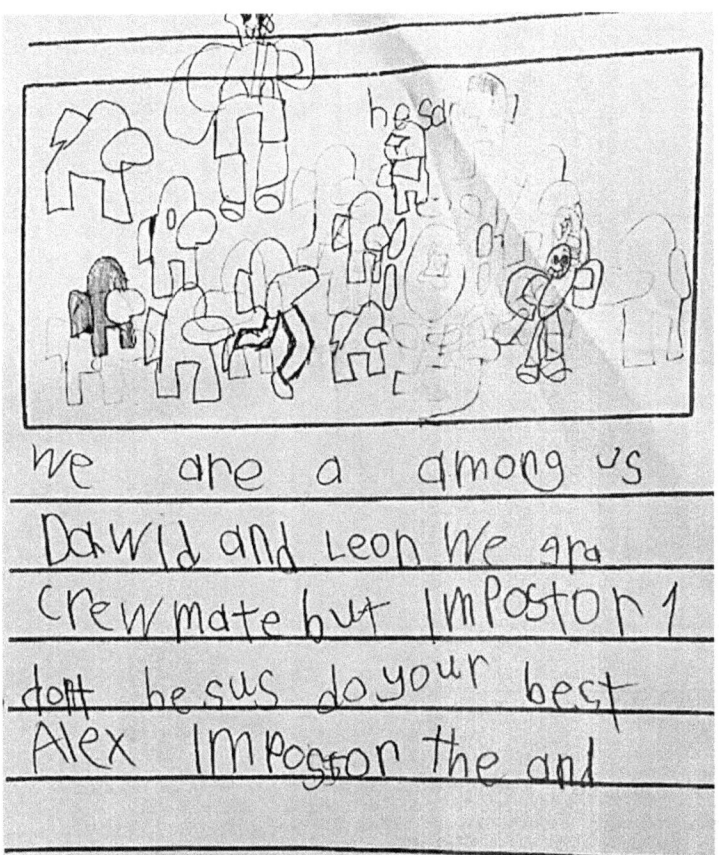

we are a among us
Dawid and Filip we gra
crewmate but impostor
I don't he sus (says) do
your best Alex impostor
the and (end)

Figure 11.3 Filip's writing sample – January

middle and end are clearly present, and some features of the narrative are present (e.g., a basic setting – the big house – and the presentence of characters) though more description would be welcomed. High-frequency words such as *were, fighting, big, house* and *kill* are spelled correctly, while phonetic spelling is also used to good effect, and attempts such as *knine* (knife) and *missd* (missed) are decodable, meriting a Level 4 for spelling on the rubric. There is an emerging awareness of the role of full stops, though there is a tendency to overuse them (something that often occurs as pupils apply a new skill). Filip's writing now merits a Level 3 on capitalisation and punctuation, as, while full stops are generally present at the end of sentences, capital letters are still not used consistently. Audience awareness continues to develop as Filip provides the reader with more relevant details.

Clearly, Filip has made good improvement over a relatively short period of time, and can be expected to improve further as he benefits from writing instruction described in Box 11.3, and is given opportunities to apply what he has learned. Some work on sentence structure, incorporating the use of capital letters at the beginning of sentences would help with conventions. Mentor texts can be used to further develop Filipe's vocabulary and his understanding

256 Teaching and Assessing Writing in the Primary School

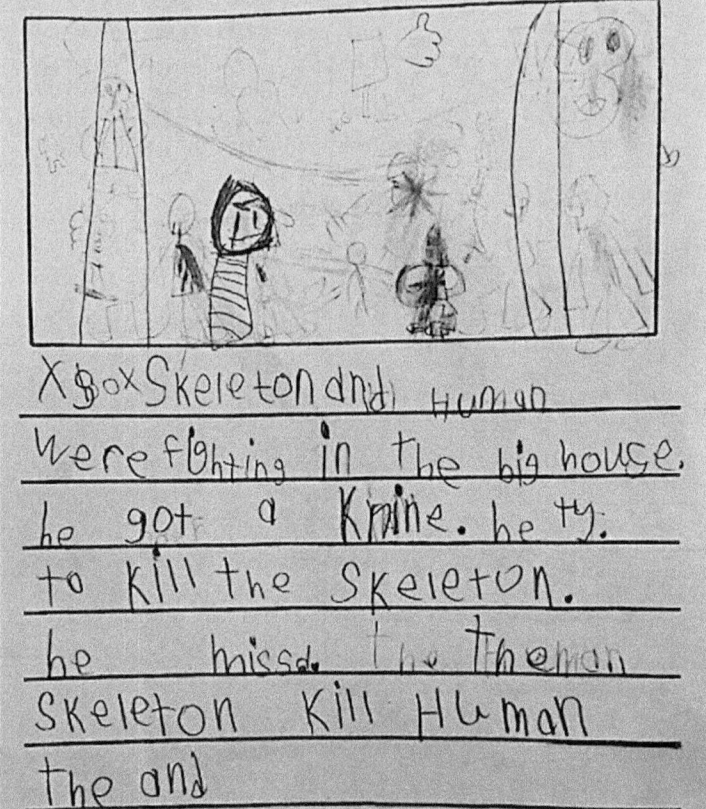

Xbox Skeleton and Human were fighting in the big house. he got a knine (knife). He ty (try). to kill the skeleton. he missd. the skeleton kill Human the and

Figure 11.4 Filip's writing sample – February

of language patterns in sentences and he can begin to consider the use and impact of language in his own texts.

Conclusion

The focus of the current chapter was on addressing the needs of diverse writers, including those with learning difficulties, those for whom English is an additional language, and those in socioeconomically disadvantaged circumstances. A particular issue arises when children experience a number of risk factors, such as educational disadvantage combined with English as an additional language, or multiple learning difficulties. In almost all cases, it is necessary draw on assessment procedures to identify where the underlying difficulty lies, what the children's strengths and weakness are, and how best to address them. This is consistent with differentiation, where the teacher adapts learning by focusing on the needs of individual students or groups of students with similar needs. Indeed, the Writing Workshop provides a good framework for this, as min-lessons and conferences can be used to differentiate instruction and address particular difficulties. Key ideas such as metacognition, self-regulation, motivation and self-assessment will continue to be important for all writers, including those who or struggling and/or have particular difficulties.

In many cases, struggling writers will benefit from mainstream instructional approaches that have been adapted to address their needs, though teachers may require additional professional development to support them in doing so. In a small number of cases, it will be necessary to implement more specialised programs that are designed to address difficulties in specific aspects of writing, such as spelling, handwriting or composition, and again some additional training may be required by teachers prior to implementation.

Although this chapter emphasised the importance of language, and oral language in particular, in the writing development of children with EAL, oral language is important for all writers, including those in disadvantaged circumstances. Hence, an integrated approach to writing instruction, in which oral language plays a key role, alongside reading, is very important.

Reflect, Connect, Act

Identify a spelling or writing intervention targeted at a key at-risk group (Lavan & Talcott, 2020 provide several examples).

- Describe the target group for the intervention.
- Identify the main steps in the intervention and comment on them based on what you have learned in this book.
- Summarise the research evidence for the intervention.
- Identify any challenges that might need to be addressed in implementing the intervention with the group you have selected.

Share your outcomes with other teachers.

Suggestion for Further Reading

Fitts, S., Bowers, E., & Keisler, L. (2016). Writing instruction for English learners: Examining instructional practices in fourth-grade classrooms. *NABE Journal of Research and Practice, 7(1)*, 106–141. https://doi.org/10.1080/26390043.2016.12067806

Note

1 In the United States, the term 'learning disability' may be used instead of 'learning difficulty'. In practice, in the context of writing, both terms suggest a difficulty that is specific to spelling, handwriting or writing more generally (i.e., despite the provision of opportunity to learn, children struggle with aspects of writing).

12 Planning for Writing across a School

This chapter explores how a school culture of writing which balances the cognitive and affective dimensions of literacy and nurtures children as writers can be created and sustained. It opens with a brief overview of aspects of writing addressed in previous chapters. Next, it provides some insights into how to get started on a whole-school approach to writing. It draws on our experiences of working collaboratively with schools through the *Write to Read* project, the research on professional development (PD) that shaped our approach and the use of our rubric to support schoolwide conversations around writing development and its application to capture evidence of growth in writing.

> **Reflect and Connect**
>
> 1 Do you have a personal philosophy of writing pedagogy? In what ways might your identity and history as a writer influence your planning and pedagogy?
> 2 Does your school have a whole-school approach to writing? Does it align with your philosophy of writing development?
> 3 How do you learn best? What kinds of professional development have you engaged in?
> 4 What do you think are key features of professional development that can support schools in developing a whole school framework for writing?

Despite its importance to children's literacy development and achievement, writing remains the under-represented language form in research and practice. It is no surprise then that concerns about children's writing development are 'common across the globe...the typical teacher does not devote enough time to writing and writing instruction' (Graham & Rijlaarsdam, 2016, pp. 278–281). Though teachers report that they are aware of effective teaching practices and adaptations, they use them infrequently (about once a month), which is not often enough to truly impact the quality of writing (Gilbert & Graham, 2010; Troia & Graham, 2017). While it is not clear why this might be the case, some insights come from teachers' self-reports which indicate they find it a challenge to meet the needs of all learners in today's diverse classrooms and in particular, the needs of struggling writers (US: Troia et al., 2009;

Ireland: Kavanagh et al., 2015; UK: Dockrell et al., 2016). Graham (2019) argues that children do not have access to the instruction they need and deserve. It is also likely that policy shifts have impacted practice with unintended negative consequences for writing instruction. In many jurisdictions, time for authentic writing has been squeezed out as curricula have become more tightly prescribed and standards set. Dyson (2020), writing about shifts in teaching in the US, notes that writing is increasingly taught through 'textbook-driven, skill-oriented lessons' and argues that 'using composing to practice and showcase one's skills is not the intention-driven "real" writing that furthers meaning-making' (p. 123), while Barrs (2019) criticises the 'grammatical complexity and ostentatious vocabulary' emphasis in the writing curriculum in England which, she contends, results in writing that is 'inflated and unconvincing' (Barrs, 2019, p. 18).

Graham's extensive body of research highlights that classroom writing practices are influenced by teachers' beliefs and values, attitudes towards writing, and their knowledge of writing development and writing pedagogies. Cremin and Oliver (2016) examined teachers' attitudes to writing, their sense of themselves as writers and the potential impact of teachers engaging in writing on pedagogy and student outcomes in writing. They concluded that while the evidence base is not strong, teachers' conceptualisation of what counts as writing tends to be narrow and attitudes towards writing can be compromised by low self-confidence, negative writing histories and tensions around positioning themselves as writers in classrooms. On the other hand, teachers can be explicit role models for children when they write alongside them in the classroom. Teachers with a strong sense of self-efficacy and positive attitudes towards writing are better able to engage struggling writers and enhance their writing quality (Graham & Harris, 2002). Such teachers are more likely to possess a 'growth mindset' (Yeager & Dweck, 2020) and are better able communicate to learners that improvement occurs with sufficient effort (Ekholm et al., 2018). Such teachers are also likely to be better able to create classroom conditions for authentic writing to occur and for students to flourish and develop as writers.

Like teacher engagement, research also highlights that the affective dimensions of writing (attitude, motivation, engagement, self-efficacy, self-regulation, value), are important mediators of children's participation in each stage of the writing process (planning, translating, revising, publishing) (see Chapter 1) and on writing development. Knowledge of motivational strategies is essential teacher knowledge for writing as research indicates that children disengage from classrooms disconnected from their needs (Christenson et al., 2012). This is less likely to occur when classrooms support student agency which Vaughn (2020) defines as 'a student's ability to have ideas, intentions, and to exert influence and take actions to expand the learning context' (p. 115).

How then, given the many challenges outlined and the breadth and depth of knowledge required by teachers, can we change how writing is taught so that children receive the instruction they need and deserve? While individual teachers can and do make a difference to children's writing, the impact is magnified if a research-informed vision for writing is developed and implemented across a whole school (Graham, 2019).

We have found working in a collaborative reciprocal research-university partnership is a valuable way for schools and universities to learn from and with each other. On the *Write to Read* project, each school is assigned a literacy coach (a teacher with a master's level qualification in literacy with extensive experience teaching in schools designated as disadvantaged). To develop an understanding of the realities and complexities of each particular school context, coaches generally visit fortnightly in year one of the change process, less often in year two and strive to build strong collaborative relationships with teachers. We work with the whole school from the outset and collaborate with teachers and the school leadership to design and implement a research-informed framework tailored to their school context. Coaches engage in evidence-based multifaceted professional development which includes meeting with teachers to build research-informed 'content and pedagogical content knowledge' (Shulman, 1987) for writing, in-class demonstrations and non-evaluative observations (Joyce & Showers, 2002), provision of professional readings to support practice (e.g. Au et al., 2008), assessment tools for writing and using them to inform planning and practice (Kennedy & Shiel, 2022, 2024) and adopting an inquiry stance to trialling new approaches (Cochran-Smith & Lytle, 2009).

Though access to a coach who visits regularly may not be easily available to schools, it is still possible for a school to improve practice by discovering and harnessing internal expertise. In the Irish context, School Self-Evaluation (SSE, DE, 2022) is a requirement for all schools and lays out a systematic process for initiating and evaluating changes to practice. It can be used as a framework for embarking on a whole school process of change. Schools typically have a literacy coordinator (a post of responsibility) – a teacher in the school whose role it is to promote literacy development across the school. Literacy co-ordinators have the potential to support teachers in refining their practice (e.g. advising on resources, facilitating dialogue among staff, modelling and demonstrating new pedagogies and observing, scaffolding and coaching teachers). Literacy coordinators usually have a special interest in literacy and may have additional qualifications. Along with other likeminded colleagues, they can be a catalyst for initiating and supporting whole school change (see Chapter 1: Caoimhe Shiel's (*Write to Read* coach) account of supporting change in her junior school). We have found that establishing leadership teams in schools to drive the process in between professional development sessions is effective (see Box 12.2 below, Annemarie Roche's (*Write to Read* coach) account of developing literacy leadership in schools).

Participation in PD is not a guarantee that professional learning will take place and that practice will change. As King et al. (2022, citing Timperley et al., 2007, p. 233) highlight, 'PD is not something that is "done" to teachers, rather it involves teachers as active participants responsible for their own learning' (p. 5). Thus, the process of PD is as important as content and pedagogies; it should empower teachers as professionals (Kennedy & Shiel, 2010). It is our view that by forming a professional learning community, teachers and schools can begin to source and develop additional expertise to support the desired changes. A goal of this book is to support the process and to provide in one volume an accessible review of the research on writing and prompts on how to use it to develop a responsive, comprehensive and engaging framework for a whole school approach to writing.

Early Moves: Maximising the Affordances of Classrooms Across a School

Our work with schools has shown us that 'writing development is influenced by the affordances of classrooms which can either constrain and hinder it or propel it forward' (Kennedy & Shiel, 2022, p. 127). Equally, school cultures and structures can have the same effect, as Dyson contends 'none of us have unencumbered agency; we are all constrained

Planning for Writing across a School 261

and empowered by the institutional structures within which we live,' (2020, p. 123). Creating a coherent and empowering whole-school approach to writing requires an openness to new ideas and a willingness to reflect on practice and embrace new ways of thinking and doing.

The challenge is to ensure school-wide professional conversations occur regularly and focus on building progression and continuity in writing across the school without compromising teacher autonomy and creativity. Such an approach to change honours the notion of lifelong learning, and the professionalism and autonomy of teachers as critical decision-makers who are creators of curriculum rather than consumers of it (Au et al., 2008; Kennedy, 2014). PD that cultivates a spirit of experimentation and an attitude of 'let's try a new idea and evaluate how it works' is more effective and successful than PD that prescribes or scripts changes (Kennedy, 2014). Hord (2008, p. 12) refers to this as 'relational' support. She contends that 'trust is a significant factor for the community [of teachers] and leaders should take steps to build this important capital' (p. 12). Teachers are more likely to try new approaches, ask questions, debate issues and request help when there is a sense that we are all learning together. Teachers participating in our research have highlighted how they have found the process intellectually stimulating and have enjoyed the social dimension of learning that occurs (see Kennedy, 2014; Kennedy & Shiel, 2024). As one teacher noted:

> *You have more to talk about, and also, we are trying out, we're experimenting on things and trying it as a whole group. Not just ourselves... I suppose we are more excited about trying new things as well, we like talking about it. Even we'd be talking about it on the way home and everything! I think it is good like that to talk with other people 'cause you learn more.*

Teacher collaboration within and across levels is pivotal to developing and sustaining a school vision and a research-informed whole school coherent framework for writing that honours students' identities, languages and cultures (Dyson, 1993, 2020; Kelly et al., 2020). School leadership can signal a value on collegial conversations and ensure that the essential infrastructure to support change is established. Graham (2019) argues that principals also

---

BOX 12.1 DEVELOPING INFRASTRUCTURE FOR A WHOLE-SCHOOL APPROACH TO WRITING

- Establish leadership teams across class levels
- Balance composition of the teams
- Establish who will be responsible for setting up a timetable for coach/literacy coordinator input (sharing new content; modelling, observing; planning)
- Decide how often the coach will visit and how long each session will be
- Decide on whether the sessions will be during/after school or both
- Establish procedures for internal team planning after input
- Encourage the principal to participate in PD
- Lay foundations for relational trust
- Establish cross-class level discussions 3-4 times a year

need professional development on how to lead change and need to understand the theory, research and practice underpinning changes. Certainly, in our work with schools, when the principal participates and actively engages in PD alongside teachers, the change process is more successful and moves at a faster pace. These dimensions are critical to successful change efforts (Guskey, 2000; Lipson et al., 2004).

Developing Infrastructure to Support Change

The process of change should begin with a consideration of the degree to which current teacher practices align with the research base on writing and an examination of what is working well and what might need greater attention. A prerequisite for success is the allocation of time whereby all colleagues in the school can come together at regular intervals to build a shared understanding of the changes and commit to working together to develop a framework suitable for the school context. Coaches will need to work with teachers to focus on new content (learning about new methods/assessment tools; planning and troubleshooting questions which have arisen). Consideration will need to be given to how best to share this knowledge. Perhaps at times it should be communicated at a whole school meeting; other times it might be best to group teachers (e.g., JI teachers on their own initially; SI/1st; 2nd/3rd/4th; 5th/6th) to work with the coach. The configuration of the groupings may change at different points of the year, in order to best address children's stage of development and the needs of teachers. A key to successful school-based PD is the provision of time and space for teachers to meet outside of the PD to consider implications, debate issues, reflect on changes to practice and plan forward for the next steps (Cordingley et al., 2015). Guskey (2002) highlights that many PD initiatives falter when the infrastructure to support the change has not been considered. In establishing leadership teams (Box 12.1), consider the composition of the team e.g., experienced teachers, newly qualified teachers, teachers with additional qualifications in literacy and teachers with good levels of experience at a particular level. This last point is important as our research has shown that pedagogical content knowledge (PCK) is situated and teachers who are comfortable with new approaches at one class level will not necessarily feel confident if teaching a different class level, as this teacher who was new to teaching Junior Infants noted:

> *Really, it's like starting afresh with a new grouping... 'I know how to do this with 2nd or 3rd and 4th, but it's a new kind of programme to do it with a different age grouping'.*
>
> (Junior Infant teacher)

Changing class levels on a yearly basis is common in the Irish context and this represents both a challenge (to adapt new approaches to a new class level) and an opportunity (to further develop expertise in using existing knowledge to respond to the needs of children at a new class level).

Teachers have reported that they have enjoyed being part of a whole school approach, particularly one which built collegiality, making them feel part of an engaged community of learners working towards common goals:

> *We're all working the same system, rather than each teacher closing her door and working in her own way. It's nice, you walk into any classroom, and you can go around and*

read the writing...and see what's going on in the rooms...I think it makes maybe things in school feel more like a community thing than, yeah. You don't really feel alone on it either.

(5th/6th class teacher)

> **BOX 12.2 *WRITE TO READ* LITERACY COACH, ANNE MARIE ROCHE, OUTLINES HOW SCHOOLS HAVE CREATED ORGANISATIONAL ROUTINES TO ALLOW LITERACY COORDINATORS AND CORE TEAM MEMBERS TO DEVELOP AS LEADERS IN LITERACY**
>
> **Literacy Coordinator**
>
> In Irish primary schools, literacy is led by a teacher assuming the role of literacy coordinator. Often held as a post for which an additional allowance is paid, this teacher is the liaison with the literacy coach and school staff.
> Duties for this role tend to include:
>
> - Leading the development of literacy planning
> - Sourcing and maintaining high-quality resources and sharing these with fellow teachers
> - Organising Continuing Professional Development (CPD)
> - Supporting assessment at a classroom and school level
> - Supporting staff induction in literacy practice
> - Liaising with stakeholders to drive change processes at a school level
> - Monitoring and evaluating literacy teaching and learning
>
> The role of literacy coordinators has evolved considerably since we first began working with schools. In the early days, coaches liaised with coordinators to plan and implement in-school support sessions. Acting as an agent for the school, coordinators conveyed updates and concerns gathered from the staff during 1-1 meetings with the literacy coach. This information combined with anecdotal feedback notes from teacher sessions was used to inform ongoing staff PD. Although this operated as a successful arrangement, literacy coaches considered different approaches which allowed for increased input from a wider cohort of teachers using a distributed leadership perspective.
>
> **Core Team**
>
> As a result of these considerations, a selection of schools was invited to assemble a core team to work with the literacy coach. Core teams comprised of four or five teachers and represented a variety of class levels. Whilst some teachers held an additional qualification in a literacy-related field, most had an interest in literacy teaching and were willing to adopt the role.

> School principals and literacy coordinators assembled the core team in different ways. Some identified and approached those with interests and talents in literacy teaching. Others invited teachers to self-nominate.
>
> Core teams met with the literacy coach at regular intervals over the school year. Literacy coaches supported these teams intensively in the initial phases. Principals generally arranged for these sessions to take place during school time which demonstrated the value placed on the process. Almost immediately, the quality of feedback and discussion on the change process improved. Literacy coaches gained a greater insight into the challenges that teachers were facing. Core teams worked with the coach to identify priorities for the school year and collaborated to design an improvement plan. Teachers on core teams shared the workload and assumed a variety of roles on the team. Acting as liaisons to teachers working at the same class level, they shared information and resources and gathered feedback.
>
> The core team also received advance PD and input on new initiatives prior to the whole school's input. This proved to be particularly successful as these teachers felt more equipped to support colleagues when new dimensions were introduced at the school level. Some took on pilot studies in their classroom to trial approaches and invited others in to observe.
>
> Literacy coaches observed that there was greater investment in the coaching process with the inclusion of a wider cohort of staff. Core team members often identified different concerns to those shared by the literacy coordinator. Literacy coordinators were supported to delegate responsibility.
>
> These changes led to an increased momentum in the coaching process. Schools with core teams successfully created a culture for all teachers in a school to work together in a new way. By facilitating professional development and other key organisational functions, a wider group of teachers was invited to develop their skills as leaders, which positively impacted on teaching and learning in the classroom.

Once the nuts and bolts of PD have been established and there is consensus amongst staff to begin, the focus can shift to building teacher capacity for new approaches to the teaching of writing. Graham (2019) has distilled the research on effective writing pedagogy into five main principles that he contends are key to changing how writing is taught:

- Writing frequently for real and different purposes
- Supporting students as they write
- Teaching the needed writing skills, knowledge, and processes
- Creating a supportive and motivating writing environment
- Connecting writing, reading, and learning

These have been explored in detail across the previous chapters of this book and can form the basis of whole school sessions and facilitate discussion within and across class levels. How to use the book to begin the process is outlined in the following sections.

Writing Frequently for Real and Different Purposes

Time for writing is often the first contentious issue to be discussed and agreed on across a school. As has been highlighted in Chapters 1 and 6, children's writing is unlikely to develop to its potential without the allocation of sufficient time for them to compose. Teachers are the gatekeepers of time and pedagogical foci in classrooms; what they value is what receives time and attention. Research internationally indicates writing instruction rarely receives the attention it needs and deserves (Brindle et al., 2016; Graham, 2019). Graham et al. (2012b/2018) recommend a minimum of an hour a day from first class, of which 30 minutes of the hour should be devoted to explicit teaching and the other 30 minutes for children to work on their texts. Inadequate time to write and incubate ideas (Cutler & Graham, 2008; Graham, 2019), limits opportunities for engagement to develop, or a sense of a writing community to emerge (Graham et al., 2012b; Calkins & Ehrenworth, 2016).

BOX 12.3 EXPLORE HOW TIME IS CONFIGURED

1. In what ways is writing enacted in my classroom? During literacy time and/or integrated across the curriculum?
2. What proportion of literacy time is allocated to writing? Are oral language, reading and writing meaningfully integrated?
3. Do I *teach* writing *every day* or less often?
4. How much time do I give each writing lesson?
5. Does writing occur at the same time daily? What time will work best for my class?
6. Is the time allocation aligned with the research findings? If not, where could I reconfigure and carve out more time?

Time allocation confers a value and a priority on the activity and learners quickly pick up on the subtle message this conveys when a daily predictable block of writing becomes an essential part of their school day. Time is also needed for a sense of 'flow' (Csikszentmihalyi, 1975) to develop. Too many gaps between writing sessions interrupt the flow, making it difficult for writers to reconnect with their thought processes from the previous session, and it is very likely that young writers will have lost focus and interest in the piece. To give writing more time, teachers may need to be convinced that it is needed and worth the time allocation. Using the questions in Box 12.3 as a reflective tool and keeping a log or diary across a week can illuminate how time is actually being spent and inform discussions on how time might be increased.

Reflecting on the value of writing by creating belief statements about writing can reinforce its value and importance to overall literacy development. Box 12.4 provides an example of what the belief statements might look like. The belief statements may prompt further discussion and are a call to action to rethink how time is used and how it could be better used. Some ways to consider addressing time issues include:

> **BOX 12.4 OUR BELIEF STATEMENTS ABOUT WRITING**
> - Writing supports development in oral language and reading
> - Writing supports children to clarify their thinking
> - Writing supports children to learn across the curriculum
> - Writing allows children to demonstrate their learning
> - Writing allows children to develop specialised language or language about writing
> - Writing is a social endeavour and requires a supportive environment
> - Writing is complex; it has many subskills
> - Writing is a process and develops over time
> - Writing gives children a voice and supports creativity and imagination
> - Writing is a life skill
> - Writers need choice and agency over their writing topics

- Integrating the teaching of oral language, reading and writing within an instructional block rather than teaching them in separate lessons (see Chapters 1, 2, 6, 8)
- Identifying genuine links and synergies across curricula: for example, link report or persuasive writing into a thematic inquiry in history or geography; link procedural writing into a science or mathematics lesson (see Chapters 7 and 8)
- Minimising the time children spend completing workbook pages or worksheets practising writing conventions (grammar, spelling and punctuation) in isolation – these skills should be integrated in the context of children's compositional writing when they are ready for the skill and have shown a need for it in their writing (see Chapter 9).

A further consideration is how time, once allocated, is used. Establishing a predictable structure for the writing workshop will create the conditions to support writer engagement (see Chapter 6) and response to writing, and allow instruction on the crafts, processes and conventions of writing to occur in authentic ways according to writers' stages of development and assessed needs.

Greater time allocation is one critical ingredient for improving writing quality, but it must be combined with student choice and agency overwriting if they are to write for real and different purposes, the second part of Graham's (2019) first principle. As Reeve and Shin (2020) argue: 'all students have interests, goals, and dreams. To be intrinsically motivated and to embrace intrinsic growth strivings is simply a part of the human motivational architecture' (p. 151). The extent to which writing is purposeful, and writers are given agency over topic choice, and time to revisit, craft and share writing, will determine whether children see themselves as writers participating in a vibrant writing community, or if they see writing as a school activity or a teacher assigned task to be completed. Dyson (2020, p. 123, citing Britton, 1993) captures the difference nicely:

> What children use [oral and written] language for in school must be "operations" and not "dummy runs" …. [Children] must practice language in the sense in which a doctor

"practices" medicine and a lawyer "practices" law, and not in the sense in which a juggler "practices" a new trick before he performs it. This way of working does not make difficult things easy … [but it makes them] worth the struggle.

(p. 130)

Teachers consistently report that autonomy over writing topic is key to children's engagement as indicated by this teacher: *I'll say, 'take out your Write to Read folder' and they love that. Their enthusiasm for writing now is, they love to write. The ownership plays a part'.*

Intrinsic motivation flourishes when children are facilitated to engage in writing on self-chosen topics (see Box 12.5 for prompts to help with reflection on children's writing agency).

BOX 12.5 CONSIDER WRITER CHOICE, ENGAGEMENT AND AGENCY

1 Do children have control over writing topics, or do I assign writing tasks?
2 To what extent can children engage in writing across a range of genres and disciplines on topics of personal interest and curiosity?
3 To what extent do children have opportunities to collaborate and choose with whom they would like to partner?

When time and choice come together, writers begin to develop their 'voice', which Graves (1994) contends is the part of the self that pushes the writing ahead, *the dynamo in the process, …voice is the engine that sustains writers through the hard work of drafting and redrafting* (p. 81/82). This is only possible when children know that their choices will be respected and valued and that they can count on a supportive classroom environment where they can share their writing intentions, drafts, struggles and successes and seek help from teachers and peers when needed.

Supporting Students as they Write

As has been highlighted in Chapter 10, support for writers as they write, occurs through peer and teacher conferences and through a daily share session. The art of conferencing is often a new skill for teachers to acquire and, as outlined by Roisin O'Shea, *Write to Read* coach (Chapter 10, Box 10.1), it takes time for it to develop, for each teacher to develop a style that works for them and the children, and also for writers to become comfortable discussing their writing with teacher and peers.

In whole school planning sessions, it is helpful if teachers share their experiences of conferencing, what they find easy or challenging, what is working well and what isn't and if the conferencing is feeding into planning for instruction. Pooling ideas on how to conference more effectively and sharing anchor charts with each other can be a valuable way for teachers to build a sense of community amongst themselves and to support each other in embedding new practices into their teaching. Teachers should consider how anchor charts might look across a variety of class levels (see Chapter 10: Figures 10.1, 10.2 and 10.5).

> **BOX 12.6 LEARNING TO CONFER**
>
> 1. Do I make time for conferences daily?
> 2. Have I explained to children the purpose of a conference?
> 3. To what extent do I *listen* to writers during a conference? Is the balance 80/20 in favour of children?
> 4. What kinds of questions am I asking? Do they show the writer I value their ideas? Have I modelled for children the kinds of language structures for responding during a conference?
> 5. Do I focus on writer's intentions rather than on the accuracy of conventions?
> 6. Do I have a system for keeping track of conferences (e.g., a tally)?
> 7. On what basis are children selected for a conference?
> 8. Do I have a way to record useful information from the conference?
> 9. Are conferences informing my planning?
> 10. Have I modelled for children how to peer conference?

In advance of a professional learning community, teachers could read sections of Chapter 10 pertaining to conferencing and sharing sessions. Boxes 12.6 and 12.7 can prompt teachers to share their experiences and consider how to address challenges and deepen their understanding. It can also lead to further discussion on how to build oral language and scaffold the language of response according to children's stages of development. Learning how to create a dialogic interaction in conferences and throughout the shared session entails a shift in role for teachers. For many it is an experience that has changed their perspective on literacy teaching:

> *I just think it's ignited a love for teaching literacy more so… that I'm just a facilitator at times, that they can learn a lot from each other. They really do enjoy choice and when they have the freedom to write about what they want and read what they want…*
>
> (5th class teacher)

There is nothing worse than a child standing at the top of a room, reading their work aloud and either they can't be heard by all present or children are not actively listening to the writer or indeed both. It is essential that the foundations for a successful share session are laid at the outset. Both conferencing and the share session are invaluable in building the academic language structures that show insight into the craft of writing. Exploring the language of response (see Tables 10.1 and 10.2, Chapter 10) can offer ways to establish an effective share session. Such 'dialogic metatalk' (Myhill, 2021) gives children a language for responding to writers, for talking about writing and in so doing supports them to be better able to go 'inland' to listen and respond to their own consciousness and thoughts as they compose and reflect on their writing. Learning to listen and give feedback feeds forward to the writer how an audience has perceived a text and where there might be gaps, which is helpful in 'identifying dissonances between the author's intended meaning and the text produced' (Philippakos & MacArthur, 2016, p. 419). It prompts children to consider aspects of their writing that may need to be revised.

BOX 12.7 ESTABLISHING EFFECTIVE SHARE SESSIONS

1. Do I reserve 5-10 minutes daily for the share session? Why/why not?
2. Is sharing on a voluntary basis?
3. Have I set the tone for the share session?
4. Have I modelled for children how to show a writer they are actively listening? (body language)
5. Have I modelled *active listening* by (a) identifying craft; (b) asking a pertinent question of the writer; (c) seeking clarification?
6. Have I created anchor charts to scaffold the interaction?
7. Have I made specific links between reading fluency techniques and writers reading their text (part of the text) aloud?
8. Have I a system in place to keep track of who shares?
9. Have I a system in place to keep anecdotal notes during the share session?
10. Have I provided opportunities for children to share with a wider audience? (e.g., other classes, the principal, assemblies, parental celebrations)

Witnessing how peers are wordsmithing and constructing their texts is a powerful way for writers to learn from each other and to consider possibilities for their own writing. Children are more likely to invest in writing and have a desire to hone the quality of their writing when they experience such support while writing. These daily experiences shape their attitudes to writing and support them in discovering their voice' and unique way of putting words on paper. Such experiences are what make 'young children's composing, or any constructive and creative act, wilful and intentional, that is, "real"' (Dyson, 2020, p. 119). Such experiences honour the individual and social dimensions to writing which Camacho et al. (2021) posit are key to writing motivation. When the basic structures of the Writing Workshop are in place and it is running smoothly, increased attention can be given to mini lesson content, methods for teaching mini lessons, and other forms of assessment beyond those associated with conferences and reading children's work.

Teaching Writing Processes, Knowledge and Skills Through Mini Lessons

In our work with schools, we have found that the concept of mini lessons is new for most teachers. Keeping mini lessons 'mini' and focused on just one teaching point is a challenge initially as is the need to ensure the lesson is tailored to children's zone of proximal development (Vygotsky, 1978) so that they can stretch to the next step along the path towards reaching their writing potential. As we have seen in previous chapters, writing is not a unitary skill but a complex problem-solving process (McCutchen et al., 2008). As Deane et al. (2008) highlight:

> [A] writer can confront a staggering hierarchy of problems, including how to generate and organize task-relevant ideas; phrase grammatically correct sentences that flow; use correct punctuation and spelling; and tailor ideas, tone, and wording to the desired audience.
> (p. 3)

For teachers new to teaching writing on a **daily** basis, it can be daunting to decide on content for a lesson every day. In working with the whole staff in a professional learning community, it is helpful to use Chapter 6, Figure 6.2 to reflect on key messages about how to plan and teach mini lessons and get the balance right so that the message to children is that mini lessons support them as writers and offer techniques that they can borrow to enhance the quality of their writing (Box 12.8).

> **BOX 12.8 PLANNING AND TEACHING MINI LESSONS**
>
> 1. I have planned a mix of mini lesson types and organisational groupings across a week
> 2. I have kept the mini lessons brief (10-15 min.)
> 3. I have prioritised craft lessons over conventions lessons
> 4. I have used an appropriate mentor text (quality children's literature to underpin lesson content) long enough for my think-aloud and a short, guided practice for children
> 5. The mentor text was at an appropriate level
> 6. I have framed craft and process mini lessons as invitations, not prescriptions for writing, *and* conducted these lessons with the whole class
> 7. I used the gradual release of responsibility model for craft and process lessons
> 8. I adopted a discovery approach to small group convention lessons
> 9. I have co-constructed anchor charts with children to capture key aspects of mini lessons and displayed them in the classroom as visual reminders of learning
> 10. I have designed templates for children to keep a record of mini lesson content in their writing folder (see Chapter 10: Table 10.4 and Table 10.5 for examples)
> 11. I have kept a record of my mini lessons and annotated texts in my writing folder for future reference

In our experience, sourcing the mentor texts is something that teachers found challenging and with which they wanted further support (see Kennedy & Shiel, 2024 for a discussion). Responsibility for sourcing texts can be divided across teachers of varying class levels and a bank of materials can be built up for sharing across the school. Some schools have put a system in place for this as highlighted by this teacher:

> *It's so embedded in the school you see...a bank of resources and things have been built up... We introduced a folder in each classroom, so if you're someone who found something that's great for narratives, you keep a copy, you know so you could show other people (literacy coordinator)*

Research indicates that teacher knowledge of children's literature is not strong (Cremin et al., 2024) and teachers can name few current authors or recently published titles for children in either fiction or non-fiction informational texts. Learning how to stay up to date and where to find reliable reviews of children's books is a key skill for teachers to develop.

Sourcing Mentor Texts

Creating a timeline of major book awards and regularly reviewing the winning books for fiction, poetry, nonfiction and illustration is a good start (Table 12.1). The Children's Book Council (CBC, US) and Children's Books Ireland (CBI) are two organisations that ensure children's voices are heard, with awards given to books chosen by children. CBI publishes the *Inis* magazine (x 3 annually), the only publication in Ireland completely devoted to children's and young adults' literature. It contains reviews of new titles and feature articles with authors and illustrators. CBI also publishes a range of free resources useful for teachers, including their annual guide to the latest children's books published to coincide with the start of the new school year, themed book lists, and idea and activity packs designed to promote creativity (https://childrensbooksireland.ie/what-we-do/our-publications). The Horn Book Inc (https://www.hbook.com/page/about-the-horn-book) in the US is also an invaluable resource where you will find articles, reviews, blogs, newsletters and reference to the bimonthly Horn Book Magazine. Additionally, the International Board on Books for Young People (IBBY) produce a refereed quarterly journal devoted to children's literature: https://www.ibby.org/bookbird.

Table 12.1 Archives of award-winning books for children

Website	Overview
https://www.nypl.org/blog/2023/01/30/winners-newbery-caldecott-king-belpre-ala-awards	New York Public Library: links to all major awards for children in one place (e.g., Newbery, Caldecott, Coretta Scott King, Pura Belpré, Robert Sibert medal and many more!)
https://www.cbcbooks.org/readers/reading-lists/ccba	Children's Book Council (CBC) US contains links to all previous CBC Children's Choice Book Awards
https://yotocarnegies.co.uk/archive	Archives of previous medal winners and resources: Yoto Carnegie/Kate Greenaway: Illustration Yoto Carnegie: Writing
https://www.ibby.org/awards-activities/awards/hans-christian-andersen-award	Archive of Award-winning children's books: International Board Books for Young People (IBBY) Hans Christan Andersen (body of distinguished Honour List (Writing, Illustration, Translation)
https://discoveririshkidsbooks.ie	A one-stop shop for books and advocacy: Irish authors, illustrators, publishers: updated lists by age level, award winners, resources
https://www.literacyireland.com/laibiennialbookawards	Archives: Biennial Literacy Association of Ireland award: Irish published children's books
https://childrensbooksireland.ie/what-we-do/kpmg-childrens-books-ireland-awards	Archives: annual Children's Books Ireland (CBI)/KPMG; includes Children's Choice Awards

Table 12.2 Criteria for the NCTE Orbis Pictus Award and ALA Robert Sibert Medal Award

https://ncte.org/awards/orbis-pictus-award-nonfiction-for-children/	http://www.ala.org/alsc/awardsgrants/bookmedia/sibertmedal
Accuracy–facts: current, complete, balance of fact and theory, varying points of view, stereotypes avoided, author's qualifications adequate, appropriate scope, authentic detail	Clear, accurate, stimulating facts/concepts/ideas in appropriate presentation for subject and audience
Organization–logical development, clear sequence, interrelationships indicated, patterns provided (general-specific, simple-complex)	Appropriate organization/ documentation. Supportive features: index, table of contents, timelines
Design–attractive, readable, illustrations complement text, placement of illustrative material appropriate and complementary, appropriate media, format, type	Excellent, engaging, and distinctive visual presentation; The book must be a self-contained entity, not dependent on other media for enjoyment.
Style–writing is interesting, stimulating, reveals author's enthusiasm for the subject; curiosity and wonder encouraged, appropriate terminology, rich language	Excellent, engaging, distinctive use of language; Significant contribution: how well the work elucidates, clarifies and enlivens its subject.
Each nomination should: be useful in teaching grades K-8; encourage thinking and more reading; model exemplary expository writing and research skills; share interesting/timely subject matter; appeal to a wide range of ages.	Respectful of/of interest to children. Respect for children's understanding, abilities, and appreciation. Children range from birth to 14 years.

There are also several prestigious awards for high-quality nonfiction books for children that value content, form, design, illustration and respect for children. As can be seen from Table 12.2, the criteria for the National Council for Teaching English (NCTE) Orbis Pictus Award and American Library Association (ALA) Robert Sibert Medal Award place significant emphasis on the craft of writing as well as the currency, authenticity and accuracy of the content.

Books in the mentor text library should include diverse author writing styles and formats. Using the metaphor of a mirror, a window and a doorway, the International Literacy Association Position Statement on the characteristics of culturally sustaining and academically rigorous classrooms (ILA, 2017, citing Bishop, 1990) highlights the importance of school and classroom libraries being representative of the cultures and identities of children in the school. They argue that 'culturally proficient literacy educators ensure that the **mirror** they make part of their classroom for each student reflects common human experiences as well as those that are unique and singular' (ILA, 2017, p. 2). Encountering culturally authentic books mirroring their lives provides children with opportunities to develop insights into their own personal and cultural experiences, provides a **window** into the lives of others offering the potential to foster empathy and understanding of different perspectives, and opens **doorways** to new horizons and possibilities for children. The website www.wowlit.com is a good site for teachers to explore literature from around the world.

Methodologies for Teaching Mini Lessons

Learning to source mentor texts to support children in acquiring strategies and techniques for writing is a key skill, but attention must also be given to how to use the literature in a way that is authentic and offers up options to children rather than prescriptions of techniques that must be included in their writing. This is key to ensuring that motivation to write is not constrained, given that explicit teaching has been identified as having a 'bright and dark side' in terms of its impact on motivation (de Smedt et al., 2019).

While examining the *Write to Read* rubric will provide ideas for the kinds of *content* to include in mini lessons (ideas, word choice, organisation, voice, elements of genre, conventions), it is important that teachers master two key methodologies introduced in Chapter 6 and elaborated with examples in Chapters 7, 8, 9 and 10. First, the Gradual Release of Responsibility Model (GRRM: Pearson & Gallagher, 1983; Fielding & Pearson, 1994) is an important approach to teaching the processes and crafts of writing to the whole class, while a Discovery Approach (Graves, 1994) is helpful in teaching the conventions of writing in small groups, which have been formed on the basis of formative assessment data.

As with any new learning, teachers first need opportunities to build their confidence and self-efficacy in using the methodologies. It is best to start with one method at a time. Bandura (1995) suggests that to foster self-efficacy a range of experiences is required including: (a) vicarious experiences; (b) social persuasion; (c) mastery experiences; and (d) attention to physiological and emotional states. When these experiences are included in PD initiatives, they have the potential to influence teacher attitudes, beliefs and values (Liou & Canrinus, 2020; King et al., 2022) as well as their practice. **Vicarious** experiences can be created by having teachers read and reflect on the sample lessons outlined in Chapters 7, 8, 9, 10. The lessons provide vignettes of actual classroom practice and the kinds of dialogue, resources and sequencing to use in lessons which will support teachers to envision how they might attempt to put the methodology into action in their own classrooms. Similarly, watching videos of mini lessons (highlighted in several chapters) serves the same purpose. **Social persuasion** occurs when coaches share their experiences of successfully implementing mini lessons in their own classrooms and schools. This is particularly powerful as Write to Read coaches teach in contexts similar to that of the school they are supporting which can reassure teachers that this approach can work well in their classrooms too and motivate them to give it a go if coaches model or demonstrate within classrooms in the school (see Chapter 1, Caoimhe Shiel's (*Write to Read* coach) account of modelling for teachers in her own school). Teachers have particularly valued the demonstrations they witnessed by *Write to Read* coaches as shared in the following comments:

> She did a little bit of modelling, talking around things, and that was terrific. To see it in action and to see the children react to it.
>
> (5th/6th teacher)

> I really found that fabulous, to see demonstration lessons and stuff. ___ would come in and do different things. She'd show you something, and then you'd really remember it when you've seen it.
>
> (1st class teacher)

Mastery experiences can be built by providing teachers with opportunities to collaboratively plan lessons based on the new approaches, experiment with teaching them and then debriefing with a coach or peers to discuss how the lesson went. Multifaceted PD ensures that teachers will have a high level of success as they introduce new practices into their repertoire of teaching strategies, contributing to a positive **emotional** state as lessons go well. As Bandura (1995, p. 3) points out: 'successes build a robust belief in one's personal efficacy'. Each success no matter how small builds teacher efficacy, and none is more powerful than seeing the effect of change on children's engagement

> *I think it was a combination of confidence growing because teachers, their knowledge was growing, and seeing the results from the kids from every little bit they did, they could see it was working.*
>
> (Literacy coordinator)

The association between teacher expectations and student performance has long been a focus of research and analysis (e.g., Rosenthal & Jacobson, 1968; Jussim & Barber, 2005). Rubie (2007) reported that teachers' class-level expectations may be more significant for student learning than expectations at the level of the individual. PD can change teacher beliefs, assumptions about learning and expectations for children:

> *but it's definitely changed my way of teaching, how I approach teaching writing...that's been huge for me...when I was teaching Junior Infants before W2R, part of it could have been that I probably didn't think that they could go that far, you know? But once you see that it's possible, you're really able to bring them on.*
>
> (Junior Infant teacher)

Encouraging teachers to adopt an inquiry-as-stance (Cochran-Smith & Lytle, 2009) to their teaching as they begin to try out new approaches and assessment tools are essential to support critical reflection as they examine what worked well, what didn't, what might need to be refined, how well the children responded and if the mini lessons actually transfer into the writing (Box 12.9).

BOX 12.9 EARLY PD ACTIVITIES: BUILDING TEACHER CONFIDENCE WITH THE GRRM

- During PD sessions teachers should read and reflect on the exemplar GRRM craft lessons and teacher notes provided in Chapters 8 and 10; Discuss with colleagues the ways in which the model is similar and different to their current practice.
- Discuss key features of the GRMM; teachers should work in pairs or small groups to create a checklist for an effective craft and process lesson based on the exemplars.
- Using the structure, teachers should collaboratively plan some word choice and process lessons for the class they are currently teaching.

- Discuss how a word choice craft lesson differs according to class level.
- Watch the mini lesson videos on the *Write to Read* website to see a craft lesson in action.
- Following the PD session, teachers should try out the lessons in their classrooms and keep a note of what went well, what might need to change and children's responses.
- At the start of the next PD session, teachers can debrief and share what they learned from their experiences. Use the prompts in Box 12.10 to reflect deeply on GRRM lessons.
- Plan further craft lessons using the *Write to Read* rubric for inspiration;
- As relational trust builds, coaches and teachers can observe each other teaching lessons and provide feedback to each other.
- Build a bank of mini lessons and mentor text extracts and create a digital archive of lessons and resources over time.

The PD experiences highlighted here align with the research base that advocates PD in writing should ensure that teachers experience the writing strategies they will employ (Graham, 2019; Slavin et al., 2019) as such experiences have been found to influence teachers' beliefs about writing, their dispositions toward writing and writer identity, which it is argued increases the likelihood that they will write, enjoy writing, see the value of writing and enjoy teaching it (Graham, 2019).

BOX 12.10 TEACHING WITH THE GRADUAL RELEASE OF RESPONSIBILITY MODEL

1. I began the mini lesson with a statement rather than a question when I gave the **Explanation** *at the start of the lesson*
2. The brief explanation highlighted the *what* and *why* of the lesson
3. I chose an appropriate mentor text and preplanned my **demonstration** (think-aloud) to show my thinking process on how the author had used the technique and why
4. I observed and listened to children as they worked in pairs on the **guided practice** and took note of who got it and who needed more reinforcement
5. We constructed the anchor chart together
6. I invited children to try the technique during **independent** writing time.
7. We finished the workshop by **reflecting** and **setting goals** after the share session
8. I built children's **metacognitive awareness** (declarative, procedural and conditional) by bookending the mini lesson with **Explain** and **Demonstrate** and **Reflect/set goals**

The GRRM model (Box 12.10) when used well brings strategies to a more conscious level so that learners may better internalise them and know when to call upon and use them when working independently (see Chapters 8 and 10).

As teachers, we are primed to start lessons with questions to establish children's prior knowledge but doing so in this case will divert attention away from the main focus and elongate the mini lesson, unintentionally stealing writing time. In our experience, teachers have found it hard to shake off the questioning habit in this instance.

It is important that mini lessons using the GRRM are brief and focused with memorable examples highlighted drawing on high-quality mentor texts (Box 12.10). Carefully planning the mini lessons using a decontextualised academic language register is a powerful tool for enhancing children's oral language and scaffolding their use of this kind of language across genres. Teachers have remarked that it has given children a deeper understanding of language registers and genre features:

> *The children have a really, really top understanding, in my opinion, of the different genres, a lot more so than other children I would have had that I've taught in a different setting They've a great theoretical understanding of what they're doing. That's the difference.*
>
> (5th class teacher)

BOX 12.11 TEACHING WITH THE DISCOVERY APPROACH

1. I convened the small group on the basis of assessment (reading children's work and conference notes)
2. I began by explaining to the group: *'Today we are focusing on... I have noticed that in your writing you...*
3. I chose a text that had several examples of the target skill used correctly
4. I asked questions to help the children speculate:

    - Why is the (target punctuation) used here?
    - How did the author know to put it there?
    - How does it help the reader to read the piece of text?
    - What's the hard bit?
    - What's the confusing bit?
    - How will we remember to use it in our writing?

5. We constructed the anchor chart together
6. Children applied what they learned to their current writing piece
7. Children engaged in peer scaffolding and helped each other identify and correct errors
8. We concluded by reflecting on what we learned, when and why we would use the target punctuation; what was easy/hard; we set goals to improve accuracy
9. Children kept a record of the lesson in the mini lesson section of their writing folder for future reference
10. I have kept a record of small group mini lesson participation and kept the mentor texts for future reference

Lessons on the conventions of writing are often the main focus of writing lessons at the primary level, indicating an overemphasis on secretarial skills (e.g. grammar, spelling and punctuation) at the expense of authorial skills (Daffern et al., 2017). Furthermore, such skills are often taught in a one-size-fits-all approach through workbook pages divorced from the context of children's own writing. Learning how to address skills in a meaningful way is another shift in practice for teachers (Box 12.11, Box 12.12). Small group mini lessons convened on the basis of formative assessment are more effective in transferring

> **BOX 12.12 EARLY PD ACTIVITIES: BUILDING TEACHER CONFIDENCE WITH THE DISCOVERY APPROACH**
>
> - Ask teachers to bring three samples of children's writing to the PD session representative of children whom they consider to be high, middle and low-achieving writers in relation to conventions, specifically punctuation. In the PD session, they should make a list of what punctuation marks each child is using accurately, all of the time, some of the time, or rarely.
> - Make a note of which children are **not** experimenting or using punctuation to the level expected for their stage of development (see **Rubric: Conventions** component).
> - During PD sessions teachers should read and reflect on the exemplar convention lessons and teacher notes provided in Chapter 9; Discuss with colleagues the ways in which the approach is similar and different to their current practice.
> - Discuss key features of the Discovery Approach. In pairs or small groups, teachers should create a checklist for an effective lesson using the exemplars.
> - Using the structure, teachers should collaboratively plan some punctuation lessons for the class they are currently teaching.
> - Discuss expectations for conventions according to class level. Explore the Conventions component and sub-components of the *Write to Read* Rubric.
> - Following the PD session, teachers should try out the lessons in their classrooms and keep a note of what went well, what might need to change and children's responses.
> - At the start of the next PD session, teachers can debrief and share what they learned from their experiences. Use the prompts in Box 12.11 to reflect on the lessons.
> - Keep a record of mini lessons and hold children accountable for self-correcting errors for the conventions taught in mini lessons.
> - Build a bank of mini lessons, mentor text extracts and create a digital archive of lessons and resources over time. These can be shared at a whole school level.
> - Read Chapter 9 and reflect on how they will monitor and address other conventions such as spelling and handwriting.

skills into children's compositional writing. Small group mini lessons mean children are in a group when they have demonstrated a need and a readiness for a particular skill. Guiding children to hypothesise on the purpose of the convention and to consider its value (Graves, 1994), inducts children into a mindset that conventions are signposts for the reader and an element of author craft or, as Myhill et al. (2012) puts it, a 'design tool' to enhance writing quality. Teachers should make it a habit to convene small groups on one day of the week and children not involved in the lesson can use the time to concentrate fully on their writing (see Chapter 9).

Graham's (2019) principle four (create a supportive and motivating writing environment) and principle 5 (connect writing, reading, and learning) are naturally embedded within writing workshops that are research-informed and enacted consistently and daily. The conferencing and share sessions along with peer feedback, peer and self-assessment when revising writing, and mini lessons targeting the crafts, processes and skills of writing according to children's assessed needs and stages of development all support the evolution of classrooms into an engaged community of writers. Mini lessons naturally integrate oral language, reading and writing across genres as children are engaged in reading and responding to mentor texts, considering how best to use the techniques in their writing, and reading and responding to a wide range of texts (print, digital and =multimodal) as they engage in inquiries across the curriculum. In sum, research-informed writing workshops are an effective framework in which to systematically integrate and embed Graham's (2019) five principles for effective writing instruction. The following sections address how teachers and schools may begin the process of planning.

Teacher Planning for Writing

As teachers' comfort levels increase in managing and operationalising a writing workshop their focus can shift onto longerterm planning to accommodate the needs of children at their class level(s) and to satisfy curriculum requirements. Graham contends that 'good instruction requires rich and interconnected knowledge about subject matter and content, students' learning and diversity, and subject specific as well as general pedagogical methods' (2019, pp. 284-285). Such knowledge is exemplified in learning to attend to craft, process and conventions mini lessons and diversifying methodologies and groupings to best serve the range of writers in the class. In the examples below, monthly plans developed by *Write to Read* coaches are presented and demonstrate how processes, crafts and conventions are balanced over a month. The first example shows a plan for an early year's class using shared and interactive writing as the main approach which can be used as a starting point for initiating writing with children in Junior/Senior Infants (Box 12.13). The second (Box 12.14) is focused on a literary approach to report writing in a 6th class (examples of writing from this unit of work can be seen in Chapters 8 and 10). A brief overview of each week is provided and some of the mentor texts that were used to support the craft and process dimensions of the unit of work are highlighted. The small group mini lessons are not included here, as they were specific to the needs of children in that particular class.

BOX 12.13 BEGINNING AT THE BEGINNING: INTRODUCING SHARED WRITING, INTERACTIVE WRITING AND THE WRITING WORKSHOP

Caoimhe Shiel, Class Teacher, Support Teacher, Write to Read Coach. You can read about how she inspired change in her own school in Chapter 1

Introduce shared writing as soon as possible in infants, where the teacher acts as a scribe and models writing on the easel. The students orally contribute to the composition of the text, with the teacher drawing upon early literacy skills whilst demonstrating the writing process.

Later in the year, when the children have begun their phonics programme, as well as their handwriting programme, the teacher can begin interactive writing with the children. The teacher will lead the lesson but share the pen with children. This builds student confidence when moving towards independent writing with the introduction of the writing workshop.

In this planning grid, a writing workshop was initially introduced three days a week and interactive writing was continued twice a week to ease this transition towards more independent writing.

Week 1	Introducing Interactive Writing in the Classroom Link to weekly big book
Monday	Draw and label a picture (e.g. a character from a big book- hat, coat, boots, legs), model writing left to right. Invite children to listen to the sounds in recorded words, and to write some of the more dominant sounds (move beyond initial letter sounds as soon as possible).
Tuesday	Draw and label a picture (e.g., the setting from a big book: tree, woods, path, cave, bush). Model writing labels with a focus on correct letter size. Invite children to write some words, drawing on the letter sounds they know.
Wednesday	Draw and label a picture retelling the *beginning* of the story. Write a sentence on lines under the picture box. Model where to start writing words on the top line and then move down. Invite children to listen to the sounds in words, and to write some letter sounds or high-frequency words (use the class word wall).
Thursday	Draw and label a picture retelling the *middle* of the story. Write 2 sentences on lines under the picture box. Demonstrate writing words that sit on the line. Invite children to write some letters/words. Highlight the capital letter at the beginning and the full stop at the end.

Friday	Retell the story – Draw and label a picture retelling the *end* of the story. Write 2+ sentences on lines under the picture box. Emphasise spaces between words using a finger space. Invite children to use a finder space before writing initial letter sounds in words.
Week 2	Integrated **interactive writing** with other subjects to show a range of genres e.g. recount, procedural, poem
Monday	**Recount** of the weekend: label the picture and write 3 to 5 sentences. Model directionality. Emphasise a continuous sentence over 2 lines and model rereading this feature of the text.
Tuesday	**Link to SEE (Social and Environmental Education)** Map of the school area. Draw and label a simple map of the area surrounding the school (e.g. road, park, shop, crèche, post box). Encourage invented spelling: sounding out words (e.g., spelling creche as cresh, etc)
Wednesday	**Link to PE Physical Education):** Procedural writing: How to Play Horses and Jockeys Game. Draw and label a diagram of the game. Make a list of equipment needed.
Thursday	**Link to PE:** Procedural writing – How to Play Horses and Jockeys Game continued. Begin writing steps (focus on 'bossy verbs' – place, run, catch, count, etc.)
Friday	**Poem:** Write a short poem with the children (can link to SEE or feature a new phonics sound taught earlier in the week). Write the text with the children and focus on fluency when rereading (taking note of any punctuation e.g. full stops, commas, exclamation marks or question marks). Display in classroom for children to refer back to.
Week 3	**Introducing the Writing Workshop alongside Interactive Writing**
Monday	**Writing workshop Day 1** *Organisational Mini Lesson* – Structure: Mini lesson, independent writing, sharing, writing name and date on work. Use an anchor chart to explain parts of the lesson. Model drawing a picture, labelling and writing a sentence of a narrative text in the mini lesson. Allow choice of writing paper and pencils and explain children have complete choice of writing topics during independent writing time. Explain why names and the date need to be on the work. Model asking questions and praising specific aspects of writing during the share session.
Tuesday	**Interactive Writing** Summarising a big book story – Draw and label a picture summarising the weekly big book story. Write sentences also. Invite children who were reluctant or struggling to write independently in writing workshop the previous day to share the pen with you to build confidence in their writing abilities.

Wednesday	**Writing workshop Day 2** *Organisational Mini Lesson:* Storing work, introducing conferencing During the mini lesson, explain to the children that they may want to continue their work or start a new piece. Model storing previous work in personal folder to keep as a learning portfolio. During independent writing time, once children are settled, explain that you will be speaking to different children about their writing during each lesson and begin conferencing (keep conference notes to inform future planning). Continue modelling, asking questions and praising work during the share session.
Thursday	**Interactive writing:** Link to big book. Use large sentence strips under pictures of various parts of the story and write a summary sentence for each one. Display for the children to refer back to. Emphasise aspects of writing that you have noticed need attention when children are writing independently in writing workshop (e.g., spaces between words, directionality, stretching words and linking letters to dominant sounds, punctuation).
Friday	**Writing workshop Day 3** *Organisational Mini Lesson focus on share session:* Model planning to write (think, draw, label) and write as on the previous day in mini lesson. Continue toconference during independent work. Focus on the share session: have all children turn knee-to-knee and eye-to-eye initially to share with partners and then invite individual children to share (children can choose to not share). Model how to comment on others' work to the class e.g. two stars and a wish. Sometimes it can be useful to start a share session anchor chart to display ideas or comments e.g., I wonder, I noticed, I like, etc. Encourage children to be specific in their comments.
Week 4	**Continuing the Writing Workshop alongside Interactive Writing**
Monday	Interactive writing: Link to big book. Use a story planning map to fill in details about the weekly big book (character, setting, beginning, middle and end). Can use words or full sentences. Display for the children to refer back to.
Tuesday	**Writing workshop Day 4** *Process lesson- planning for writing:* Model using a simple planning grid to come up with story ideas (focus words include characters, setting, beginning, middle and end). Continue with conferencing during independent writing time and add to the sentence starter anchor chart during the share session.
Wednesday	**Writing workshop Day 5** *Process lesson- planning for writing continued:* Continue modelling using a simple planning grid to come up with story ideas (focus words include characters, setting, beginning, middle and end) and link these to a checklist at the bottom of the writing page. Show children how to tick off these features as they include them in the story. Continue with conferencing during independent writing time and add to sentence starter anchor chart during the share session.

Thursday	**Interactive writing** Link to a photo display e.g. of children during **Aistear**[1] play time. Label pictures of children and write sentences describing what they are doing e.g., Alice and Ben are in roles in the shop. Try to link to a skill that children are struggling with e.g. capital letters in names.
Friday	**Writing workshop Day 6** **Skills Mini lesson**- e.g. capital letters for names: Explain to children that you are going to continue with your stories but that you will call up groups of children to work on a certain skill instead of conferencing during independent writing today. Call up children struggling with a common skill e.g. capital letters in names on labels or in sentences and model this with a small group at the easel before calling up a different group (groups are convened based assessment of writing to date). Add to sentence starter anchor chart during the share session.

BOX 12.14 USING MINI LESSONS TO DEVELOP USE OF FIGURATIVE LANGUAGE, POETIC DEVICES, IMAGERY AND QUOTES (5TH AND 6TH CLASSES)

Stephen Brett is currently the Principal of a DEIS school in South Dublin. He is a literacy coach on the Write to Read project. Stephen initiated this work as he found that children were not transferring mini lessons learned in units of study on fiction, into their non-fiction informational writing. In Chapter 8 you can find examples of children's work which emanated from the monthly plan outlined here.

In **week one,** the main focus of my mini lessons was firstly to hook the reader in the opening paragraph and secondly to demonstrate the use of figurative language as a technique for creating a powerful introduction e.g., painting a scene, opening with a question, using dialogue or a surprising fact.

Week 1	Monday	Tuesday	Wednesday	Thursday	Friday
Writing Interesting Hooks Figurative language **Reading** Summarising Determining Importance	**Mini lesson** Taking notes from a video **Mentor text** *Butterflies,* Seymour Simon **Templates** Concept map Definition map	**Mini lesson** Creating a hook for the reader **Mentor text** *The Boy who Harnessed the Wind:* William Kamkwamba	**Mini lesson** Variety of hooks **Mentor texts** *The Pebble in my Pocket:* Meredith Hooper; *Bugged: How Insects Changed History:* Sarah Albee	**Mini lesson** Figurative/ Descriptive language **Mentor text** *Our Solar System* Seymour Simon (2014) *Frogs:* Nic Bishop	Small group mini lessons according to assessment

In **week two**, the focus shifted to the use of poetic devices. Mini lessons based on 'Show Don't Tell' (where the writer makes reference to the different senses) helped strengthen the visual aspect of the descriptive nonfiction. This enabled writers to home in on the sensory details of their topic. The purpose of this was to help instil vivid images in the writer's mind and use emotive language to bring the writing to life.

Week 2	Monday	Tuesday	Wednesday	Thursday	Friday
Writing Imagery Show – don't tell Turning facts into scenes **Reading** Visualising Questioning	**Mini lesson** Imagery **Mentor text** *Drowned City: Hurricane Katrina and New Orleans:* D. Brown. **Activity:** KWL (Students document what they know about a topic, what they want to know, and what they have learned in the end).	**Mini lesson** Comparing different authors' styles **Mentor texts** *Locomotive:* B. Floca; *Frogs:* N. Bishop	**Mini lesson** Show don't tell **Mentor text** *The Shyest Fish in the Sea:* N. Butterworth	**Mini lesson** Facts into scenes **Mentor text** *The Girl from the Tar Paper School:* T. Kanefield; *Star Stuff: Karl Sagan and the Mysteries of Cosmos:* S. Sisson	Small group mini lessons based on assessment needs

In **week three**, the focus moved to imagery, precise language and transitional phrases. The focus on imagery allowed children to condense the poetic devices focused on in week one and week two. The focus on precise language helped to create a strong mental picture whilst also giving depth to the language piece. It is a craft that many nonfiction writers use, and I wanted to bring the writers' attention to this as it is a wonderful technique within nonfiction. The use of transitional phrases helped with the fluidity of the piece. This was important as the purpose of the study was to take the reader on a visual journey so sequencing the events and using such phrases enabled children to achieve this goal.

Week 3	Monday	Tuesday	Wednesday	Thursday	Friday
Writing Imagery Precise language Transitional phrases **Reading** Drawing Inferences Making Predictions	**Mini lesson** Drawing on the senses **Mentor text** *One Tiny Turtle:* N. Davies **Activity:** Two column sheet	**Mini lesson** Drawing on the senses **Mentor text** *Drowned City: Hurricane Katrina and New Orleans:* Dan Brown	**Mini lesson** Precise language **Mentor text** *The Shyest Fish in the Sea:* Nick Butterworth *Snakes:* N. Bishop	**Mini lesson** Precise language **Mentor text** *Monsieur Marceau:* L. Schubert; *The Snake Scientist:* S. Montgomery; *Locomotive:* B. Floca.	Small group mini lessons according to assessment

In **week four**, the focus turned to sentence length, using quotes from different sources and creating circular endings. In week five, children were also encouraged to use checklists and to begin revising a piece for publication following self and peer assessment. Children were also supported to begin considering the best format for publication. Some chose to develop a narrated PowerPoint and selected images to accompany their work. Others chose to write a narrative and some chose to also turn their report into a found poem.

Week 4	Monday	Tuesday	Wednesday	Thursday	Friday
Writing Varying Sentence length Effective Endings Using quotes **Reading** Synthesising Connections	**Mini lesson** Compare & Contrast **Mentor texts** Whales: S. Simon; Dolphins: S. Simon; **Activity:** Venn Diagram	**Mini lesson** Using Quotes **Mentor text** Game Changers: The Story of Serena and Venus Williams: L. Cline-Ransome	**Mini lesson** Sentence Length **Mentor text** 30 Minutes over Oregon: A Japanese Pilot's WW11 Story: M. Tyler Nobleman	**Mini lesson** Endings **Mentor texts** Sharks: S. Simon The Big Blue Whale: N. Davies; Spiders: Nic Bishop	Finalising first drafts Selecting a piece for publication Developing a checklist for revision

Mentor Texts used in Unit of Study

- Albee, S. (2014). *Bugged: How Insects Changed History*. Bloomsbury USA Children's. ISBN-13: 978-0802734228
- Hooper, M. (2015). *The Pebble in my Pocket*. Frances Lincoln Children's Books (Revised edition 5th). ISBN-13: 978-1847807687
- Bishop, N. (2007). *Spiders*. Scholastic; Illustrated edition. ISBN-13: 978-0439877565
- Bishop, N. (2008). *Frogs*. Scholastic Nonfiction; Illustrated edition. ISBN-13: 978-0439877558
- Bishop, N. (2012). *Snakes*. Scholastic Nonfiction; Illustrated edition. ISBN-13: 978-0545206389
- Brown, D. (2017). *Drowned City: Hurricane Katrina and New Orleans*. HMH Books for Young Readers. ISBN-13: 978-0544586178
- Butterworth, N. (2006). *The Shyest Fish in the Sea*. Candlewick Press, U.S. ISBN-13: 978-0763629892
- Cline-Ransome, L. (2018). *Game Changers: The Story of Serena and Venus Williams*. Simon & Schuster/Paula Wiseman Books; Illustrated edition. ISBN-13: 978-1481476843
- Davies. N. (2008). *The Big Blue Whale*. Walker Books. ISBN-13: 978-1406312577
- Davies, N. (2015). *One Tiny Turtle*. Walker Books. ISBN-13: 978-1406364637
- Floca, B. (2013). *Locomotive*. Atheneum/Richard Jackson Books; Illustrated edition. ISBN-13: 978-1416994152
- Kanefield, T. (2014). *The Girl from the Tar Paper School*. Harry N. Abrams, 1st edition. ISBN-13: 978-1419707964
- Kamkwamba, W. & Mealer, B. (2009). *The Boy who Harnessed the Wind*. William Morrow & Co. ISBN-13: 978-0061730320

- Montgomery, S. (2001). *The Snake Scientist*. Clarion Books; Illustrated edition. ISBN-13: 978-0618111190
- Nobleman, Tyler, M. (2018). *30 Minutes over Oregon: A Japanese Pilot's WW11 Story*. Clarion Books; Illustrated edition. ISBN-13: 978-0544430761
- Schubert, L. (2012). *Monsieur Marceau*. Flash Point. ISBN-13: 978-1596435292
- Simon, S. (2019). *Dolphins* (Smithsonian-Science). Harper Collins; Illustrated edition. ISBN-13: 978-0064462204
- Simon, S. (2019). *Whales* (Smithsonian-Science). Harper Collins, revised edition. ISBN-13: ISBN-13: 978-0060877118
- Simon, S. *Sharks* (Smithsonian-Science). Harper Collins, revised edition. ISBN-13: ISBN-13: 978-0060877132
- Simon S. (2011). *Butterflies*. Harper Collins; Illustrated edition. ISBN-13: 978-0061914935
- Simon, S. (2014). *Our Solar System*. Harper Collins; Revised edition. ISBN-13: 978-0061140105
- Sisson, S. (2014). *Star Stuff: Karl Sagan and the Mysteries of Cosmos*. Roaring Brook Press; Illustrated edition. ISBN-13: 978-1596439603

Later Moves: Building Progression in Writing Across a School

A Whole School Approach to Assessment of Writing

Effective writing instruction is more likely to occur 'when goals, curriculum, instructional methods, and assessment are aligned' (Graham, 2019, p. 288). A starting point for PD on assessment is a school-wide conversation about what makes a text 'good' (Box 12.15). It is interesting to hear teachers discuss the qualities that they look for in a piece of writing. Such conversations reveal teachers' values and underlying philosophies of writing. These values transmit to children and may unintentionally convey mixed messages about writing that are counter-productive to good quality writing. Some teachers highlight the secretarial skills, others the authorial dimensions, while in reality a focus on both is needed.

To truly build progression in writing, it is essential that teachers develop a very good understanding of developmental pathways in writing and have ways to systematically assess writing development to build an accurate picture of writing quality across the school (see Chapter 5). Calkins et al. (2019) have argued that rubrics may be viewed as learning pathways in that they can be aligned vertically across class levels in a school and horizontally across genres. If linked to instruction and national curricula, they can not only enhance student writing but also 'function as significant professional development both for expert and new teachers' (p. 174). The *Write to Read* rubric fulfils both functions and has been found to be a valid and reliable instrument to track growth in writing across class levels over time (Kennedy & Shiel, 2022). Templates for summarising performance across grade levels using the *Write to Read* rubric can be found in Appendix 5.2.

Rubrics can 'help explain terms and clarify expectations' (Crusan, 2010, p. 43). The *Write to Read* rubric gives teachers professional language for thinking and talking about writing

> **BOX 12.15 PD ACTIVITY: WRITING ASSESSMENT AND WRITING QUALITY**
>
> 1. Ask teachers to discuss in small groups what makes a piece of writing stand out for them. What do they appreciate in a text? What is important? What is not so important?
> 2. Ask them to discuss how they assess writing. How do they know if writing is improving? How do they know if writing is reaching, exceeding or falling short of expectations for their class level? Do they assess process as well as product? How often do they assess writing? In what ways does assessment data inform teaching and learning?
> 3. Create a mind/concept map of the responses and discuss similarities and differences in perspectives. Guide teachers to consider strengths and weaknesses and highlight any gaps.

development across key components of writing (ideas, organisation including genre features, word choice, voice, conventions). It supports them in developing an understanding of appropriate expectations or norms for their class level and a greater appreciation of a continuum of writing growth. The rubric presents high-level content and benchmarks across dimensions of writing that teachers typically haven't considered possible for young children in particular, and so raises their expectations for what children can accomplish from an early stage of development. In working with schools on using the rubric, and in trialling it in their own classes, our coaches have reported responses such as the following:

> *A few were like, there's so many aspects to writing you just don't think to break down that much at that level but it can be broken down which is great. Yeah, like word choice has word level, sentence level and imagery... They were like, I didn't even think to consider that.*
>
> *I suppose what I've noticed just I think in terms of myself and setting expectations, like the Word Choice component completely springs to mind in terms of how early we'd like to see certain things and probably how little we teach them as teachers at early stages of writing.*

Comments such as these demonstrate how powerful a rubric can be for PD. It can create a certain level of 'cognitive dissonance' (Thompson & Zeuli, 1999) and can be a catalyst for teacher reflection, challenge assumptions about writing development and raise expectations for what children are capable of achieving in writing.

It is important that as part of a whole school approach to writing, time is provided for teachers at the same class level and a class level above and below to come together to examine writing samples in a particular genre and to evaluate them using the rubric. Sharing data in this way is essential to build a picture of children's writing strengths and aspects for further development. It also helps to build coherence and progression in writing (across

Planning for Writing across a School 287

genres), to track growth over time and to inform short and long-term planning as indicated by this teacher:

> The W2R rubrics, they're great I find for using them to plan. You're looking and kind of saying, okay, here's where they are, here's where I want them to go, so this is what I'm going to teach.
>
> (2nd class teacher)

Before comparing writing across class levels, it is important for teachers to first develop an understanding of the structure of the rubric and to become comfortable in using it to score writing samples. The samples of writing shared in Chapters 5 and 8 can be used for that purpose. Teachers will find it less intimidating to rate samples of writing that are not from their own class and school. The samples in Chapter 5 have been scored and discussed in the chapter while those in Chapter 8 have been discussed but the scores have not been given. These professional conversations lay the groundwork for discussions across class levels so teachers can begin to establish class-level expectations and consider progression from one class level to the next.

BOX 12.16 PD ACTIVITY: DEVELOPING FAMILIARITY WITH THE *WRITE TO READ* RUBRIC (1)

1. Ask teachers to read the rubric carefully to familiarise themselves with the content and language. Ask teachers to read the three texts in Chapter 5 and in pairs to assign a score for each subcomponent. Scores can be recorded on post-it notes and then compared with those assigned in Chapter 5.
2. **Samples in Chapter 5:**
   - 5.1: Fiction: *The Spoocy Cave (Senior Infants/Kindergarten)*
   - 5.2: Persuasive: *Letter of Complaint (3rd class)*
   - 5.3: Fiction: *The War (6th class)*
3. The samples in Chapter 8 span a range of classes at the primary level: from Junior and Senior Infants (4–6-year-olds) to 2nd class (7–8-year-olds) and 6th class (12–13-year-olds). Begin with the samples from the youngest writers, then move to the 2nd class and finish with the two 6th class samples. This will give an idea of how writing might develop across different class levels. Teachers can work in pairs or small groups to assign a score for each subcomponent, record it on a post-it and then compare and agree scores.
4. **Samples in Chapter 8:**
   - 8.2a–8.2e: Fiction: *A Wondeeful(wonderful) Night in the Park* (Senior Infants)
   - 8.3: Informational writing: *Rhino* (Senior Infants)
   - 8.7: Persuasive Writing: *Summer is Best* (Junior Infant)
   - 8.8: Persuasive Writing: *The Country or the City is Best* (Senior Infants)
   - 8.9 Persuasive Writing: *Letter of Complaint* (6th Class)
   - 8.10a/8.10b: Informational Writing: *The Life of a Bat* (6th class)
   - 8.11a/8.11b: Informational/Persuasive writing: *Fantastic France* (2nd class)

As teachers become more comfortable with the rubric and with discussing writing quality, the next step is to begin an analysis of writing in their own school (Box 12.17). Rather than trying to analyse the writing of every child in every class, it is easier to begin with a representative sample (for example, three samples one high, middle and low achiever selected at random at each class level) and to focus on one specific genre.

BOX 12.17 PD ACTIVITY: DEVELOPING FAMILIARITY WITH THE *WRITE TO READ* RUBRIC (2)

1. Decide on a genre; Ask teachers to select one high-, middle and lower-achiever
2. Anonymise the samples by deleting any identifiers (e.g. name of child, room number, class level) and randomly assign a number to each sample.
3. Make enough copies of the samples; teachers work on scoring in small groups
4. Choose one or two components of the rubric for focus (e.g., *word choice* and *voice*).
5. Ask teachers to read the texts and in groups to assign a score for each of the sub-components. Record their scores on post-it notes and stick on texts.
6. Give them a few minutes to complete the task and then feedback the scores.
7. Record the scores for each sample on an Excel sheet and display:

Word choice Sample 1	Group 1	Group 2	Group 3	Group 4	Group 5	Group 6
Word level						
Sentence level						
Imagery						
creative						
language use						
Voice Sample 1						
Audience						
Risk-taking						
Style						

8. Repeat the process for another 2 components e.g. ideas, organisation & genre, and then finish with conventions.
9. Discuss any discrepancies in scores and ask teachers to give a rationale for the score that they have given and how they resolved any issues as they worked with their partner.
10. Discuss the trajectory of scores. Are they as expected? What was interesting? Surprising? How different were the scores in more senior classes? Were some components/subcomponents stronger than others? Where are the strengths/weaknesses?

Whole School Planning

In developing a whole school plan for writing, it is important to have all teachers involved in shaping the plan and creating the framework across grade levels. A dynamic approach to planning is needed, as whole school plans will need to be reviewed and updated yearly, in the light of new assessment data and any changes to curriculum that have occurred. As the writing workshop embeds across the school, children's writing will develop, necessitating a revision of content and expectations for writing across class levels, particularly for the first few years of implementation. We have found, for example, that what children in first class (six to seven years) in year one of implementation can produce will be very different in quality from the writing of children in first class in year three of implementation, as the latter will have experienced writing daily for three years.

The rubric analysis across class levels in a school can demonstrate where there might be overlap or a lack of progression in writing at senior class levels. In looking at writing across class levels, the rubric has demonstrated for teachers the need to 'up the ante' (Pressley et al., 2001) and hold themselves and children accountable for higher levels of sophistication in writing. As this teacher highlighted:

> *One of the issues that we had in my school was, just let's use poetry as an example. Everybody was doing similes; everyone was doing alliteration. Nobody was doing other poetic devices. I'd argue the level of similes that were happening in First class would not be too far away from the level of similes that was happening in Sixth class.*
>
> (6th class teacher)

That teacher went on to emphasise that a whole-school approach and sharing of assessment data and writing samples school-wide is critical if teachers are to *'up their game'* and truly push up the quality of writing: *So, you're not starting afresh, you're not rehashing things that have basically been covered. You'd be able to you know, keep the ball rolling for want of a better word'.*

An effective way to trace development is to maintain portfolios of children's writing and to pass them on from one year to the next so that the next year's teacher can see children's stage of development and aim to push the writing on to the next level. In one partner junior school (four to seven-year-olds), teachers invited children to select pieces for the portfolio and justify their choices and the portfolio transitioned with the children to the senior school:

> *So, they're just like clipped together for the month and then usually they'll come up and tell you why and you write it down at the bottom of their portfolio and some of the writing we keep in a file in the school for the three years, just to see the progression across more than one year...which is nice, especially when we hand them over to the senior school.*
>
> (Junior Infant teacher)

As noted in Chapter 6, in developing a whole school plan for writing it is important to consider how the various genres will be distributed across the year (See Chapter 6, Table 6.1). Revisiting genres more than once annually allows for further development of a genre and transfer of mini lessons from one genre to the next. Teachers should have assessment data to hand and the rubric for easy reference and use them to inform the mapping of mini lessons for each class level in a particular genre. Meaningful links can be made across other curricula to enrich and authentically integrate genres. The plan shared above for 6th class can act as a template for considering how to record which crafts and processes will be addressed over the month. Consider in what ways the second monthly plan for the genre could extend and build on this one and also the prerequisites needed for children to be able to respond to the mini lessons (e.g., to have already engaged with descriptive writing and creative use of language and imagery in fiction, recount or persuasive). Notice also in the writing plan above, that the links with reading are briefly highlighted. Additionally, the children are writing on topics that they have chosen and are interested in researching and the mini lessons are there to support them in realising their ambitions for their texts, not as a prescription.

Affective Dimensions of the Change Process

As with any change process, teachers will experience a variety of emotions (fear, anxiety, motivation, excitement, expectations) which may range from positive to negative (Rawdon, 2020). There is increasing awareness in PD research of the importance of the affective dimensions of PD in impacting teachers' beliefs, attitudes, sense of self-efficacy and practice. As a literacy coordinator shared with us, some teachers will embrace change right away and enjoy the challenge and others will take longer to adapt:

> *You know, some people will love it and take to it and do over and above and then others will come slower to it. You have to balance that with the different skill levels and different, you know, with teachers as well, so you kind of just have to work with what you have.*
> (Literacy coordinator)

Teacher confidence, identity and self-efficacy are intrinsically linked to their emotions, personality and prior experiences with writing (Graham, 2018) which may be positive or negative. Consider the following responses shared by teachers at various stages of the implementation process:

> *To be honest, writing is one I'm not really confident on as a teacher…*
> *Funny enough, I enjoy teaching it more now.*
> *I remember from myself back in school, I hated creative writing because it was sort of like, 'here, write'. Even now I don't like it… I was a bright intelligent kid, why didn't I like it? It was because it was like here's just a blank paper…We break it down, we show them actually how… I tend to find I could do it all day. You want to give the time to it because it's going so well.*

If a school-wide approach to writing is to successfully develop, confronting teachers' writing histories and providing a safe space for them to talk about both positive and negative experiences is important, particularly as research shows that teachers who are less confident as writers and do not enjoy it give it less attention (Box 12.18). Being aware of your colleagues' feelings will help you to work more closely with them. As Graham (2018, p. 273) points out:

> *I propose that writing cannot be fully understood without considering how the communities in which it takes place and those involved in creating it evolve, including how community and individuals reciprocally influence each other.*

BOX 12.18 AFFECTIVE DIMENSIONS OF PD

- Consider the various levels of teacher experience in the school. How might support need to differ for each level?
- Consider how to encourage open dialogue so that teachers can feel comfortable expressing opinions
- Encourage teachers to discuss their writing history and how it influences their teaching of writing
- How might teachers be supported to develop a positive writing identity?

Research indicates that PD should also consider teachers' career stage and existing knowledge base (King et al., 2022). As indicated in the quotes below, newly qualified teachers may have encountered research and process-based approaches to writing pedagogy in their college courses but may not have implemented them if they were not evident in the school in which they found employment. Additionally, they may be grappling with other professional dimensions of teaching in this, their first year of teaching.

> You learn a certain amount in college about how to teach literacy and what to do…I don't know what it is, you kind of come into a school and if it's not going on, I don't know why you slip back. You end up going with what is going on in the school.
>
> (mid-career teacher)

> I think when you're a young teacher as well I felt clueless, so it was nice to have kind of a routine to become accustomed to…It gives a real focus to my planning, as well as to children's learning.
>
> (Newly-qualified teacher)

Hall and Hord (1987) in their *Concerns-Based Adoption Model (CBAM): A Model for Change in Individuals*, conceptualised the change process as a series of stages that teachers pass through as they engage with change resulting in the need for varied levels and kinds of support. Initially teachers' questions are more '*self-oriented*' i.e. they are concerned about how the proposed changes will affect them personally. From there, concerns become more '*task-oriented*', and teachers focus on management and organisational issues so things run more efficiently and smoothly. Change does not occur in a linear fashion but rather in a dialectical manner 'moving back and forth between change in beliefs and change in classroom practice' (Cobb et al., 1990, reviewed in Villegas-Reimers, 2003). Each new topic brings new demands on teachers, and they need continued support as they experiment and work out the difficulties. As with any change process, there will be bumps along the road and it will take time for all pieces to fall into place and to feel like a practised symphony. Next, they move toward 'impact-oriented queries' where they focus more on the students and less on themselves and consider if the changes are working well for learners, and if there are any adaptations needed (Box 12.19).

> **BOX 12.19 DIVERSE LEARNERS**
>
> 1. Observe how different children behave and concentrate during the workshop. Which children are thriving? Which children need further scaffolding?
> 2. Where might the roadblocks be? How could you adapt your mini lessons to ensure these children can benefit (e.g. reinforcing concepts in a follow-up small group, using more visuals, shorter texts, planning templates, pair work)
> 3. Take a close look at their writing samples. Are there particular skills they are missing?
> 4. Consult with children. Ask them what they are finding difficult and if they have suggestions on what might help them. Integrate their views into any adaptation.

At this point, teachers will focus more on refining practice to differentiate mini lessons to support diverse learners (see Chapter 11 and read Annemarie Roche's (*Write to Read* coach) account of adapting the workshop for children for whom English is an additional language. Finally, even when the changes have become routine for teachers, they need continued support to focus on student learning and to maintain the changes made over time. It is also important to consider how teachers new to the school each year who are new to writing workshops can be inducted into the whole school approach to maintain continuity. New colleagues have appreciated the range of supports which partner schools have put in place from sharing resources to inviting teachers to observe in their classrooms, which, as one teacher who regularly modelled in her own classroom and in the classroom of a new teacher highlighted, a 'modelled lesson is very powerful':

> *So, I got to observe it being carried out in some of the classrooms, observing other teachers, and the staff are really supportive*
>
> *Like I just handed over my folder to ___ in 3rd class and said, look, here's the strategies, take what you might find useful. The writing – here's the genres, maybe some resources that I use for mini lessons even just a list of 100 mini-lessons, just for him to start off with.*

Conclusion

The capacity to write well is fundamental to success in school and supports individuals in discovering and reaching their potential in life. While few become literary giants, writing plays a fundamental role, be it major or minor, in whatever career path is chosen in life. Yet writing often does not receive the time it needs and deserves in classrooms. Our work with whole schools has taught us that teachers learning together can have a powerful effect on pupils' agency, engagement, voice, creativity and development as writers. Working collaboratively with our research team has energised and inspired teachers and school leaders and instilled a 'can do' attitude to make a difference to children's lives and attainment. We leave the last word to a principal in a partner school: '*I think it affirmed for me, that if the right structures are put in place, resources and thinking, something amazing can happen.*' We hope this book contributes to this endeavour.

Reflect, Connect, Act

1. Examine your termly/yearly plan for writing. What are the strengths of the planning? What might need to be adjusted? Consider:
    - How the plan aligns with the research base on writing.
    - The balance between process/craft/skill mini lessons.
    - The balance of genres: attention to fiction, recount, poetry, persuasive, informational writing.
    - The balance between whole class and small group mini lessons.
    - The range of assessment tools used: balance of formative and summative.
    - Links between assessment and mini lessons.
    - The level of choice and agency provided to children.
    - Links with the national literacy curriculum learning outcomes.
    - Links within and across curricular areas (e.g. oral language, reading and writing in English, other languages and across disciplines).
    - Affordances of digital and multimodal tools.
    - Attention to the needs of children with writing difficulties.

2. With colleagues examine a school plan for writing. What are the strengths? What might need to be adjusted? Consider the:
    - Progression in (a) craft development and (b) skill development across genres, and the level of challenge and expectations across class levels for emergent, developing and advanced writers.
    - Formative and summative assessment of writing within and across class levels.

3. With colleagues, consider the school infrastructure to support the school as a professional learning community for writing. Consider the:
    - Time for professional conversations about writing within and across class levels.
    - Time for teachers to collaboratively plan for writing.
    - Time for teachers to observe and demonstrate lessons and support each other's practice in teaching writing.

Note

1 *Aistear* is an early childhood curriculum framework (National Council for Curriculum and Assessment, 2009; literature review to update Aistear, French G. & McKenna, G. (2022); https://ncca.ie/media/5915/literature-review-to-support-the-updating-of-aistear-the-early-childhood-curriculum-framework-jan-2023.pdf)

Appendix A

Partial W2R Writing Assessment Rubric – Word Choice

Word Choice	Level 1	Level 2	Level 3	Level 4	Level 5	Level 6	Level 7
Word Level	Symbols are used to represent words and meaning is unclear without the child's input.	Labels, captions are present and/or lists of words.	May use environmental print and regular words (Tier 1), or words from familiar contexts (TV, film, games), in patterned sentences.	As previously mentioned, uses simple everyday adjectives and/or varied verbs (Tier 2) (e.g., *walked* for *went*; *delicious* for *nice*) are used occasionally to make the text interesting. In informational text disciplinary language begins to appear (e.g., *antennae, aphid*).	As previously mentioned, some adjectives beyond basic level are used to make text interesting (in at least one part of the text) (e.g. *extraordinary, desperate, amazing, enormous*) and verbs (e.g. *peeked, plucked, swooped pounced, whispered camouflaged, whispered*). Informational text describes rather than just tells (e.g., *A ladybird is a small red beetle with black spots*).	As previously mentioned, uses more advanced adjectives and varied verbs more consistently (e.g. in more than one part of the text). In informational text, description is more precise and combines with disciplinary language (e.g., *Black rhinos have a hooked upper lip that they use to pluck leaves off bushes and trees*).	As previously mentioned uses along with some experimentation precise nouns to make text interesting (e.g., *cottage* for *house*, *stool* for *chair, catastrophe* for *a bad event, croissant* for *roll, the evil witch decided to make an elixir*). In informational texts, disciplinary words are used consistently and descriptive words are precise and apt.

Word Choice	Level 8	Level 9	Level 10	Level 11	Level 12	Level 13	Level 14
Word Level	As previously mentioned, uses a combination of advanced and varied adjectives, verbs, adverbs and precise nouns consistently and correctly, and appropriate to the genre.	As previously mentioned, uses a variety of appropriate descriptive language for particular effect to suit the context/genre (e.g., character setting, plot in narrative; descriptions/explanations in informational text; argument in persuasive writing)	As previously mentioned, demonstrates awareness of audience as well as the context/genre in selecting appropriate descriptive language.	As previously mentioned, uses descriptive language drawing on at least one of the senses so the reader can see, hear, smell, feel, taste in at least one part of the text or level of descriptive vocabulary continues to build, appropriate to the genre and grade level.	As previously mentioned, uses descriptive language which draws on the senses in two or more parts of the text but is not overused (e.g.,---a precise noun is used instead of an adjective, a precise verb instead of an adverb, to suit the author's purpose) or descriptive vocabulary is further strengthened and is appropriate to the author's purpose and genre.	Makes highly effective use of most of the dimensions of descriptive language outlined previously.---Quality of vocabulary builds on previous levels.	Exceptional use of each of the dimensions of descriptive vocabulary.---Creative, imaginative and apt use of language is evident:---The overall quality of the language distinguishes it from level 13.

Appendix A 297

	Level 1	Level 2	Level 3	Level 4	Level 5	Level 6	Level 7
Word Choice							
Sentence Level	Symbols are used to represent words and meaning is unclear without the child's input.	Labels, captions are present and/or lists of words.	Simple sentences (e.g., *I like to...*) begin to emerge. May be patterned sentences.	Patterned sentences are more complex (e.g., *I like ... because...*) and are complete. In informational text: facts are in simple sentences (e.g. *A ladybird can fly and crawl. It has spots and antennae.*).	As previously mentioned, sentence openers begin to show variety. Has moved beyond patterned sentences.	Sentence openers show variety and sentences begin to vary in length. In informational text, sentence structure is varied (e.g., with intentional use of the present tense/ timeless verbs: *Rhinos mark their territory by soaking a bush with their urine*).	As previously mentioned, variety in sentence openers and sentence length adds to the overall text.—Informational text: timeless verbs/ present tense is used consistently; comparisons may be drawn (e.g. *Rhinos have weak eyesight but excellent hearing*).

	Level 8	Level 9	Level 10	Level 11	Level 12	Level 13	Level 14
Word Choice							
Sentence Level	Writer begins to experiment with description beyond the word level; descriptive details begin to cluster across a few sentences.	Sentence openings begin to show sensitivity to the language register of the genre (e.g., narrative, report, informational, persuasive).—Experiments with multi-clause sentences.	Sentence openings show greater sensitivity to genre language register. More complex (multi-clause) sentences appear consistently in different parts of a text.	Makes effective use of genre-specific sentence openings.—More complex, elaborated sentences appear regularly and enhance the descriptive impact and flow of text.	Makes effective use of genre-specific sentence openings. More complex, elaborated sentences appear regularly and enhance the descriptive impact.	As previously mentioned, sentences are used with increasing effect. Descriptive details are more memorable and hold reader interest.	Sentence openings, structure, length and complexity vary for effect and work convincingly throughout to create a unique and memorable text suited to genre and audience.

Word Choice	Level 1	Level 2	Level 3	Level 4*	Level 5	Level 6	Level 7
Imagery and Creative Language Use	Symbols are used to represent words and meaning is unclear without the child's input.	Reliance on picture (if present) to connect with the reader and/or lack of details in text (e.g., see cat).	Little or no use of imagery as phrases, lists or sentences are basic and connect to the reader in a general way (e.g., I like the big cat).	Experiments with simple descriptive language or literary phrases (e.g., Yummy in my tummy) or two simple adjectives for effect (e.g., A plump pink pig, a big bad wolf).	Descriptive elements go beyond simple adjectives/verbs, as simple figurative language such as similes/alliteration may appear (e.g., I was like a bomb exploding with excitement, I faced my fears, I fell into a deep sleep, tickled like a paintbrush).	Uses more than one literary phrase or example of figurative language to enhance the piece of writing and engage the reader (e.g., Mat swooped into the night; It was a wonderful night in the park; no trouble to be seen; the frog is as small as my fingernail).	Literary phrases or examples of figurative language are used more consistently in more than one part of text to create vivid mental pictures (I was so nervous I felt like there were ants crawling around my stomach; after all the pictures, my jaw was aching).

Word Choice	Level 8	Level 9	Level 10	Level 11	Level 12	Level 13	Level 14
Imagery and Creative Language Use	Uses literary phrases and instances of figurative language more effectively, including one or more of the following: – alliteration–simile–metaphor–or– Uses grade-level appropriate nouns and verbs in at least one part of longer texts.	Uses two or more literary phrases and instances of figurative language to create a particular effect/emphasis. Devices include: – alliteration–simile/metaphor–irony/hyperbole–personification–or– Sustains use of grade-level precise nouns and verbs in at least half of the text.	As previously mentioned, uses a wider range of literary phrases and instances of figurative language appear more consistently across the text and create vivid images for the reader–or– Sustains use of grade-level precise nouns and verbs across the full text.	A wider range of literary phrases and instances of figurative language appear more consistently across the text and create vivid images for the reader and Sustains use of grade-level precise nouns and verbs across the full text.	As previous and matches language to genre. Evidence of emergence of 'word-consciousness' (i.e., appropriate and inventive use of words) to create unique images.	As previously mentioned.... word consciousness evidenced by judicious use of wide range of imagery/literary phrases/figurative language across a text to create particular moods, scenes, events arguments, which linger in.	Strong evidence of more sophisticated word consciousness (i.e., apt and inventive use of words) to suit the genre, author's style, purpose and intended audience and engage the reader from start to finish.

Appendix B
Class-level Scoring Template for W2R Rubric (All Components)

Punc = Punctuation; Conv = Conventions; Gram = Grammar; BMEP = Beginning, Middle, End; Trans/Conn = Transitions and Connectives/Paragraphing; WordC = Word Choice; Sent = Sentence; Aud = Audience.

	Conventions				Organisation			Ideas		Word Choice			Voice		
Date	Sur-name/ Initial	Class	Spell	Punc	Gram	BMEP	Trans/ Conn	Genre	Main Ideas	Details	WordC	Sent	Imag-ery	Aud	Risk	Style

References

Abbott, M. (2001). Effects of traditional versus extended word-study spelling instruction on students' orthographic knowledge. *Reading Online, 5*(3).

Akhavan, N., & Walsh, N. (2020). Cognitive apprenticeship learning approach in K-8 writing instruction: A case study. *Journal of Education and Learning, 9*(3), 123-142. https://doi.org/10.5539/jel.v9n3p123

Alamargot, D., & Chanquoy, L. (2001). Development of expertise in writing. In G. Rijlaarsdam (Series ed.), *Through the models of writing* (9, pp. 185-218). Dordrecht-Boston, London: Kluwer Academic Publishers. https://doi.org/10.1007/978-94-010-0804-4_7

Alamargot, D., & Fayol, M. (2009). Modelling the development of written composition. In R. Beard, D. Myhill, M. Nystrand, & J. Riley (Eds.), *Handbook of writing development* (pp. 23-47). London: Sage.

Alberti, N., Howell, J., Mullis, J., Turner, J., Twe, K., Chant, K., Talyor, K., Saunders, K., Olsen, L., Meyer, M., Ong, N., Davis, R., Hill, S., & Woodward, S. (2021). *Co-creating multimodal texts with young children*. University of Southern Queensland. Retrieved from https://usq.pressbooks.pub/multiliteracies/

Allott, K. (2019). *Assessing children's writing: A best practice guide for teachers*. Sage.

All-Party Parliamentary Group Inquiry. (2021). *Speak for change: Final report from the oracy all-party parliamentary group inquiry*. Retrieved from https://www.education-uk.org/documents/pdfs/2021-appg-oracy.pdf

Arold, B. W., & Shakeel, M. D. (2021). *The unintended effects of the Common Core Standards on non-targeted subjects* (working policy paper). Harvard Kennedy School. Retrieved from https://www.hks.harvard.edu/sites/default/files/Taubman/PEPG/research/PEPG21_03.pdf

Aronson, M. (n.d.). *Transcript from an interview with Marc Aronson*. Retrieved from https://www.readingrockets.org/books/interviews/aronson/transcript

Aronson, M., & Zarnowski, M. (2015). Teaching nonfiction with confidence: Learning to love inquiry. Accessed at: https://www.olaweb.org/assets/CSD/ira_finalcorrex.pdf.

Atwell, N. (1998). *In the middle*. Portsmouth, NH: Boynton Cook.

Au, K., Raphael, T., & Mooney, K. C. (2008). What we have learned about teacher education to improve literacy achievement in urban schools. In L. C. Wilkinson, L. M. Morrow, & V. Chou (Eds.), *Improving literacy achievement in urban schools: Critical elements in teacher preparation* (pp. 159-184). Newark, DE: International Reading Association.

Australian Curriculum, Assessment and Reporting Authority (ACARA). (n.d.). *NAPLAN national results*. Author. Retrieved from https://www.acara.edu.au/reporting/national-report-on-schooling-in-australia/naplan-national-results

Australian Education Research Organisation. (2022, March). *Sentence combining: Improving sentence quality, complexity and variety*. Author. Retrieved from https://www.edresearch.edu.au/sites/default/files/2022-04/aero-sentence-combining-practice-guide-190422.pdf

Bacon, N. (2019). *The well-crafted sentence: A writer's guide to style* (3rd ed.). Bedford/St. Martins.

Bandura, A. (1997). *Self-efficacy: The exercise of control*. W H Freeman/Times Books/Henry Holt & Co.

Bandura, A. (1995). Exercise of personal and collective efficacy in changing societies. In A. Bandura (Ed.), *Self-efficacy in changing societies* (pp. 1-45). Cambridge University Press.

Banerjee, B., Yan, X., Chapman, M., & Elliott, H. (2015). Writing keeping up with the times: Revising and refreshing a rating scale. *Assessing Writing, 26*, 5-19. https://doi.org/10.1016/j.asw.2015.07.001

Barbot, B., Tan, M. & Randi, J., & Santa-Donato, G., & Grigorenko, E. (2012). Essential skills for creative writing: Integrating multiple domain-specific perspectives. *Thinking Skills and Creativity, 7*, 209-223. https://doi.org/10.1016/j.tsc.2012.04.006

Barnes, E., Nì Chiaràin, N., & Nì Chasaide, A. (2017). Departures from the "norm": Orthography and morphology of Irish impact on literacy instruction and acquisition. In M. Wilson & G. Mehigan (Eds.), *Exploring the literacy landscape* (pp. 22-20). Literacy Association of Ireland.

Barrs, M. (2000). The reader in the writer. *Reading, 34(2),* 54-60. https://doi.org/10.1111/1467-9345.00135

Barrs, M. (2019). Teaching bad writing. *English in Education, 53(1),* 18-31. https://doi.org/10.1080/04250494.2018.1557858

Bazerman, C. (2016). What do sociocultural studies of writing tell us about learning to write. In C. A. MacArthur, S. Graham, & J. Fitzgerald (Eds.), *Handbook of writing research* (2nd ed., pp. 11-23). The Guilford Press.

Bear, D. R., Invernizzi, M., Templeton, S., & Johnston, F. (2012). *Words their way: Word study for phonics, vocabulary, and spelling instruction* (5th ed.). Boston, MA: Pearson.

Beauvais, L., Favart, M., Passerault, J.-M., & Beauvais, C. (2014). Temporal management of the writing process: Effects of genre and organizing constraints in grades 5, 7, and 9. *Written Communication, 31(3),* 251-279. https://doi.org/10.1177/0741088314536361

Beck, I. L., McKeown, M. G., & Kucan, L. (2008). *Creating robust vocabulary: Frequently asked questions.* Guilford.

Bereiter, C., & Scardamalia, M. (1987). *The psychology of written composition.* Lawrence Erlbaum Associates.

Berninger, V. W., Fuller, F., & Whitaker, D. (1996). A process model of writing development across the life span. *Educational Psychology Review, 8(3),* 193-218. https://doi.org/10.1007/BF01464073

Berninger, V. W., & Swanson, H. L. (1994). Modifying Hayes and Flower's model of skilled writing. In E. Butterfield (Ed.), *Children's writing; Toward a process theory of development of skilled writing* (pp. 57-81). JAI Press.

Berninger, V. W., Vaughan, K., Abbott, R. D., Begay, K., Coleman, K. B., Curtin, G., Hawkins, J. M., & Graham, S. (2002). Teaching spelling and composition alone and together: Implications for the simple view of writing. *Journal of Educational Psychology, 94(2),* 291-304. https://doi.org/10.1037/0022-0663.94.2.291

Berninger, V. W., & Winn, W. D. (2006). Implications of advancements in brain research and technology for writing development, writing instruction, and educational evolution. In C. MacArthur, S. Graham, & J. Fitzgerald (Eds.), *Handbook of writing research* (pp. 96-114). Guilford.

Berninger, V., Abbott, R., Nagy, W., & Carlisle, J. (2010). Growth in phonological, orthographic, and morphological awareness in grades 1 to 6. *Journal of Psycholinguistic Research, 39(2),* 141-163. https://doi.org/10.1007/s10936-009-9130-6

Bhowmik, S., & Kim, M. (2021). K-12 ESL writing instruction: A review of research on pedagogical challenges and strategies. *Language and Literacy, 23(3),* 165-202. https://doi.org/10.20360/langandlit29530

Biemiller, A. (2005). Size and sequence in vocabulary development: Implications for choosing words for primary grade vocabulary instruction. In A. Hiebert & M. Kamil (Eds.), *Teaching and learning vocabulary: Bringing research to practice* (pp. 223-242). Erlbaum.

Bilton, C., & Duff, A. (2021). *Improving literacy in key stage 2: Guidance report* (2nd ed.). Education Endowment Foundation. Retrieved from https://d2tic4wvo1iusb.cloudfront.net/production/eef-guidance-reports/literacy-ks2/EEF-Improving-literacy-in-key-stage-2-report-Second-edition.pdf?v=1709995674

Bilton, C., & Tillotson, S. (2020). *Improving literacy in key stage 1: Guidance report* (2nd ed.). Education Endowment Foundation. Retrieved from https://d2tic4wvo1iusb.cloudfront.net/production/eef-guidance-reports/literacy-ks-1/Literacy_KS1_Guidance_Report_2020.pdf?v=1709999417

Bintz, W. P., & Ciecierski, L. M. (2017). Hybrid text: An engaging genre to teach content area material across the curriculum. *The Reading Teacher, 71(1),* 61-69. https://doi.org/10.1002/trtr.1560

Bishop, N. (n.d.). Retrieved from https://www.nicbishop.com/

Bishop, N. (2008). *Frogs.* Scholastic Nonfiction.

Bodrova, E., & Leong, D. (2006). Vygotskian perspectives on teaching and learning early literacy. In S. Neuman & D. Dickinson (Eds.), *Handbook of early literacy research* (Vol. 2, pp. 243-268). Guilford Press.

Boscolo, P., & Ascorti, K. (2004). Effects of collaborative revision on children's ability to write understandable narrative texts. In L. Allal, L. Chanquoy, & P. Largy (Eds.), *Revision cognitive and instructional processes. Studies in writing, 13* p. 157-170. Dordrecht: Springer. https://doi.org/10.1007/978-94-007-1048-1_10

Braddock, R., Lloyd-Jones, R. & Schoer, L. (1963). *Research in written composition.* National Council of Teachers of English.

Breetvelt, I., van den Bergh, H., & Rijlaarsdam, G. (1994). Relations between writing processes and text quality: When and how? *Cognition and Instruction, 12(2)*, 103-123. https://doi.org/10.1207/s1532690xci1202_2

Brindle, M., Graham, S., Harris, K. R., & Hebert, M. (2016). Third and fourth grade teacher's classroom practices in writing: A national survey. *Reading and Writing: An Interdisciplinary Journal, 29*, 929-954. https://doi.org/10.1007/s11145-015-9604-x

Bruning, R. H., & Kauffman, D. F. (2016). Self-efficacy beliefs and motivation in writing development. In C. MacArthur, S. Graham, & J. Fitzgerald (Eds.), *Handbook of writing research* (2nd ed., pp. 160-173). Guilford Press.

Burger, J. (2013). *Springsteen on Springsteen: Interviews, speeches, and encounters.* Omnibus Press.

Butterworth, C. (2014). *See what a seal can do.* Walker Books.

Calkins, L. (1986). *The art of teaching writing.* Heinemann.

Calkins, L. (1994). *The art of teaching writing* (5th ed.). Heinemann.

Calkins, L. McCormick. (2000). *The art of teaching reading.* Pearson.

Calkins, L. & Ehrenworth, (2016). Growing extraordinary writers: Leadership decisions to raise the level of writing across a school and a district. *The Reading Teacher, 70(1)*, 7-18, Wiley https://doi.org/10.1002/trtr.1499

Calkins, L. Ehrenworth, M., & Akhmedjanova, D. (2019). Creating formative assessment systems in the teaching of writing, and harnessing them as professional development. In H. Andrade, R. E. Bennett, & G. Cizek (Eds.), *Handbook of formative assessment in the disciplines* (pp. 173-206). Routledge.

Camacho, A., Alves, R. A., & Boscolo, P. (2021). Writing motivation in school: A systematic review of empirical research in the early twenty-first century. *Educational Psychology Review, 33*, 213-247. https://doi.org/10.1007/s10648-020-09530-4.

Carlson, J. (n.d.). *13 writing strategies for ELL students. Better writing, less groaning.* Retrieved from https://kid-inspired.com/13-writing-strategies-for-ells/#BN-b3d757ed0cec529f

Casey, L. B., Miller, N. D., Stockton, M. B., & Justice, W. V. (2016). Assessing writing in elementary schools: Moving away from a focus on mechanics, *Language Assessment Quarterly, 13(1)*, 42-54. https://doi.org/10.1080/15434303.2015.1136311

Centre for Literacy in Primary Education. (2015-16). *The writing scale.* Author. Retrieved from https://clpe.org.uk/system/files/2021-09/CLPE%20WRITING%20SCALE%20REBRAND.pdf

Chauvin, R., & Theodore, K. (2015). Teaching content-area literacy and disciplinary literacy. *SEDL Insights, 3(1)*, 1-10. https://sedl.org/insights/3-1/

Cho, B., Woodward, L., & Li, D. (2018). Epistemic processing when adolescents read online: A verbal protocol analysis of more and less successful online readers. *The Reading Teacher, 53(2)*, 197-221. https://doi-org.dcu.idm.oclc.org/10.1002/rrq.190

Chomsky, C. (1979). Approaching reading through invented spelling. In L. B. Resnick & P. A. Weaver (Eds.), *Theory and practice of early reading* (pp. 2, 43-65). Erlbaum Associates.

Christenson, S. L., Reschly, A. L., & Wylie, C. (Eds.). (2012). *Handbook of research on student engagement.* New York: Springer.

Clark, C., Bonafede, F., Picton, I., & Cole, A. (2023). *Children and young people's writing in 2023.* National Literacy Trust. Retrieved from https://nlt.cdn.ngo/media/documents/Writing_in_2023.pdf

Clark, D. (2023). *Percentage of pupils whose first language is known or believed to be other than English in England from 2015/16 to 2022/23.* Retrieved from https://www.statista.com/statistics/330782/england-english-additional-language-primary-pupils/

Clark, S. K., & Lott, K. (2017). Integrating science inquiry and literacy instruction for young children. *The Reading Teacher, 70(6)*, 701-710. https://doi.org/10.1002/trtr.1572

Clay, M. (1993). *Reading recovery: A guidebook for teachers in training.* Heinemann Education.

Clay, M. (2002). *An observation survey of early literacy achievement* (2nd Ed.). Heinemann.

Cochran-Smith, M., & Lytle, S. L. (2009). *Inquiry as stance. Practitioner research for a new generation.* New York: Teachers College Press.

Cohen, J. A., Casa, T. M., Miller, H. C., & Firmender, J. M. (2015). Characteristics of second graders' mathematical writing. *School Science and Mathematics, 115(7)*, 344-355. https://doi.org/10.1111/ssm.12138

Colonnese, M. W., Amspaugh, C. M., LeMay, S., Evans, K., & Fields, K. (2018). Writing in the disciplines: How math fits into the equation. *The Reading Teacher, 72(3)*, 379-387. https://doi.org/10.1002/trtr.1733

Concannon-Gibney, T. (2019). Immersing first graders in poetry: A genre study approach. *The Reading Teacher, 72(4)*, 431-443.

Cordingley, P., Higgins, S., Greany, T., Buckler, N., Coles-Jordan, D., Crisp, B., Saunders, L., & Coe, R. (2015). *Developing great teaching: Lessons from the international reviews into effective professional development*. Teacher Development Trust. Retrieved from https://tdtrust.org/wp-content/uploads/2015/10/DGT-Full-report.pdf

Crammond, J. (1998). The uses and complexity of argument structures in expert and student persuasive writing. *Written Communication, 15(2),* 230-268. https://doi-org.dcu.idm.oclc.org/10.1177/0741088398015002004

Cremin, T., Mukherjee, S. J., Aerila, J., Kauppinen, M., Siipolo, M., & Lähteelä, J. (2024). Widening teachers' reading repertoires: Moving beyond a popular childhood canon. *The Reading Teacher, 77(6),* 833-841. https://doi.org/10.1002/trtr.2294

Cremin, T., Myhill, D., Eyres, I., Nash, T., Wilson, A., & Oliver, L. (2020). Teachers as writers: Learning together with others. *Literacy, 54(2)* p.49-59.

Cremin, T., & Oliver, L. (2016). Teachers as writers: A systematic review. *Research Papers in Education, 32(3),* 269-295. https://doi.org/10.1080/02671522.2016.1187664

Crusan, D. (2010). *Assessment in the second language writing classroom*. Ann Arbor: The University of Michigan Press.

Csikszentmihalyi, M. (1975). *Beyond boredom and anxiety: Experiencing flow in work and play*. San Francisco, CA: Jossey-Bass.

Cuff, B. M. P. (2019). *A review of approaches to assessing writing at the end of primary education: Drawing on historical and international practices*. Ofqual. Retrieved from https://assets.publishing.service.gov.uk/media/5c9cdfd0e5274a5278f2755d/International_primary_writing_review_-_FINAL_28.03.2019.pdf

Culham, R. (2018). *Teach writing well: How to assess writing, invigorate instruction and rethink revision*. Routledge.

Cunningham, P. M., & Cunningham, J. W. (2002). What we know about how to teach phonics. In A. E. Farstrup & S. J. Samuels (Eds.), *What the research has to say about reading instruction* (3rd ed., pp. 78-109). International Literacy Association.

Cunningham, P. M., & Hall, D. P. (1994). *Making words: Multilevel, hands-on developmentally appropriate spelling and phonics activities*. Good Apple

Cutler, L., & Graham, S. (2008). Primary grade writing instruction: A national survey. *Journal of Educational Psychology, 100(4),* 907-919. https://doi.org/10.1037/a0012656

Daffern, T. (2016). What happens when teachers use metalanguage to teach spelling? *Reading Teacher, 74(4),* 423-434. https://doi.org/10.1002/trtr.1528

Daffern, T., Mackenzie, N. M., & Hemmings, B. (2015). The development of a spelling assessment tool informed by Triple Word Form Theory. *Australian Journal of Language and Literacy, 38,* 72-82. https://doi.org/10.1007/BF03651958

Daffern, T., Mackenzie, N. M., & Hemmings, B. (2017). Predictors of writing success: How important are spelling, grammar and punctuation? *Australian Journal of Education, 61(1),* 75-87. https://doi.org/10.1177/0004944116685319

Daffern, T., & Mackenzie, N. M. (2020). Theoretical perspectives and strategies for teaching and learning writing. In T. Daffern & N. M. Mackenzie (Eds.), *Teaching writing: Effective approaches for the middle years* (pp. 15-32). Routledge.

Dahlström, H. (2021). Students as digital multimodal text designers: A study of resources, affordances, and experiences. *British Journal of Educational Technology, 53(2),* 391-407. https://doi.org/10.1111/bjet.13171

Dalton, B. (2012). Multimodal composition and the common core standards. *The Reading Teacher, 66(4),* 333-339. https://doi.org/10.1002/TRTR.01129

Dalton, B. (2014/2015). Level up with multimodal composition in social studies. *The Reading Teacher, 68(4),* 296-302. https://doi.org/10.1002/trtr.1319

Datchuk, S. M., & Kubina, R. M. (2013). A review of teaching sentence-level writing skills to students with writing difficulties and learning disabilities. *Remedial and Special Education, 34(3),* 180-192. https://doi.org/10.1177/0741932512448254

Datchuk, S., Kubina, R., & Mason, L. (2015). Effects of sentence instruction and frequency building to a performance criterion on elementary-aged students with behavioral ocncerns and EBD. *Exceptionality, 23,* 34-53. https://doi.org/10.1080/09362835.2014.986604

de Abreu Malpique, A., Valcan, D., Pino-Pasternak, D., & Ledger, Susan. (2023). Teaching writing in primary education (grades 1-6) in Australia: A national survey. *Reading and Writing, 36,* 119-145. https://doi.org/10.1007/s11145-022-10294-2

Deane, P., Odendahl, N., Quinlan, T., Fowles, M., Welsh, C., & Bivens-Tatum, J. (2008). *Cognitive models of writing: Writing proficiency as a complex integrated skill*. Educational Testing Service.

Department for Education. (2013). *The national curriculum in England: Key stages 1 and 2 framework document*. Author. Retrieved from https://assets.publishing.service.gov.uk/media/5a81a9abe5274a2e8ab55319/PRIMARY_national_curriculum.pdf

Department for Education. (2020). *English proficiency of pupils with English as an additional language*. Author. Retrieved from https://assets.publishing.service.gov.uk/media/5e55205d86650c10e8754e54/English_proficiency_of_EAL_pupils.pdf

Department of Education. (2022). *Looking at our School 2022: A quality framework for primary schools and special schools*. Author

Derewianka, B. (2015). The contribution of genre theory to literacy education in Australia. In J. Turbill, G. Barton, & C. Brock (Eds.), *Teaching writing in today's classrooms: Looking back to looking forward* (pp. 69-86). Australian Literary Educators' Association.

De Smedt, F., Graham, S., & Van Keer, H. (2019). The bright and dark side of writing motivation: Effects of explicit instruction and peer assistance. *The Journal of Educational Research, 112(2)*, 152-167. https://doi.org/10.1080/00220671.2018.1461598

De Smedt, F., & Van Keer, H. (2017). Fostering writing in upper primary grades: A study into the distinct and combined impact of explicit instruction and peer assistance. *Reading and Writing, 31(2)*, 325-354. https://doi.org/10.1007/s11145-017-9787-4

Dobinson, K. L., & Dockrell, J. E. (2021). Universal strategies for the improvement of expressive language skills in the primary classroom: A systematic review. *First Language, 41(5)*, 527-554. https://doi.org/10.1177/0142723721989471

Dockrell, J. E., Marshall, C., & Wyse, D. (2015). *Evaluation of talk for writing* https://educationendowmentfoundation.org.uk/uploads/pdf/Talk_for_Writing.pdf

Dockrell, J. E., Marshall, C. R., & Wyse, D. (2016). Teachers' reported practices for teaching writing in England. *Reading and Writing, 29*, 409-434. https://doi.org/10.1007/s11145-015-9605-9

Dolch, E. W. (1936). A basic sight vocabulary. *The Elementary School Journal, 6(36)*, 456-460.

Dombey, H. (2006). Phonics and English orthography. In M. Lewis & S. Ellis (Eds.), *Phonics, practice, research, policy* (pp. 95-104). Chapman.

Duthie, C., & Zimet, E. K. (1992). Poetry is like directions for your imagination. *The Reading Teacher, 46(1)*, 14-24.

Dweck, C. S. (2007). The perils and promise of praise. *Educational Leadership, 65(2)*, 34-39.

Dwyer, B. (2020). *Internet research and inquiry cycle. Support materials for teachers*. Dublin: National Council for Curriculum and Assessment (NCCA). Retrieved from https://www.curriculumonline.ie/getmedia/494184f0-d17b-468d-8173-23c4e5513d4d/Internet-research-and-inquiry-cycle.pdf.

Dwyer, B., Burke, P., & Kennedy, E. (2022). *Pedagogical strategies, approaches and methodologies to support disciplinary literacy at primary and post-primary levels*. Ireland: Department of Education. https://doi.org/10.5281/zenodo.7881295

Dyson, A. H. (1993). *Social worlds of children learning to write in an urban primary school*. Teachers College Press.

Dyson, A. H. (2020). This isn't my real writing: The fate of children's agency in too-tight curricula, *Theory into Practice, 59(2)*, 119-127. https://doi.org/10.1080/00405841.2019.1702390

Ehri, L. (2005). Phases of development in learning to read words by sight. *Journal of Research in Reading, 18(2)*, 116-125. https://doi.org/10.1111/j.1467-9817.1995.tb00077.x

Ehri, L. C. (2020). The science of learning to read words: A case for systematic phonics instruction, *Reading Research Quarterly, 55(S1)*, S45-S60. https://doi.org/10.1002/rrq.334

Ehri, L. C., & Nunes, S. R. (2002). The role of phonemic awareness in learning to read. In A. E. Farstrup & S. J. Samuels (Eds.), *What the research has to say about reading instruction* (3rd ed, pp. 110-139).). Newark, DE: International Literacy Association.

Ekholm, E., Zumbrunn, S., & DeBusk-Lane, M. (2018). Clarifying an elusive construct: A systematic review of writing attitudes. *Educational Psychology Review, 30(3)*, 827-856. https://doi.org/10.1007/s10648-017-9423-5

Fancher, L. A., Priestley-Hopkins, D. A., & Jeffries, L. M. (2018). Handwriting acquisition and intervention: A systematic review. *Journal of Occupational Therapy, Schools & Early Intervention, 11(4)*, 454-473. https://doi.org/10.1080/19411243.2018.1534634

Fayol, M. (2016). From language to text: The development and learning of translation. In C. MacArthur, S. Graham, & J. Fitzgerald (Eds.), *Handbook of writing research* (2nd ed., pp. 130-143). Guilford Press.

Feng, L., Lindner, A., Ji, X. R., & Malatesha Joshi, R. (2019). The roles of handwriting and keyboarding in writing: A meta-analytic review. *Reading and Writing, 32(1)*, 33-63. https://doi.org/10.1007/s11145-017-9749-x

Fearn L. & Farnan, N (2007). When is a verb? Using functional grammar to teach writing. *Journal of Basic Writing* 26, 1-26. CUNY. DOI: 10.37514/JBW-J.2007.26.1.05

Ferretti, R. P., & Lewis, W. E. (2019). Argumentative writing. In S. Graham, C. A. MacArthur & M. Herbert (Eds.), *Best practices in writing instruction* (3rd ed., pp. 135-161). Guilford Press.

Fielding, L. G., & Pearson, P. D. (1994). Reading comprehension: What works. *Educational Leadership, 51(5)*, 62-68.

Fitts, S., Bowers, E., & Keisler, L. (2016). Writing instruction for English learners: Examining instructional practices in fourth-grade classrooms. *NABE Journal of Research and Practice, 7(1)*, 106-141. https://doi.org/10.1080/26390043.2016.12067806

Fitzgerald, J., & Teasley, A. B. (1986). Effects of instruction in narrative structure on children's writing. *Journal of Educational Psychology, 78(6)*, 424-432. https://doi.org/10.1037/0022-0663.78.6.424

Fletcher, R. J. (1993). *What a writer needs*. Heinemann.

Fletcher, R. J., & Portalupi, J. (1998). *Craft lessons: Teaching writing K-8*. Stenhouse.

Flower, L., & Hayes, J. R. (1981). A cognitive process theory of writing. *College Composition and Communication, 32(1)*, 365-387. https://doi.org/10.2307/356600

French, G. & McKenna, G. (2022). *Literature review to support the updating of Aistear the early childhood curriculum framework*. National Council for Curriculum and Assessment. https://ncca.ie/media/5915/literature-review-to-support-the-updating-of-aistear-the-early-childhood-curriculum-framework-jan-2023.pdf

Friddle, K. A., & Ivey, G. (2023). Motivate and engage our youngest writers. *Reading Teacher, 77(3)*, 300-309. https://doi.org/10.1002/trtr.2251

Fry, E. B. (1984). *The reading teacher's book of lists*. Prentice Hall.

Furey, W. M., Marcotte, A. M., Wells, C. S., & Hintze, J. M. (2017). The effects of supplemental sentence-level instruction for fourth-grade students identified as struggling writers. *Reading & Writing Quarterly, 33(6)*, 563-578. https://doi.org/10.1080/10573569.2017.1288591

Gadd, M., & Parr, J. M. (2017). Practices of effective writing teachers. *Reading and Writing: An Interdisciplinary Journal, 30(7)*, 1551-1574. https://doi.org/10.1007/s11145-017-9737-1

Gamble, N. (2019). *Exploring children's literature: Reading for knowledge, understanding and pleasure* (2nd ed.). Sage.

Garcia, N., Abbott, R., & Berninger, V. (2010). Predicting poor, average, and superior spellers in grades 1 to 6 from phonological, orthographic, and morphological, spelling, or reading composites. *Written Language & Literacy, 13(1)*, 61-98. https://doi.org/10.1075/wll.13.1.03gar

Gentry, J. R. (2000). A retrospective on invented spelling and a look forward. *The Reading Teacher, 54(3)*, 318-332. https://www.jstor.org/stable/20204910

Gilbert, J. & Graham, S. (2010). Teaching writing to elementary students in grades 4 to 6: A national survey. *Elementary School Journal, 110*, 494-518. https://psycnet.apa.org/doi/10.1086/651193

Gillespie Rouse, A. (2019). Instruction for students with special needs. In S. Graham, C. A. MacArthur & M. Hebert (Eds.), *Best practices in writing instruction* (3rd ed., pp. 361-384). Guilford Press.

Goldman, S. R., Britt, M. A., Brown, W., Cribb, G., George, M., Greenleaf, C., Lee, C. D., Shanahan, C., & Project READI. (2016). Disciplinary literacies and learning to read for understanding: A conceptual framework for disciplinary literacy. *Educational Psychologist, 51(2)*, 219-246. https://doi.org/10.1080/00461520.2016.1168741

Gombert, J. E. (1992). *Metalinguistic development*. University of Chicago Press.

Gonzalez-Frey, S. M., & Ehri, L. C. (2021.) Connected phonation is more effective than segmented phonation for teaching beginning readers to decode unfamiliar words. *Scientific Studies of Reading, 25(3)*, 272-285. https://doi.org/10.1080/10888438.2020.1776290

Goodwin, A. P., & Ahn, S. (2013). A meta-analysis of morphological interventions in English: Effects on literacy outcomes for school-age children. *Scientific Studies of Reading, 17(4)*, 257-285. https://doi.org/10.1080/10888438.2012.689791

Gough, P., & Tunmer, W. (1986). Decoding, reading, and reading disability. *Remedial and Special Education, 7*, 6-10.

GOV.UK. (2023). *Key stage 2 attainment. National headlines*. Author. Retrieved from https://explore-education-statistics.service.gov.uk/find-statistics/key-stage-2-attainment-national-headlines/2022-23

Graham, S. (1999). The role of text production skills in writing development: A special issue - I. *Learning Disability Quarterly, 22(2)*. https://doi.org/10.2307/1511267

Graham, S. (2006). Writing. In P. A. Alexander & P. H. Winne (Eds.), *Handbook of educational psychology* (pp. 457-478). Lawrence Erlbaum Associates Publishers.

Graham, S. (2018). A revised writer(s)-within-community model of writing. *Educational Psychologist, 53(4)*, 258-279. https://doi.org/10.1080/00461520.2018.1481406

Graham, S. (2019). Changing how writing is taught. *Review of Research in Education, 43*, 227-303. https://doi.org/10.3102/0091732X18821125

Graham, S., Berninger, V. W., Abbott, R. D., Abbott, S. P. and Whitaker, D. (1997) Role of mechanics in composing of elementary school students: a new methodological approach. *Journal of Educational Psychology, 89*, 170-182. https://doi.org/10.1037/0022-0663.89.1.170

Graham, S. (2025). The writer(s)-within-community model. In C.MacArthur,S. Graham, & J. Fitzgerald, J. (Eds.). *Handbook of writing research* (3rd Ed). Guilford.

Graham, S., Bollinger, A., Booth Olson, C., D'Aoust, C., MacArthur, C., McCutchen, D., & Olinghouse, N.(2012b/2018). *Teaching elementary school students to be effective writers: A practice guide* (NCEE 2012-4058). Washington, DC: National Center for Education Evaluation and Regional Assistance, Institute of Education Sciences, U.S. Department of Education. Retrieved from https://ies.ed.gov/ncee/wwc/publications_reviews.aspx#pubsearch.

Graham, S., Gillespie, A., & McKeown, D. (2013). Writing: Importance, development, and instruction. *Reading and Writing, 26(1)*, 1-15. https://doi.org/10.1007/s11145-012-9395-2

Graham, S., & Harris, K. R. (2002). The road less travelled: Prevention and intervention in written language. In K. Butler & E. Silliman (Eds.), *Spelling, reading, and writing in children with language learning disabilities* (pp. 219-237). Erlbaum.

Graham, S., & Harris, K. (2005). *Writing better: Effective strategies for teaching students with learning difficulties*. Brookes.

Graham, S., Harris, K. R., & Mason, L. (2005). Improving the writing performance, knowledge, and self-efficacy of struggling young writers: The effects of self-regulated strategy development. *Contemporary Educational Psychology, 30(2)*, 207-241. https://doi.org/10.1016/j.cedpsych.2004.08.001

Graham, S., & Harris, K. R. (2005). *Writing better: Effective strategies for teaching students with learning difficulties*. Baltimore, MD: Brookes Publishing Company.

Graham, S., Harris, K. R., & McKeown, D. (2013). The writing of students with learning disabilities, meta-analysis of self-regulated strategy development writing intervention studies, and future directions: Redux. In H. L. Swanson, K. R. Harris, & S. Graham (Eds.), *Handbook of learning disabilities* (2nd ed., pp. 405-438). Guilford Press.

Graham, S., Harris, K. R., & Santangelo, T. (2015). Research-based writing practices and the common core: Meta-analysis and meta-synthesis. *The Elementary School Journal, 115(4)*, 498-522. https://doi.org/10.1086/681964.

Graham, S., & Harris, K. (2019). Evidence-based practices in writing. In S. Graham, C. A. MacArthur, & M. Hebert (Eds.), *Best practices in writing instruction* (3rd ed.). Guilford.

Graham, S., & Hebert, M. (2011). Writing to read: A meta-analysis of the impact of writing and writing instruction on reading. *Harvard Educational Review, 81(4)*, 710-744. https://doi.org/10.17763/haer.81.4.t2k0m13756113566

Graham, S., Kiuhara, S. A., & MacKay, M. (2020). The effects of writing on learning in science, social studies, and mathematics: A meta-analysis. *Review of Educational Research, 90(2)*, 179-226. https://doi.org/10.3102/0034654320914744

Graham, S., Liu, X., Bartlett, B., Ng, C., Harris, K. R., Aitken, A., Barkel, A., Kavanaugh, C., & Talukdar, J. (2018). Reading for writing: A meta-analysis of the impact of reading interventions on writing. *Review of Educational Research, 88(2)*, 243-284. https://doi.org/10.3102/0034654317746927

Graham, S., McKeown, D., Kiuhara, S., & Harris, K. R. (2012). A meta-analysis of writing instruction for students in the elementary grades. *Journal of Educational Psychology, 104(4)*, 879-896. https://doi.org/10.1037/a0029185

Graham, S., & Perin, D. (2007). A meta-analysis of writing instruction for adolescent students. *Journal of Educational Psychology, 99(3)*, 445-476. https://doi.org/10.1037/0022-0663.99.3.445

Graham, S., & Rijlaarsdam, G. (2016). Writing education around the globe: Introduction and call for a new global analysis. *Reading and Writing: An Interdisciplinary Journal, 29(5)*, 781-792. https://doi.org/10.1007/s11145-016-9640-1

Graham, S., & Sandmel, K. (2011). The process writing approach: A meta-analysis. *The Journal of Educational Research, 104*(6), 396-407. https://doi.org/10.1080/00220671.2010.488703

Graham, S., & Santangelo, T. (2014). Does spelling instruction make students better spellers, readers, and writers? A meta-analytic review. *Reading and Writing: An Interdisciplinary Journal, 27*(9), 1703-1743. https://doi.org/10.1007/s11145-014-9517-0

Grainger, T., Goouch, K., & Lambirth, A. (2005). *Creativity and writing. Developing voice and verve in the classroom.* Oxon: Routledge.

Graves, D. (1981). Patterns of child control of the writing process. In D. H. Graves (Ed.), *A case study observing the development of primary children's composing, spelling, and motor behaviors during the writing process, final report* (pp. 177-188). University of New Hampshire.

Graves, D. H. (1983). *Writing: Teachers and children at work.* Heinemann Educational.

Graves, D. H. (1989). *Investigate nonfiction.* Heinemann Educational

Graves, D. H. (1994). *A fresh look at writing.* Heinemann Educational.

Graves, M., & Watts-Taffe, S. M. (2002). The place of word consciousness in a research- based vocabulary programme. In A. E. Farstrup & S. J. Samuels (Eds.), *What the research has to say about reading instruction* (3rd ed., pp. 140-165). Newark, DE: International Reading Association.

Guskey, T. R. (2000). *Evaluating professional development.* Thousand Oaks, CA: Corwin.

Guskey, T. R. (2002). Professional development and teacher change. *Teachers and Teaching: Theory and Practice, 8*(2), 381-391. https://doi.org/10.1080/135406002100000512

Hale, E. (2017). Academic praise in conferences. A key for motivating struggling writers. *The Reading Teacher, 71*(6), 651-658. https://doi.org/10.1002/trtr.1664

Hall, K. (2006). How children learn to read and how phonics helps. In M. Lewis & S. Ellis (Eds.), *Phonics, practice, research, policy* (pp. 9-22). Chapman.

Hall, K., & Harding, A. (2003). *A systematic review of effective literacy teaching in the 4 to 14 age range of mainstream schooling.* London: EPPI-Centre, Social Science Research Unit, Institute of Education.

Hall, G. E., & Hord, S. M. (1987). *Change in schools: Facilitating the process.* State University of New York Press.

Halliday, M. A. K. (1978). *Language as social semiotic: The social interpretation of language and meaning.* Edward Arnold.

Halliday, M. A. K. (1985). *An introduction to functional grammar.* Edward Arnold.

Halliday, M. A. K., & Hasan, R. (1989, 1997). *Language, context and text: Aspects of language in a social-semiotic perspective.* Geelong: Deakin University.

Hampton, S., & Resnick, L. B. (2009). *Reading and writing with understanding.* Washington, DC: International Reading Association.

Hanna, P. R., Hanna, J. S., & Hodges, R. E. (1965). *Phoneme-grapheme correspondences as cues to spelling improvement.* US Department of Health, Education and Welfare.

Hansen, J. (1987). *When writers read.* Portsmouth, NH: Heinemann.

Harris, K. R., & Graham, S. (1992). Self-regulated strategy development: A part of the writing process. In M. Pressley, K. R. Harris, & J. T. Guthrie (Eds.), *Promoting academic competence and literacy in school* (pp. 277-309). Academic Press.

Harris, K. R., Graham, S., & Mason, L. H. (2006). Improving the writing, knowledge, and motivation of struggling young writers: Effects of self-regulated strategy development with and without peer support. *American Educational Research Journal, 43*(2), 295-340. https://doi.org/10.3102/00028312043002295

Hawkins, L. K., & Certo, J. L. (2014). It's something that I feel like writing, instead of writing because I'm being told to: Elementary boys' experiences writing and performing poetry. *Pedagogies: An International Journal, 9*(3), 196-215. https://doi.org/10.1080/1554480X.2014.921857

Hayes, J. R. (1996). A new framework for understanding cognition and affect in writing. In C. M. Levy & S. Ransdell (Eds.), *The science of writing: Theories, methods, individual differences, and applications* (pp. 1-27). Lawrence Erlbaum Associates, Inc.

Hayes, J. R. (2006). New directions in writing theory. In C. A. MacArthur, S. Graham, & J. Fitzgerald (Eds.), *Handbook of writing research,* (pp. 28-40). The Guilford Press.

Hayes, J. R., & Flower, L. (1980). Identifying the organization of writing processes. In L. W. Gregg, & E. R. Steinberg (Eds.), *Cognitive processes in writing: An interdisciplinary approach* (pp. 3-30). Hillsdale, NJ: Lawrence Erlbaum.

Hayes, J. R., & Olinghouse, N. G. (2015). Can cognitive writing models inform the design of the Common Core State Standards? *The Elementary School Journal, 115(4)*, 480-497. https://doi.org/10.1086/681909

Heard, G., & McDonough, (2009). *A place for wonder reading and writing nonfiction in the primary grades*. Routledge, Taylor and Francis.

Hillocks, G., Jr. (1986). *Research on written composition: New directions for teaching*. Urbana, IL: National Council of Teachers of English

Hord, S. M. (2008). Evolution of the learning community. *Journal of Staff Development, 29(3)*, 10-13.

Huxford, L. (2006). Phonics in context: Spelling links. In M. Lewis & S. Ellis (Eds.), *Phonics, practice, research, policy* (pp. 83-94). Chapman.

International Dyslexia Association. (n.d.). *Understanding dysgraphia*. Retrieved from https://dyslexiaida.org/understanding-dysgraphia/

International Literacy Association. (2017). *Position statement and literacy leadership brief: Characteristics of culturally sustaining and academically rigorous classrooms*. Author.

International Literacy Association. (2020). *Position statement and policy brief, no. 9457: Phonological awareness in early childhood literacy development*. Author.

Ippolito, J., Dobbs, C. L., & Charner-Laird, M. (2019). *Disciplinary literacy inquiry and instruction*. Learning Sciences International.

James, K. H., & Engelhardt, L. (2012). The effects of handwriting experience on functional brain development in pre-literate children. *Trends in Neuroscience and Education, 1(1)*, 32-42. https://doi.org/10.1016/j.tine.2012.08.001

Jones, S.M., Myhill, D.A & Bailey, T.C. (2013). Grammar for writing? An investigation into the effect of contextualised grammar teaching on student writing. *Reading and Writing, 26*, 1241-1263. https://doi.org/10.1007/s11145-012-9416

Jonsson, A., & Svingby, G. (2007). The use of scoring rubrics: Reliability, validity and educational consequences. *Educational Research Review, 2(2)*, 130-144. https://doi.org/10.1016/j.edurev.2007.05.002

Jouhar, M. R., & Rupley, W. H. (2021). The reading-writing Connection based on independent reading and writing: A systematic review. *Reading & Writing Quarterly, 37(2)*, 136-156. https://doi.org/10.1080/10573569.2020.1740632

Joyce, B., & Showers, B. (2002). *Student achievement through staff development* (3rd ed.). Alexander, VA: Association for Supervision and Curriculum Development.

Jussim, L., & Barber, K. M. (2005).Teacher expectations and self-fulfilling prophecies: Knowns and unknowns, resolved and unresolved controversies. *Personality and Social Psychology Review, 9(2)*, 131-155, Lawrence Erlbaum Associates Inc. https://doi-org.dcu.idm.oclc.org/10.1207/s15327957pspr0902_3

Kavanagh, L., Shiel, G., Gilleece, L., & Kiniry, J. (2015). *The 2014 National Assessments of English Reading and Mathematics. Volume 11. Context Report*. Educational Research Centre.

Kear, D. J., Coffman, G. A., McKenna, M. C., & Arbrosio, A. L. (2000). Measuring attitude towards writing: A new tool for teachers. *The Reading Teacher, 54(1)*, 10-23. https://www.jstor.org/stable/20204872

Kelly, K., Becker, W., Lipscomb, G., & Robards, A. (2020). Centring culture through writing and the arts: Lessons learned in New Zealand. *The Reading Teacher, 74(2)*, 147-158. https://doi.org/10.1002/trtr.1918

Kennedy, E. (2014). *Raising literacy achievement in high-poverty schools: An evidence-based approach*. New York: Routledge.

Kennedy, E., Concannon-Gibney, T., & Dwyer, B. (2022). *Pedagogical strategies, approaches and methodologies to support literacy in the primary school: A review of research*. Ireland: Department of Education. https://doi.org/10.5281/zenodo.7881327

Kennedy, E., Dunphy, E., Dwyer, B., Hayes, G., McPhillips, T., Marsh, J., O'Connor, M., & Shiel, G. (2012). *Literacy in early childhood and primary education (Children aged 3-8 years). Commissioned research report*. National Council for Curriculum and Assessment. Retrieved from https://www.erc.ie/documents/oral_language_in_early_childhood_and_primary_education_3-8_years_.pdf

Kennedy, E., & Shiel, G. (2010). Raising literacy levels with collaborative on-site professional development in an urban disadvantaged school. *The Reading Teacher, 63(5)*, 373-383. Themed Issue on Urban Education: International Reading Association. https://doi.org/10.1598/RT.63.5.3

Kennedy, E., & Shiel, G. (2019). *Writing pedagogy in the senior primary classes: Knowledge, skills and processes for writing*. NCCA.

Kennedy, E., & Shiel, G. (2022). Writing assessment for communities of writers: Validation of a rubric to support formative assessment of writing in Pre-K to Grade 2. *Assessment in Education: Principles, Policy and Practice, 29(5)*, 1-23. https://doi.org/10.1080/0969594X.2022.2047608

Kennedy, E., & Shiel, G. (2024). The teaching of writing in the *Write to Read* literacy framework in low-SES primary schools in Ireland. *Reading & Writing*, Special Issue: *Teaching Writing, 37(6)*, 1-29. https://doi.org/10.1007/s11145-023-10510-7

Kent, S. C., & Wanzek, J. (2016). The relationship between component skills and writing quality and production across developmental levels: A meta-analysis of the last 25 years. *Review of Educational Research, 86(2)*, 570-601. https://doi.org/10.3102/0034654315619491

Kervin, L., & Mantei, J. (2016). Digital writing practices: A close look at one grade three author, *Literacy, 50(3)*. https://doi.org/10.1111/lit.12084

King, F., French, G., & Halligan, C. (2022). *Professional learning and/or development (PL): Principles and practices. A review of the literature*. Ireland: Department of Education. https://doi.org/10.5281/zenodo.7250425

Kintsch, W. (1998). *Comprehension: A paradigm for cognition*. Cambridge: Cambridge University Press.

Kress, G. (2003). *Literacy in the new media age*. Routledge.

Kovalcik, B., & Certo, J. L. (2007). The poetry café is open! Teaching literary devices of sound in poetry writing. *The Reading Teacher, 61(1)*, 89-93. https://doi.org/10.1598/RT.61.1.10

Laminack, L. (2017). Mentors and mentor texts: What, why, and how? *The Reading Teacher, 70(6)*, 753-755. https://doi.org/10.1002/trtr.1578

Lane, R., Parrila, R., Bower, M., Bull, R., Cavanagh, M., Forbes, A., Jones, T., Leaper, D., Khosronejad, M., Pellicano, L., Powell, S., Ryan, M., & Skrebneva, I. (2019). *Formative assessment evidence and practice literature review*. Australian Curriculum and Assessment Reporting Authority, Educator Services Australia, and the Australian Institute for Teaching and School Leadership.

Langer, J. (2011). *Envisioning literature: Literary understanding and literature Instruction* (2nd ed.). New York: Teachers College Press.

Lavan, G., & Talcott, J. (2020). *Brooks's What works for literacy difficulties? The effectiveness of intervention schemes* (6th ed.). The School Psychology Service Ltd. Retrieved from https://www.theschoolpsychologyservice.com/wp-content/uploads/2020/11/What-Works-for-Literacy-Difficulties-6th-Edition-2020.pdf

Leland, H. C., Harst, C. J., & Smith, K. (2005). Out of the box: Critical literacy in a first-grade classroom. *Language Arts, 82(5)*, 257-268.

Levy, C. M., & Ransdell, S. (1995). Is writing as difficult as it seems? *Memory & Cognition, 23(6)*, 767-779. https://doi.org/10.3758/BF03200928

Limpo, T., & Graham, S. (2020). The role of handwriting instruction in writers' education. *British Journal of Educational Studies, 68(3)*, 311-329. https://doi.org/10.1080/00071005.2019.1692127

Liou, Y., & Canrinus, E. T. (2020). A capital framework for professional learning and practice. *International Journal of Educational Research, 100*. https://doi.org/10.1016/j.ijer.2019.101527

Lipson, M. Y., Mosenthal, J. H., Mekkelson, J., & Russ, B. (2004). Building knowledge and fashioning success one school at a time. *The Reading Teacher, 57(6)*, 534-545.

Liu, Y., Fisher, L., Forbes, K., & Evans, M. (2017). The knowledge base of teaching in linguistically diverse contexts: 10 grounded principles of multilingual classroom pedagogy for EAL. *Language and Intercultural Communication, 17(4)*, 378-395. https://doi.org/10.1080/14708477.2017.1368136]

Lowe, K., & Bormann, F. (2012). U-can write: Working with struggling writers. *Literacy Learning: The Middle Years, 20(2)*, 22-28.

Lu, X., & Kim, S. (2021). A systematic review of collaborative writing implementation in K-12 second language classrooms. *TEFLIN Journal, 32(1)*, 50-71. https://doi.org/10.15639/teflinjournal.v32i1/50-71

Mackenzie, N. M., & Scull, J. A. (2015). Literacy: Writing. In S. McLeod & J. McCormack (Eds.), *Introduction to speech, language and literacy* (pp. 398-445). Oxford.

Madden, N. A., Slavin, R. E., Logan, M., & Cheung, A. (2011). Effects of cooperative writing with embedded multimedia: A randomized experiment. *Effective Education, 3(1)*, 1-9.

Martin, J. R. (1985). *Factual writing: Exploring and challenging social reality* (pp. 149-166). Deakin University Press. Geelong, Victoria: Deakin University Press.

Martin, J. R. (2001). Language, register and genre. In A. Burns & C. Coffin (Eds.), *Analysing English in a global context: A reader*. Routledge.

McCarrier, A., Pinnell, G. S., & Fountas, I. (2000). *Interactive writing: How language and literacy come together in K-2*. Heinemann.

McCutchen, D., Teske, P., & Bankston, C. (2008). Writing and cognition: Implications of the cognitive architecture for learning to write and writing to learn. In C. Bazerman (Ed.), *Handbook of research on writing: History, society, school, individual, text* (pp. 451–470). Taylor & Francis Group/Lawrence Erlbaum Associates.

McEvoy, E. (2014). *Exploring the impact of a cross-curricular approach on inquiry-based report writing and on the historical thinking of sixth-class pupils*. Unpublished master's thesis, Dublin City University.

McGaw, B., Louden, W., & Wyatt-Smith, C. (2020). *NAPLAN review final report, State of New South Wales (Department of Education)*. State of Queensland (Department of Education), State of Victoria (Department of Education and Training), and Australian Capital Territory.

McLean, E. (2022). *Writing and writing instruction: An overview of the literature*. Australian Education Research Organisation. Retrieved from https://www.edresearch.edu.au/sites/default/files/2022-02/writing-instruction-literature-review.pdf

McMaster, K. L., Kunkel, A., Shin, J., Jung, P. G., & Lembke, E. (2018). Early writing intervention: A best evidence synthesis. *Journal of Learning Disabilities, 51*(4), 363–380. https://doi.org/10.1177/0022219417708169

Martin, J. R. (1985). *Factual writing: Exploring and challenging social reality*. Deakin University Press.

Miller, S. (2021). *Selecting and evaluating children's literature*. Presentation, DCU Library, December, 2021.

Moats, L.C. (2005). How spelling supports reading. *American Educator, 29*, 12–43. https://www.aft.org/ae/winter2005-2006/moats

Montessori, M. (1912). *The Montessori method*. New York: Schocken Books.

Montessori, M. (1964). *The Montessori method*. Cambridge, MA: Bentley Publications.

Moyles, J. (1989). *Just playing? The role and status of play in early childhood education*. Open University Press.

Murphy, P., Wilkinson, I., Soter, A., Hennessey, M., & Alexander, J. (2009). Examining the effects of classroom discussion on students' comprehension of text: A meta-analysis. *Journal of Educational Psychology, 101*, 740–764. https://psycnet.apa.org/doi/10.1037/a0015576

Murphy, D. (2016, April, 27). How do we develop a writing identity? *Two Teachers Writing*. Retrieved from https://twowritingteachers.org/2016/04/27/writing-identity/

Murray, D. M. (1990). *Shoptalk: Learning to write with writers*. Portsmouth, NH: Heinemann.

Myhill, D. A., Jones, S. M., Lines, H., & Watson, A. (2012). Re-thinking grammar: The impact of embedded grammar teaching on students' writing and students' metalinguistic understanding. *Research Papers in Education, 27*(2), 139–166. https://doi.org/10.1080/02671522.2011.637640

Myhill, D. (2021). Grammar reimagined. Foregrounding understanding of language choice in writing. *English in Education, 55*(3), 265–278. https://doi.org/10.1080/04250494.2021.1885975

Myhill, D., Cremin, T., & Oliver, L. (2023a) The impact of a changed writing environment on students' motivation to write. *Frontiers of Psychology, 14*, 1212940. https://doi.org/10.3389/fpsyg.2023.1212940

Myhill, D., Cremin, T., & Oliver, L. (2023b). Writing as a craft: Re-considering teacher subject content knowledge for teaching writing. *Research Papers in Education, 38*(3), 403–425. https://doi.org/10.1080/02671522.2021.1977376

Myhill, D., & Watson, A. (2014). The role of grammar in the writing curriculum: A review of the literature. *Child Language Teaching and Therapy, 30*(1), 41–62. https://doi.org/10.1177/0265659013514070

Myhill, D., Watson, A., & Newman, R. (2020). 'Thinking differently about grammar and metalinguistic understanding in writing'. *Bellaterra Journal of Teaching & Learning Language & Literature, 13*(2), e870. https://doi.org/10.5565/rev/jtl3.870

National Assessment of Educational Progress. (NAEP). (2012). What does the NAEP writing framework measure? *Measure Up, 16*(2-4), 2. Retrieved from https://samplebox.westat.com/idea_rfa/media/NSSC/MeasureUp_Elem_Winter12.pdf

National Assessment of Educational Progress. NAEP. (No date). *2017 writing*. Author. Retrieved from https://nces.ed.gov/nationsreportcard/writing/2017writing.aspx

National Commission on Writing. (2003). *The neglected "r": The need for a writing revolution*. New York: College Entrance Examination Board.

National Council for Curriculum and Assessment (NCCA). (2005). *An evaluation of curriculum implementation in primary schools: English, mathematics and visual arts*. Author. https://assets.gov.ie/25382/d967a57f78894843b3983e354d132e64.pdf

NCCA. (2008). *Primary curriculum review: Phase 2 (Gaeilge, Science, SPHE)*. Retrieved from https://www.ncca.ie/media/2267/primary_curriculum_review-_phase_2_final_report_with_recommendations.pdf

NCCA. (2019). *Primary language curriculum. English medium schools*. https://www.curriculumonline.ie/getmedia/2a6e5f79-6f29-4d68-b850-379510805656/PLC-Document_English.pdf

NCCA. (n.d.). *Primary language curriculum. Progression continua. English medium schools*. Author. Retrieved from https://www.curriculumonline.ie/getmedia/87033bef-fa59-41e0-87e4-4f9126e61821/Progression-Continua.pdf

National Commission on Writing. (2003). *The neglected "r": The need for a writing revolution*. New York: College Entrance Examination Board.

National Council of Teachers of English (NCTE). (2016). *Professional knowledge of the teaching of writing*. Urbana, IL: National Council of Teachers of English. Retrieved from https://ncte.org/statement/teaching-writing/

National Governors Association Center for Best Practices & Council of Chief State School Officers. (NGACBP & CCSSO). (2010a). *Common core state standards for English language arts and literacy in history/social studies, science, and technical subjects*. Authors. Retrieved from https://thecorestandards.b-cdn.net/ELA_Standards_1.pdf

NGACBP & CCSSO. (2010b). *Common core state standards for English language arts and literacy in history/social studies, science, and technical subjects. Appendix B: Text exemplars and sample performance tasks*. Authors. Retrieved from https://www.nysed.gov/sites/default/files/programs/standards-instruction/appendix-b-text-exemplars-and-sample-performance-tasks.pdf

NGACBP & CCSSO. (2010c). *Common core state standards for English language arts and literacy in history/social studies, science, and technical subjects. Appendix C: Research supporting key elements of the standards & glossary of key terms*. Authors. https://achievethecore.org/page/1192/ccss-ela-literacy-appendix-a-research-supporting-key-elements-of-the-standards-glossary-of-key-terms

National Institute of Child Health and Human Development (NICHHD). (2000). *Report of the National Reading Panel. Teaching children to read: An evidence-based assessment of the scientific research literature on reading and its implications for reading instruction*. Reports of the subgroups (NIH Publication No. 00-4769). Washington, DC: US Government Printing Office.

Naumann, A., Stirling, T., & Borthwick, A. (2011). What makes writing good? An essential question for teachers. *The Reading Teacher, 64*(5), 318-328. https://doi.org/10.1598/RT.64.5.2

Needham, T. (2021, May 10). The development of writing expertise: From telling to crafting. *Thoughts about Teaching*. Retrieved from https://tomneedhamteach.wordpress.com/2021/05/10/the-development-of-writing-expertise-from-telling-to-crafting/

New London Group. (1996). A pedagogy of multiliteracies: Designing social futures. *Harvard Educational Review, 66*(1), 60-92. https://doi.org/10.17763/haer.66.1.17370n67v22j160u

Ogle, D. M. (1986). K-W-L: A teaching model that develops active reading of https://psycnet.apa.org/record/1986-22966-001

O'Halloran, C. L., & Schleppegrell, M. J. (2016). Writing "voice" in children's science arguments: Aligning assessment criteria with genre and discipline. *Assessing Writing, 30*, 63-73. https://doi.org/10.1016/j.asw.2016.06.004

Oireachtas Library & Research Service. (2020). Education in Ireland: Statistical snapshot. *Houses of the Oireachtas*. Retrieved from https://data.oireachtas.ie/ie/oireachtas/libraryResearch/2020/2020-04-03_l-rs-infographic-education-in-ireland-a-statistical-snapshot_en.pdf

Olinghouse, N. G., & Wilson, J. (2013). The relationship between vocabulary and writing quality in three genres. *Reading and Writing, 26*(1), 45-65. https://doi.org/10.1007/s11145-012-9392-5

Olson, C. B., & Godfrey, L. (2019). Narrative writing. In S. Graham, C. A. McArthur & M. Herbert (Eds.), *Best practices in writing instruction* (3rd ed., pp. 81-107). Guilford Press.

Ouellette, G., & Sénéchal, M. (2017). Invented spelling in kindergarten as a predictor of reading and spelling in Grade 1: A new pathway to literacy, or just the same road, less known? *Developmental Psychology, 53*(1), 77-88. https://doi.org/10.1037/dev0000179

Pajares, F., Johnson, M. J., & Usher, E. L. (2007). Sources of writing self-efficacy beliefs of elementary, middle, and high school students. *Research in the Teaching of English, 42*, 104-120. https://www.jstor.org/stable/40171749

Pajares, F., & Valiante, G. (2006). Self-efficacy beliefs and motivation in writing development. In C. A. MacArthur, S. Graham, & J. Fitzgerald (Eds.), *Handbook of writing research* (pp. 158-170). Guilford Press.

Paris, S. G. (2005). Reinterpreting the development of reading skills. *Reading Research Quarterly, 40(2)*, 184-202. https://doi.org/10.1598/RRQ.40.2.3

Parr, J., & Timperley, H. (2010). Feedback to writing, assessment for teaching and learning and student progress. *Assessing Writing, 15*, 68-85. https://doi.org/10.1016/j.asw.2010.05.004

Paris, S. G., Lipson, M. Y., & Wixson, K. K. (1994). Becoming a strategic reader. In R. B. Ruddell, M. R. Ruddell, & H. Singer (Eds.), *Theoretical models and processes of reading* (pp. 788-811). International Reading Association.

Parsons, S. A., Ives, S. T., Fields, I. R., Barksdale, B., Marine, J., & Rogers, P. (2023). The Writing Engagement Scale: A formative assessment tool. *The Reading Teacher, 77(3)*, 278-289. https://doi.org/10.1002/trtr.2244

Pasquarella, A. (2019). Best practices in writing instruction for English language learners. In S. Graham, C. A. MacAurthur, & M. Hiebert (Eds.), *Best practices in writing instruction* (pp. 385-405). Gilford.

Patiño, J. F., Calixto, A. L., Chiappe, A., & Almenarez, F. T. (2020). ICT-driven writing and motor Skills: A review. *International Electronic Journal of Elementary Education, 12(5)*, 489-498. https://www.iejee.com/index.php/IEJEE/article/view/1074

Pearson, P. D., & Gallagher, M. C. (1983). The instruction of reading comprehension. *Contemporary Educational Psychology, 8(3)*, 317-344. https://doi.org/10.1016/0361-476X(83)90019-X

Perfect, K. A. (1999). Rhyme and reason: Poetry for the heart and head. *The Reading Teacher, 52(7)*, 728-737. https://www.jstor.org/stable/20204675

Philippakos, Z. A., & MacArthur, C. A. (2016). The effects of giving feedback on the persuasive writing of fourth- and fifth-grade students. *Reading Research Quarterly, 51(4)*, 419-433. https://doi.org/10.1002/rrq.149

Pressley, M., Allington, R. L., Wharton-McDonald, R., Collins Block, C., & Mandel Morrow, L. (2001). *Learning to read: Lessons from exemplary first-grade classrooms*. Guildford.

Putman, R. S. (2017). Using research to make informed decisions about the spelling curriculum. *Texas Journal of Literacy Education, 5(1)*, 24-32. Retrieved from https://www.semanticscholar.org/paper/Using-Research-to-Make-Informed-Decisions-about-the-Putman/ad1de4c484b7d467bb20e7743f3d086757e3e0f5

Puzio, K., Colby, G. T., & Algeo-Nichols, D. (2020). Differentiated literacy instruction: Boondoggle or best practice? *Review of Educational Research, 90(4)*, 459-498. https://doi.org/10.3102/0034654320933536

Pytash, K. E., & Morgan, D. N. (2014). Using mentor texts to teach writing in science and social studies. *The Reading Teacher, 68*, 93-102. https://doi.org/ 10.1002/trtr.1276

Rawdon, C., Sampson, K., Gilleece, L., Cosgrove, J., St. Patrick's College (Dublin, I., & Educational Research Centre. (2020). *Developing an evaluation framework for teachers' professional learning in Ireland: Phase 1, desk-based research*

Read, C. (1975). Children's categorization of speech sounds in English. ERIC Clearinghouse on Reading and Communication Skills and National Council of Teachers of English https://files.eric.ed.gov/fulltext/ED112426.pdf

Reeve, J. M., & Shin, S. H. (2020). How teachers can support students' agentic engagement. *Theory in Practice, 59(2)*, 150-161. https://doi.org/10.1080/00405841.2019.1702451

Rietdijk, S.,Van Weijen, D., Janssen, T., Bergh, H., & Rijlaarsdam, G. (2018). Teaching writing in primary education: Classroom practice, time, teachers' beliefs and skills. *Journal of Educational Psychology, 110(5)*, 640-663. https://doi.org/10.1037/edu0000237

Rijlaarsdam, G., Couzijn, M., Janssen, T., Braaksma, M., & Kieft, M. (2006). Writing experiment manuals in science education: The impact of writing, genre, and audience, *International Journal of Science Education, 28(2-3)*, 203-233. https://doi.org/10.1080/09500690500336932

Rinehart, R., & Kuhn, M. (2023). Building better questions. *Science and Children, 60(3)*, 68-70. January/February. http://dx.doi.org/10.1080/00368148.2023.12291858

Roche, M. (2015). *Developing children's critical thinking through picturebooks: A guide for primary and early years students and teachers*. Routledge.

Rogoff, B. (1990). *Apprenticeship in thinking: Cognitive development in social context*. New York: Oxford University Press.

Rose, J. (2006). *Independent review of the teaching of early reading. Final Report*. Department for Education and Skills, England. Retrieved from https://dera.ioe.ac.uk/id/eprint/5551/2/report.pdf

Rose, D., & Martin, J. (2012). *Learning to write, reading to Learn: Genre, knowledge and pedagogy of the Sydney School*. Equinox Publishing.

Rosenblatt, L. M. (1978). *The reader, the text, the poem: The transactional theory of literary work*. Carbondale: Southern Illinois University Press.

Rosenblatt, L. M. (1988). *Writing and reading: The transactional approach*. Technical Report 416: Center for the Study of Reading, University of Illinois, Urbana-Champaign.

Rosenthal, R., & Jacobson, L. (1968). Pygmalion in the classroom. *The Urban Reivew*, 3(1), 16-20.

Rothery, J. (1996). Making changes: Developing an educational linguistics. In R. Hasan & G. Williams (Eds.), *Literacy in society* (pp. 86-123). Longman.

Routman, R. (2004). *Writing essentials: Raising expectations and results while simplifying teaching*. Portsmouth, NH: Heinemann.

Rubie, C. M. (2007). Classroom interactions: Exploring the practices of high and low expectations teachers. *British Journal of Educational Psychology*, 77, 289-306. https://doi.org/10.1348/000709906X101601

Saddler, B. (2013). Best practices in sentence construction skills. In S. Graham, C. A. MacArthur, & J. Fitzgerald (Eds.), *Best practices in writing instruction* (2nd ed., pp. 238-256). Guilford Press.

Saddler, B. (2018). Writing a true sentence. Writing syntactical sophistication through sentence-level writing instruction. *Perspectives on Language and Literacy*, Spring. Retrieved from www.DyslexiaIDA.org

Saddler, B., & Graham, S. (2005). The effects of peer-assisted sentence-combining instruction on the writing performance of more and less skilled writers. *Journal of Educational Psychology*, 97(1), 43-54. https://doi.org/10.1037/0022-0663.97.1.43

Saddler, B., Moran, S., Graham, S., & Harris, K. (2004). Preventing writing difficulties: The effects of planning strategy instruction on the writing performance of struggling writers. *Exceptional Children*, 12(1), 3-17. https://doi.org/10.1207/s15327035ex1201_2

Santangelo, T., & Graham, S. (2016). A comprehensive meta-analysis of handwriting instruction. *Educational Psychology Review*, 28(2), 225-265. https://doi.org/10.1007/s10648-015-9335-1

Santangelo, T., Harris, K., & Graham, S. (2016). Self-regulation and writing: Meta-analysis of the self-regulation processes in Zimmerman's and Risemberg's model. In C. A. MacArthur, S. Graham, & J. Fitzgerald (Eds.), *Handbook of writing research* (2nd ed., pp. 174-193). Guilford Press.

Scarborough, H. S. (2001). Connecting early language and literacy to later reading (dis)abilities: Evidence, theory, and practice. In S. Neuman & D. Dickinson (Eds.), *Handbook for research in early literacy* (pp. 97-110). Guilford Press.

Schunk, D. H., & Zimmerman, B. J. (2007). Influencing children's self-efficacy and self-regulation of reading and writing through modelling. *Reading and Writing Quarterly*, 23, 7-25. https://doi.org/10.1080/10573560600837578.

Schwellnus, H., Cameron, D., & Carnahan, H. (2012). Which to choose: Manuscript or cursive handwriting? A review of the literature. *Journal of Occupational Therapy, Schools, & Early Intervention*, 5(3-4), 248-258. https://doi.org/10.1080/19411243.2012.744651

Scott Sheldon, J. B., Shumaker, J. B., Sheldon-Sherman, J., Schumaker, J., & Sheldon-Sherman, B. (1998). *Fundamentals in the sentence writing strategy. Instructors' manual*. University of Kansas.

Scottish Government. (2011). *Curriculum for excellence. Literacy and English. Experiences and outcomes*. Author. Retrieved from https://education.gov.scot/media/qhxmxnfq/literacy-english-eo.pdf

Scull, J., Mackenzie, N. M., & Bowles, T. (2020). Assessing early writing: A six-factor model to inform assessment and teaching. *Educational Research for Policy and Practice*, 19(2), 239-259. https://doi.org/10.1007/s10671-020-09257-7

Sedita, J. (2019, December 1). *The strands that are woven into skilled writing*. Retrieved from https://keystoliteracy.com/wp-content/uploads/2020/02/The-Strands-That-Are-Woven-Into-Skilled-WritingV2.pdf

Shanahan, T. (2016). Relationships between reading and writing development. In C. A. MacArthur, S. Graham, & J. Fitzgerald (Eds.), *Handbook of writing research* (2nd ed., pp. 194-207). The Guilford Press.

Shanahan, T. (2019). *Disciplinary literacy in the primary school*. National Council for Curriculum and Assessment. Retrieved from https://ncca.ie/media/4679/disciplinary-literacy-in-the-primary-school-professor-timothy-shanahan-university-of-illinois-at-chicago-1.pdf

Shanahan, T., & Shanahan, C. (2012). What is disciplinary literacy and why does it matter? *Topics in Language Disorders*, 32, 1-12. https://doi.org/10.1097/TLD.0b013e318244557a

Shuell, T. J. (2021). Learning theories and educational paradigms. In N. J. Smelser & B. Baltes (Eds.), *International encyclopedia of the social and behavioral sciences* (pp. 8613-8620).

Shulman, L. S. (1987). Knowledge and teaching: Foundations of the new reform. *Harvard Educational Review*, 57(1), 1-22.

Simon, S. (2014). *Our solar system* (Revised Edition). Collins.

Sippola, A. E. (1995). K-W-L-S. *The Reading Teacher, 48*, 542-543.

Slavin, R. E., Lake, C., Inns, A., Baye, A., Dachet, D., & Haslam, J. (2019). *A quantitative synthesis of research on writing approaches in grades 2 to 12*. Best Evidence Encyclopaedia (BEE) Center for Research and Reform in Education, Johns Hopkins University.

Smagorinsky, P. (1987). Graves revisited: A look at the methods and conclusions of the New Hampshire study. *Written Communication, 4(4)*, 331-342. https://doi.org/10.1177/0741088387004004001

Smith, B. E. (2014). *Composing across modes: Urban adolescents' processes responding to and analyzing literature*. Unpublished doctoral dissertation. Nashville Tennesee.

Snowling, M. J. (2000). *Dyslexia* (2nd ed.). Blackwell.

Standards and Testing Agency. (2018). *Teacher assessment frameworks at the end of key stage 2*. Author. Retrieved from https://assets.publishing.service.gov.uk/media/637ba0b0e90e072854bcab87/2018-19_teacher_assessment_frameworks_at_the_end_of_key_stage_2.pdf

Strand, S., Malmberg, L., & Hall, J. (2015). English as an additional language and educational achievement in England: An analysis of the national pupil database. Educational Endowment Foundation, Unbound and the Bell Foundation. Retrieved from https://www.bell-foundation.org.uk/app/uploads/2017/05/EALachievementStrand-1.pdf

Templeton, S., & Morris, D. (1999). Theory and research into practice: Questions teachers ask about spelling. *Reading Research Quarterly, 34(1)*, 102-112. https://doi.org/10.1598/RRQ.34.1.6

Templeton, S., & Morris, D. (2000). Spelling. In M. L. Kamil, P. B. Mosenthal, P. D. Pearson, & R. Barr (Eds.) *Handbook of reading research: Volume III* (pp. 525-544). Lawrence Erlbaum Associates Publishers.

Thompson, C., & Zeuli, J. S. (1999). The frame and the tapestry: Standards-based reform and professional development. In L. Darling-Hammond & G. Sykes (Eds.), *Teaching as the learning profession: Handbook of policy and practice* (pp. 341-375). Jossey-Bass.

Torgerson, C., Brooks, G., Gascoine, L., & Steve Higgin, S. S. (2019.) Phonics: Reading policy and the evidence of effectiveness from a systematic 'tertiary' review, *Research Papers in Education, 34(2)*, 208-238. https://doi.org/10.1080/02671522.2017.1420816

Tracey, B., Reid, R., & Graham, G. (2009). Teaching young students strategies for planning and drafting stories: The impact of self-regulated strategy development. *Journal of Educational Research, 102(5)*, 323-331. https://doi.org/10.3200/JOER.102.5.323-332

Traga Philippakos, Z. A., & Moore, N. S. (2020). Formative assessment on writing: Affordances and challenges in elementary settings. In C. Martin, D. Polly, & R. Lambert (Eds.), *Handbook of research on formative assessment in Pre-K through elementary classrooms* (pp. 282-306). Hershey, PA: IGI Global.

Troia, G., & Graham, S. (2017). Use and acceptability of adaptations to classroom writing instruction and assessment practices for students with disabilities: A survey of Grade 3-8 teachers. *Learning Disabilities Research & Practice, 32*, 257-269. https://doi.org/10.1111/ldrp.12135

Troia, G. A., Lin, S. C., Monroe, B. W., & Cohen, S. (2009). The effects of writing workshop instruction on the performance and motivation of good and poor writers. In G. A. Troia (Ed.), *Instruction and assessment for struggling writers: Evidence-based practices* (pp. 77-104). Guilford Press.

Troia, G. A., Shankland, R. K., & Wolbers, K. A. (2012). Motivation research in writing: Theoretical and empirical considerations. *Reading & Writing Quarterly, 28(1)*, 5-28. https://doi.org/10.1080/10573569.2012.632729

Ukrainetz, T. A., Nuspl, J. J., Wilkerson, K., & Beddes, S. R. (2011). The effects of syllable instruction on phonemic awareness in preschoolers. *Early Childhood Research Quarterly, 26(1)*, 50-60. https://psycnet.apa.org/doi/10.1016/j.ecresq.2010.04.006

Van Der Heide, J. (2017). Classroom talk as writing instruction for learning to make writing moves in literary arguments. *Reading Research Quarterly, 53(3)*, 323-344. https://doi.org/10.1002/rrq.196

Vasquez, V. M., Janks, H., & Comber, B. (2019). Critical Literacy as a way of being and doing. *Language Arts; Urbana, 96(5)*, 300-311.

Vaughn, M. (2018). Making sense of student agency in the early grades. *Phi Delta Kappan, 99(7)*, 62-66. https://doi.org/10.1177/0031721718767864

Vaughn, M. (2020). What is student agency and why is it needed now more than ever. Student agency: Theoretical implications for practice [themed journal issue]. *Theory into Practice, 59(2)*, 109-118. https://doi.org/10.1080/00405841.2019.1702393

Villegas-Reimers, E. (2003). *Teacher professional development: An international review of the evidence*. UNESCO: International Institute for Educational Planning.

Vygotsky, L. S. (1978). *Mind and society: The development of higher psychological processes* (M. Cole, V. John-Steiner, S. Scribner, & E. Souberman, Eds. & Trans.). Cambridge, MA: Harvard University Press (Original work published 1934).

Wagner, B. J. (1999). *Building moral communities through educational drama*. Ablex.

Wang, H., & Troia, G. A. (2023). How students' writing motivation, teachers' personal and professional attributes, and writing instruction impact student writing achievement: A two-level hierarchical linear modelling study. *Frontiers in Psychology, 14*, 1213929. https://doi.org/10.3389/fpsyg.2023.1213929

Watson, G. (2014). *Developing reading fluency through repeated reading procedure*. Unpublished master's thesis, Dublin City University.

Welsh Kruger, M., & Enriquez, G. (2023). Maths and picture books: Story, math anxiety, and building joy. *The Reading Teacher, 72(3)*, 379-387. https://doi.org/10.1002/trtr.1733

Williams, C. (2018). Learning to write with interactive writing instruction, *The Reading Teacher, 71(5)*, 523-532. https://doi.org/10.1002/trtr.1643

Williams, C., & Beam, S. (2019). Technology and writing: Review of research. *Computers & Education, 128*, 227-242. https://doi.org/10.1016/j.compedu.2018.09.024

Williams, K. J., Walker, M. A., Vaughn, S., & Wanzek, J. (2017). A synthesis of reading and spelling interventions and their effects on spelling outcomes for students with learning disabilities. *Journal of Learning Disabilities, 50(3)*, 286-297. https://doi.org/10.1177/0022219415619753

Wixson, K. K., Valencia, S. W., Lipson, M. Y., Risko, V. J., Paratore, J., Reinking, D., & Hruby, G. J. (2020). *Children experiencing reading difficulties what we know and what we can do*. International Literacy Association, Literacy Leadership Brief.

Wohlwend, K. E. (2011). *Playing their way into literacies: Reading, writing, and belonging in the early childhood classroom*. Teachers College Press.

Wood Ray, K., & Glover, M. (2008). *Already ready: Nurturing writers in preschool and kindergarten*. Heinemann Educational.

Wooten, D.A., Liang, L.A. & Cullinan, B.E. (Eds.) (2018). *Children's literature in the reading program: Engaging young readers in the 21st Century* (5th ed.). Guilford Press.

Wright, T. S., & Gotwals, A. W. (2017). Supporting kindergartners' science talk in the context of an integrated science and disciplinary literacy curriculum. *Elementary School Journal, 117(3)*, 513-537. https://doi.org/10.1086/690273

Wright, K. L., Hodges, T. S., Dismuke, S., & Boedeker, P. (2020). Writing motivation and middle school: An examination of changes in students' motivation for writing. *Literacy Research and Instruction, 59(2)*, 148-168. https://doi.org/10.1080/19388071.2020.1720048

Wyse, D. (2019). Choice, voice and process – Teaching writing in the 21st century: Revisiting the influence of Donald Graves and the process approach to writing. *English in Australia, 53(3)*, 82-91.

Wyse, D., Jones, R., Bradford, H., & Walport, M. A. (2018). *Teaching English, language and literacy* (4th ed.). Routledge.

Yeager, D. S., & Dweck, C. S. (2020). What can be learned from growth mindset controversies? *American Psychologist, 75(9)*, 1269-128. https://doi.org/10.1037/amp0000794

Young, R., & Ferguson, F. (2022a). *The science of teaching primary writing*. The Writing for Pleasure Centre.

Young, R., & Ferguson, F. (2022b). *The Writing for Pleasure Centre's grammar mini lessons for 5-11 year olds* (2nd ed.). The Writing for Pleasure Centre.

Young, R., & Ferguson, F. (2023). *Sentence-level instruction: Lessons that help children find their style and voice. For 3-11-year-olds* (2nd ed.). Writing for Pleasure Centre.

Zimmerman, B. J. (2000). Attaining self-regulation: A social cognitive perspective. In M. Boekaerts, P. R. Pintrich, & M. Zeidner (Eds.), *Handbook of self-regulation* (pp. 13-39). Academic Press. https://doi.org/10.1016/B978-012109890-2/50031-7

Zimmerman, B. J. (2001). Theories of self-regulated learning and academic achievement: An overview and analysis. In B. J. Zimmerman & D. H. Schunk (Eds.), *Self-regulated learning and academic achievement: Theoretical perspectives* (pp. 1-37). Lawrence Erlbaum Associates Publishers.

Zimmerman, B. J., & Kitsantas, A. (2002). Acquiring writing revision and self-regulatory skill through observation and emulation. *Journal of Educational Psychology, 94(4)*, 660-668. https://doi.org/10.1037/0022-0663.94.4.660

Index

Note: **Bold** page numbers refer to tables; *italic* page numbers refer to figures and page numbers followed by "n" denote endnotes.

de Abreu Malpique, A. 65
achieved curriculum 56, 57, 66-67, 69, 89
additional language 64, 150, 166, 236, 245, 249, 250, 252, 256, 292
aesthetic stance 139, 147, 155, 225
Aistear 3, 293n1
Alamargot, D. 6, 10
Alberti, N. 54
alliteration 152, 161, 227, 289
alphabetic principle 30, 187, 188
anchor charts 4, 57, 97-102, 107, **108**, 112, *113*, 129, *130*, *136*, 143, *144*, 149, 155, 162-165, *169*, 200, 202, 203, 211-212, 218-222, 228-231, 234, 269-270, 275-276, 280-282
argumentative/persuasive texts 48-49
Aronson, M. 121, 138
assessment, writing 18, 21, 56, 66, 67, 69-89, 221, 283, 285; formative 70-82; self-efficacy and motivation 85-86; summative 86-89; whole school approach 285-288
Australia 19, 40, 59, 65, 67, 86
Australian Education Research Organisation 28
autism spectrum disorders (ASD) 236

balanced sentences 27
Bandura, A. 273, 274
Barbot, B. 5
Barrs, M. 65, 259
Bear, D. R. 30, 187
Because of Winn Dixie (Camillo) 116
Beck, I. L. 150

beginning writers 7, 9, 72
belief statements 265, 266
Belsen camp 50-51
Bereiter, C. 6, 9, 10, 16, 225, 237
Berninger, V. W. 6, 8-9, 13, 14, 16, 33, 97
Biemiller, A. 149
Bintz, W. P. 41
body language 46, 168, 218, 269
Bruning, R. H. 12
'business as usual' approach 18
Bussis 190

Calkins, L. 2, 84, 149, 285
Camacho, A. 33, 269
Camillo, Kate di 115; *Because of Winn Dixie* 116
Certo, J. L. 49
change process 260, 262, 264, 290, 291
Chanquoy, L. 10
characters 45, 46, 75, 81, 86, 119, 131-135, 164, 279, 281
checklist dolch list *195*
children's early writing development 5
children's literature 270-272
Ciecierski, L. M. 41
Clark, C. 66
Clark, S. K. 53
classroom context 31-33
classrooms, designing *100*
cognitive models 10, 16
community model 6, 10, 11, 16
complex sentences 27, 28, 81, 82, 199, 200, 243

comprehension 1
Concannon-Gibney, T. 49
conferencing, teacher's perspective 217-218
constrained skills 179, 199
content knowledge 25, 45, 53, 236, 245
convention game 203-204
conventions 60, 61, 69, 70, 72-74, 179, 180, 188, 199, 201, 204, 277, 278
conventions mini lessons 178-207; accuracy in writing, genres 178-207; constrained and unconstrained skills, balancing attention 178-179; context of writing, supporting development 180; grammar and punctuation, addressing 198-204; integrating phonemic awareness, phonics, spelling and handwriting 188-198; interactive writing 180-181; role of spelling and transcription, writing workshop 185-198; shared writing approach 180; spelling development, assessment and pedagogy 185-188; transitioning to writing workshop 181-185; writing samples to inform teaching of conventions 205-206
cooperative learning 20, 21
core teams 263-264
craft mini lessons 146-177; developing 'voice' 152-156; engaging lead 162-167; prioritising 146-147; text structure, craft across genres 160; text structure, signifying 161-162; Write to Read rubric, enhance genre knowledge 168-177; Write to Read rubric, planning for text structure 167; Write to Read rubric, planning for voice 156-160; write-to-read rubric, planning for word choice 151-152
Crammond, J. 123
creative writing 5
Cremin, T. 35, 119, 148, 225, 259
critical life skills 123, 169
critical literacy 15, 137
Csikszentmihalyi, M. 91
Culham, R. 71
curriculum, writing 22, 24, 56-69, 259, 261, 265, 266; development 18, 56; documents 40, 56, 57, 59, 69, 200; England's National Curriculum 59-61; implementation 64-66; intended writing curriculum 57; Ireland's Primary Language Curriculum 61-64; United States Common Core Standards 57-59

Daffern, T. 31, 96, 188
Dalton, B. 54, 232
Datchuk, S. M. 243
Deane, P. 269
declarative metacognitive knowledge 8
DEIS schools 217, 282
Derewianka, B. 44, 51, 168, 244
desktop alphabet *196*
De Smedt, F. 8, 31, 34, 124
detention (poem) 117, *117*
developed sentences 27
dialogic metatalk 268
dialogic writing workshop 99
digital tools 231, 232
direct instruction 2, 22, 124, 149, 224, 236, 243, 247
disciplinary literacy 15, 52-53, 55
disciplinary writing 40-55
discovery approach 200, 201, 270, 273, 276, 277; building teacher confidence with 277; teaching with 276
discrete skills 2
diverse learners 235, 292
diverse writers: addressing needs of 235-257; children with special needs and struggling writers 236-245; educational disadvantage and writing development 248-256; English as additional language, writers 245-248
Dockrell, J. E. 65
domain or topic knowledge 15
Duthie, C. 49
Dwyer, B. 231
Dysgraphia 244-245, 249
Dyson, A. H. 259, 266

effective share sessions 269
effective writing pedagogy 18-39; children's spelling development, supporting 29-31; experimental studies of 20-21; fluency in writing sentences 27-29; handwriting and typing/keyboarding 36-38; knowledge base 25-26; policy-focused research reviews 24-25; process outcomes studies 22-24; strategy instruction and writing development 35-36; teaching grammar to improve 26-27; writers' agency and identity 34-35
Elkonin boxes *189*
engagement 6

England's National Curriculum 59-61
English as additional language (EAL) 245-248, 257
English grammar 58, 66
English grammar, punctuation and spelling (EGPAS) 66
English language 185, 192, 199, 235
Enriquez, G. 52
experimental studies 15, 18, 20, 21, 24
explicit instruction 28, 34, 38, 44, 46, 124, 237, 238, 247

Fancher, L. A. 37
Fayol, M. 6, 237
Feng, L. 37, 38
Ferguson, F. 26, 27, 34, 43, 45
Ferretti, R. P. 48
field 43, **44**, 45
figurative language 156, 228, 282
Fitzgerald, J. 46
five-finger recount plan 133, *135*
Fletcher, R. J. 151
focused sentences 27
formative assessment, writing 2, 64, 69-83, 88, 89, 99, 130; feedback impact, writing development 82-83; portfolios 84; progression steps 84-85; scoring rubrics for 71-73; think-aloud assessments 84; Write to Read (W2R) writing rubric 73-82
Furey, W. M. 243

Gadd, M. 19, 22
generating ideas 3, 5-7, 10, 14-16, 19-21, 31-32, 34, 36-38, 44, 46-47, 52, 57-60, 71, 73-81, 84-87, 91, 94-95, 100, **102**, 106-109, 111, 112, *113*, 114, 115, 117, 120, 124, **125**, 127, 129, 131, 135, **137**, 141, 143, 159, 164, 170, 180, 184, 186, 196, 205, 208, 214-216, 225, 226, 235-237, 244, 246-248, 254, 257, 261, 267, 273, 281, 287
genre-based approaches: origins of 40-43, **44**; to supporting writing development 40-43, **44**
genres 4, 15, 32, 40-55, **41**, 43, 44, 47, 49, 51, 55, 63, 81, 92, 146, 147, 152, 168, 288, 289; accuracy in writing, developing 178-207; argumentative/persuasive texts 48-49; challenges, basis for writing instruction 51; evaluating, revising and publishing writing 208-234; generating, planning and drafting writing 106-145; informational texts 46-47, **48**; main text genres 44-45; narrative texts 45-46; poetry 49-50; teaching genre, perspectives 44; word choice craft mini lessons, developing 149-150; word consciousness, quality literature 147-149; writing quality, developing and enhancing 146-177
Gentry, J. R. 187
Gillespie Rouse, A. 236, 237, 244
goal setting 8
Godfrey, L. 45
Goldman, S. R. 136
Gough, P. 13
gradual release of responsibility model (GRRM) 28, *96*, *108*, 125, 138, 149, 200, 234, 244, 270, 274-276
Graham, S. 1, 5, 12, 15, 21, 29, 35, 37, 38, 44, 64, 82, 92, 116, 124, 198, 206, 237, 238, 243-245, 249, 250, 259, 261, 264-266, 278, 290
Grainger, T. 107, 124, 146
grammatical complexity 65, 259
graphic organisers 42, 125, 133, 141, 143; for informational text **43**; narrative text 42, **42**
Graves, D. H. 2, 7, 19, 91, 99, 117, 119, 139, 146, 159, 199, 200, 206, 214, 225, 267
Guskey, T. R. 262

Hale, E. 69
Hall, G. E. 291
Hall, K. 19, 207
Halliday, M. A. K. 40, 43
handwriting instruction 37, 238, 245
Harding, A. 19, 207
Harris, K. R. 8, 116, 237
Hasan, R. 43
'have-a-go' cards 197, **198**
Hawkins, L. K. 49
Hayes, J. R. 7, 13
Heard, G. 121, 162
Hebert, M. 1
historical inquiry 122
Hord, S. M. 261, 291
Huxford, L. 186

informational genres 168
informational writing *159*, 175
instructional approaches 24, 28, 64, 257

interactive writing 279-282
International Dyslexia Association (IDA) 244-245
Ippolito, J. 170
Ireland 40, 67, 77, 84, 92
irregular target word 193

Jonsson, A. 71
Jouhar, M. R. 16
junior infant drawing *108*

Kauffman, D. F. 12
Kennedy, E. 24, 73
Kent, S. C. 29
King, F. 260
Kintsch, W. 136
knowledge 6; crafting 9, 10; functions and purposes of texts 15; transforming 9, 10; universal text attributes 15
knowledge-telling strategy 9
Kubina, R. M. 243

Langer, J. 45
language 10, 26, 43, 51, 58, 61, 146, 147, 149, 151, 152, 156, 185, 245, 247, 266, 268, 282, 283
language comprehension skills (LC) 13
language features 43
Lavan, G. 245
learning difficulties 24, 235-238, 245, 256
learning disabilities 19-20, 257n1
learning to confer 268
less-skilled writers 9
letter sound relationships 191
Lewis, W. E. 48
lexical knowledge 17n2
Limpo, T. 37
literacy coordinators 260, 263, 264, 270, 274, 290
literacy development 3, 149, 186, 247, 250, 260, 265
literacy teaching 24, 36, 263, 264, 268
Liu, Y. 246
long-term memory 7
Lott, K. 53
lower secondary schooling 9

MacArthur, C. A. 83
Madden, N. A. 20
Martin, J. R. 43

mastery experience 12
May 191, 192
McDonough 121
McGaw, B. 67
McLean, E. 24, 72
McMaster, K. L. 36, 238
mentor texts 32, 43-44, 54-55, 97, 147, 148, 151, 153, 200, 221, 253, 255, 270, 276, 278, 282-284
metacognition 33
metacognitive knowledge 9, 235
meta knowledge 15
Miller, S. 148
mini lessons: artefacts of personal relevance 117; classroom talk to support writing development 208-209; creating lists of topics 112-114; current events, tuning 123; drawing, play, popular culture and reading 107-111; figurative language, poetic devices, imagery and quotes 282-285; generating ideas 107; genre-specific planning and drafting strategies 124-125; imagining characters 119; inspiration for writing 107-111; learning why writers write 116-117; links with reading 136-138; methodologies for teaching 273-278; narrative graphic organisers, children' stage of development 131-135; planning and drafting narrative texts 125-135; planning and teaching 270; process 106-123, 208-234; publishing writing 231-234; scaffolding interaction, share session 209-214; scaffolding peer and self-assessment 221-224; scaffolding talk, writing conference 214-219; social context, nurturing 208-209; strategies for taking notes 138-145; supporting writers to choose topics 107-123; tapping into inquiry 120-123; teacher as writer 119; teaching researching, planning and drafting, informational texts 135-143; teaching writers proofreading strategies 230; teaching writers to evaluate writing 219-221; teaching writers to plan and draft writing 124; teaching writers to revise writing 224-228, **229**; teaching writing processes, knowledge and skills through 269-278; think, draw, label, write strategy 126-131; transfer to fiction writing, evidence **158**; transfer to non-fiction/informational writing **160**, **173-174**; writing folder and writer notebook 114-115
mixed ability grouping *122*

Moats, L.C. 185
mode 43, **44**, *45*
Moore, N. S. 84
more skilled writers 9
morphological representations 30
motivation 6, 12-13, 31-33
Moyles, J. 107, 186
multiliteracies 53-54
multimodal texts 40-55
Murphy, D. 34
Myhill, D. A. 5, 25, 26, 33, 151, 198, 278

NAPLAN assessment programme 67
narrative texts 41, 42, 44-46, 74, 82, 167, 244, 280
Needham, T. 9, 10, 15
non-fiction, craft 148
non-fiction authors **121**
not so simple view of writing 13-14

offline planning 6
O'Halloran, C. L. 152
Olinghouse, N. G. 150
Oliver, L. 35, 225, 259
Olson, C. B. 45
on-demand writing 2
online planning 6
oracy 208
oral language 1, 2, 14-16, 52, 61, 90, 92, 97, 99, 149, 257, 265, 266; skills 15, 215
organisation of writing/text 2, 7, 10, 14, 21, 40-41, 44-47, 60, 70-74, 76, 77, 80-81, 124, 147, 161, 167, 177, **226**, 236-237, 273, 278, 288, 301
orthographic knowledge 29
orthographic representations 30
O'Shea, Roisin 267
Ouellette, G. 187

pair work *195*
Pajares, F. 33
Paris, S. G. 97, 179
Parr, J. M. 19, 22
Parsons, S. A. 85
Pasquarella, A. 246, 247
patterned sentences 75, 112, 184, 254
pedagogical content knowledge 147, 260, 262
pedagogy, writing 18-20, 264
peer assessment 209, 248, 284

Perfect, K. A. 49
Perin, D. 35, 198, 244
persuasive writing 123, 166, 168, *171*, 175, 287; sub-genres of 168
Philippakos, Z. A. 83
phoneme-grapheme relationships 238-242
phonetic spellings 254, 255
phonological representations 30
picture mapping 133
PIEW (PILOT, IMPLEMENT, EMBED, WAITLIST) model 4
plain letter cards 239, 240
poetry 49-50
pre-planning 6
primary language curriculum 40, 61-64
procedural knowledge 8, 15, 33, 53
process writing, elements of 3
professional development (PD) 21, 24, 35, 64, 249, 250, 258, 262, 264; activities 274-275, 286-288
Putman, R. S. 185, 186
Puzio, K. 249

reading 14-16
reading-writing connections 16
record of leisure reading *111*
record of writing topics *111*
recursive cycles 2
Reeve, J. M. 266
register variables 45
research, children's writing 18-19; case studies 19-20
responsive teaching 19
rhetorical knowledge 17n2
Rijlaarsdam, G. 160
Roche, M. 137
Rosenblatt, L. M. 139, 147, 152
Rose Report 13
Rubie, C. M. 274
Rupley, W. H. 16

Saddler, B. 27, 28, 237, 243
Sandmel, K. 21
Santangelo, T. 13, 29, 37
Scarborough, H. S. 14
Scardamalia, M. 6, 9, 16, 225, 237
Schleppegrell, M. J. 152

Schunk, D. H. 12, 31
Schwellnus, H. 37
scoring rubrics 10, 13, 69-72, 86, 250
Scott Sheldon, J. B. 243
Scull, J. 109
Sedita, J. 14
self-efficacy 12-13, 18, 31
self-regulated strategy development (SRSD) 8, 21, 33, 35, 36, 243
self-regulation 12-13, 31
Sénéchal, M. 187
shared writing 279-282
Shiel, G. 73
Shin, S. H. 266
short-term memory 6, 7
Shuell, T. J. 36
simple view of reading 13
simple view of writing 13, 14
skilled writers 6, 9, 225
skills-based writing 2
Slavin, R. E. 21, 198, 249
Smagorinsky, P. 20
small group skills lesson 200-206
Smith, B. E. 232
social engagement 86
social persuasion 12, 273
speech conventions 201-203
spelling development 29-31, 96, 185, 187
stage models of writing development 187, 188
Strand, S. 245
strategy instruction 26, 35, 38, 106-107, 124, 237
strephosymbolic child 190, 207n1
student-facing checklists 84-85
subgenres 40, 41, **41**, 47, 168
summative assessment, writing 69-70, 86-89
Svingby, G. 71
Swanson, H. L. 6, 8, 9, 13, 16, 33, 97
syntactical knowledge 17n2
systemic functional linguistics 43

Talcott, J. 245
teacher knowledge 146, 148, 270
teacher's anecdotal notes **71**
teaching grammar 18, 25, 26, 65, 66, 198
teaching/learning cycle 45
teaching writing 1; basic principles for 19; broad approaches to 1-5; 'genre' approach 4; meta-analyses of research 21-22; process approach 2; recommendations **25**; and supporting writing development **23**; traditional approach 2; works clearinghouse recommendations for **23**; see also individual entries
Teasley, A. B. 46
tenor 43, **44**, 45
think-draw-label-write-add-detail approach 251
Thompson 67
time allocation 265, 266
Tracey, B. 124
Traga Philippakos, Z. A. 84
transcription skills 9, 14, 29, 179, 186, 206, 236
translation process 7
triple words form theory 30
Troia, G. A. 96, 245
Tunmer, W. 13

United States Common Core Standards 48, 57-59
upper primary grades 9

Valiante, G. 33
Van Keer, H. 8, 31
Vaughn, M. 34, 259
vicarious experience 12
visual displays *100*
vocabulary knowledge 14, 149

Wagner, B. J. 49
Wanzek, J. 29
Watson, A. 198
Welsh Kruger, M. 52
whole-school approach, developing infrastructure 261
Williams, K. J. 238
Wilson, J. 150
Winn, W. D. 14
word choice 28, 72, 73, 75, 79, 82, 149-151, 167, 180, 185, 219, 286, 288
working memory 7, 9, 10, 13, 14, 16, 25, 37, 96, 124, 244
workshop, writing 2, 3, 90-105, **102**, 104, 179, 185, 209, 217, 219, 278-282, 292; classroom teacher, advice 104; essential resources, sourcing 100-102; implementing in my school 3-4; materials for writing 102, 104; mini lesson pedagogies 96-99; mini lessons 95-99; oral lan-

guage, supporting 99; pedagogies to support writers 95–99; routines, establishing 100–102; structuring writing time 94, 94–95; successful research-informed, building blocks 90–95; time and choice 90–93; typical structure of 99

Wright, K. L. 33

writer's voice 10, 27, 45, 61–63, 72–77, 79, 81, 91, 107, 123, 141, 155–157, 164, 167, 177, 202, 205, 224, 267, 269, 273, 286, 288

Write to Read project 50

Write to Read (W2R) rubric, class-level scoring template 301; familiarity 287, 288; partial W2R writing assessment rubric, word choice 295–300

writing: Berninger and Swanson's cognitive model of 6–8; community, components 11; complexity of 5; conferences 85; co-ordination and management 6; creative 5; defined 5; development 40–55; development, Bereiter and Scardamalia's model of 8–9; Graham's writer(s) within community model 10–11; models of 6–11; needs of children, second class 250–253; as a product 2; proficiency 1; programme, components 19; quality 286; *see also individual entries*

writing across school: affective dimensions, change process 290–292; affordances of classrooms, maximising 260–262; building progression in 285–292; developing infrastructure to support change 262–264; planning 258–293; sourcing mentor texts 271–272; supporting students 267–269; teacher planning for writing 278; whole school planning 289–290; writing frequently, real and different purposes 265–267

Writing: Teachers and Children at Work (Graves) 19, 20

Writing Wings with Multimedia (WWM) 20, 21

Wyse, D. 20, 47

Young, R. 26–27, 34, 43, 45

Zarnowski, M. 138

Zimet, E. K. 49

Zimmerman, B. J. 12, 31

For Product Safety Concerns and Information please contact our EU
representative GPSR@taylorandfrancis.com
Taylor & Francis Verlag GmbH, Kaufingerstraße 24, 80331 München, Germany

www.ingramcontent.com/pod-product-compliance
Lightning Source LLC
Chambersburg PA
CBHW060257240426
43661CB00060B/2816